THE BOSS

BOOKS BY ROBERT ST. JOHN

The Boss
Ben-Gurion
Foreign Correspondent
Through Malan's Africa
This Was My World
Tongue of the Prophets
Shalom Means Peace
The Silent People Speak
It's Always Tomorrow
From the Land of Silent People

AUTHOR'S NOTE

The Arabic expression for President is *El Rayis*. But in colloquial Arabic the same word, given a slightly different intonation, *El Rayiis,* is the equivalent of boss. Strangers address Gamal Abdel Nasser as Mr. President, but his wife, his friends, and his subordinates call him the Boss.

Because the Arabic language has its own alphabet, there is no standard English-language spelling for Arabic words. Common nouns are spelled herein as they are most usually reproduced in English. An attempt has been made to spell all proper names as their owners spell them in transliteration.

The Egyptian pound has been translated into dollars at two dollars to the pound, the current rate on the free-money market.

Most of the quotations ascribed to Gamal Abdel Nasser are from his interviews with the author, or from conversations recalled by his associates. The rest are from his own written works and his speeches.

APPRECIATION

These are the people on three continents who supplied the stories, checked the facts, decided the spellings, gave of their time, and deserve thanks:

UNITED ARAB REPUBLIC

Gamal Abdel Nasser
Abdel-Nasser Hussein, the father
Az el-Arab, a brother
Khalil Hussein Khalil, an uncle
Taha Hussein, an uncle
Attia Hussein, an uncle
Mohamed Hassanein Heikal, editor in chief, *Al Ahram*
Abdel-Hakim Amer, Vice-President, Minister of Defense
Hussein Shafei, Minister of Social Affairs
Zakaria Mohieddin, Minister of the Interior
Ali Sabri, Minister of State for Presidential Affairs
Mohamed Hatem, Deputy Minister of State for Presidential Affairs
Abbas Radwan, Minister of the Interior, Southern Region
Ahmed Naguib Hashem, Minister of Education, Southern Region
Tewfik Abdel-Fattah, Minister of Social Affairs, Southern Region
Dr. Mahmoud Gohary, Controller General of Confiscated Property
Machmud el Gayar, Director of President's Office for Internal Affairs
Amin Shaker, Director of President's Office for Public Affairs
Abdul Moneim Shafei, Under Secretary, Ministry of Social Affairs
Shukri el Kuwatly, former President of Syria
Brigadier Anwar Hashem, commandant, Mankabad
Mahmud Abdel Latif, former Supreme Court Justice
Abdel Latif el Gayar, Mayor of Khatatba
Mohamed Maher Aly Aly, Mayor of Beni Mor
Sheik Garab, his first teacher
Omm Gharib, childhood friend
B. Boutros-Ghali, professor, Cairo University
Dr. Ali el-Gritly, chairman, Bank of Alexandria
Ahmed Fouad, administrateur-délégué, Banque Misr
Mustafa Amin, publisher, *Akhbar el Yom*
Mohamed Hassan el-Zayat, U.N. Advisory Council for Somaliland
Colonel Abd Elrahim Aggag, writer
Gamil Acknoukh Fanous, farmer

Nawal Mehallawi, *Al Ahram*
Taghi Nasr, former Foreign Minister of Iran
Youssef Sahagh, *Al Ahram*
Henri Habib Ayrout, S.J., author of *The Fellaheen*
Sa'ad Afra, Director of Information
Aly Hamid Fawzi, European section, Department of Information
Mary Azouri, writer
Aly Khairy, director, Helwan Observatory
Dr. Nour Ragai, lawyer
Anwar el Sadat, secretary general, National Union
Wilton Wynn, bureau chief, Associated Press
Frank Kearns, CBS correspondent
Raymond A. Hare, former American Ambassador
Albert E. Peterson, Assistant Information Officer, U.S. Embassy
William A. Lovegrove, Cultural Officer, U.S. Embassy
John Foley, First Secretary, U.S. Embassy
Joe Alex Morris, Jr., New York *Herald Tribune* correspondent
Maurice Guindi, UPI correspondent
Welles Hangen, NBC correspondent
Jay Walz, New York *Times* correspondent
Mahmaud Salah Zohny, reporter, *Rosa Youssef*
Abel Sabit, editor, *Egyptian Economic & Political Review*
Dorothy Spoffard, U.S.I.S. librarian

ELSEWHERE

Mustafa Kamel, U.A.R. Ambassador, Washington
Mohamed Habib, U.A.R. Press Officer, Washington
Salah el Din Mel Charaoui, Councilor, U.A.R. Embassy, Athens
Marcelle de Botton, Paris
Joy Tabet, Beirut
John Crawford, Geneva, Switzerland
Dr. Sathi Solimon, Geneva, Switzerland
Howard Daniel, Geneva, Switzerland
Thorstein Guthe, Geneva, Switzerland
Honor McCusker, librarian, U.S.I.S., Athens

Also a certain number of opponents of Gamal Abdel Nasser who prefer that
their names not be mentioned.

CONTENTS

CHAPTER 1

THE MOST MEMORABLE MOMENT

A message from the control tower at Port Said reported that the temperature in the city was already over a hundred in the shade, although it still was only midmorning. As they approached the ground it almost seemed possible to see the heat rising in shimmering waves to envelop the plane.

The instant the door was opened the inside temperature went up twenty or thirty degrees. But this was no time for thinking of physical discomfort. Today Egyptians were celebrating the final defeat of colonialism, after twenty-three centuries of occupation and exploitation. Today here at Port Said they were going to show the world how they felt about the departure of the last Britisher from their soil.

The first man out of the plane was a tall, broad-shouldered army officer with a crescent-shaped scar in the center of his forehead, a close-trimmed mustache, and black hair that curled tightly to his head. He smiled as he waved his right hand to the throng that had come to the airport to greet him.

"Long live Gamal Abdel Nasser!" they shouted as soon as they recognized him.

Today would not soon be forgotten by this man with the insignia of a lieutenant colonel on his uniform. He had dreamed of such a celebration as this for thirty years, since he first became infected as a small boy with the contagion of Egyptian nationalism. In his imagination all these years he had never doubted that the leader who would bring about the departure of the last foreigner would be named Gamal Abdel Nasser.

It seemed to take hours to go the short distance from the airport to the center of the city. The population of Port Said was less than two hundred thousand, but people had poured in from all over Lower Egypt until the streets were now solid masses of humanity. Policemen swung their clubs trying to clear a way for the car. Men in long robes called *galabiyas* ignored physical danger as they fought with each other to get close enough to touch him. Some even persisted in trying to kiss him.

1

Once the men guarding the car lost control completely and the crowd that pressed in became so dense he almost suffocated.

Finally they reached Navy House, the formidable building the British had used as headquarters during the seventy-four years of their occupation. The crowd cheered when he greeted General Abdel-Hakim Amer and several other members of the Revolutionary Command Council.

Nine MIGs flew overhead in tight formation as the climax of the day approached. Out in the harbor a twenty-one-gun salute was fired by an Egyptian frigate of British origin, surrounded by five small torpedo boats built in Yugoslavia.

"This is the most memorable moment in a lifetime," he told the crowd as he took an Egyptian flag in his hands, held it up for everyone to see, kissed it, then raised it slowly over Navy House.

The tens of thousands within range of his voice took this as a signal to show how they felt about this new freedom he had won for them. The din was almost enough to break a man's eardrums. It seemed to make the flimsy buildings along the street tremble on their foundations. When he held up his hand for silence so he could continue his speech, they cheered and shouted louder than ever. He could only smile and wait for their energy to become dissipated.

As he waited he thought back over the path to this pinnacle. In three years he had risen from an obscure army officer to become Egypt's Prime Minister. He had planned and directed a revolution that rid the country of a lazy King and a corrupt regime, and it was done with a minimum of bloodshed. He had wrested power from a general who had not been content to remain a figurehead in the new government. He had kept his promise to the Egyptian people: that he would drive out the last vestige of colonialism. Never in modern times had Egypt been in such an advantageous position as she was today. Not only was the detested foreigner gone, but the land of the Nile was now almost strong enough and independent enough to humble those who once had humbled her. Under his leadership she was playing a reckless but so far successful game that he called "positive neutrality," meaning that Egypt was pitting the East against the West and collecting from both sides. From the Soviet Union war equipment was flowing in by the thousands of tons: submarines, tanks, planes, heavy artillery, anything he asked for. The United States, wary, was trying to outbid Russia for the privilege of helping Egypt build a great dam. Smaller countries on both sides of the Cold War, as well as a few uncommitted nations, were vying with each other to trade their manufactured goods for Egyptian cotton. Technicians and experts from all over the world were coming to help Egypt join the twentieth century. Books, opera companies, ballet troupes, athletic teams, and learned lecturers were pouring in.

Publicly it could never be put this way, but Egypt, under his guidance, had most of the world eating from her hand, a happy thought for a nation that for so many centuries had been humiliated by so many different people.

Gamal Abdel Nasser raised his head a little higher and thrust out his jaw a little farther as he stood on the platform in front of Navy House in Port Said, listening to the continuing acclaim of his countrymen.

The story had had its beginning hundreds of years ago in a small village called Beni Mor, although that was not actually the place of his birth.

CHAPTER 2

THE TRIBE OF THE BITTER ONES

Beni means "tribe of" and Mor means "bitter," so the village bearing this name on the edge of the Nile in Upper Egypt is the home of the Tribe of the Bitter Ones. The Bitter Ones were not Egyptians but Arabs who trekked here between five hundred and a thousand years ago from the Arabian peninsula. That is the ancestral background of Gamal Abdel Nasser. When the leaders of other Arab countries say that Arab nationalism should not be directed from Cairo on the ground that Egyptians are not really Arabs at all, they are partly right. When they say that Nasser himself is an Egyptian and not an Arab, they are partly wrong.

The train for Beni Mor starts from Cairo's central railroad depot, which is on a public square dominated by a gargantuan statue of Rameses III, found years ago lying on its side in the sand twenty miles away and transported here to remind Egyptians of their Pharaonic past. The train crosses almost immediately to the west side of the great muddy Nile. The first stop is Giza, a spot on the desert where three men who lived nearly three thousand years before Christ built resting places for their embalmed bodies commodious enough to house all the food and other items they thought they would need during an afterlife of indeterminable duration.

The express for Beni Mor leaves just as the rising sun begins to strike the tip of the half-billion-ton Great Pyramid, making it seem an incandescent source of light. Half an hour out of Cairo the train passes close enough to Sakkara for passengers to see a monument at least a hundred years older than the wonders of Giza: King Zoser's Step Pyramid, a staircase to heaven, the world's first major building in stone.

It is fitting that the traveler to Beni Mor should begin his trip with these reminders of Pharaonic achievement rather than with a last look at Cairo's radio and television towers, or the modern Babylonian structure called the Nile Hilton Hotel, for Cairo and the twentieth century are being left behind; ahead lies Upper Egypt, where a great civilization flourished thousands of years before Nasser's revolution.

4

Men from Upper Egypt are called *Saïdis*. In some circles of Cairo it is customary to use the word contemptuously. A few thousand years ago it would have been a compliment, for the best art, the greatest learning, the foremost intellectual accomplishments of the world were centered for a time hundreds of miles south of Cairo. But today when a Cairene says Saïdi he refers to a man from that part of Egypt that has stood still since ancient days, making almost no use of modern instruments to lessen the drudgery of life, with only mud-hut architecture, a death rate equaled in few other places inhabited by man, a birth rate so high that it frightens politicians and Malthusians alike, and a scale of living that is the lowest anywhere in the world.

In most parts of Upper Egypt it never rains. Life exists here only by grace of the Nile. The belt of green, nearly a thousand miles long, varies in width from half a mile to fifteen. Beyond on either side is the stifling, suffocating desert. In this narrow valley and the Delta live twenty-four million people, eighteen million of them rooted to the soil. The green is the result of artificial irrigation. At flood season the Nile is dammed so its water will cover the fields and leave them not only soaked with moisture but covered with eight tons per acre of rich silt, washed off the hillsides of Central Africa.

During the rest of the year water must be raised from the river or canals by mechanical means. For three or four thousand years the men of Upper Egypt have done this principally with a *shadoof*, a long pole with a ball of mud at one end for a weight and a bucket suspended from a rope at the other, set on a forked stick for a fulcrum and operating like a seesaw. It takes at least two days to water a single acre this way, and the result is that the peasant spends most of his life standing barefooted in oozy mud, either making or repairing the earth walls of his irrigation ditches or raising the water exactly as it was done before the time of the biblical prophets. A few Saïdis use a slightly more advanced device, a screwlike machine for raising water by turning a crank, which they call a *tamboor*. Occasionally the quiet of the Nile Valley is broken by the sound of a gasoline engine. But pump and engine cost five hundred dollars, and in Upper Egypt the annual average income per family is forty dollars.

Six hours south of Cairo the train comes to Assyut, capital and largest city of Upper Egypt; population, one hundred thousand. Across the river and two canals and then several miles northeast is Beni Mor. On the canals great wooden boats called *feluccas* are used for transport. Their sails reach high into the blue sky but often they hang limp, so the boatmen spend much of their time on tow paths pulling their boats with stout ropes, their backs so bent, the effort so great that their faces almost touch the ground. This is Upper Egypt, 1960.

Here most of the green is on the west side of the river, as are the railroad, the only large city, the towns, and most of the villages. Accordingly, it is an insult to say that a man is from the east bank, a *charky*. The people of Beni Mor are east-bankers.

The village itself is hidden by a circle of giant date palms that always seem to be swaying slightly, even when there is not a trace of wind. These trees provide food and shade, as well as material for roofing, for brooms, and for the stuffing of mattresses, while the pollen of the male date palm, mixed with water, is considered an unexcelled cure for the barrenness of a wife. Inside the circle of palms there are five thousand people living just about as the peasants of ancient Egypt lived. Not a square inch of the precious land in this green belt must be wasted, so the houses are crowded together. The streets are so narrow that new-model automobiles from America scrape first the houses on one side and then those on the other. The same soil that gives these people their living also gives them their shelter, for all their houses are made of mud.

The streets are strewn with dung and refuse. If the roadway is not wet with the urine of animals, it is so dry that the slightest scuffing of feet raises a cloud of gray-brown dust. The houses form one large confused mass, compact and shapeless. Most are one story and have no windows.

The predominating color of Beni Mor is an unrelieved, dull, gray brown. The roads are that color, the fields, the skin of the peasants, the dust that rises in swirls whenever an animal or human moves, and the hide of the *gamus,* that lumbering water buffalo that spends its time splashing around in the canals when not being worked. Even the spirit of the people seems a dull gray brown.

In Beni Mor there is no electricity, no sewage system, no running water in the houses. All water, for whatever purpose, was dipped from the canals until three years ago, when an artesian well was sunk, a pump imported, and a line of spigots installed in a public square. Here, as elsewhere in rural Egypt, the people are reluctant to use "artificial water." During the months of flood the Nile is the color of a cup of black coffee into which one teaspoon of cream has been stirred. The *fellahin,* or peasants, believe that their men are more potent, their women more fertile when the Nile is high, so most marriages take place during this season.

These are a superstitious people, and most of their beliefs have some connection with the river that rules their lives. When a woman's time approaches, she makes her way the quarter or half mile from Beni Mor village down to the river and swallows some of the mud on its shore, to assure a satisfactory birth. If a man feels he is about to die he will go to the river's edge and dip out a last handful of the powerful water and drink it. If a child is critically ill, his mother will take him to the Nile and throw in food to feed the river and order the child to repeat an old prayer: "O Nile, let my strength be as great as your depth." The fellahin argue that the water of the Nile is rich, that artesian water has no "body" to it. But the "body" of Nile water is not only the dark brown mud from the hills of Central Africa. The river and the eighteen thousand miles of canals are the only sewage system available in most of Egypt. They are also the community bathtubs, the only available washing machines, the kitchen sink in which the community washes its pots and pans, and the community garbage dump as well as the community drinking fountain.

In the canals and ditches the water is further polluted by the bilharzia parasite, which enters the body through the skin, lodges in bladders and intestines, and wears down the stamina of almost all the fellahin.

The people of Beni Mor, along with most other fellahin, are also afflicted with ancylostomiasis, a disease that might disappear if the village had a sewage system, but here, as elsewhere in Upper Egypt, humans relieve themselves as animals do, when and where the urge occurs.

The birth and death rates in Beni Mor are about what they are in other Upper Egyptian villages, double the rates in America. During an average year 225 babies are born here, while a hundred men, women, and children (especially children) go off to receive their final judgment from Allah. This, happening all over Egypt, gives the country another half million stomachs a year to worry about.

Although Egypt is twice the size of California, the band of green, plus the several oases in which life can exist, comprises less than 4 per cent of the total land. It is as if in the United States only Montana were habitable, with the other forty-seven continental states useless desert.

Upon the death of a father in Egypt it is the custom for his land to be divided equally among his sons. Because of the ever increasing population, the size of each farm grows considerably smaller with each passing generation, and so there is less and less land to feed each family.

Except for three mosques and one Coptic church there is nothing in Beni Mor to relieve the gray-brown dreariness of it. Beni Mor is a pilgrimage spot for Copts. Once a year they come from all over Upper Egypt to this particular village to pay their respect to St. George, after whom the local church and small monastery are named.

Most of the Moslems of Beni Mor belong to one of four families, and because outsiders are seldom taken in marriage nearly all the Moslems of Beni Mor are somehow related to each other, so that it is almost impossible for a man to marry a local girl who is not his cousin, in one way or another.

In Beni Mor, as in Cairo and throughout the rest of Egypt, nomenclature is a confused and confusing matter, for few people have family names. The full name of the President of the United Arab Republic is Gamal Abdel Nasser Hussein Khalil Sultan. (A hyphen belongs between Abdel and Nasser, for it is a single name, but by custom in the United States the hyphen has been dropped.) Gamal is his own given name; Abdel-Nasser was his father's given name; Hussein his grandfather's; Khalil his great-grandfather's; and Sultan his great-great-grandfather's. There has never been a family name, such as Smith or Jones. The general rule is that a male child takes his father's string of names, drops off the last one, and adds his own at the beginning, although he has the right to carry through life with him as many of the other names tagged on as he pleases. A girl is given a name that she puts ahead of whatever her father is called.

In the eighteenth century the ancestor named Sultan established himself in the northeast corner of the village, near where a new mosque has just been built, and for nearly two hundred years his descendants have held onto this corner.

One of Sultan's sons was Khalil Sultan. One of Khalil Sultan's sons was Hussein Khalil, who died only a few years ago at the age of 107. They still boast about him in Beni Mor. There was a man! He had three wives, the last a girl in her twenties when he married her on his sixty-fifth birthday. He had his last child by her when he was ninety.

One of Hussein Khalil's other children is Abdel-Nasser Hussein, father of the President, who today lives in Alexandria, and who himself has sired nine children in addition to Gamal.

Besides Abdel-Nasser Hussein, four other sons of Hussein Khalil are still alive: Taha Hussein, age thirty, who laughs heartily whenever he explains that he was conceived just before his father's ninetieth birthday; Sultan Hussein; Khalil Hussein Khalil, who retains his grandfather's name at the rear as well as at the front; and Attia Hussein. These are the four uncles of Gamal Abdel Nasser.

Taha and Attia have remained fellahin and still live in the family home, which is a few yards down a narrow dirt road from the new mosque. It is made of mud, like all the others, and animals occupy part of it, but it has a second story, which sets it a little apart.

Khalil Sultan, when he was alive, owned seventy *feddan,* approximately seventy acres. But the inexorable process of division among heirs has cut the farm down so much that Taha and Attia now have only twelve feddan between them. (They would have even less if the other boys had not gone off to the city to live.) Twelve feddan around Beni Mor, where land is worth up to a thousand dollars a feddan, make Taha and Attia much better off than most. There are still, despite their nephew's land reforms, several million fellahin who own no more than two feddan, which is barely enough to support a family, and many have not even that.

When a distinguished guest comes to Beni Mor, all the rugs in the village—which are not many—are borrowed and scattered around on the floor of the community house. Chairs placed against the four walls are occupied by the *ohmda,* or mayor, and other representatives of the four leading families. All of them come in the traditional village dress, the galabiya, a loose-fitting garment of Egyptian cotton that begins at the neck and almost touches the ground. Some galabiyas are plain white and look like old-fashioned nightshirts, some are of striped material, and others, for holidays and formal occasions, are dark. Under this garment the fellah wears a pair of loose-fitting drawers with a drawstring at the waist and a vest fastened high up on the neck with small buttons. Although their galabiyas, all cut from the same pattern, make for uniformity, each man's degree of imagination is shown by what he wears on his head. First he puts on a skull cap and over it winds a piece of cloth. The color of the cloth, its length, how it is wound, and then what is done with the loose end reveal the individuality of each man. Sometimes the cloth is pure white, or a plain dark color, but often it is some faded pastel shade. The longer the cloth, the more impressive the size of the turban.

The men sitting so straight around the four walls of the community house have the same dignity of bearing that the sculptors of Pharaonic days succeeded in preserving in stone. They are exceedingly handsome, considering the diseases that plague their bodies. Down through the millennia they have been invaded, conquered, pillaged, held in servitude, exploited, subjected to all the punishments of man and nature, yet they have survived. They have even adopted the religion and the language of some of the invaders without surrendering their individuality.

The men of Beni Mor are nearly all heavily built, but never fat. They average almost six feet in height. Their ankles, necks, and wrists are thick, their faces broad, their foreheads and hips narrow. They have thick noses, full lips, heavy jaws. Their faces generally wear a blank expression, as if they were not really part of the world that swirls around them. In Cairo people who call themselves Egyptians vary in skin pigmentation from the pale pink white of an Anglo-Saxon to a black almost as intense as that of a person from Ghana. But these men of Beni Mor are uniform in pigmentation: a pleasant beige color. Most of them have short-cropped mustaches, for to them this is a sign of virility.

The custom used to be that at all receptions small cups of thick, sugary Turkish coffee would be served. Today they pass around bottles of Coca-Cola. Before the advent of this American invention the fellah, forbidden by the Koran to drink alcohol, spent all his spare money on coffee and tea. The monotony of his work, the insufficiency of his diet, the pains in his body, the perpetual exhaustion caused by disease—all these troubles were assuaged by an excessive intake of caffein.

Babies are taught to drink tea before they are weaned. In Beni Mor and other Upper Egyptian villages they make tea as they do Turkish coffee, by boiling the powder or leaves in water, along with a large amount of sugar. This thick sirupy concoction is the narcotic of the fellah. It may ruin his stomach and disrupt his finances but he will starve himself and his family, if necessary, to save money to buy tea.

The sun of Upper Egypt is blindingly bright. There is rarely a cloud to soften its rays. It bakes the earth for fourteen or fifteen hours a day. But the fellah works under it, from sunup to dark, bareheaded, barefooted, squinting his eyes, his face swarming with flies, the air he breathes heavy with dust that no rain ever comes to settle. When the wind is strong it brings sand from the desert that bites the skin and makes the eyes more bloodshot than ever.

The fellah may have a piece of paper that says he owns the land he works, but actually the land owns him. The Koran does not command him to take the seventh day for rest, so he observes the Day of the Prophet with work as usual.

The wife of a fellah is almost unique among country women in not being able to sew. If her husband needs a new galabiya, poor as he is he must hire a tailor. His wife is not adept enough with a needle even to do simple mending.

Although the fellah works long and diligently, he seems to take neither pride nor joy in what he does.

He is illogical in his striving for logic. There is the story of the ohmda who says to the fellah's small son:

"Go to your father, my lad, and tell him that the Bey, to whom he owes money, is waiting here for him. If your father is not at home, tell him to come all the same, because the Bey knows very well that he *is* at home."

The fellah makes no attempt to hide his fatalism. One of his favorite expressions is *"In cha Allah* [If it is God's will]." By using this phrase he will avoid ever giving a definite answer.

"Will your cotton be ready for delivery next week?" you may ask him.

"In cha Allah."

"Will you be able to repay your loan when it falls due next month?"

"In cha Allah," is the inevitable reply.

Cairo is the capital of his country, but Cairo is almost two hundred thirty miles away and so it is as foreign to him as San Francisco. Nothing that happens there really interests him unless it has to do with irrigation or restrictions on the amount of land that can be planted to cotton. Universal suffrage, democracy, Israel, communism, birth control, even Arab nationalism are just words that have little connection with his life.

He understands only the present; only that which is immediately at hand. He waits to buy seeds until the day for sowing has arrived. He sends for a doctor after it is too late. His wife fills the kerosene lamp only after it has grown dark.

These are the kinfolk of Gamal Abdel Nasser. Occasionally some of them escape from their dusty villages, but they take a part of the gray-brown world with them wherever they go.

Two who escaped more than half a century ago were brothers, Khalil Hussein Khalil and Abdel-Nasser Hussein. As small boys they went from Beni Mor to attend school in Alexandria. While they were there, their mother died in Beni Mor, so they stayed on in the city. As a result, the history of Egypt was changed, for one of these men sired Gamal Abdel Nasser and the other introduced him to the ways of revolution.

CHAPTER 3

CAESAR WAS AMBITIOUS

On the fifteenth day of January 1918, there was confusion in a small mud-brick house on a narrow, unpaved street in the Bacos section of Alexandria, for here, a few days earlier than expected, a child was born. The mother was the young wife of the thirty-year-old postmaster of the area, Abdel-Nasser Hussein. The house they lived in consisted of a hall and three rooms, one of them occupied by Khalil Hussein Khalil, who now, owing to the successful birth, was an uncle. Behind the house there was a small yard where chickens were kept. In front, masses of people swirled past the doors. Alexandria's population in those days was less than half a million, but in Bacos people seemed jammed even closer together than in Beni Mor. There was manure in the streets here, too, for donkeys and dogs and sometimes sheep and goats wandered through the narrow thoroughfares, and humans added their refuse. But here there were no fields to escape to. Vegetable stands, meat markets, small shops of all kinds lined the roadway.

Abdel-Nasser Hussein had done well for a boy from the country. Here in Alexandria he had acquired education enough to become a civil servant and already was in charge of a small post office. Few people in a section so poor as this either sent or received letters, and his salary, the equivalent of thirty dollars a month, was nothing to boast about, but he was, after all, a postmaster, and he had married well. His wife's name was Fahima. She was the daughter of Mohamed Hammad, who had his own roots back in Upper Egypt but was now a well-known Alexandria contractor, engaged in the business of transporting goods on the canals. His daughter had acquired some of the qualities of the people of this seaport city, which actually was more foreign than it was Egyptian or Arabic, with its large Greek, Italian, and Jewish colonies, its sprinkling of Maltese, French, Bulgars, and Austrians, and its Mediterranean culture. The newborn child inherited a certain amount of curiosity, romanticism, and daring from his mother, to balance the pride, stubbornness, and fatalistic resignation from his paternal side.

12

The postmaster and his wife decided to call their first-born Gamal Abdel Nasser. In the Koran there is a verse listing ninety-nine names for Allah, among them *Nasser,* "the one who helps you to win victory." So the postmaster's son would be "Gamal, slave of the one who helps you to win victory," a name that might someday be an asset.

Gamal was six months old when the family moved to a different house. This was the beginning of many years of peregrination. The boy's ancestral roots might be back in Beni Mor, but he was so repeatedly being transplanted during his early years that he never felt at home anywhere, and this affected his entire outlook on life. Today he remembers "only as if they were shadows" the many places he lived in as a child. The house in which he was born is unmarked, and he has no idea what street it is on. His father and his uncle are not sure, either.

There was a crisis in the family when Gamal was only two years old, much too young to understand its seriousness. One day Uncle Khalil Hussein Khalil vanished. When it finally came out that he had been arrested by British secret police for organizing anti-British demonstrations, his brother, Abdel-Nasser, was greatly disturbed. After all, he was a civil servant, and if they connected him with the trouble he might find himself suddenly out of work. Uncle Khalil went off to prison for several years and there were no repercussions, but it made Gamal's father determined that no other member of his family would get mixed up in politics.

A second child, Az el-Arab, arrived when Gamal was three, but Fahima's favorite was always her first-born—and the attachment between them grew stronger by the year.

Gamal's first serious trouble with his father occurred when the family was living in Alexandria. There was a windmill in the back yard to pump water, and a reservoir that Gamal used as a wading pool. He was intrigued by the idea that if you dug deeply enough you could reach water, so he started digging a well of his own. When his father came home that night he ordered the boy to stop, and to fill up the hole at once. Instead, Gamal put several boards over the opening and disguised them by sprinkling earth over them. Then each day while his father was away he would continue his digging. One night his father fell into the hole and almost broke both legs. Early the next morning, spurred by his father's fury, Gamal filled up the hole.

Postmaster Abdel-Nasser Hussein was shifted several times, finally to Khatatba, a village forty miles up into the Delta from Cairo. Gamal was six, Az el-Arab was three, and another boy, Leisy, was about to be born when the family moved to Khatatba. The post office was at one end of a street of small shops, near the railroad tracks. Behind the post office in the same building were living quarters for the postmaster and his family, behind that a small garden, and behind that, sand; the start of the great Western Desert.

Here in Khatatba a new sort of life began for Gamal. There were poverty and squalor, as there had been everywhere else they had lived, and the houses were just as dark and dreary, and the filth in the roads was no different, but this was the country; here he was introduced to birds and animals, and saw trees, cotton plants, corn, things he had never known about before. There were more camels here than he had ever seen, and cactus plants that grew to a height of ten or twelve feet. Several kilometers from the post office was an immense farm owned by Mobarek Bey el Gayar, the first man Gamal ever met with the title of *bey*. He was so important that the government had made him ohmda of seven villages. He owned several thousand feddan of land and employed hundreds of fellahin. Gamal's father and he became good friends, and sometimes when he came to the post office he would let Gamal ride his donkey. At four o'clock each Sunday morning the postmaster would awaken Gamal and take him to the Gayar farm for a few hours of shooting. Often they returned home with enough birds to feed the family for days. There was no school at Khatatba except a kindergarten for children of railroad employees, which Gamal attended. At Khatatba he met a foreigner for the first time, the only Englishman in the village, who when he became lonely for someone to talk to in his own language would come to the post office and sit across the table from Abdel-Nasser Hussein and gossip for an hour or two. Gamal, who was soon to develop such strong feelings about British colonialism and Britons in general, has always remembered his "first Englishman" as a gentle and kindly man who gave him his first dog, named Bobbie. It was kept in a kennel behind the post office and, being female, was soon supplying pets for many other boys in the village.

In the Khatatba school Gamal not only learned to read and write but also received his first instruction in the Koran. He was awed by its accounts of heaven and hell, and one day after school he and the son of the teacher, who was in his class, had a discussion.

"What do you think about hell?" he asked his little friend.

"I'm frightened of it," the boy replied.

"So am I. I don't want to go to hell."

"Me neither."

"But it says in the Koran that everybody goes to hell if he makes even one little sin," Gamal pointed out.

"How can we avoid it, even one small sin?"

"Do you remember how it says that little children under seven who die don't get punished?"

"Yes. Why?"

"How old are you?" Gamal asked.

"Six."

"Me, too."

"Then if we die before next year we'll be all right!" his friend exclaimed triumphantly.

"But maybe we won't die. I don't feel as if I was going to die."

"Me neither."

"I've got an idea," Gamal said brightly.

"What is it?"

"If we kill ourselves right now, before we get to be seven, then we won't have to go to hell."

"But maybe killing yourself is a sin."

"What difference? If we're not seven we can't do any sins yet. That's what the Koran says."

"But how do we kill ourselves?"

Gamal thought a long time before he figured out an answer. In the post office, on his father's desk, there was a large lump of wax, used to seal letters. Something his father had said gave him the idea that the wax was poison, so that afternoon he stole it while his father's back was turned, and the two boys, hiding behind the schoolhouse, each ate half of it. When the last trace of the wax was gone, they lay down side by side on the ground to wait for death. Every few minutes one turned to the other and asked, "Do you feel as if you were dying?"

They agreed that they felt queer, but after one hour when death had not come, although they had severe pains in their stomachs, they went home, confessed, and were lectured on the seriousness of stealing government property and on not taking the Koran so literally.

While the family was living in Khatatba, Gamal's mother went home to Alexandria to see her parents and took him with her. It was a trip he never forgot because one evening he and his mother went to the Theater Zizinia, near the Mohamed Aly Palace, and saw an operetta about life under the Ottomans. It was the first time Gamal had ever been in a theater, and it would be the last time for years. All he knew then about the music was that he liked it, especially a song about the sun rising as the farmers start off to the fields.

After two years at Khatatba, Gamal completed his kindergarten course and his parents decided to send him to Cairo to begin his schooling in earnest. Uncle Khalil Hussein Khalil was out of prison now and was working for the government department that handled religious property, so Gamal went to stay with him in the capital. Khalil's living quarters were three rooms in a large building occupied by nine other families, all Jewish, on a street called Musky Seka el Gidada, which in those days was the chief shopping thoroughfare of the old Arab quarter of Cairo. With Uncle Khalil lived Mahmud Abdel Latif, a boy of fifteen who had joined Khalil's household years earlier, after the sudden death of his father. Despite the difference in their ages the two boys became close friends, Mahmud acting as guide for the younger one, showing him the wonders of this noisy, pulsating city. Gamal was used to the confusion and clamor of Bacos and to the rural pandemonium of Khatatba, but this was different. Here were more than a million people, the greatest concentration of human beings anywhere in the Middle East, packed so tightly together that even making just the normal motions of life seemed to cause friction.

The quarter was most exciting at night when the kerosene lanterns and electric lights on the stalls made a glare that was blinding. Some of the best craftsmen in the East were here, crowded into a few square feet of space apiece, working sixteen hours a day. The street was full of taxicabs with horns that were always blowing, trucks whose drivers kept up a running volley of curses, wagons driven by men who whipped their horses and mules without mercy and shouted at the animals in Arabic dialects that Gamal had never heard before.

In the shops and in the stalls along the sidewalks a man could buy almost anything, if he just had the money: phonograph records, secondhand clothes, rusty knives, bed quilts in a dozen violent colors, miniature camels made of leather especially for tourists, shoes fit for a king, pieces of silk, worn-out sewing machines, antiques from the Orient, inlaid silverwork, anything you could think of carved out of ivory, gold jewelry, tin bathtubs, rusty nuts and bolts, bright-colored calico. This was Musky Seka el Gidada, a street out of *The Thousand and One Nights* for Gamal.

The school he attended, El Nahassin, was in what the guidebooks called "the most picturesque part of the city," which meant that most of the men wore galabiyas, that even those in city clothes had red felt tarbushes on their heads, that the women covered their faces with black veils. Here were Bedouins from the desert, sheikhs, Persians, Syrians, Levantine merchants, Jews, Turks, traders from the Orient, and, of course, tourists. There were many ancient religious buildings in this quarter. In whatever direction Gamal looked he could see minarets and domes, and frequently during the day he could hear muezzins calling the faithful to prayer.

"Picturesque" referred to the *souks,* to the great market called Khan Khalil. Mahmud took him there often: miles of narrow streets that crisscrossed each other and zigzagged in odd directions. Many of them were covered over, so you had the impression you were going on and on in one vast building. There was one street just of goldsmiths; another of men who made things from tin; another of men and boys who cut intricate designs in copper, then pounded silver into the grooves; another of saddlemakers. Each man had his own shop, but usually it was so minuscule that there was not even room for a chair, and the artisan had to sit on the floor, his legs curled up under him.

There were wonderful smells: the odor of strong spices shipped here in large burlap sacks from places in Africa or the Far East, fresh wood shavings, newly tanned leather, food being fried in olive oil, incense, and then other odors not so pleasant, but all mixed together they were the smells of Khan Khalil and the souks and the street called Musky Seka el Gidada.

Gamal loved it at first, but he soon discovered it was also dirty and unpleasant to live in. Here there was a lack of toilet facilities, not much running water, too little living space for so many people, not enough food that was nourishing, babies who were sick.

Mahmud took him to a place called Al Azhar, and told him that this was the oldest university in the world, built as a mosque almost a thousand years ago and almost immediately converted into a place of learning, where the purity of the Arabic language and the true teachings of the Prophet were to be guarded. There were thousands of boys and men from all thirty countries of the Moslem world studying here. You could see them by first removing your shoes and then wandering into the ancient mosque and looking around. They sat cross-legged on carpets on the cold floor, their lips constantly moving as they memorized the Koran.

When Friday afternoon came and it began to grow dark, which was a sign to the Jews that their holy day had begun, the people in the house on Musky Seka el Gidada would often ask Gamal or Mahmud to put on their lights for them, orthodox rules not permitting them to do any work for the next twenty-four hours, not even so much as lighting a kerosene lamp or turning an electric button. Mahmud obliged them, but Gamal usually refused.

"Why don't you do it for them?" Mahmud would ask.

"Why should I?" was always the answer Gamal gave.

Otherwise they lived in peace with their neighbors, these two young Moslem boys in a street sprinkled with Jewish shopkeepers and craftsmen, in a house where they and Uncle Khalil were the only ones who did not celebrate Shabbath starting at sundown on Friday.

The high point of Gamal's first year in Cairo was the parade that went right through Musky Seka el Gidada on its way to Mecca. It was the annual religious rite called El Mahmal. Every year during the eleventh month of the lunar year, Silkada, the holy cloth was taken to the holy city. The parade began at Abbassia because that was the suburb northeast of Cairo where the Army had its headquarters, and a crack cavalry regiment always accompanied the cloth to guard it from thieves. There was also a caravan of camels, one of them bearing a richly decorated canopy. It took dozens of soldiers to carry the magnificent cloth, which was woven of pure gold thread. The cavalrymen were resplendent in their glittering uniforms. This was the first large group of soldiers Gamal had ever seen and he could not stop talking to his friend about them.

"Did you see, Mahmud, how shiny the skin of the horses was? Did you see the silver things the men wore on their shoes to make the horses go faster? Did you see——"

The boys watched from the window of Uncle Khalil's flat until the last soldier was out of sight, then ran down into the street, squirmed their way through the crowds, and finally caught up with the parade again, following it all the way to Hussein Mosque, where the cloth was blessed, then to the railroad station, where men and animals were loaded onto a train that would take them to Suez; there they would board a ship for the long journey through the Canal and down the Red Sea toward Mecca. Everything about the event fired Gamal's imagination, but when he talked about it later to Mahmud it was the soldiers he always mentioned.

Uncle Khalil could not afford a servant, and often it was late at night before he returned to the flat, and Mahmud's teacher sometimes kept him after school, so Gamal was left to look after himself much of the time. He was a child of the street; of this dirty, crowded, intense street, full of shouting, pushing, noisy people who bargained and haggled and made the air vibrant with their high-pitched excitement. It seldom rained and it was never very cold, so home for Gamal was what home was for most of these people, a place to sleep. Those who had no homes, and there were many, would sleep curled up anywhere, even in the middle of a sidewalk.

Uncle Khalil had a charge account with a Greek grocer who was instructed to give Gamal and Mahmud anything they asked for. So the boys often ate standing in the doorway of the shop or wandering the street, with black olives and bread and cheese in their hands.

By this time Gamal's character had begun to be formed. He already had a passion for secrets and intrigue. Often he would not take even Mahmud into his confidence. The simplest affairs became matters of plot and counterplot, cloaked in dark mystery.

Already, at the age of eight, he was fiercely independent. He objected to having to submit to authority of any kind. He seemed to resent anyone being in a position to give him orders or even make requests: his father, his teachers, the policemen on the streets, the Jews in the building who asked him to turn on their lights, sometimes even Mahmud. He resented more than anything else someone trying to make a decision for him.

"I will decide myself," he would often say, and after that there was no arguing about it.

Once Mahmud said to him, "You are the most stubborn and obstinate boy I ever met!"

Gamal smiled and made no defense. He had positive ideas of his own on almost every subject. He was always asking why, and many of the answers he received failed to satisfy him. He generally thought carefully before answering even the simplest question. He kept himself extremely neat and clean, considering the circumstances in which he was forced to live. He was always calm, and seemed to overcome quickly his fear of the big city.

Each Thursday the pupils of the El Nahassin school were taken on a sight-seeing expedition by their teachers. One week they went to Giza to inspect the great stone pyramids, but these made little impression on Gamal. He was happy to be out in the open and have a holiday from school, that was all.

On another Thursday they spent hours going through the Egyptian Museum, but this vast warehouse of ancient treasures made even less impression on him. He was not enough interested ever to go back again. The next time he visited the museum was after the revolution, on some state occasion.

Yet Gamal remembered well a story they read in school that year— about an English lad named Horatio Nelson, who was in the crew of a ship. The captain called for volunteers for a dangerous task. Before anyone else could step forward young Horatio did; he was given the mission, even though he was very young, and carried it out successfully, thus becoming a hero. It was difficult for Gamal to connect himself with ancient Egypt and a civilization that had been dead for thousands of years, but he imagined himself quite easily in the shoes of young Nelson. He was, like many a boy of eight, a hero in search of a role.

On Sundays, when government offices were closed, the boys were with Uncle Khalil, and sometimes he told them of his experiences in prison. This was better than reading books. At this age Gamal was not nearly so interested in the reason his uncle was opposed to the British as in stories of the plotting and conniving he had done. During the year Gamal lived with his uncle he received many practical lessons in how to be a revolutionary, and they provided him substance for innumerable boyhood dreams.

He wrote frequently to his mother in Khatatba, for her answers kept him from being homesick. He liked his life in the city but he did miss his mother. He often thought of their evening at the operetta, and in one letter promised her that when the school year was over he would take her to the theater again. During the winter his mother wrote that she was going to Alexandria to have a baby. That was the last letter he had from her. He kept writing but she never replied. Occasionally a letter came from his father telling how busy his mother was with the children and her housework. The baby had come all right, and they had named him Shawky.

When the school year ended, Gamal went back to Khatatba. Instead of his mother there was another woman in the house taking care of the children. When he asked where his mother was, everyone was silent. After a few moments his father said quietly, "She's dead, Gamal. She died a few days after Shawky was born."

When Gamal finally spoke he asked, "Why didn't you write and tell me?"

He does not remember what his father answered. He left the post office building and walked alone through the yard and out onto the desert. This was his first experience with death. He had never been a joyful, happy child. There was too much of Beni Mor in him for that. But now he began to grow even more reserved—pensive, grave. From this day on death would be a frightening thing for him. The brutality of it would often make him hesitate before making a decision.

The gulf between Gamal and his father widened. After a short time at Khatatba he asked if he might go to Alexandria to live with his maternal grandparents. His father agreed, so that autumn a sad-faced nine-year-old boy entered the Attarene Primary School of Alexandria. Perhaps because of the unhappiness that overwhelmed him, he failed to pass grade two and had to repeat it the next year. Then he failed grade three. His father, now postmaster at Suez, not only had remarried but had begun to have children by his second wife. He agreed that Suez was no place for his eldest son, but neither was Alexandria, he said, for the grandparents obviously were spoiling Gamal. Although the boy was now twelve, he still had not passed his third-grade primary examinations, so his father sent him back to Uncle Khalil in Cairo.

The next spring, he did pass, receiving a certificate that said he had completed the three-year primary course and was now ready for secondary school.

That summer, he went to Alexandria to spend the vacation with his grandparents. One hot July evening he saw a crowd of men and boys streaming through the streets toward Mohamed Aly Square, which was a few blocks back from the waterfront and so large that it was always used for demonstrations. He had no idea what the reason for the outpouring was but he joined the shouting, jostling throng. When they reached the square and the leaders began to make speeches, he understood little of what they said. But it was all very exciting. There were Egyptian policemen and British policemen, and many soldiers. Some of the officers were swinging clubs. Thousands of men and boys were milling around. Then shots were fired over the heads of the demonstrators. A man screamed and fell, wounded. Gamal was in the thick of it, shouting, too, although he still didn't know what he was demonstrating for or against. It was enough for him that he was opposing the police and the British. These were the same people Uncle Khalil was against, so he *must* be on the right side.

Suddenly a large hand seized hold of his collar and he found himself in the grasp of the law. He was put in a police van with dozens of others, not any of them as young as he. He was a little frightened but very proud at being the youngest. They were taken to a nearby police station, where they were all searched, then put into cells. There were half a dozen men in Gamal's cell. After the door had been locked and the guard had left, he turned to a young man beside him.

"What were we demonstrating about?" he asked.

The young man looked at him in surprise. "You mean you don't know?"

The demonstration, he explained to Gamal, had been organized by Misr el Fatat, the Young Egypt party, an extreme, ultranationalistic group that had the blessing of Benito Mussolini, copied the Italian fascists in many ways, and even wore green shirts, supplied secretly from Rome, it was said. This particular demonstration was directed against the British because of what had recently happened at Mansura.

They were locked up until morning. Some of the others slept, but Gamal kept the young man awake all night with questions. He had no desire to sleep. He was not even hungry, although he had missed his evening meal. He was more excited than he had ever been in his life. He was a revolutionary now, just as his uncle had been. Much of what his young cellmate said made no sense to him. But he was happy, just being here. In a certain way he was a hero, too.

The next morning, his grandfather came and obtained his release. When his father heard that his eldest son now had the start of a police record, he decided to put Gamal in a place where he would have no further opportunity to mix in politics, either by accident or design. He sent him to a boarding school in the health-resort city of Helwan, thirty-two kilometers up the Nile from Cairo.

During his first year at Helwan, Gamal had malaria, which may have caused him to fail his classes. The next year, he repeated the courses and passed them all except English. Then he went back to Alexandria, again lived with his grandparents, and entered a school called Ras-el-Tin. He was a handsome boy by now, tall for his age, with broad square shoulders.

At Ras-el-Tin he failed again. This time it may have been because he often absented himself from school to go to a moving-picture theater and watch films of war and adventure. The frequent failures in school were annoying his father, who insisted that he continue at Ras-el-Tin and repeat the year's work. Instead, against his father's specific orders, he enrolled in a private institution called the Farida School. He hoped that if he passed his father might forgive him.

He did pass, but his father, now working in a post office in Cairo, decided his son had better come back under the parental roof, submit to parental discipline, and have some parental guidance, so he sent for the boy.

It was now 1934. Gamal, sixteen, was beginning to feel like a man. He was already as tall as his father, impatient with life, not interested much in what they were trying to teach him in school, eager to be part of the important world of adults. He had been going to school for ten years and had passed only one secondary and three primary grades.

His father lived now in Khamis el Adtz Street, in the heart of the Jewish quarter called Koronofisch. There were no other Moslems in the street, but he was required to live there to be near the branch post office in which he worked. The apartment he had rented consisted of four rooms and a miniature balcony overlooking the street. It was a crowded and not very happy home for Gamal. His own brothers were eight, ten, and thirteen. There were several small half brothers and sisters. Gamal had little social or intellectual exchange with either his father or his father's new wife, and he spent no more time than necessary in the house. There were several mosques not far away; inside any one of them, away from the noise and confusion of the street, it was quiet and a man could think. Others went there to talk with Allah or recite verses from the Koran. Gamal went there to read and try to figure out some of the problems that troubled him.

Before the school year began, he met some youthful members of the Young Egypt party who persuaded him to join. He paid a year's dues in advance with money he obtained from his father without telling him specifically what he wanted it for. Then he received a membership card and was assigned to help the cause by doing odd jobs for the newspaper that Young Egypt had just begun to publish.

Older members were trained in the making and throwing of bombs. The organization was under the constant surveillance of the police and agents of the palace. Its membership list was a bizarre mixture of youthful idealists, political opportunists, rogues, and scoundrels.

As soon as school began, Gamal discovered the important role secondary schools played in the political machinations of opposition parties. Their aim seemed to be to keep the country in a constant state of agitation. The more demonstrations and disturbances, the better. And the way to set off trouble was to spread word through the larger secondary schools that at a certain hour on a certain day the pupils were to arm themselves with sticks, stones, any weapons they could find, and march out of their classes, defying their teachers and threatening them, if necessary, although most of the teachers, overworked and underpaid, were not reluctant, even before sticks were brandished in their faces, to have a holiday.

The students from Gamal's school then went in mob formation to Opera House Square, where they met the students from other secondary schools. They surged through the street of fancy shops, Kasr el Nil, patronized largely by foreigners, around the great circle called the Midan of Ismailia, past the Semiramis Hotel, where they would taunt foreigners enjoying their afternoon whiskey or drinking tea on the broad veranda, then past the British Embassy, always under heavy guard, then through Garden City with its great villas owned by rich foreigners and illustrious Egyptian beys and pashas, then over one Nile River bridge onto Rhoda Island, and finally over another into Giza and thus to the grounds of the university. Once they were on the campus, the object was to persuade the thousands of university students to join in the demonstration or, failing this, to embarrass them into it.

If a teacher, in an effort to maintain a modicum of discipline in the classroom, interfered too much with such activities, he was called an imperialist, a friend of the British, a colonial stooge.

As a member of Misr el Fatat, Gamal now had a prominent part in organizing demonstrations, first in his own school and then in all the secondary schools in his area. Once he spent three days and three nights in Abdin jail because he and some other Young Egypt workers were caught trying to set up a youth camp on the desert near the pyramids without permission. He was enjoying his new career. It gave him a feeling of importance and provided a degree of compensation for the mother he had lost, the home life he lacked, the parental affection he needed but no longer received.

During his fourth class of secondary school he joined the dramatic society. The play they produced that year was Shakespeare's *Julius Caesar*. Because it was about politics, albeit politics nearly two thousand years dead, it was of interest to most of the boys in El Nahda school; because it was well larded with plot and conspiracy it was especially appealing to Gamal.

After they had read the script, there was a long dispute over who should get which part. Many wanted to be Marcus Brutus and do the stabbing. Others, Gamal among them, wanted a chance to make Antony's great speech to the Romans over Caesar's body. But Gamal was assigned the title role. For one night he would be Julius Caesar, the Roman dictator who would be killed by some of his best friends because they were afraid that under him the people were about to lose their liberty.

During the weeks of rehearsal he was happier than he had ever been. He would walk up and down Khamis el Adtz Street, reciting his lines half aloud. The teacher had told them to "try to live your parts," to imagine they were actually the characters they portrayed. So after he had memorized the words Gamal concentrated on giving them the force he thought they deserved. He felt very important as he recited:

> "I rather tell thee what is to be feared
> Than what I fear,—for always I am Caesar."

With all the other noises there were in the street, no one paid much attention to the tall young man with black curly hair who strode up and down, his head bent, his lips constantly moving. And those who passed by seemed completely unaware that they were brushing elbows with a great Roman general.

The closer it came to January 19, 1935, the day the play would be presented at the Printania Theater, the more excited he grew and the oftener he went over his lines.

Abdel-Nasser Hussein was in the audience on the evening of the performance. He hardly recognized the commanding figure who came striding onto the stage as soon as the curtain went up on Act I, Scene 2. Gamal remembered all his lines, which made his father proud. When the dramatic moment of assassination came, Caesar shouted, *"Et tu, Brute?"* in a bloodcurdling way. As he fell dead, Abdel-Nasser Hussein jumped up to run to his son's aid. But then the corpse twitched slightly and he returned to his seat, aware again that it was all a play.

After the curtain went down, Gamal stood in the wings to hear the speech of Brutus:

"Romans, countrymen, and lovers! hear me for my cause; and be silent. . . . If, then, that friend demand why Brutus rose against Caesar, this is my answer,—Not that I loved Caesar less, but that I loved Rome more. . . ."

He was listening now to the kind of patriotism the Young Egypt party preached. It was almost like being in Abdin Square at a political rally. Only this was in some ways more exciting. . . . Now Antony was making his wonderful oration:

> "Friends, Romans, countrymen, lend me your ears;
> I come to bury Caesar, not to praise him.
> The evil that men do lives after them;
> The good is oft interred with their bones . . ."

It seemed to have something to do with Egypt and his own life, although at seventeen he was not sure how to translate Caesar and Brutus and all they said into twentieth-century terms.

This school year was the busiest period of young Gamal's life so far. Besides his other activities, he already had the reputation of being willing to sacrifice anything for his fellow members in the Young Egypt party. He would walk halfway across Cairo instead of taking a tram and then contribute to the party the money his father had given him for fare. He carried bundles of papers to save the party's having to hire someone to do it. When he heard that the printer was threatening to close down the paper unless the printing bill was paid at once, Gamal went to the man and used all his charm and oratorical ability to get the printer to give the paper a few more days to meet its debt.

Each year, pupils in the secondary schools were required to read one English book and were examined on it at the end of the year. The book for 1934–35 was *The Scarlet Pimpernel,* by Baroness Orczy. Romance, adventure, and resolution were there between the covers. The Scarlet Pimpernel was a hero like the hero he wanted to be someday. The Scarlet Pimpernel had a sense of humor. That was one reason he liked him, for, he thought, "We Egyptians also have a sense of humor. We are always telling jokes and laughing. I like the book because here is a man who seems fit for nothing, yet he turns out to be a leader. When the crisis comes, he is stubborn and strong. We are like that, too. We seem to be good for nothing, yet when a crisis arrives we show ourselves."

School records state that Gamal Abdel Nasser passed all his fourth-year courses, which is technically true. Actually he failed most of them, but the principal, impressed by his popularity and his basic intelligence, let him slip by.

One day in the summer of 1935 a minor political crisis arose that Gamal felt he should discuss with the chairman of the Young Egypt party, so he walked halfway across the city (as usual, to save the tram fare) and presented himself at the chairman's office. First he was told an interview was impossible because he had made no appointment in advance. But he was so insistent that a secretary finally admitted him to the presence of the leader, who sat behind a desk reading a copy of the party paper. He hardly looked up.

"Gamal Abdel Nasser, sir."

"Yes. What can I do for you?"

Before Gamal could answer, he started talking again.

"Our paper is going to be a great success. Our circulation is up thirty per cent over last month. We have reserves of three hundred pounds. In another year our profits should reach ——"

Something about the man's attitude incensed young Gamal. He left the chairman's office without even mentioning why he had come. That night, he resigned from Misr el Fatat.

"I have sacrificed a great deal for Young Egypt," he explained to a minor party leader, "but not any more. I believed in the party, until I saw the chairman sitting there counting his profits. He was behaving just like any other party leader. When I heard the way he talked about money rather than ideals and principles and aspirations I was no longer interested."

It was the first disillusionment of a young idealist. It was the start of his cynicism about party politicians, which would increase from year to year and would someday lead him to order the elimination of all political parties, good and bad alike. But at seventeen Gamal was not yet condemning them all. He switched from Misr el Fatat to the Wafd party and was soon busy organizing demonstrations again.

There was a place for everyone in the Wafd party. Only in Egypt could such an all-inclusive political party have existed. In it were fellahin and pashas, boys and men in galabiyas, Anglophiles and Anglophobes, conservatives and revolutionaries, intellectuals and irresponsible rabble-rousers. Each new recruit was welcome to try to pull the party in whatever direction he thought best, while behind the scenes pashas bought and sold influence and made profit out of power.

As the school year began, Gamal realized he had only one chance of graduating. In all Egyptian secondary schools pupils were required to take either a scientific or a literary course. Gamal had chosen the former, but now he realized he had made a mistake. He would never be able to get mathematics through his head. He had been passed from fourth grade to fifth only because of a friendly principal. But the time for baccalaureate examinations was approaching. They would be given by the government, and there would be no chance to influence marks by personality. So he switched to the literary section, against his father's advice, knowing that geography, history, and literature would be easier for him.

Through his reading he acquired several new heroes, one of them the founder of modern Egyptian nationalism, Mustafa Kamel. He followed this patriot's career step by step. Kamel had gone to Paris to study law. There he became secretary to a French politician, from whom he learned to hate the British. Kamel returned home to Egypt and founded the Nationalist party, as well as a newspaper to express the party's ideas. He worked mostly among the youth of the country, Copt and Moslem alike. Kamel was a perfect hero for Gamal, and he regretted only that Kamel was not now alive, so that he could become one of his disciples.

That year, he also read *The Soul Regained,* a novel combining romance, sentimentality, and patriotism in a mixture that delighted him. The book was by a contemporary writer, Tewfik Hakim. In it an English character described Egyptian peasants as being little better than beasts of burden. A Frenchman, defending them, declared:

"These people lack only one thing, a leader who will personify their hopes and their dreams, and who will be a symbol of their great ideal. When this man suddenly appears, the world will be astonished to see a people who have been united for centuries only by suffering and sacrifice accomplish a new miracle of the pyramids."

Here indeed was a role crying for a hero. Gamal read the passage many times.

During his last year at the Nahda school, he was in constant and bitter dispute with the headmaster, an Englishman who tried to counteract the inflammatory anti-British speeches Gamal made between classes to his fellow pupils with facts about what Britain had done to raise the intellectual and material standards of the Egyptian people. The headmaster became the personification of all he was fighting against, which may have been one reason he spent so little time attending classes— only forty-five days out of the entire school year.

One day during a geography lesson the teacher, lecturing about the importance of climate on the character of a people, said, "Those who live in a temperate climate, for example, are possessed of great self-control, and for this reason they are qualified to govern other people. England is a good example."

Gamal jumped to his feet. "Professor, I don't agree with you. You call it a virtue. I call it a bloody vice!"

One Sunday, soon after the school year began, the British Foreign Secretary delivered a speech in London designed to dampen Egyptian hopes for any change in what they called their "colonial status."

All day Monday secondary school pupils and university students streamed through the streets of Cairo, some with banners, some with school flags, others just milling about, shouting their feelings. Gamal was in the middle of it.

On Wednesday, Gamal adressed his fellow pupils as soon as they arrived at El Nahda, suggesting that they take their flag and parade from school to school, urging other secondary boys to join them in another day of demonstrations. As they were leaving their own school, their English headmaster tried to remonstrate with them. Eyewitnesses did not agree, later, about what actually happened. One published report said the teacher fired several bullets from a revolver over the heads of the young rebels, hoping to "bring them to their senses," and that in revenge they destroyed his automobile, parked beside the school.

After they were joined by pupils from several other schools they stormed through the city, shouting ugly slogans at anyone who looked like a foreigner. They crossed the small bridge onto Rhoda Island, then stampeded to the bridge that would take them across the other branch of the Nile and onto the university campus. But the police had outwitted them. This bridge turned on a pivot to permit the feluccas, with their immensely tall sails, to pass. When Gamal and his fellow demonstrators arrived, the bridge was open to boat traffic and the police were grinning over their easy victory.

Some of the students jumped into the water. Some tried to rent boats to get across the river. Others, Gamal among them, made an attempt to seize control of the mechanism by which the bridge could be closed.

The police started swinging clubs, the students throwing stones. Then more police arrived, armed with rifles. An officer named Lotus, second in command of British security forces, came in an open car. The students pelted him with stones. He fell, severely wounded. The police with rifles opened fire. One student was shot through the head and died immediately. Another received a volley in his stomach and was taken to a hospital, where he died later. More troop reinforcements arrived and surrounded the entire area.

It was the time of Ramadan, which meant that good Moslems had not eaten since the night before. Gamal, in the thick of the fighting, suddenly felt extremely weak. He turned to two students beside him and said, "They've got us surrounded. There's no way for us to get through police lines. They're going to arrest every one of us."

"What can we do?" one of them asked.

"We must hide in some building inside the circle and hope they don't find us," Gamal decided.

The three boys sneaked into the garden of an apartment house and were about to crawl under some bushes when an elderly lady saw them and asked what they were up to. Gamal gave her such a dramatic reply that she took them to her fourth-floor apartment and hid them. Half an hour later, looking out the window, she saw police officers entering the building, so she gave each boy a pair of pajamas and told them to change quickly. When the police came to make a search of her apartment, she insisted the boys were her own sons and had not been out of the house all day. After she was sure the police had finished their roundup she let them dress and go their way.

A political meeting had been called for that evening by the Wafd party, to commemorate the attempted rebellion of 1919. It was to be held in front of the home of the late Prime Minister Saad Zaghlul on Falaki Street, which had become so much of a symbol since his death that it was called Beit el Umma, the Home of the Nation.

By the time Gamal arrived, a crowd had gathered in Falaki Street. To give the event an aspect of importance a *sewan* had been erected, an immense square tent made of many pieces of bright-colored quilted cloth hung over a framework of poles. Saad Zaghlul's widow was present. So was Mustafa el Nahas, whom everyone called Nahas Pasha, the man who had become leader of the Wafds after the death of Zaghlul. He made the principal speech. Egyptians, he said, would fight and die as long as a single Englishman remained on Egyptian soil. His oratory ignited the crowd. Young Gamal reacted just as the others did. The throng left the meeting place and swarmed through the streets in a series of disorganized demonstrations. The King's police and the British security forces were ready. Clubs were swung, shots rang out. Someone held up a handkerchief dripping with blood and shouted a curse. The sight of blood always has a strong effect on an Egyptian crowd. The demonstrators began to stone the police. Suddenly something hit Gamal on the head. He was never sure afterward whether it was a bullet from a policeman's gun or the blow of a well-aimed club, but his forehead seemed to be split wide open and blood was running into his eyes, down his nose, into his mouth, all over his clothing. He could hardly see. Someone carried or dragged or led him (he was not certain which) into the nearby office of a newspaper, *Al Guihad*. Those who looked at the wound thought he should be taken at once to a hospital, but the boy kept saying "No! No!" He was sure that if they took him to a hospital he would be arrested, and he had a great fear of arrest. Perhaps because he knew how his father would react.

"Just wash it and bandage it," he pleaded. "Let me go home quickly, before the police take me!"

The wound was so deep that Gamal Abdel Nasser would bear the scar of it for the rest of his life, although official photographs would be retouched so it would never show. It was almost three inches long, a little to the left of center on his forehead and just below the hairline. It was the shape of a crescent.

Abdel-Nasser Hussein was first worried then provoked when his son arrived home late that night with a white bandage around his head, which advertised to anyone with eyes to see that he had been in trouble. He was even angrier the next day when *Al Guihad*, describing the fracas, listed among the night's casualties the Minister of War, who had somehow been struck in the head by a policeman's baton, and Gamal Abdel Nasser, student, wounded on the forehead.

It was the first time that the boy's name had appeared in print.

Abdel-Nasser Hussein's concern was that the publicity would result in the loss of his post office position. That was what prompted him to telephone his brother Khalil, whose work with the department of religious property had taken him to El Mahalla el Kubra, one of the largest towns of the Delta, seventy-five miles north of Cairo. Khalil agreed that to save Gamal from being arrested or getting into further trouble it would be wise to get him out of the capital. So Gamal took his fifth-grade books to El Mahalla el Kubra and during the weeks he was in hiding there began to prepare in earnest for the annual tests.

Because of the demonstrations, the government closed all Cairo schools for a month. During that time the British Government took one more forward step, under pressure. It agreed to negotiate a treaty of full independence for Egypt.

In the wave of celebrations and self-congratulations that followed, youth was given part of the credit for forcing London's hand. Others thought that their fight now was over, but when Gamal came back from his exile in the Delta he told anyone who would listen, "Nahas is right. We have not won while there is a single British soldier left on the soil of our country."

When he tried to rejoin his class at El Nahda, the headmaster informed him that because of a complaint lodged against him by the police he was inadmissible.

Gamal's classmates signed and presented a petition for his return to the school. When it was rejected, they announced a general strike and went so far as to pile their desks in the courtyard and threaten to burn them. The headmaster gave in, but the pupils declared, knowing they were now in a position of power, that Gamal would not return to school unless the headmaster personally went for him in a horse-drawn carriage. Thus the young rebel returned.

Now that he was taking a literary course, he had to write many compositions. Other students often were reprimanded because theirs were so short, but Gamal had the opposite trouble. He could never stop writing until he reached the last page of the composition book. Until now he had not thought much about a career. During his last year in school, however, he considered becoming a professional writer and made one serious literary effort. On the first page of the composition book he wrote, as if it were the title shot of a film:

Gamal Abdel Nasser Presents

A Patriotic Novel

ON THE ROAD TO FREEDOM

It was a story of the invasion of the Mediterranean seaport of Rosetta by the British in 1805 and their defeat at the hands of Egyptian irregulars. The romantic-minded young author introduced a love affair between an Egyptian soldier and the daughter of the Arab governor of Alexandria, and spiced the tale with espionage agents, plots, counterplots, and miscellaneous embellishments reminiscent of many early Hollywood films. In just twenty pages he managed to crowd five chapters and introduce fifteen major characters. The fifth chapter concluded —at the bottom of the last page of the composition book—with one character saying to another, "If you agree to marry your son to my daughter, I will free you from the debt you owe me, as well as the compounded interest. And you know that my daughter is beautiful."

That was as far as Gamal ever went with the story: five chapters and 2900 words from the start he became bogged down in what he said were "certain complications about the plot." Or it may have been just that he reached the last page of the composition book.

The percentage of students who passed the government baccalaureate examinations in the spring of 1936 was very low, because of the excessive amount of time that had been taken up that year with extracurricular political activity. But Gamal Abdel Nasser was one of those who did pass. His father was as much surprised as he was pleased.

A few weeks after graduation Britain and Egypt signed the 1936 Treaty of Alliance, which some historians claimed was the greatest event for Egyptians since the Arab invasion. It recognized the equal status of the two countries. No British troops were to be permitted anywhere in Egypt except along the Canal. In no way were they to infringe upon the national sovereignty of Egypt, and they were to remain only until the Egyptians themselves were in a position to assure safety of navigation.

This seemed to put an end to Gamal's activities as an agitator. At least his days of schoolboy demonstrations were over. Now to find a career. First he applied for admittance to the Royal Military Academy, Egypt's West Point or Sandhurst. If Egypt was to be a sovereign nation, there should be opportunities, Gamal thought, in the Army. His application was rejected. He had no impressive family connections, no sponsors, no particular recommendations. And so, instead, he followed the practice of many other young men who wanted to rise above the social and economic status of their parents. He entered the law school of Fouad University in Cairo. Law was respectable, and the yearning for respectability and status among the middle class was so great that a majority of all university students were studying law. In each of the classes Gamal attended, there were hundreds of students sitting, taking notes. Sometimes as many as a thousand.

Gamal left law school after a few months. Many reasons for his departure have been given by others, among them that he decided he had no aptitude for law. To this his answer is: "I left before any examinations were held, so how could I know whether I liked it? The rule I had always followed was never to study until just before examinations. So when I left I knew nothing yet about whether I liked law."

The real reason is much more understandable. There was unending friction between Gamal and his stepmother. He and his father were not even speaking to each other. If he remained a student in law he would have to live at home, perhaps for a long time, because with so many new lawyers being turned out each year only a few ever found positions in law offices. But if he undertook a military career he would be sent to distant places. He would live away from home, in army barracks. Thus he could escape.

He asked for and received an appointment with the Under Secretary of State for War and presented his case. He admitted he had a police record. He admitted he had organized demonstrations. He said he had no letters of recommendation from beys or pashas. But he wanted to serve in the Army. The general, apparently won by the boy's serious intensity, told him to report before an examination board on a certain day in March. When the day came, Gamal found that the general himself was seated behind the desk, in charge of the examiners. Four hundred young men applied for admission. Only forty were to be accepted.

He was much surprised when he read the list of the successful candidates in the papers and saw his name among them. So was his father. Surprised but not angry, as he had been the first time his son's name appeared in print.

"The Army may be the making of him," Abdel-Nasser Hussein said to his brother, Khalil Hussein Khalil.

CHAPTER 4

THE CUT OF THE KNIFE

"...and you are now commissioned a second lieutenant."

The young man who saluted, then held out his hand to take his certificate of graduation from the Egyptian Royal Military Academy was twenty years old, almost six feet tall, clean-shaven, exceptionally broad of shoulder. He had a deep scar almost in the center of his forehead. He seldom smiled, although when he did his expression was warm and friendly. Throughout his sixteen months at the Academy on the perimeter of Cairo he had been called by his classmates "the somber cadet." During those months he had grown from a boy to a man.

Everything had conspired against his acquiring a sound basic education: the death of his mother, the trouble with his father and stepmother, the lack of any place he could look upon as home, the distractions of politics. But during his time at the Academy he had been free of all these handicaps, so he read as much as possible when he was not on the field drilling or studying military subjects. The academy library was a good one, and included even the most up-to-date books in English. But Gamal's literary interest was limited almost exclusively to Egypt and the Middle East: Egypt yesterday, today, tomorrow, though yesterday to him meant only the immediate past. He still had no interest in mummies, hieroglyphics, ancient art, or dead splendor. Mustafa Kamel was still his hero. He was trying to carry on his own political thinking from where Kamel had left off upon his death. His interest was so intense that often, after lights out, he would read under the covers by flashlight.

As a result of the 1936 treaty with Britain, the Egyptian Government had opened the Academy to boys from all classes of society, regardless of wealth, family, position. Gamal and his classmates were the first group of the "new officers" graduated. They had been given an accelerated course because they were needed in the field. As they were sent off to their first posts they were told that theirs would be the task of making something better out of the Egyptian Army than a second-rate police force.

35

Second Lieutenant Gamal Abdel Nasser—now nicknamed Jimmy—was posted to the Fifth Battalion at Mankabad, a military station on the edge of the desert in Upper Egypt, just across the river and a few miles up the road from Beni Mor. Here he had his first close association with British army officers. For the next six years he would be dealing with them. To him many of them seemed third-rate; away from home, unhappy, forced to serve time in an uncomfortable and strange part of the world, and bored by a life of inaction, they seemed to be poor advertisements for their country. They had to have their afternoon tea promptly at five, no matter what was happening. Many of them looked down on Egyptians as members of a lesser breed because of the color of their skin and because their broken English was so often unintelligible. They called the Egyptians "wogs" and "gippies," not caring that the words were offensive. They issued impossible orders and handed out unfair punishments. They strutted; they were pompous. Such were the observations of Lieutenant Gamal Abdel Nasser and his friends. There were, of course, exceptions, but the young Egyptian officers were not interested in exceptions. At Mankabad he began to feel the Anglophobia to which he had been exposed secondhand in the writings of Mustafa Kamel. There he also met some Egyptians for whom he had no respect, his superior officers.

"They were overfed, lazy, and selfish. They spent their time eating, drinking, gambling, carousing, smoking hashish, and engaging in many different forms of tyranny and corruption. They had the most unmilitary-shaped stomachs I ever saw on army officers anywhere. They were fawning and subservient to the British Military Mission, and a disgrace to the uniform they wore. They spent money that belonged to the Egyptian Army on food and drink for themselves."

Gamal Abdel Nasser was no neophyte rebel. He had already defied his father, his stepmother, his schoolteachers, the police, British security officers, and the Egyptian Government. But it was significant that his first real intrigue, his first act of plotting, was against his superior officers at his first military post. He was so incensed by their behavior that he tried to organize a cabal against them. There were nearly three thousand soldiers and officers at Mankabad, and this young man so fresh from the Academy went among them spreading criticism of the senior officers and making no secret of his contempt for them. This never burst into open rebellion because he was soon sent on maneuvers to El Cherif, twenty miles farther away from the Nile and civilization.

It was in the shadow of this hill that the first seeds of the revolution of 1952 were planted. All day long the young officers drilled, worked, played at war. By nighttime they were tired, but they often sat around a campfire in front of their tents and talked. Anwar el Sadat was one of them, a soft-speaking, amiable young man with coal-black hair, a large bushy mustache, and an intense, crisp way of talking. He was eleven months younger than Gamal but had graduated from the Academy ahead of him.

"I despise the British more than anyone on earth!" Sadat announced one night to those around the campfire.

There were mutterings of agreement.

"You all know about Zahram, don't you?" he continued. "Well, I was brought up listening to the song of Zahram. My grandmother used to sing it to me, and for her it was not just another song. She came from Dinshawai. You know what happened there, don't you? It's one of the saddest chapters in our entire humiliating history. In 1906—that was the year before Lord Cromer finally left—may his soul roast in hell— some British Army officers went hunting pigeons at Dinshawai and somehow one of their bullets set fire to a field of ripe summer wheat. When the fellahin saw the flames they began to chase the British officers. One of the officers fell. It was later determined that he had died of a sunstroke. But the British authorities, instead of compensating the fellah for the loss of his wheat, ordered a trial of the villagers for bringing about the death of the officer. They built a gallows in the center of the village even before a single witness was heard. The judge ordered six villagers to be flogged, then hanged in public view. After it was all over, the villagers composed a song about Zahram. He was the first of the six to be hanged, a handsome fellow, if my grandmother was right, tall, powerful, with the muscles of a giant. All the girls of the village loved him. That's what the song said, anyway." He paused, then said angrily, "Do I hate the British? You're damn right I do!" After a moment, in a voice soft with venom, he added, "Someday I'm going to get even with them for what they did at Dinshawai. I don't yet know how, but my day is going to come."

Another young officer, explaining that he was from Alexandria, took up the complaint:

"Why should this country of ours be run *by* foreigners and *for* foreigners? That's what I want to know. They don't even consult us. In Alexandria I know foreigners who have lived there all their lives and still they don't speak a single word of our language. Is that right? They exploit our country and take our wealth off to Europe to spend. The worst of it is they don't even seem a little grateful. Most of them actually despise us. That's the worst."

At Mankabad there was no one to temper this xenophobia; no one to answer their bitter arguments, to point out that the development of Egypt had often been achieved by foreigners despite the apathy of some Egyptians and the greed of others.

Around the campfire they talked about how sick Egypt was; about the restlessness of educated young men like themselves; about the frequent changes of power among the politicians; about their contempt for the existing order. Young Gamal listened more often than he talked, and did a lot of thinking during these months on the desert.

Among those who sat in on the discussions was another recent graduate of the Academy, Zakaria Mohieddin. He was hesitant about expressing his opinions, but he made it clear that he was on the side of the rebellious young men.

Before Gamal left Mankabad, he received an invitation to visit Beni Mor. His father had never taken him there and never suggested a visit to him. Gamal knew why. Abdel-Nasser Hussein and his father had quarreled, just as Gamal Abdel Nasser and his father had. His father and grandfather had quarreled so bitterly that Abdel-Nasser Hussein no longer visited Beni Mor, and he had no desire for his son to honor the family by going there. But somehow word reached Beni Mor that a handsome young member of the clan was stationed at Mankabad, so a cousin came over and insisted on taking Gamal back for a visit.

They gathered in the *duwar,* or community house, to greet him and passed him a gold-covered box of tinsel-wrapped chocolates and a small cup of thick Turkish coffee. They stared at him, trying to see if he resembled his father's family. They asked him about Abdel-Nasser Hussein and his second wife, and how many more children he had, and about Uncle Khalil.

Gamal, on his side, carefully examined the place of his ancestral roots and scrutinized his relatives. He met his grandfather, Hussein Khalil, who that year was celebrating his hundredth birthday. He also met Taha, who was his uncle, although he had just reached the age of ten, and Attia, who had remained a fellah.

In his smart military uniform, his head full of revolutionary ideas, he may have wondered how much he had in common with those fellahin who lived their gray-brown life so close to the soil and so far removed from political activity. Yet these were the people who were really being exploited. These were the victims of the system he wanted to overthrow.

However, Gamal Abdel Nasser did not ever again go to Beni Mor for a real visit, although he paused there briefly fifteen years later when he was on an official tour of Upper Egypt.

In 1939 the world was on the verge of a catastrophic war. But in Alexandria a bright young second lieutenant was being prepared for duty in the Anglo-Egyptian Sudan, place of exile for Egyptian officers in disfavor or disgrace. The rebels of Mankabad had been scattered. Their superior officers, suspicious of all their talk, had arranged for them to be sent off in divergent directions.

The night Gamal Abdel Nasser arrived in Alexandria he was greeted by another lieutenant who, being the duty officer and knowing Nasser was coming, personally made a room ready for him.

"Lieutenant Abdel-Hakim Amer, sir," he said smartly, as he presented himself.

Gamal smiled. They had known each other slightly at the Academy, for Amer had been in the class behind him. He remembered that this slim, impulsive young man had been nicknamed Robinson because of his fondness for the Robinson Crusoe type of story. Amer had his roots even deeper in the soil of Upper Egypt than Nasser, for he had been born in a village halfway between Cairo and Beni Mor. In many ways they were different, yet they instinctively liked each other and that night as they sat talking a friendship began.

The next year, France fell. Dunkirk. The start of Nazi air raids on Britain. And in Khartoum two young lieutenants were busying themselves with the most routine of army duties, in a city that was hardly a city, hundreds of miles from anything familiar.

From Khartoum they were transferred forty-five kilometers farther south, to Jabal al Awlia, on the White Nile, where Egypt had built a dam she guarded with her own troops. Amer and Nasser were the only officers there. They had adjoining rooms, ate together, hunted wild birds together, shared their books and newspapers. The friendship between the impulsive, unpredictable Amer and the cool, almost phlegmatic Nasser grew stronger. Much of the time they talked about the future of Egypt, and Amer suggested they should try to affect that future by working somehow within the Army.

"But let's remember that we are not politicians," he cautioned.

"And I'm not sure we want to be," Nasser replied.

"But if we can get enough young army officers to think as we do, something may come of it."

The seeds planted at Mankabad were beginning to take root.

In September, Italians under Grazziani took Sidi Barrani, sixty miles inside Egypt. Late that year, Nasser and Amer were transferred from the Sudan back to Cairo.

When Churchill succeeded Chamberlain as Prime Minister he promptly demanded that the Egyptian Army be withdrawn from all front-line positions. This the Egyptian Army considered an insult to its reputation, and there was loud grumbling. Nasser and Amer heard that the pyrotechnical Anwar el Sadat wanted to do more than grumble. After leaving Mankabad he had been sent to the Western Desert and was in one of the two Egyptian divisions ordered to turn in their arms and withdraw. What he wanted to do was stage an armed revolt against the British, but cooler heads persuaded him that his time for revenge had not yet come. When he arrived in Cairo he conferred at once with Nasser.

"We must organize!" he declared. "The British are going to lose the war. We must be ready to take over when they are forced out."

The pro-Axis sympathies of most Egyptians at this time were not based alone on the conviction that the Germans and Italians were going to win the war. Nor alone on the Arab proverb: "He who is the enemy of my enemy is my friend." The ideology of the two totalitarian powers was ready-made for a country like Egypt. It reassured the wealthy pashas and beys who were amassing fortunes out of the war and wanted to keep their money. But at the same time the mumbo jumbo of the "socialism" they dispensed fascinated the masses of the poor, the ignorant, and those easily taken in by slogans. There was something in it for every Egyptian. Military men such as young Lieutenant Nasser were impressed by the might of the Wehrmacht and the Luftwaffe, by the military genius that had so quickly brought about the fall of Warsaw, Copenhagen, Oslo, Brussels, Paris, Athens, Belgrade.

One day Sadat told Nasser and Amer of a chance meeting he had had with a man he thought they could use, Sheikh Hassan el Banna, a watch-repairer by trade, now founder and Supreme Guide of an organization calling itself the Moslem Brotherhood. Some people looked upon him as a saint, others as an eccentric. He went about Cairo wearing a long red cloak that partially hid his face. He boasted that he made an average of fifteen hundred speeches a year. As a small boy he had written leaflets, which he nailed to the doors of mosques, calling on all good Moslems to give up the wearing of gold rings and silk clothes. Then he began a practice of getting up while it was still dark and going from house to house, arousing people indiscriminately because he thought it was time for them to get ready to say their prayers by the first light. He wrote patriotic poetry and campaigned against equal rights for women. As he grew older he rented three of the largest cafés in Cairo and entertained his audiences with vivid descriptions of the tortures of hell. In 1928 he began organizing the Moslem Brotherhood. Its stated objective was to seek the moral perfection of the individual and a regeneration of society. Branches set up all over the country organized industrial enterprises to bring in funds for the movement, raised money to build mosques, gave courses in physical training, engaged in an intensive study of eschatology, supported a newspaper of their own, and began building schools in which the principles of Islam would receive due stress.

The more fanatic of the brethren often outdid the Supreme Guide in their religious ardor. Not only did they aim to set up a theocratic state, by violent means if necessary, but many wanted to expel from the country every single foreigner, to punish women who so much as peeked from behind their veils, and to go back to the old Koranic penalties for adultery, theft, and murder.

The organization's initiation ceremony took place in a room lighted dimly by candles. The initiate, holding the Koran in one hand and a revolver in the other, swore an oath of loyalty, obedience, and secrecy. Then, as an advertisement of his membership, he would try to grow a small wisp of a fuzzy chin beard.

Sadat, the rebel soldier, was not much interested in these activities of El Banna and his followers. "But," he kept saying, "there is no reason why we should not make use of this highly organized band."

Nasser and Amer discussed it and then asked Sadat to have a talk with El Banna. Several days later Sadat reported that he had had a long conference with the Supreme Guide in his villa on the edge of the city, a place he described as being "shrouded in mystery, its walls lined with marble, and with a library full to the very ceiling with books."

The mystic leader had boasted that all Egypt was flocking to his banner, rich and poor, intellectuals and workers, fellahin and city people. He impressed his visitor as being a fanatic and a clear thinker, both at the same time. He had hinted that the Brotherhood was about to set up ammunition dumps and engage in paramilitary training. He had used the expression "shock battalions." This was the part of the conference that Sadat stressed to Nasser.

The Supreme Guide declared that the Brotherhood was a strictly indigenous organization, yet Sadat noticed that in his speeches and writings he often referred to events in Germany, Italy, and Turkey. He obviously admired the Nazis, the Fascists, and the Turkish Nationalists. He seemed to approve of the way power had been consolidated in Turkey by the elimination of political parties. He reminded Sadat that Italy had been "brave enough" to defy most of the world when sanctions were imposed upon her during her invasion of Abyssinia. He said Egypt was using this new invention, the radio, to corrupt the people with songs about love and sex, whereas Hitler had used it to enlighten his people.

Nasser's decision was that they should infiltrate the Brotherhood with their own young officers and keep a close eye on it. Someday it might be useful. He delegated Sadat as the go-between.

One evening Sadat reported he had made another contact. The Supreme Guide had arranged for him to meet General Aziz el Masri, who had been deposed as Egyptian Chief of Staff at the insistence of the British because they doubted his loyalty to the Allied cause. The rendezvous was arranged with much secrecy. El Banna gave Sadat a piece of paper on which was written an address. When Sadat found the place, it turned out to be a dental clinic. There the old general was waiting.

"He is a little man," Sadat told Nasser. "A little man with a passionate temperament, tremendous energy, and a will of iron."

He had fought in the Balkan wars and again in Libya with the Turks against the Italians. He had been tutor to the boy Farouk in England but later fell into disfavor.

"Why?" Nasser asked.

"Because someone persuaded young Farouk that General Masri was intending to poison Queen Nazli, Farouk's mother," Sadat replied. Then he continued, "The general says he will give us his support. He says he believes in young officers. He says, 'Look what Napoleon did when he was only thirty!' "

But before the conspirators could make any more progress, Amer was transferred to Mankabad and Nasser was sent to that key defense point on the Western Desert called El Alamein.

El Alamein was a dreary post in 1941. Nasser was not at all happy there. There was war to the west, war to the north, confusion back home, but at El Alamein there was only sand, boredom, and mutual contempt between British and Egyptian officers. He missed his friend, the unpredictable Amer, and he missed, too, the excitable Sadat.

One day in March he received by grapevine a sensational piece of news. A Nazi agent had sneaked through enemy lines and arrived one night at the home of General Aziz el Masri with plans for the deposed Chief of Staff to collaborate with the Germans. There was no hurry. But the agent explained how Masri could communicate his reply when he had made up his mind.

While the old general was debating the offer, a new message from the Nazis suggested they send a plane for Masri. The general accepted. The plane would have R.A.F. markings and would arrive at dawn on Saturday. If it received the correct recognition signals from the ground it would land at an appointed place, close to Oasis Road. The general would come aboard quickly and be landed behind German lines a few minutes later.

About the middle of the week Sadat, who was supposed to see that the plan was carried through, was ordered to the Western Desert. To avoid going he played ill. But he overdid it. His illness was so convincing that he was placed in a military hospital in Cairo, under guard.

On Saturday, just before dawn, a plane with R.A.F. markings flew low over Oasis Road. When it received no recognition signals it returned to its base. General Aziz el Masri had not forgotten. His automobile had broken down on the way to the rendezvous.

Several weeks later at El Alamein, Nasser received even more dramatic news. Embarrassed by what had happened, General Masri had made his own plans to get out of Egypt by Egyptian plane. His two pilots would be members of the Egyptian Air Force, trained by the British but friendly to the Axis. One was Abdul Moneim Abdul Raouf, a reckless young flying officer. He was a friend of Sadat and through Sadat had become a friend of Nasser. He was an enrolled member of the Moslem Brotherhood and in Sadat's absence served as the principal link between Nasser and El Banna. The other pilot was Hussein Zulfi-car Sabry, a small, wiry young squadron leader who had been a classmate of Sadat and Zakaria Mohieddin at the Academy. Now he was second in command of King Farouk's private aircraft. Nasser heard a rumor at El Alamein that Farouk knew of Masri's desire to go over to the Nazis and that he was the one who had assigned Sabry to fly the general. The young man was a crack pilot, but on the take-off his plane hit a post and was almost demolished. Both pilots and the general were arrested. They were now in jail awaiting trial.

The next report Nasser received was that Raouf, Sabry, and the general had been found guilty of high treason and would probably spend the rest of their lives in prison. Sadat, now out of hospital, his fake illness cured, sent him this message:

"Except for ill luck we would have joined forces with the Axis, struck a quick blow at the British, and perhaps have helped win the war. Better luck next time!"

By 1942 the Nazis were sweeping across Russia. The Japanese had sunk the best part of the American fleet at Pearl Harbor and had captured Manila. In Egypt, on February 4, British authorities were informed that King Farouk was about to appoint as Prime Minister Aly Maher, known as "Hitler's man." Just before dusk on this day the square in front of Abdin Palace, in the heart of Cairo, was suddenly filled with the thunder of war. A squadron of British tanks and armored vehicles converged on the palace. Three tanks charged the wrought-iron palace gates and forced an entrance, although there really was no opposition. The British Ambassador, Sir Miles Lampson, surrounded by South African officers with drawn pistols, entered the palace, found the cowering King, and presented him an ultimatum: appoint Nahas Pasha, the Wafd political leader, Prime Minister within twenty-four hours or quit the country.

Psychiatrists have advanced the theory that the shock of February 4 brought about a complete change in the character of Farouk: he began to be nervous and depressed, irascible and often violent; he even changed physically from an attractive man to a prematurely aged, fat figure.

More important for Egypt was the change that came over Gamal Abdel Nasser and the other young officers who were beginning to look to him for guidance. At Mankabad, in the Sudan, in Cairo, and at El Alamein he had had considerable personal contact with British officers, most of them with more education, more sophistication, more culture than he had. And somehow they seemed to make him feel it. Perhaps not always intentionally. He also felt the centuries of humiliation bred into his core, the degradation to which his people had been subjected by one conqueror, one occupier after another. For hundreds of years uncomplaining fellahin had taken the oppression stoically and lived to see the invader absorbed or eventually driven out. But now, finally, a generation had arisen that would not accept such treatment with meekness and resignation.

The question of whether the British had a right, at such a critical moment as this, to protect themselves against the Trojan-horse maneuver Farouk and his Nazi friends were preparing was not the point under consideration by the young rebels. It was the method they used to do it. If Sir Miles Lampson had not sent tanks charging into the courtyard of Abdin Palace on February 4, 1942, some other event might have acted as the catalytic agent for Gamal Abdel Nasser, but this action was what did it.

"I am actually glad for the incident," he wrote to one of his brothers. "This is the cut of the knife which has given back life to our young officers."

To a friend he wrote: "I am ashamed that our army has not reacted against this attack and that she has accepted it, but I am glad that our officers, who until now think only of amusing themselves, at last begin to speak of revenge."

The more he thought about it the more furious he became, for in another letter he wrote: "I flame with anger. . . . This shock has put souls into some bodies. They have learned there is something called dignity."

In this same letter he used so vile a word in referring to the British that an Egyptian newspaper left a blank when it printed the letter. Then he added: "I believe the Imperialists hold a weak, one-trump hand. They are simply bluffing and bullying us. Had they felt there were Egyptians ready to shed their blood and meet force with force, they would have beat a hasty retreat, like a harlot rebuffed."

In 1942 Nasser and his officer friends had no strong feeling either for or against Farouk. But in this case he was an Egyptian symbol who had been spat upon. When he lost face in the eyes of the world, so did they. Now Farouk, the King, was virtually a prisoner within his own palace and Egypt was no better than an occupied country, they said. But, more important, the Egyptian Army, their army, had been revealed to the world as a weak and useless thing. This was the great mortification. One squadron of tanks had captured a country without a shot being fired. Not a single Egyptian soldier had offered to shed a drop of blood to protect his sovereign from ignominy. What a story for an Egyptian officer to tell his children!

Angry and frustrated, many of the men gathered at the Officers' Club in Zamalek on Gezira Island and just talked. A middle-aged staff officer, Lieutenant Colonel Mohamed Naguib, sent in his resignation, saying he did not wish to continue his association with an army that could not defend its king. The resignation was rejected. Two young lieutenants, Abdel Latif Baghdady and Salah Salem, presented themselves to the

Chief of the Royal Cabinet and offered their services, to perform whatever task, no matter how dangerous, the King might think up for them. Anwar el Sadat, man of violence, began talking about dynamite and assassination.

But Gamal Abdel Nasser on February 4, 1942, quietly started planning revolution. They would need an organization, so he began to create one aimed at seizing power—somehow, someday. He decided to call himself and his associates the Free Officers. Free because they would owe allegiance to no one. No one except him. Free because they would form no alliances, make no promises, have no ideology, no program. Only to seize power. The Free Officers would be a secret society, with no one knowing its size, its leaders, its membership. No one except him. And perhaps Amer. On that day Gamal Abdel Nasser began to devote his life —all his energy, all his time, all his spare money—to laying the groundwork for revolution.

In July the Germans were advancing toward the Caucasus. In the East, Singapore, Hong Kong, Malaya, the Dutch East Indies had fallen. At Tobruk twenty-five thousand British soldiers had been captured. The Afrika Korps was racing across North Africa. Soon it would be pounding at the gates of Alexandria. The Luftwaffe had the sky almost to itself. In Cairo the street mob was chanting, "Rommel! Rommel! Rommel!" The British were talking of evacuation. The Embassy was burning its secret papers.

Sadat, with the permission or perhaps even at the suggestion of Nasser, who had now been transferred to Cairo, went to see El Banna. He reported that the Supreme Guide had wept and fumbled with his prayer beads and said his soul was moved by the vision of Egypt in arms, marching, delivering herself from her bondage. But after this bit of emotionalism he suggested that the Free Officers join the Moslem Brotherhood and quietly submerge themselves in his movement that was serving Allah as well as Egypt.

"That is not the way," Nasser decided. "We may have the same objective, but we must remain Free Officers. Completely free."

They talked about whether they should have any definite political orientation, and Sadat said, "I have always mistrusted theories and purely rational systems. I believe in the power of concrete facts and the realities of experience. My political ideas have grown out of the personal experiences of oppression, not out of abstract notions. I am a soldier, not a theoretician, and it is by the empirical process that I have come to realize that my country must have a political system which responds to its essential needs and reflects its true spirit."

Nasser never got himself tangled up in such a verbose explanation of opportunism, but he did agree that there would be less possibility of controversy among the Free Officers, less danger of breaking up into splinter groups, if they agreed only on the need to bring about a change. This was a shrewd decision.

One hot evening that same summer two young officers in British uniform arrived by military car at Sadat's home. The spokesman introduced himself in perfect Arabic as Hussein Gaafer. He told his story cautiously at first. His real name was Herr Appler and he had been born in Egypt of a German mother and an Egyptian father. His companion was Herr Sandy. They were Nazi agents sent by Rommel to establish an intelligence center in Cairo. They had crossed the desert in a jeep with British markings. Strapped around their waists was almost a quarter of a million dollars in counterfeit British bank notes, manufactured by the Germans. They also had a powerful radio transmitter in the car.

Sadat introduced them to Raouf, and tried to help them with their espionage problem. They changed their British uniforms for civilian clothes and their counterfeit money, a little at a time, for good Egyptian bank notes. They might have succeeded in their mission if they had not taken up residence on a Nile houseboat with an Egyptian dancer who had been the mistress almost simultaneously of a British officer and an American reporter. Their eventual exposure quickly led to the arrest of a young Egyptian officer who was also involved, but for several months no one connected Sadat or Raouf with them. Then Winston Churchill went through Cairo on his way to the Moscow Conference of August 1942 and asked to see the two Nazi prisoners. For him they talked. Shortly afterward Sadat was arrested, court-martialed, and sent to a prison camp in Upper Egypt.

By this time the Free Officers' organization was beginning to take form, and one of the first assessments Nasser collected from the members went to pay Sadat's family the equivalent of fifty dollars a month during the entire two years he was in prison.

By December the tide of battle was turning everywhere. The Russians had halted the Germans at Stalingrad. The British had won at El Alamein. Nearly three hundred thousand Allied troops had landed in North Africa.

About this time Nasser, now a captain, was appointed an instructor in the Military Academy and Amer became an instructor in the Army School of Administration. This gave both of them an excellent opportunity to look over young officers and cadets and select for the Free Officers those who seemed to have rebellion in their souls.

In the spring Nasser learned that Sadat had been transferred to a British-supervised prison at Zeitun, on the edge of Cairo. There Sadat and five other inmates hatched a plot. They made a hole in the floor of their quarters, dropped down into a rabbit hutch, brushed themselves off, and headed for the city. The plan was that Sadat and one of the others would go to the apartment of a French lady, who they were sure would hide them, and next morning they would take a taxi to Abdin Palace, where they would try to see Farouk and complain of the way the British were treating Egyptian prisoners. The other four were to remain in hiding until they received word that Sadat and his companion had succeeded. Then they, too, would surrender and go back to prison.

"We made the plan like a military operation," Sadat later boasted to Nasser, but it was far from a success. The French lady took them in but kept them awake all night arguing. She had saved fifteen hundred pounds so she could leave Egypt, which she detested, but she insisted that the two convicts take the money and escape themselves. She would eventually find a way to get more. Exhausted from trying to resist her generosity, the pair went to the palace in the morning in a state of great weariness. There they were refused audience with the King and were taken into custody. Several hours later they were back in their prison cells. The other four escapees were caught, one by one, during the ensuing month.

Earlier this same year Amer, during a serious political discussion with Nasser, suddenly interrupted himself and said, "Gamal, I am going to get married."

"I have noticed that your mind has been wandering lately," his friend replied with a laugh.

In other parts of the world the following year, 1944, was a time of unprecedented violence. There were furious land, sea, and air battles in the Pacific. France was invaded by the Allies. At the Battle of the Ardennes Bulge the Americans and Germans between them lost a quarter of a million men, dead and captured.

In Egypt, military instructor Gamal Abdel Nasser spent most of his time, when he was not lecturing to his students, in private talks with men he thought would make good revolutionaries. He had to operate with caution, for British agents were everywhere, and they had many well-paid Egyptian informers. As he plotted and planned he became an able judge of men. He developed methods for testing the sincerity and honesty of those with whom he spoke. He seldom did the talking. If he were to express opinions, they might agree in order to draw him out or trap him. He preferred to let the young cadets and officers express themselves to him. He was looking for men who were not merely critical but who burned with a crusading desire to help create a new order. Yet he quickly veered away from men who had any fixed ideology. He signed up few he knew to be Communists or Moslem Brothers. He wanted officers who were uncommitted to anyone or anything else; uncommitted even to political, economic, or religious patterns of thought.

One of the instructions he gave to each new member was to arouse sentiment against the British in every possible way. Cadets and officers off duty, in civilian clothes, should talk so they could be overheard in cafés, on trams, even in mosques. Those Egyptian army officers and politicians who were sycophants of the British must be held up to public scorn. Every humiliation the British heaped upon the Egyptians must be denounced, every mistake they made magnified. Army men and civilians alike must be reminded, repeatedly, of what had happened on February 4, 1942. Any military reverse the British suffered should be exploited.

Nothing was ever committed to writing. The books he had read, the films he had seen, the true stories he had heard convinced him that words on paper had wrecked more plots and cost more lives than anything else. So Gamal Abdel Nasser began training himself to remember names, addresses, dates, places. Never at any time was there a membership list of the Free Officers. He and Amer were the only ones who knew all the names. Others knew some. Some may have known many. Most knew only a few.

Nasser's tactics of listening instead of talking and conferring with members one at a time gave each Free Officer the feeling that it was "me and Nasser." This was to cause complications later when dozens of them would each claim that for years he had been the principal aide and main support of the chief. Yet the ego-inflating device had great value in those early years.

Amer and Nasser had a friend, Abdel-Hamid Kazem, who lived in Abbassia, not far from the Academy. He was the owner of a small rug factory, one of the few friends outside the Army either of them had.

Often the two young officers went together to the Kazem home. Abdel-Hamid had a sister, Tahia, an attractive, dark-haired girl who managed the household for him. She had been born in Cairo, one of three daughters of a successful tea merchant. When he died he left her some stocks and bonds, from which she drew a monthly income of about two hundred dollars. Her mother and one sister also were dead. Her other sister was married, so she lived with Abdel-Hamid, her only brother.

When Nasser first met Tahia, she was twenty-one and he was twenty-five. They spoke together only casually, for he was much more interested in serious discussions with her brother. But Amer, after he married, tried to play matchmaker, often suggesting to Abdel-Hamid that Tahia and Gamal would make an excellent pair.

"Oh no, she wouldn't be the least interested in Gamal!" he always replied.

Some months later Gamal himself approached Abdel-Hamid. Again, perhaps not wanting to be deserted by his sister and left alone, he replied, "Oh no, I don't think she'd be interested."

"Would you dare to ask her?" Gamal challenged.

The brother did, and a few months later Gamal and Tahia were married in the presence of a few of her close friends, her brother, and some of Gamal's army officer companions. It was not a marriage that grew out of a great romance, yet they settled down to a comfortable and happy life together, Tahia contentedly occupying herself with her home, her husband, and the children who soon began to arrive in close succession, while Gamal devoted most of his time and energy to his obsession: laying the groundwork for revolution. He was happy to have a home and someone to take care of him who never questioned him about his extraordinary comings and goings.

Lieutenant Zakaria Mohieddin, who had been at Mankabad with Nasser, was one of the first men he signed up for the Free Officers. A couple of years later Mohieddin brought to his chief a brilliant young cousin, Khaled, who became one of the few avowed Communists Nasser ever took into the secret military order. Then, early in 1944, Khaled introduced to Nasser a boyhood friend, Ahmed Fouad, a dynamic young lawyer with an extensive knowledge of Marxism and a large library on political, social, and economic subjects. From him Nasser borrowed many of the books he read during the years before the revolution. Most of them had a strong left-wing orientation.

Late in the year the pro-Allied government of Nahas Pasha fell, and as a result most political prisoners were released. Among the exceptions was Anwar el Sadat, who was told he would have to wait until the end of the war. In protest he organized a hunger strike of his fellow prisoners. It was a success for several days, then the authorities persuaded all the others to break their fast. Sadat grew lean and feeble. Finally he was transferred to a hospital on the east bank of the Nile. On the third day, weak though he was, he managed to escape. British and Egyptian police and secret agents searched futilely for him month after month. He outwitted them by remaining constantly on the move. Sometimes he was in remote villages of Upper Egypt. Then in the Delta. Sometimes right in Cairo itself. He made no attempt to see Nasser, but sent word that he was alive and just waiting for the psychological moment to appear and collect his revenge.

In 1945 everyone knew that Germany was almost finished. Just before American troops streamed across the Rhine, the Egyptian Government declared war on both Germany and Japan. It was only a gesture, made to place Egypt at the peace table, but Ahmed Maher, the Prime Minister responsible, was immediately assassinated by the Moslem Brotherhood.

A few days later his successor, Nokrashy Pasha, called on the British Ambassador and tried pounding the table. The Ambassador shrugged his shoulders and reminded the new Prime Minister that there was still a war in progress. He suggested that Egypt hold up its demands until a more propitious moment. Nationalist forces used the story of this rebuff to stir public indignation, and it brought Sadat out of hiding. He was thin, nervous, and excited as he shook hands with Nasser.

"I couldn't stay away any longer. I know what's happened. I think the time has come," he said.

"The time . . . ?"

"The time to collect my revenge."

Nasser smiled.

"I have it all very carefully planned," Sadat explained. His scheme was to blow up the sprawling yellow-stone buildings of the British Embassy in the heart of Cairo at a time when the Ambassador and his entire staff would be in their offices.

Nasser, as he sat listening to his friend, was faced with the necessity of making the first of a long line of life-or-death decisions. Starting now and perhaps for the rest of his life he would be in a position to decide whether a man should live or die. Sometimes it would be a question of whether a certain human being should be assassinated. Later the question would be whether a man should be hanged by the neck as punishment for a political act.

His most enthusiastic supporters contend that he is a mild and gentle man; that the loss of his mother when he was nine instilled in him a fear of death (not only of dying himself but of inflicting death on others) that has served as a nonsanguinary influence on him throughout his life. Others, while still praising him for his moderation in ordering the taking of human lives, contend that the motivation is more pragmatic than psychological; that his extensive reading about revolutions convinced him murder does not pay; that he who lives by assassination is likely to die by an assassin's weapon himself; that if one enemy is executed, ten new and even bitterer enemies may be created among the survivors; that you can sometimes make an ardent supporter out of an enemy if you are not too hasty in taking his life.

Sadat, today still one of Nasser's close friends and political associates, left his meeting with the military instructor that day clear in his own mind as to why Nasser vetoed his plan.

"Do you remember 1924?" Nasser asked him. "Do you remember the terrible British reprisals after the murder of Sir Lee Stack, the Governor-General of the Sudan, and the Sirdar of the Egyptian Army? No, Anwar, I am against your plan to blow up the Embassy. We must not give them a chance for a repetition of 1924."

In March 1945, on Britain's initiative, all the Arab nations formed an organization to be called the Arab League, ostensibly to achieve greater Arab unity. Nasser and his Egyptian nationalists were suspicious, and warned that anything organized on instructions from London, or even with British blessing, must be avoided like a plague.

On April 28 Benito Mussolini was caught and killed by a mob. The next day in a bunker in Berlin, Adolf Hitler committed suicide. Eight days later the war in Europe ended. Egypt was left in a state of social, political, and moral confusion. Sadat was impatient with Nasser's caution. What was the sense of their organization if they kept temporizing? Egypt's political horizon should be extended now from the Persian Gulf to the Atlantic seacoast; from the Indian Ocean to the plateaus of Central Asia.

Partly because of this pressure, Nasser reorganized his movement. Henceforth there would be a civilian auxiliary to the Free Officers, and Sadat would head it. He would recruit his followers mostly from university students. They would be under Nasser's general direction but would have a degree of autonomy.

The Free Officers themselves would be divided into cells of five or ten

members each. Twenty cells would form a section. In principle no Free
Officer would know the name of other Free Officers except members of
his own cell. This would prevent anyone, wittingly or unwittingly, from
giving away information. It would be like a great web. He, Nasser,
would be the spider in the center. He could follow threads leading him
to any member of the organization, for all the threads eventually led to
him. The principle was that one man had to know everything, and the
less the others knew the better.

The Free Officers' most important secret was the identity of their
leader, and it was a secret so well kept that out of the several hundred
Cairo newspapermen—accustomed to prying into matters such as this
—only one knew, until long after the revolution, that the quiet-spoken
man with the scar on his forehead was the founder and chief.

Five sections were organized, dealing with economic affairs, personnel,
security, terrorism, and propaganda. The principal duty of the economic
section was to look out for dependents of Free Officers who might be
killed or sent to prison, to purchase arms and equipment, and to collect
an initial contribution of two months' salary from each member, which
would be called a loan. The personnel unit would keep track of the activities of all members and investigate any reports of desertions. The
security unit would issue the password (which was frequently changed),
punish violations of rules, and screen new recruits. The terrorism section
would set up a clandestine factory to make small arms and Molotov
cocktails. Ten thousand empty bottles were obtained from a Cairo
wholesaler and a work unit spent evenings filling them with explosives.
They were to be used whenever the necessity arose, but mainly to help
drive the British out of Egypt. The propaganda section would prepare
and distribute leaflets.

In October, Sadat began to form his secret civilian auxiliary. Because
he was an often frustrated terrorist, his first idea was to prepare a list
of men to be assassinated. He placed former Prime Minister Nahas
Pasha at the top and began to draw up a plan that was put into action
on December 11. As Nahas was driving through a crowded Cairo street,
one of Sadat's men threw a bomb under his automobile. Sadat had
based his calculations on a maximum speed of thirty miles an hour,
because of the usual density of traffic at this hour in the neighborhood.
But the car was moving at forty-five miles an hour, so the bomb exploded after Nahas was safely away. Instead of killing Britain's best
friend among the politicians it wounded a number of British soldiers in
a truck that happened to be following the Nahas car.

The report of the assassination attempt appeared in newspapers all over the world, and Nasser knew it was the work of his friend and aide, yet there was neither a reprimand nor an order to desist from such tactics, for Sadat immediately began to plan his next adventure in sudden death.

By now General Masri was out of prison, so Nasser went to visit him. The general was in his early seventies, and the hardships of the prison term had aged him, but young Nasser found the old man stimulating. He had strong feelings and he expressed them without inhibition. His hatred of the British, now that they were on the winning side of the war, was even greater than in the days when he had tried to help the almost victorious Nazis.

"The cream of the scum!" was one of his favorite expressions for them.

Nasser discussed with the general the idea Sadat kept propounding: that the Free Officers should co-operate more closely with the Moslem Brotherhood.

"Moslem Brotherhood?" Masri snorted. "Moslem Brotherhood? That's nothing but a damn bunch of fanatics. Stay away from them!"

The second time Nasser came to call, the general looked him over slowly, from his curly black hair to his well-shined shoes, and said, "For all I know, you may be a secret police officer, trying to trap me into incriminating myself."

As Nasser started to protest, the general held up his hand. "Well, even if you are, I like to talk to you," he said with a smile.

During the next seven years Nasser frequently called on the general. The old man talked to him about many things: war, revolution, politics. He was intelligent and well versed in Middle Eastern history. Often Nasser sat and listened to him for hours. Gradually the old general became the patron saint of the Free Officers and, in Nasser's words, their "spiritual leader."

By 1946 war in the Pacific as well as war in Europe had ended, yet British and American men in uniform still swarmed the streets of Cairo and Alexandria day and night. This, said Gamal Abdel Nasser, was in violation of the treaty of 1936. Many other Egyptians thought so, too. National resentment grew daily, and it did not help the national inferiority complex to be told that Egypt had declared war only to get in on the spoils. Newspaper editors wrote vitriolic articles. Tempers boiled. There were casualties every day from mob violence. Schoolboys and university students organized themselves into secret societies whose declared purpose was to harry anyone in a foreign uniform. Members of one band specialized in roaming the streets of Cairo at night, looking for intoxicated British soldiers and sailors, who would be bashed over the head with clubs and left in the gutter. No attempt was made to rob them. That was not the purpose.

In other countries schoolboys talked of sports, or films, or girls. In Egypt in those days they were interested only in what they glorified by the name "politics." In Alexandria a gang of young men killed six British soldiers. An Egyptian judge, an old revolutionary, gave some of the culprits long prison sentences. Five days later he himself was assassinated.

The Free Officers and the Moslem Brotherhood agreed about the British. Both advocated complete evacuation of all foreign troops from the country. Only their methods differed. In 1946 the Supreme Guide called for war against foreign culture as well as foreign troops: "Shun your British friends. Boycott their businesses. Withdraw from societies and clubs in which they are members. Stop speaking their language. Stop reading their books."

The action units of the Brotherhood went even further. They smashed windows that bore French or English signs, rioted in cinemas that failed to put Arabic sound tracks on imported films, threw acid in the faces of Egyptian women so "heathen" as to go out in public unveiled, and threatened to bomb all girls' schools. They even warned the editor of the Arabic edition of the *Reader's Digest* that, unless he used his magazine to propagate the beliefs of Islam, bombs would be planted in his office. And everyone knew that the Brothers were building an arsenal of machine guns, bombs, hand grenades, and rifles to use when the time came.

Hate was riding Egypt.

Anwar el Sadat, humiliated by his own bungling, was determined to stage-manage a successful assassination, so he picked the second man on his list, Amin Osman Pasha, former Minister of Finance in the Nahas cabinet.

"I selected him because I knew that whatever happened to him he would find no pity among real Egyptians. He had been raised and educated by the British. He had made a speech saying Egypt was wedded to England in a Catholic marriage; there could never be a divorce; even if England, the husband, left Egypt, we must be faithful and not think of permanent separation. This speech wrote his fate."

Osman Pasha had formed a club called the Renaissance Organization, its aim being "eternal co-operation with England." It had second-floor quarters in a building in the center of Cairo. Sadat made what he called a "reconnaissance" and then a plan.

On the night selected for the assassination, Osman arrived by taxi and had his right foot on the first of four steps leading into the building when one of Sadat's squad called out, "Osman Pasha!"

Sadat ordered them to do this, "because I never liked the idea of shooting a man in the back."

Osman turned. Three bullets entered his body. Sadat and his squad escaped, but after a few days four of them were arrested and confessed. Then the entire organization he had recruited with Nasser's permission was rounded up, himself included. The soft-speaking specialist in assassination was given a long prison sentence, and without him the civilian terrorist branch of the Free Officers quickly disintegrated.

At this critical moment in his own career and in the history of Egypt, Gamal Abdel Nasser had to divide his time between his classroom work at the Academy, his revolutionary activities, and his home. There was now a new member in the household, Huda, a black-haired daughter with large serious eyes, who had arrived just three days before her father's birthday in January.

In May 1946 the British Labour government proposed that all British forces and equipment be evacuated from Egypt. This caused a storm in the British Parliament. Nevertheless, on the Fourth of July, 170 years after Americans rid themselves of colonial status, a ceremony was held at the Citadel overlooking Cairo. The British General Officer Commanding handed the Egyptian Chief of Staff a silver key to the city.

Some of the Free Officers argued that after this ceremony and the retirement of the British from Cairo their objective had been realized and they might as well disband. Nasser indignantly silenced such talk.

"When the last British soldier has left our soil—and that includes the Canal—we can speak of having won."

There were thousands of foreign troops in the Canal Zone, and so the agitation continued. In one of Cairo's main squares demonstrators built a huge bonfire of all the British books they could find. During this time Gamal Abdel Nasser continued to hold quiet private talks with young officers who had a glint of rebellion in their eyes.

In November he received word that he had passed his examinations for admission to the Staff College. It would be a two-year course, leading to appointment as a staff officer. The teacher would become a pupil again.

Early the next year, twelve months and a few days after the arrival of Huda, a second daughter was born. Tahia suggested they name her Mona, "the Desired One," to show that there had been no disappointment that Mona had not been a boy. Her brother Abdel-Hamid had died suddenly, and she and Nasser agreed they would give his name to the first son born to them.

"Next time," Tahia said after Mona came.

In the spring of 1947 the United Nations held a special session in an attempt to solve the Palestine problem. Another investigating committee went to the scene and returned recommending partition. The General Assembly in November approved a plan for dividing Palestine into an Arab state and a Jewish state of almost equal size.

Neither Gamal Abdel Nasser nor his Free Officers displayed much concern at first. Palestine was far removed from the problems in which they were interested. It was, as Egypt had been, a British-occupied piece of land. The first reaction of many of Nasser's friends to the U.N. plan was that it ordered the British to quit Palestine, and this was good. Now if *they* could just find a way to get rid of the British, who still were so deeply entrenched along the Canal.

CHAPTER 5

TELL THE BURIAL SQUAD

Haj Amin al-Husaini, Grand Mufti of Jerusalem, gave considerable aid to the Nazis during World War II and after their defeat moved his headquarters from Berlin to the Cairo suburb of Zeitun. There, as preparations were being made for carrying out the U.N. partition plan, he began to organize an invasion of a Jewish state that had not yet even been proclaimed. He had the support of the *imams*, or priests, at Al Azhar, who officially declared it a *jihad*, or holy war. To Moslems this was important, for the Koran forbids invasions, aggressions, murder, and the slaughtering of an enemy, unless it is done during a jihad, in which case any man who is killed in action immediately ascends to heaven, without having to wait for judgment on his mortal deeds.

Throughout the year that the partition of Palestine was being discussed, the Moslem Brotherhood worked diligently to excite the Egyptian people against the Jews of Palestine. They even made use of the chapter from the Koran on "Relations between Jews and Moslems" that declares:

They are smitten with vileness wherever they are found, unless they obtain security by entering into a treaty with Allah and a treaty with man ... Behold you love them and they love you not. You believe in the Scriptures and when they meet you they say we believe, but when they assemble in private they bite their fingers' ends out of wrath against you.

At first little attention was paid to the fanatics. There were about fifty thousand Jews in Cairo, Alexandria, and the other Egyptian cities, who played an important part in the life of the country. In normal times they were treated with respect and equality. Some had been Cabinet Ministers and members of Parliament. Many belonged to families that had lived in Egypt for hundreds of years. But in 1947 the atmosphere rapidly changed. Brotherhood members fanned any small sparks of religious intolerance they could find. Zionism was equated with Western imperialism. It was said that the United States was helping to create

58

Israel not because of any interest in homeless Jews but in order to get an imperialistic foothold in the Middle East.

One night Sadat asked Nasser's permission to arrange a meeting of the Free Officers at the home of the Brotherhood's Supreme Guide. Nasser hesitated, then consented.

Sheikh Hassan el Banna was fired with religious fervor. He delivered a rousing talk to the officers, then told them the plan. The Grand Mufti, collaborating with the Arab League and the Brotherhood, was organizing a full-scale invasion of Palestine.

Gamal Abdel Nasser had a serious personal decision to make that night. He had never given evidence of any strong anti-Jewish feelings. He had been brought up side by side with Jewish children. It was true that during his schoolboy days, when anti-Zionist demonstrations were held in Cairo to mourn the anniversary of the Balfour Declaration, he had joined in but, as he later wrote:

"When I asked myself at that time why I left my school so enthusiastically, and why I was so angry for this land which I never saw, I could find no answer except the echoes of sentiment."

In 1947 Captain Nasser did not at first see that the question of whether the Jews should have a homeland in the Middle East affected his objectives in any way. He was interested in Egypt and in the new army he was planning to use as the instrument of his ambitions. However, the Egyptian Army had suffered unforgettable shame on that dark day in February 1942 when it had permitted the British Ambassador to capture its King; it needed a few glorious moments, some spectacular victories in the field to overshadow that memory, to strengthen its self-respect and bolster its morale. It would be no match for any major military force, but surely with the help of several other Arab armies it could win cheap and quick victories against the Jews, who had only small underground forces and probably not much equipment, Jews who seldom in their recent history had demonstrated military aptitude. That was the way Nasser explained it to his colleagues. Also, if his Free Officers jumped quickly into positions of leadership in this crisis, the movement might win prestige that would be invaluable in the internal fight to come later. So the day after Sadat suggested it, Captain Nasser presented himself before the Grand Mufti at Zeitun.

"You will need officers to lead the men in battle and train volunteers," Nasser told him, "and there are a large number of Egyptian army officers ready to place themselves at your disposal if and whenever you so desire."

The Mufti replied that he was pleased with the spirit of Nasser and his fellow officers. "I think it will be necessary to obtain permission from the government," he added.

The government refused to give permission for Nasser's release as a Staff College student, but did permit many other Free Officers to go. No objection was raised to the departure of Moslem Brotherhood members. The government was happy to have the more fanatic Brothers elsewhere, for inside the country they were always a source of worry and trouble.

One morning Nasser and Amer went to the Cairo railroad depot to say good-by to Free Officer Kamal Hussein, who was on his way to Palestine with a group of other volunteers. After Hussein had left, Nasser did not go home at once but went instead to the editor of a daily newspaper and asked to be allowed to write a description of the departure. Then he waited at the newspaper office until a late hour to see his own words in print.

He may have felt frustrated at not being permitted to join in the guerrilla war already being fought against a state that did not yet exist, but he soon found an outlet for his energy and emotions. Two of his Free Officers, Hassan Ibrahim and Abdel Latif Baghdady, both in the Air Force, drew up a plan in collaboration with Fawzi el Kawukji, commander of the Arab irregulars, to steal a number of Egyptian planes, fly them to Palestine, bomb Jewish strong points, then land on a secret airfield near Damascus. Only a few trusted Free Officers were let in on the secret. Nasser himself was in charge of the plot, and he seemed to enjoy this first opportunity to do some high-level conniving. But the entire scheme collapsed because, for some reason never satisfactorily explained, the signal for the take-off, which was to have come from Damascus, was never received.

Meanwhile, a series of articles appeared in the weekly Egyptian magazine *Akhar Sa'a* that caused some second thinking among the Free Officers. They were entitled, *Fire on the Sacred Land*. Their author was a twenty-four-year-old reporter, Mohamed Hassanein Heikal, who had just returned from Palestine, where he had gone as a war correspondent with the volunteers. His articles advised his fellow Egyptians to "prepare before you make a decision." He felt it his duty, he wrote, to tell the Egyptian Government and military that if and when they declared war on Israel they would find that the underground army, Haganah, was not a "disorganized gang" or "mob of bandits," as they had been called by Arab belittlers, but a well-organized army of first-class fighters. "In Palestine," he warned his people, "you will not be facing the eternal Wandering Jew."

Several hours after the magazine appeared on the streets of Cairo, the Egyptian Prime Minister telephoned the publisher, Mustafa Amin. "Send that reporter to me at once!" he demanded.

The Prime Minister first berated, then questioned Heikal. But, since the Egyptian Government as yet had no fixed policy on Palestine, no action was taken against him.

The Free Officers held many serious discussions about the articles, and Gamal Abdel Nasser filed the name Heikal in a corner of his mind.

In May 1948, when Great Britain announced the decision to give up her Palestine mandate, she declared she would not permit any United Nations force in the country to keep order until the withdrawal of her own troops had been completed.

"This," Sadat said to Nasser, "amounts to an invitation to both Arabs and Jews to settle the dispute by bloodshed."

Nasser's class in the Staff College was not due to graduate until mid-summer, but one day it was announced that "because there is a possibility your services may soon be needed," graduation would be on May 15. After this the thoughts and hopes and emotions of all the young cadets were centered on Palestine.

May 15, 1948, was a Saturday. At a ceremony in Tel Aviv the previous afternoon David Ben-Gurion had officially proclaimed the creation of the State of Israel. At midnight the British mandate over Palestine officially came to an end. At five o'clock Saturday morning Egypt went to war when two waves of her bombing planes attacked Tel Aviv. Later in the morning columns of the Egyptian Army crossed Israel's frontier and began attacks on some of the *kibbutzim*, the agricultural settlements. At the same time, Jordan's Arab Legion and units of the Iraqi, Lebanese, and Syrian armies joined in the invasion.

That afternoon in the Staff College, graduation exercises were held for a small group of officers who were several months from actually finishing their course. One was a man of swarthy complexion, thirty years old, five feet eleven and a half inches tall, with dark curly hair, broad shoulders, and a small, closely trimmed mustache. After the graduation there was a tea party. The talk was exclusively about Palestine. As soon as the tea was over, the graduates were given their assignments. They would leave in the morning. Captain Nasser would go to the Sixth Battalion as battalion staff officer, a post corresponding to that of operations officer in the American Army, which involved making out orders, keeping records, and preparing maps and plans. Amer would go to the Ninth Battalion and Zakaria Mohieddin to the First. All three battalions were on the Egyptian–Israeli frontier.

There were tears the next morning as the new Sixth Battalion staff officer said good-by to his wife Tahia, his daughter Huda, now two and a half, and Mona, a year younger. The newspaper he had glanced at while having breakfast contained Communiqué No. 1 of the Royal Egyptian Army. It claimed great air-raid damage inflicted on Tel Aviv and deep troop penetrations by land. It reiterated, however, that it all was merely "an operation designed to punish the Zionist gangs." This phrase made Nasser angry. It was belittling what he wanted to consider an important war, his first taste of action after eleven years in the Army.

Despite the tearful farewells he was in an eager mood that morning, and as he started down the stairs he kept repeating to himself, "We're going to war! We're going to war!"

Amer, Mohieddin, and Nasser shared a compartment. As soon as the train was under way, they spread out maps and began to discuss the situation.

The train took them as far as El Arish. When they arrived, it was already dark and the frontier was blacked out.

They were dismayed that there was no one to meet them and to tell them what they had to do. They did not know where their units were stationed, and they couldn't find anyone who did. They went to area headquarters, expecting it to be a beehive of activity, but it was as empty as a deserted house in a ghost town. Nasser, now thoroughly dejected, had a feeling of impending disaster.

Finally they came upon an officer trying to find food for himself. They shared with him some meat and bread they had brought from Cairo, and after he had eaten he told them that the Sixth Battalion was at Rafah; the First and Ninth were at Gaza. Amer and Mohieddin left by jeep in one direction, Nasser in another. At Rafah, Nasser's morale fell even further. The Sixth Battalion had just returned from an operation against an Israeli settlement, leaving some of their dead and wounded behind.

The more details he heard about his own battalion's first defeat the less he liked the war in which he had been so eager to fight a few hours earlier. The battalion had been given no chance to reconnoiter its objective; it had received no advance information about the Jewish settlement; it had been supplied only one Arab guide, who knew nothing about the defenses; and the soldiers were given no rest before the attack. After twelve hours the battalion commander had given the order to retreat.

That night, listening to Cairo Radio, Nasser heard an Egyptian communiqué claiming the Sixth Battalion had made a successful attack on a Jewish settlement. This angered him more. He felt the communiqué should have told the truth. He was also disturbed because the other officers, judging from their talk, considered they were involved in a political rather than a military war; there were neither plans, strategy, reconnaissance, intelligence, nor possibility of victory.

It was only the second day of the war. He had been at the front only a few hours. Yet he had lost his faith already. It especially annoyed him to hear the strength of the enemy praised. One officer told him:

"The Jews have electrically operated gun towers that rise out of the earth, fire automatically, then disappear into the ground."

"How do you know they are powered by electricity?" he demanded. "You can't say this unless you entered the settlement and examined the bases of the towers."

He was constantly plagued with doubts and fears. He blamed his own commanding officer, the General Staff, politicians in Cairo, the brilliance of enemy tactics, and fate for Egypt's military reverses.

On his second day at the front the Sixth Battalion received an order to break camp and move three kilometers down the road. Several hours later an order came to put the battalion on a train for Gaza. For him the one consolation of going to Gaza was that he would rejoin his friend Amer, because the Sixth was going to replace the Ninth. He and Amer had never been very far from each other all these years. Although he would not admit it publicly, he felt confidence in a situation if Amer was close by. Some of his friends saw it almost as a child-father relationship, this great dependence on his friend, and it seemed to be growing stronger rather than weaker.

At Gaza he confessed his apprehensions to Amer, who listened with interest but made little comment. Then as Amer left to move off with his troops he said, "Oh, by the way, here is a thousand pounds sterling. Army funds. You are supposed to use it to buy food for your battalion."

Nasser immediately went on a purchasing mission. The shops of Gaza were still well stocked with fresh cheese and the olives for which the region is famous. But it distressed him to think that someone had neglected to provide better food for his troops. He was heartsick thinking that his men would be fighting on a ration of nothing but olives and cheese. Over and over again he said to himself, "This is no war."

The next day, Amer's battalion attacked a kibbutz called Yad Mordechai. In Gaza, Nasser could hear the booming of guns. That night, the Egyptian wounded began to pour into Gaza Hospital. At the same time, Cairo Radio was broadcasting that the Egyptian Army had had a successful day and occupied the kibbutz. This lie plunged him into an even deeper gloom. The Egyptians had attacked the kibbutz in several waves, but they were set back, and to him their defeat looked like a massacre.

The following day, the First and Ninth were ordered into new positions. He was shocked and enraged when he saw the announcement of these troop movements in the Cairo newspapers before they had even begun.

A few days later the Sixth Battalion was ordered to advance to a village on the front called Usdoud.

He was happy now. "At long last," he thought, "we will meet the enemy face to face." Also, he would see Amer, whose battalion was fighting at Usdoud.

But then orders were received from Cairo to prepare to help the Jordanian Army, which was engaged in desperate battle with the Israelis at Bab el Wad. Jordanians, too, had invaded Israel. They, also, were trying to snuff out the newborn state. They and the Egyptians were allies, yet this command made him bitter again. However, a short time later the orders were countermanded.

At Usdoud he found Amer, who had been in the thick of the fighting there. He was still smiling and confident. This helped restore Nasser's morale. Amer had his bed in a trench in an orange grove. Nasser put his close by, in the same trench. They talked most of the night about the war, when they were not listening to reports from a radio set that stood between their cots.

Amer told his friend he had been ordered to attack the Israeli settlement of Nitsanim the next day.

"I'm worried about what will happen," Nasser answered.

Amer reassured him. His men's morale was high, he said, and Captain Mahmud Khalif, a Free Officer, had won a drawing to decide who should lead the attack.

In the morning the Ninth began its advance. In the afternoon Nasser learned that Khalif had been killed and Amer himself had been hit by a shell splinter.

During the twenty-seventh day of fighting Nasser received a message that a cease fire had been arranged. It would go into effect at six o'clock the next morning. Now more than ever, the officers were saying this was a political war.

That afternoon, Israeli forces cut the Egyptian supply line. A sharp battle ensued, and the Sixth Battalion reopened the road. After the enemy force had withdrawn, Nasser left his office, took a jeep to where the fighting had taken place, climbed a small hill, and stood there for some time looking over the battlefield.

"Here am I on a hillock between Majdal and Usdoud in Palestine," he thought. "I can see the blue sea on the horizon and the sun setting behind it, and close to me lie the dead bodies of the enemy. They tried to kill us but we killed them first. To the west are the scattered positions of our forces. Wide front. Scattered positions. Political war. To the south are our headquarters directing this political war. To the southeast is Cairo, but all Cairo wishes for is a halfhearted war. Far away in New York sits the United Nations Security Council, eleven men who decided among themselves that the battle should stop. And we have to obey." He took a deep breath and returned to his jeep. "What next?" he asked himself.

Often during the cease fire he went to the village of Usdoud and indulged in his habit of climbing to a height from which he could look down on everything and everyone else. At Usdoud there was a high wooden tower. From the top at night he could see moving lights on the enemy side of the line. This depressed him, for they were energetically building up their defenses, while his men had become apathetic. He complained that the Egyptian officers spent all their time writing reports of what had happened, telling Cairo how the troops had stormed enemy positions, shouting, *"Long live His Majesty, the Supreme Commander of our Army!"* But since the soldiers were completely occupied in either avoiding or returning enemy fire they could hardly think of cheering the King during battle, and Nasser objected to the fiction.

One day during the cease fire he decided to find out whether his soldiers understood what the war was all about.

"What are we doing here?" he asked one of them.

The soldier, a fellah from Upper Egypt, smiled and replied, "We are on maneuvers, sir."

"Maneuvers? Where?"

"At El-Rebeki, sir."

Nasser looked at the peasant incredulously. El-Rebeki was on the road running from Cairo across the desert to Suez, hundreds of miles away. It was where the Egyptian Army used to hold its annual maneuvers.

The conversation haunted him. If this man was typical, then the average soldiers, the fellahin, could not be much interested in the purpose of the Palestinian war.

During the weeks of U.N.-arranged peace he busied himself making entries in the diary he now was keeping, recording his depression over the war. He also made propaganda for his Free Officers movement, going among the younger men, sounding them out and selecting those who seemed deeply discontented and rebellious. He tried to get them to have confidence in him, for he was certain confidence and friendship would have their benefits in the future.

Toward the end of June he and other officers were summoned to a conference at G.H.Q., where they were told that the Sixth Battalion must be ready to attack the moment the armistice ended. This announcement caused a strange reaction in Captain Nasser as the battalion's staff officer: "I thought I was sitting in a theater with everyone on the stage trying to do his part well and overdoing it, while feeling at the bottom of his heart that it was just a part, and that he would soon become himself again, his real self."

This was not war as he had envisioned it. This was not war as they had studied it at the Staff College. Not war as he had imagined it during his eleven years in the Army. It was a play, a satire on war.

While the armistice was still in effect, he took two sergeants and wandered through an orange grove until they reached a point well inside Israeli positions. No one disturbed them, so the next day he took two company commanders over the same ground to show them the enemy had no artillery pieces that moved up and down by electric lifts, no concentration of tanks, no serious defenses at all.

When the war was resumed several days later, Saudi Arabia joined in, making it six Arab nations against Israel alone.

The Seventh Battalion, on the Egyptian front, had orders to attack. The Sixth, Nasser's battalion, would support it. But a soldier in the Seventh fired a green signal instead of a red one and caused such confusion that the entire operation had to be called off.

A few days later he was at lunch when a sergeant brought a message from headquarters. As he read it, a feeling of shock swept over him. The food in his throat seemed to choke him. The Sixth Battalion was ordered to seize the town of Juleis the next day. When he had recovered from the first impact of the order he became furious, for he had been given no opportunity to study the target. He started to protest, then decided it would be fruitless. Time was short.

There were still three or four hours before sunset, so he took some junior officers and made a reconnaissance. The Israelis saw them and opened fire with mortars. When he got back to headquarters Nasser, who had strong ideas of his own about how the attack should be mounted, had a long argument with his commanding officer, a colonel. Finally the colonel lost his temper.

"Cut out all that Staff College talk," he snapped. "Remember, I am in command."

The next morning, as the attack began, the colonel announced he was going to direct operations from the field, and ordered his staff officer to accompany him. This displeased Nasser. He said he felt they should remain at battalion headquarters while the fighting was in progress, in order to send and receive messages. But he was overruled by the colonel, and they went forward in a jeep, which almost at once got stuck in the sand. When at last they caught up with their troops they found the attack was not going well. There were four mortars that had not yet been put into action. The colonel ordered Nasser—now a major—to take charge of placing them in a forward position, from which the Jewish settlement could be shelled.

For a moment Nasser, nonplused, stood and looked at him. As staff officer it was his duty to remain with the colonel and help direct the entire operation. "This," he thought, "is a thousand times more important than a display of courage by advancing with four mortars." But he did not want the colonel to think him a coward, so he obeyed the order and went forward until they came within range of the enemy settlement.

After a short time, without waiting for another order from his C.O., he left the mortar position and started back for battalion headquarters. On the way he met an officer who told him that one of the company commanders he had taken on reconnaissance through the orange grove had been killed. At this he wept bitterly, though he knew he was also weeping because the battle was out of control.

Later that day, he again fought with his commanding officer over a tactical decision the colonel had made. When the argument ended, he decided to take a step he had been reluctant to take for a long time. He would go over the colonel's head and communicate with the commander of the brigade.

At brigade headquarters he filed a long bill of complaint against the colonel, but he did it unhappily, for he felt it was a sign that his battalion had lost its morale. During the whole night he was unable to shake off the oppressive gloom that enveloped him.

In the morning, as a result of his complaint, an order came that the colonel was to be replaced and was to return to Cairo. But Staff Officer Nasser was not satisfied for long. The next day, the Sixth was ordered to make another attempt to seize Juleis. The new commander believed what Nasser told him about the battalion's poor morale but he did not want to object to the order for fear he would be thought a coward. Nasser finally persuaded him to go to G.H.Q. and protest against the battle order. They went together. At G.H.Q. they discovered some reconnaissance photographs of Juleis that no one had thought to show them. Nasser was furious. The battalion had been saved from disaster by chance while G.H.Q. was filled with clean-shaven officers placidly sitting at their desks.

New orders were now issued to try to take the settlement of Negba. Here was the spot where Israeli convoys moving from the north paused before pushing on to supply the settlements in the Negev Desert. An east–west road crossed the Israeli north–south artery at this point. One company of Nasser's battalion was ordered to occupy this crossroads. But the company commander objected, saying it was sheer madness. Nasser agreed. Nevertheless, the order was carried out and he went with the company while it dug itself in and waited for an enemy attack. Then he decided the company no longer needed him and started back to the rear.

After going a short distance he was picked up by the staff officer of the brigade in an armored car. As they were passing a cornfield they heard a shot, so they drove into the field to investigate. There was no sign of life. As they headed back for the road Nasser suddenly felt a strange sensation in his chest. He realized he had been hit, and took out his handkerchief to stop the blood. Then a strange feeling came over him. He asked himself, "Is this the end?" He thought of his home, his family. "How will they take the news?" he wondered.

The brigade staff officer drove him to the hospital at Majdal. After a surgeon performed a minor operation with a local anesthetic he handed a small, thin piece of brass to Nasser, who couldn't believe what the doctor was saying. He had not been hit by a bullet at all. The bullet had struck the armored car and separated from its casing. It was merely a piece of the casing that had hit him.

His wound was a minor one, and when many serious casualties from the Negba battle began pouring in, he started to leave. But then he decided he was too exhausted; he needed a night's rest. Instead of sleeping, however, he lay awake all night, thinking about the war.

He decided he hated war, even the idea of war itself. He felt humanity had no right to exist if it did not strive for peace. He asked himself, "What is all this? We are spilling human blood on this battlefield. I am sitting with a friend. We separate. A few minutes later a phone rings. I lift the receiver. I am told that my friend's body has been torn by a bomb. I am not supposed to be moved by this because a soldier is not supposed to be moved on the battlefield. I have to say, 'Tell the burial squad.' " At that moment he made a promise—that if he ever became a leader in his country he would think a thousand times before he would drive Egyptian troops into war. He would never do this "unless there was no alternative, and only when honor and the integrity of the nation were threatened and nothing else could save them but a battle."

This was the same young man who only a few weeks before had gone bouncing down the steps of his home chanting, "We're going to war! We're going to war!" During his soliloquy in the dark of the night, lying on a hospital cot surrounded by gravely wounded men, he had forgotten that it was the Free Officers who had wanted this war, even before King Farouk committed the Egyptian Army to the invasion of Israel. It was he himself who had been impressed by the Supreme Guide's oratory and his talk of a jihad. It was he who voluntarily visited the Grand Mufti and offered the services of his Free Officers to help invade a neighboring state that was being created by the United Nations. Such a war was in no way "inevitable." Neither the honor nor the integrity of Egypt had been threatened.

It may have been the horrors of this minor, old-fashioned war that changed Nasser's mind, but he undoubtedly was also influenced by the feeling of doom he had had since his arrival at the front; by the failure of the Egyptian Army to achieve that glorious victory it so greatly needed to bolster its belief in itself.

In the morning he was informed that the battle for Negba had been lost. He left the hospital and returned to his own battalion headquarters. There he helped draw up a plan for the withdrawal of the company holding the crossroads.

The whole battalion was exhausted. For five nights the men had not slept. Later in the day, an order was received for the Sixth Battalion to retire and rest. They were billeted far from the front in an old British camp. The barracks had no roof or windows, but it looked like a palace to the men. Five minutes after they had gone to sleep, a messenger arrived with an order that one company was to report immediately to the village of Usdoud to help with a battle. In the morning another order commandeered a second company for duty at Iraq al-Suweidan. Nasser strongly resented these orders.

Then an SOS arrived from Gaza. Some Egyptian troops had been trapped inside an Israeli settlement in that area and help was needed. So his third and final company was dispatched. Resentment now overwhelmed him. He was the staff officer of a battalion, but there was no battalion.

That night, he heard Cairo Radio announce that the Security Council had ordered another cease fire, effective at 5 P.M. the next day. Just yesterday, lying on the hospital bed, he had expressed his repugnance of war and voluntarily taken a peace pledge, but when the Security Council made a move to halt the war and try to cement a peace, he was angry all over again. He stood in front of his camp and thought, "An order has been given for another truce, and we have to obey. Is this a real war or a game of chess?"

Later that day, he saw a dogfight between three Israeli and two Egyptian planes. One of the Egyptians was shot down. During the evening he learned that the pilot had been a man he knew, one of his old Military Academy students.

That night as he lay on his cot he thought, "This is what is going to happen to all of us, as long as the Supreme Command in Cairo and the Supreme Command on the battlefield remain what they are. Not one of us is going to have a chance to fight an honorable battle on equal footing with the enemy. We are all going to be killed in this way."

During the second cease fire he received two pieces of news that infuriated him. At the height of the fighting the Egyptian Royal Engineer Corps had been ordered to build a villa for King Farouk in Gaza. It had long been a custom of government bodies wishing to ingratiate themselves with the monarch to construct what were called "royal resthouses." There was one at the base of the pyramids at Giza. There was one under construction at the water's edge on Gezira Island. There was even one on the grounds of the Cairo Zoo. These were not small shelters from the rain. In most cases they were expensive stone buildings in which the King and his friends could enjoy themselves for a few hours or a few weeks.

He also learned that before news of the defeats started pouring in, King Farouk had ordered the construction of a new boulevard between Cairo and Heliopolis down which the victory parade would pass on the day the Egyptian Army returned home, after obliterating the State of Israel.

Finally he was given a four-day furlough, but he found Cairo an alien place, after being three months on the battlefield.

It did not seem like the capital of a country that was fighting a battle of life or death, and he felt "a strange sadness in this city which is swarming with everyday life."

On the second day of his leave he called at the hospital where Amer had had an operation on an infected hand. He took his older daughter, Huda, to the zoo. Then, on the fourth day, he returned to the roofless room in the old British barracks in Sinai that he called "my home under the glittering stars," and "spent hours at night studying them in their great heights and wandering in my dreams among their orbits."

It was now October 1948. The entire Negev had been awarded to Israel by the U.N., but fifteen thousand Egyptian soldiers were in possession of three strips of the desert, including the ancient cities of Gaza and Beersheba. Israel was cut off from contact with her settlements in the south Negev because the only road to them went through one of the Egyptian-held strips. Egypt, similarly, had difficulty supplying her forces in Bethlehem because the Israeli Army controlled an area through which the east–west road ran. As a result one of those peculiar agreements between belligerents was devised with the assistance of the U.N. truce commission. For six hours out of every twenty-four Egypt would permit Israeli convoys to go north and south, and for six hours each day Israel would permit Egyptian convoys to move east and west. It was a technical violation of this agreement in October 1948 by Egypt that gave the Israeli Army its excuse to begin a well-planned military move it called Operation Ten Plagues.

It was the time of the Great Feast for Moslems. On the morning of the first day Nasser's Sixth Battalion received a message from G.H.Q. that the enemy would probably attack sometime during the holidays. No further information or orders were received as headquarters began to prepare a reception for Princess Faiza, who was going to visit the battlefield. Nasser felt that he and his men had been completely forgotten.

At eleven o'clock on the night of the third day of the Feast, Israeli forces cut the road leading into the village of Iraq al-Manshiyya, where he and his battalion were now encamped. At 3 A.M. the battalion commander issued an order for him to lead an attack to reopen the road at the first sign of dawn.

Impatiently he stood outside headquarters, waiting for daylight. Everything was still, even Gat, the settlement opposite them. For two hours he watched this peaceful scene, and then suddenly the quiet was shattered by the awesome and terrifying sounds of enemy fire on all sides. Iraq al-Manshiyya was being shelled. Instead of leading his battalion to reopen the road he stayed to help defend the village.

At five-thirty, six tanks appeared on the horizon. Israeli forces in this area had not heretofore used tanks, so Nasser's commander had ordered all antitank guns left behind in the village of Usdoud; all except two that Nasser, in defiance of the commander, had told his men to bring along. Now he ordered the two guns into position.

He was notified that "the tanks of the enemy are progressing . . . the tanks of the enemy have penetrated our first positions . . . the tanks of the enemy are crossing into the village itself . . . the tanks of the enemy are deep inside the village. Israeli forces are now occupying a schoolhouse near headquarters."

He sent a message asking why the guns were not firing. The reply was that two artillery bombs had struck them and they were completely out of service. He ran out of headquarters, for he felt he had to deal with the situation on the battlefield. Plans and blueprints were no longer of any use.

Bombs were exploding all over the village. Everywhere there was the whirring of bullets and the confusion of battle. He saw a soldier repairing a telephone line cut in the fighting. Suddenly a bullet hit the man and he fell. Nasser turned his face away as another soldier came to replace the wounded one.

He ran to the rear to see if he could get help from a Sudanese regiment. An enemy shell fell dangerously close to him. "I have been saved by a strange fate," he said to himself as he watched it explode.

Everyone was trying to beat back the Israeli attack, drivers, clerks, even the cooks and the men who made coffee for the officers. At first it looked like a hopeless situation. But then with Biat guns they knocked out three of the Israeli tanks. This stiffened their morale. Eventually the three remaining tanks retired. A few hours later the Israelis mounted a second attack, but meanwhile Nasser had been able to get his other antitank guns from Usdoud and the enemy was repelled.

He was a different man now. The complete change that this one victory made in him was reflected in his diary: "That night, I went to inspect our soldiers. Self-confidence appeared very strong in their eyes, and an air of firm determination characterized all their movements. I was happy and proud."

The revitalized staff officer sat up all night thinking over what had happened and decided that the attack on his village must have been part of a general offensive. When morning came, he learned how correct this surmise had been. Operation Ten Plagues, as the Israelis called it, succeeded in capturing the pivotal town of Beersheba, drove the Egyptians back to Gaza, and encircled an area containing three Arab villages —Faluja, Iraq al-Manshiyya, and Iraq al-Suweidan. In this pocket were three battalions, the First, Fourth, and Sixth; four thousand men in all, Egyptians and Sudanese.

The Ninth Egyptian Battalion was the one that had lost the crossroads, thus permitting the pocket to be formed. In his notes he gave his explanation of why the Ninth had been defeated: "The commander of the battalion was on leave. The next in command was hit by a splinter and died immediately. The third in command took a car and fled with it, stopping only when he reached Ismailia on the Canal. The fourth in command left the battalion to go to General Headquarters."

The surrounded area came to be known as the Faluja pocket, a wasteland dotted with primitive mud huts, less than fifty miles due south of the Israeli city of Tel Aviv and just a short walk down the road from biblical Gath, birthplace of Goliath. The Arabs here led a squalid existence, as Nasser and his men could see. Although most of them had fled to the south in the early days of the war, there were still a thousand inside the pocket. The nearest Egyptian base was now sixty miles away. At the moment of encirclement a substantial supply of ammunition was on hand, and some food.

The commander of the holding operation was a tall, massive, good-natured Sudanese, Colonel Sayyid Taha. His skin was so dark that he was nicknamed the Black Wolf. Years after the Palestinian war, writing his memoirs of the fighting, Nasser devoted thousands of words to minute details, without a single word of praise for the Black Wolf of Faluja, although most military men considered him the real hero of the pocket.

At the start of the siege he wrote bitterly again in his diary: "Air raids were launched on our positions, forcefully and numerously. Our own air force disappeared completely. We never saw any of our planes. Enemy artillery began throwing fire on our heads, never keeping quiet for a moment. What bothered most was the number of casualties in our forces. The existence of the wounded in our midst was a tax on our nerves."

The broadcasts of Cairo Radio also upset him. He was about to destroy the wireless receiver and escape from the lies pouring out of it when news came over it that the Security Council had again ordered a cease fire. It enraged him that the Security Council, which had not acted during the five or six days the Israelis had been capturing Beersheba and creating the Faluja pocket, had taken action now that the Egyptians were isolated, surrounded in the middle of a desert.

"It is a conspiracy against us," he thought. "It is just playing with our fates, our lives, our destinies. It is a joke and a comedy."

Five and a half months had passed since that bright day in May when he left home, so eager for the adventure of war. During that time the Arab armies had failed to snuff out the new Jewish state. This cease fire was the third the U.N. had ordered in the hope of working out some peaceful solution of the conflict. It was announced on Thursday, to go into effect at 2 P.M. on Friday. Thursday morning a conference of all battalion commanders and their staff officers was called at Faluja. Colonel Taha, presiding, announced that he had received an urgent order from the Egyptian High Command for all four thousand men to withdraw. Nasser agreed with this idea, for he believed it unwise that a third of the Egyptian Army should remain under siege in a pocket closed from almost all sides. Everyone in the room agreed except Colonel Taha, but he finally said, "I will give in to the majority."

He ordered Nasser, because he had argued most vehemently for withdrawal, to draft a plan for leaving by a side road over which some of the wounded had been secretly removed. Nasser retired to a corner of the room, but while he was working on the plan, a new message came from G.H.Q.: "Previous order canceled. Keep your positions. Cease fire is in our interests."

On Saturday the Israelis closed the side road. Encirclement was now complete. At noon, when he realized what the situation was, Nasser issued an order to cut the daily ration for soldiers and officers to a quarter of normal. "We must prepare for the dark unknown future surrounding us," he told his aide.

He never forgot the first night in the pocket. The men were excited and nervous. Enemy planes flew over their positions, throwing down leaflets, and he took one of them to read. They were in Arabic, addressed to officers, N.C.O.s, and soldiers, and said:

... You see for yourselves in this country the results of false propaganda which you used to believe before you were sent here from Egypt. Your commanders and politicians described the Palestine war as easy. They promised you booty and pleasure. Where is the booty and where the pleasure? You did not find here anything but tragedy, anything except great losses, and you will never find anything else in the future. You have seen with your own eyes that the Jews know how to defend their country, that the Jews know how to fight when they are in their own land. They did not think and they will not think of occupying a country which is not theirs.

If you look on a map you will find that the Israeli armies encircle you completely. Now you have to choose: if you want to remain alive you have to surrender, and you will be returned safe to your country. You must know that those who tell you that we kill our prisoners are liars. This is the worst propaganda made by your commanders, who wait for medals and do not care about the death of thousands of their soldiers.

Then they listed by name Egyptian officers who had fled: a general at Iraq al-Suweidan, the commander at Beersheba, the commander at Hulaikat.

Nasser read the leaflet by flashlight. He made no comment on it in his diary, although he preserved the full text. Some of the words were like those he himself had been saying.

The next morning, a sergeant came to him and reported excitedly, "An enemy armored car has stopped just outside our positions. It is flying a white flag. A voice through a megaphone keeps repeating, " 'An Israeli officer asks to meet an Egyptian officer.' "

Nasser decided to confer with the Israeli. He took with him two junior officers and a sergeant armed with a tommy gun. They went to the edge of the pocket and waited for the enemy officer to walk the eight hundred yards from his car across no man's land to the Egyptian lines. When he came within speaking distance the Israeli announced in English, "I am the personal assistant to the general commander of this district. I am ordered to explain to you your situation. You are encircled, and we ask you to surrender."

The man who spoke had a small mustache, something like Nasser's, but he was very thin of face and of body.

Nasser answered curtly, "As to the situation, we know it well. But we do not intend to surrender."

The visitor then said he was Captain Yeruham Cohen, adjutant to Yesha'ya Bernstein, commander of the Israeli southern frontier. (Nasser was not aware until later that Bernstein was the underground name of Yigael Allon, commander of the force called Palmach, who had complete charge of Operation Ten Plagues.)

Cohen, switching to Arabic, said he had come with a request for negotiations with the Egyptian commander of the pocket. Nasser was skeptical, and demanded proof that this was not an Israeli trick. Finally convinced, he sent one of his junior officers to transmit the message to Colonel Taha. While they waited for his return they sat on the ground, talking, three Egyptians and a lone Jew.

"Where did you learn to speak Arabic?" Nasser asked.

Cohen smiled. "My parents are from the Yemen."

They carefully shied away from pertinent subjects until Cohen said something about conditions in Cairo. Then Nasser seemed to forget that he was talking to a soldier from the other side.

"Let me tell you about some of those men in Cairo!" he said heatedly. And for several minutes he denounced to the young Jewish captain the corruption of Egypt's political leaders.

When Colonel Taha's answer came it was that he had no objection to negotiations but would need confirmation from G.H.Q. Nasser and Cohen agreed that if permission was forthcoming the meeting between Allon and Taha would take place at three o'clock the next afternoon at the nearby kibbutz of Gat.

The next afternoon, three Egyptian jeeps flying white flags drove up to the kibbutz. Major Nasser was the first to step to the ground. He and Cohen saluted each other, then introduced their principals, Colonel Taha and Commander Allon. The Egyptian delegation also included one major and three colonels. They all looked curiously about them. The kibbutz seemed deserted, yet Nasser noticed pairs of eyes everywhere, peering at them from behind half-closed doors, from behind piles of fuel, from windows. The Israelis served food and hot drinks, then got down to business.

"Isn't it tragic," Allon began, "that two sides who bear no hatred for each other should be forced to fight each other so bitterly?"

"It is tragic, but that is the way of the world," replied the Sudanese commander, "and who are we to alter it?"

Allon tried another approach: "While your army is being wasted in a hopeless war in Israel, your own country is being ruled by foreigners, the British. We have already succeeded in getting rid of them. Don't you think maybe it's a trick the imperialists have played on you?"

Nasser smiled wryly, but said nothing.

Colonel Taha replied, "It will not be long before we get rid of them, too."

No matter what line of approach Allon tried, the Sudanese commander always answered, "As an officer my duty is to carry out the orders of my government."

Finally Allon bluntly proposed surrender of the pocket. He appealed to Taha to prevent the loss of additional lives by agreeing to an evacuation. Everyone in the room looked at the tall black Sudanese.

"There is no doubt that your position is better than ours," he said. "You have humiliated the hitherto unvanquished Egyptian Army. I realize only too well that by our continued stand I will not be able to change the military situation or save our front. But one thing I shall be able to save: the honor of the Egyptian Army. Therefore I shall fight to our last bullet and last man. Only orders from my government can stop me."

Thus the first round of negotiations ended. More food was served. Then the three Egyptian jeeps started back. On the way, Taha turned to the men beside him and said, "Whatever happens, we shouldn't shell that settlement. They did treat us well."

In another half hour the machine guns and rifles that had been quiet while the white flags were flying began their nerve-shattering chatter again.

Life inside the pocket was monotonous and dreary. At first mail and food were dropped from Egyptian planes. Then one day the Israelis shot down a supply plane, and after that mail and food had to be smuggled in by a circuitous overland route. At night it often was impossible to sleep because the enemy trained powerful searchlights on Iraq al-Manshiyya.

Nasser knew that it would be no great military advantage to the Israelis to wipe out the pocket, but there were political reasons for their trying to eliminate this last small hold the Egyptians had on the Negev Desert. If Tel Aviv argued that Israel should be entitled to hold Northern Galilee because she was in physical possession of it, then Egypt could use the same reasoning about the pocket.

The pocket had a perimeter of forty-eight miles. It was encircled by two thousand Israelis, men and girls, compared with the four thousand Egyptian and Sudanese soldiers and one thousand civilians, inside. If all two thousand besiegers were on duty at the same time and if they were placed in a circle around the pocket, there would still be forty yards between one soldier and the next. But that was not the way the Israelis operated. There were scattered guard posts watching the various approaches. Between these posts were larger gaps, which could be infiltrated, and through these gaps came the smuggled food, the mail couriers, sometimes even caravans.

Early in the siege a British major arrived at the head of a caravan of fifty camels, which provided several good meals for the trapped Egyptians and Sudanese. Most of the donkeys caught within the pocket were also slaughtered for meat. Fortunately the villagers had left behind a great deal of grain, which was made into flour and baked.

One of Nasser's Free Officers, Ibrahim Baghdady, spent his time in the pocket editing a newspaper that was passed from hand to hand until the ink was almost worn from its pages. He turned it out on his typewriter, then had someone draw cartoons for it and print the head-lines in red ink. There was front-page news about military events, a gossip column, and editorials directed against top army officers and even the Palace. The name of Gamal Abdel Nasser appeared often.

During the many weeks of encirclement the Israelis made three major attacks on the pocket. Before each of them there was a softening up by B-17s. Each time, three or four tons of bombs were dropped. Otherwise most of the planes that flew over were on propaganda missions. The leaflets they dropped—always in Arabic—tried to persuade the Egyp-tians that it was futile to hold out any longer. But they were unsuccess-ful, for the morale of the men was now much higher than it had been in the spring. Israel did not have enough troops to spare from other frontiers to capture the pocket or wipe it out, and the Egyptians knew it. And the Israelis were aware that the Egyptians knew they knew.

The defenders of the pocket had to use their ammunition sparingly, for while it was possible to smuggle in hand grenades and rifle bullets at night, when the sentries had their backs turned, shell-smuggling was beyond all possibility.

For Nasser the boredom of life in the pocket was somewhat relieved by an occasional meeting with Captain Cohen. One of the excuses for these conferences was the subject of Egyptian convoys of food and medicine. After several sessions the two men agreed on terms for the passage of such a convoy, but when it was stopped and inspected the Israelis claimed to have found ammunition as well as food and medicine, so it was turned back. That meant more negotiations between Cohen and Nasser. Finally a second convoy went through.

Several times Nasser asked Cohen how the Jewish people of Palestine had managed to get rid of the British. He wanted to know about the underground movement; what had been done to build up public opinion against the British. He talked with bitterness of the social differences in Egypt, of the poverty of the masses, of the wealth of the few. He asked questions about the kibbutzim.

Cohen discovered that just the mention of Jordan and its Arab Legion was enough to infuriate Nasser.

"Can you tell me why they never came to our help after we were trapped?" he asked. "They're so close, just over there." He pointed in the direction of the Hebron hills. He also was critical of the Palestinian

Arabs, and wanted to know why they had done so little fighting. But above all he blamed the British.

"I think we've been fooled by them once more," he told Cohen one day, then quickly added, "But it's going to be the last time, if I have anything to say about it!"

One morning during the first week of November, just after daylight, Nasser's orderly woke him up with news that two men wanted to see him. They stood in the doorway of the room, bedraggled, dirty figures. He looked at them closely and recognized his two friends and fellow Free Officers, Zakaria Mohieddin and Salah Salem.

"Where have you men come from?" he asked as he got up and greeted them with an affectionate embrace. "I thought you were on leave. How did you ever manage to get back?"

They told him a long story as they sat on the edge of his cot, smoking one cigarette after another. The Army High Command, knowing their desire to rejoin their units, had suggested they lead a caravan of food and supplies back into the pocket. They started from Gaza with two mules, a horse, and three Palestinian Arab guides. They traveled forty kilometers over rough terrain, walking at night, hiding by day. It took them two days of hiding, two nights of walking. As they approached the pocket they had to pass between two Israeli guard posts. At this critical moment one of the mules decided not to go any farther. They begged, kicked, pulled, but the mule refused to budge, so they started on without it, then the second mule got lonely for the first. The Palestinian guides made so much noise trying to coax it on that the Israeli sentries were alerted. One post sent out a jeep to investigate. They hid in a slight declivity and at first light, leaving the mules behind, sneaked their way into the pocket.

The High Command's plan was that they should stay long enough to make a detailed report on conditions inside the pocket, then leave for Gaza and Cairo by the route over which they had come.

"We need you here more than the High Command needs a report," Nasser told them.

Several days later they made their report by radio and received permission to stay.

On December 28 the Israelis made a full-scale attack on Iraq al-Manshiyya. In a short time they captured half the village. At this point Nasser put through a telephone call to Mohieddin in Faluja.

"Zakaria, your artillery has all of Iraq al-Manshiyya registered, hasn't it?"

"Yes, Gamal."

"Now here's the situation . . ." And he described the exact area captured by the enemy.

"What do you want us to do?"

"Try to ring the position the Israelis hold in our village with artillery fire. In this way we'll create a pocket within the pocket, a Jewish pocket inside an Egyptian pocket. Then we can isolate them from outside help."

Mohieddin pointed out that it was a reckless chance to take. Distances were short. Artillery was not always one hundred per cent accurate. Egyptian shells might fall into Egyptian positions. They might kill many of Nasser's own men.

"It's a chance we have to take, Zakaria."

The stratagem was a success. A number of Israelis were killed or taken prisoner.

Meanwhile there had been excitement in Cairo. On December 25 the Prime Minister had ordered the dissolution of the Moslem Brotherhood. Three days later, just as the full-scale attack on the pocket was under way, he was assassinated in the elevator of an office building by terrorists disguised as policemen.

This news competed with the report of the Egyptian victory at Iraq al-Manshiyya for the headlines in Cairo's newspapers. Radio and newspaper accounts of the battle exaggerated by many hundreds the number of Israeli soldiers who had been left dead on the streets of the village.

Seventeen days after the battle was over, the Egyptian commander gave permission to Colonel Shlomo Goren, Chief Rabbi of the Israeli Defense Forces, to cross no man's land and enter Iraq al-Manshiyya to hold a service over the graves of the Israeli soldiers who had died in the action. The rabbi was received by a young major who introduced himself as Gamal Abdel Nasser and who was exceedingly respectful.

"Our forces took nine dead back with them when they retired," the rabbi said, "and they left seventy-nine behind, who are listed as missing."

"We have five of your men prisoner," Major Nasser replied. "They are all in good condition. We buried the others, seventy-five. That makes eighty in all, one more than you mentioned."

He then took the rabbi to four graves, marked *A, B, C,* and *D.* The first two contained fifteen bodies each, *C* had twenty, and *D* twenty-five. "Your men fought bravely, Rabbi," he said. "We gave them a burial befitting soldiers. They were all buried with their identification tags, if they wore any."

The rabbi asked whether these were all the Israelis who had been killed during the battle, and Nasser replied, "We buried all your dead here, including those killed in the Height of the Bridge operation. There were no other dead."

The rabbi asked whether the Egyptians would permit the removal of the bodies. To this Nasser replied, "For hygienic reasons I would suggest waiting for some weeks."

Late in February 1949 on the Island of Rhodes representatives of Israel and of Egypt signed an armistice agreement. Under its terms the Faluja pocket would be evacuated; the retiring Egyptians would be permitted to take with them all their arms, ammunition, and supplies.

The evacuation took seventy-two hours. Nasser himself went out the first day, stopping at Rafah, where a young major, Amin Shaker, gave him his room at headquarters and made such an impression with his revolutionary talk that Nasser signed him up at once as a Free Officer.

It was March 6, a warm, springlike Sunday, when Nasser walked up the steps of the house in Cairo he had left on May 16, almost ten months earlier, singing happily to himself, "We're going to war! We're going to war!" He felt many years older now. He had seen death often and he had made a promise to Allah that he would never use slaughter as a method of settling differences.

Tahia cried when she saw him, as she had wept when he left, only this time they were tears of happiness. Mona and Huda no longer looked like babies as they ran to greet him.

A few days later all the units that had been in the pocket were ordered out for a full-dress parade through the streets of Cairo. The crowds gave them a heroes' welcome. Taha, now a brigadier, received the greatest ovation. Cairo newspapers, hungry for something to write about besides the Egyptian Army's defeat in Israel, seized on the resistance of the pocket, even comparing the four-month holdout to the defense of Stalingrad. Some of the articles also mentioned the bravery of the staff officer of the Sixth Battalion, Gamal Abdel Nasser.

But the real hero of the entire Palestinian campaign was a quiet-speaking, middle-aged officer who had tried to resign from the Army when the British surrounded Abdin Palace. Between May and December, General Mohamed Naguib had taken part in twenty-one engagements, on each occasion literally leading his troops into battle, although as senior officer he was not expected to do this.

In the Egyptian Army soldiers and officers wear on their breasts, along with their campaign ribbons and decorations, a figure that indicates the number of times they have been wounded in battle. Naguib wore the figure *3*. This increased his popularity enormously. Whenever a soldier would see the unusual *3* on an officer's chest he would whisper, "That must be Naguib!"

The story spread that around his neck he wore an amulet containing special verses of the Koran, which protected him from death. During the last days of the Palestinian war he was seriously wounded when he tried to rescue a soldier trapped in a tank. In a hospital, the blanket had been pulled up over his face and he had been pronounced dead, but a few minutes later a curious doctor, pulling back the covering to have a look at the corpse, saw a flutter of the eyelids and put him in an oxygen tent, ordered a blood transfusion, and gradually brought back life.

There was a curious postscript to the Palestinian war for the Sixth Battalion's staff officer. One day nearly eleven months after the evacuation of the Faluja pocket Nasser received word from the United Nations Mixed Armistice Commission that the Israelis had been unable to locate the four mass graves at Iraq al-Manshiyya. Yeruham Cohen, now a major and the head of the Israeli delegation to the commission, had suggested inviting Major Nasser to help them. Would he be willing to come across the frontier into Israel under the auspices of the commission and point out the graves? Nasser agreed.

It was a cold day in February. A sudden snowstorm blew up just as Nasser and his aides were crossing over into Israel, making the road impassable. It was the first snow Nasser had ever seen.

The next day they tried again. All trace of the snow was gone, and Captain Cohen was there in Iraq al-Manshiyya to greet his old friendly enemy. Cohen described the meeting:

"Without quite realizing what we were doing, we embraced each other and started right in resuming the discussion we had been having when we separated nearly a year before."

CHAPTER 6

THE KING AND EL BIKBASHI

"While maintaining the traditions of royal dignity and ceremony, traditions which in Egypt are particularly strong, King Farouk has endeared himself to his people by his democratic love of simplicity. The smiling King, himself at the wheel of his car, is a well-known and well-loved figure in and around Cairo, as well as in other parts of Egypt, where he has become the symbol of the young, modern Egypt."

That was what King Farouk himself may have thought, or wanted others to think, but it was a certain distance from the truth. These cheerfully misleading words appeared in an official book, *Egypt Throughout the Ages,* sponsored by the government and distributed around the world.

The King's "democratic love of simplicity" was revealed in many ways well known to his people. He had four principal palaces: Abdin, in the very heart of Cairo's poverty and despair; Kubbah, in a great green patch on the edge of the capital; and Ras-el-Tin and Montazah in Alexandria, with their backs to Egypt, symbolically facing the sea and Europe. Also, more royal villas, bungalows, and resthouses than anyone until now had been able to count. He had two ocean-going yachts and many smaller boats, and a squadron of personal planes. The number of automobiles bearing his golden crest fluctuated between two hundred forty and two hundred sixty. Ten of them were always Rolls Royces and some seventy-five Cadillacs. Half his cars were painted fire-engine red. No one else in the country was permitted to have a red automobile. This was so the police would never have an excuse for making the mistake of stopping a red car, thinking it might not belong to the King.

He himself was often at the wheel. When he was, chickens, goats, donkeys, camels, and even humans had to scatter quickly, for patience was not one of the monarch's most well-known and well-loved characteristics.

His fortune was often estimated at $580 million, not counting foreign investments worth many times that amount.

In Kubbah Palace alone he had more than a hundred suits, fifty canes, and one thousand fifty neckties, some with the letter *F* five inches high. Also shoes, shirts, garters, braces, underwear, and other accouterments in like quantity.

Each palace had immense safes in which he kept his collection of coins, medals, and stamps, worth many millions. He had the largest collection of paperweights in the world. He liked to stare through binoculars, especially at lovely ladies who were not aware they were being stared at, and in just one of his palaces he had seventy-five pairs of such glasses.

On the occasion of his second marriage his secretaries let it be known to other kings, princes, presidents, shahs, Arabian sheikhs, oilmen, and anyone else interested, that this time His Highness was accepting only wedding gifts made entirely of gold.

In the four main palaces there were miles of corridors, drawing rooms, marble and chrome bathrooms, anterooms, dressing rooms, bedrooms in which the beds were decorated with frolicking nymphs, a royal gymnasium, an individual playroom for each of his four children, private schoolrooms, feminine boudoirs, vaults, wine cellars, even a room without windows, hidden between two floors, where the royal jewels were secretly kept.

The recreation rooms in several of the palaces were as large as many a casino in Europe and were equipped with every device Farouk had ever encountered in his intensive investigation of gaming houses. He saw to it that guests who might be unable to afford to lose money to each other were supplied with funds for that purpose from the royal exchequer. In Kubbah Palace there was an immense board in one of his anterooms on which hung keys to more than fifty apartments in Cairo, each bearing a neat tag with the name of the young woman who had given it to him. A card file gave other details. The royal music room was almost like a cathedral, except that the instruments it housed were all played by machinery. Beside each royal bed in each of the palaces were six phones, all green. It was forbidden for anyone else in the country to have a green telephone.

Each of the palaces was crammed with pornography. There were kodachrome nudes with illuminated viewers, nude statues in conventional and unconventional poses, paintings that would not have been hung in any public gallery, an immense pocket watch that, in addition to telling time, gave a continuous performance by two unclad figures.

Many of these details of the life of the Egyptian monarch were public property long before he was forced to give up his throne. Guards, servants, and guests saw and gossiped. Each afternoon on the terrace of the Semiramis, one of Cairo's most sumptuous hotels, or in Groppi's tearoom on Kasr el Nil the ladies of Cairo would whisper to each other the latest reports as they sat for hours over their tea and pastries. The whispering created a myth—which eventually turned out to be no myth at all.

No one ever mounted a throne with more public good will than Farouk had in 1936. He was a handsome, slender boy of sixteen, attending a boarding school in England, when he received the news of the death of his father, King Fouad. He cut short his education and hurried home. The Palace quickly set to work to spoil him. Gradually he became a disappointment, then a scandal to his people. He slept for short periods during the day and roamed Cairo at night, looking for personal adventure. The reading matter on his bedside tables soon became either erotica or American comic books.

He was the largest landowner in Egypt, for his grandfather had set the pattern, owning one out of every five arable acres in the country, yet borrowing nearly half a billion dollars from Europe during the sixteen years of his rule to keep his books balanced. As Farouk grew older he turned into a coarse Falstaff who spent his country's money as if he were honor-bound to get rid of as much of it as possible. Month by month the royal waistline grew larger, the royal pate balder, and the stories they told in Groppi's lewder. He had forgotten a bit of advice his father had once given him: "It is nothing to be a prince, but it is something to be useful." He was no longer mindful that his name, Farouk, meant "He who carefully discriminates between right and wrong."

Gamal Abdel Nasser had direct personal contact with King Farouk only once. One evening in 1943 he wandered into the Officers' Club on Gezira Island, in the heart of Cairo, surrounded by the Nile. He was twenty-five years old, a first lieutenant, and had just married Tahia. Farouk was only twenty-three, but he was a King and he already had several daughters. As Nasser sat in a circle of fellow officers, Farouk joined them. After a few minutes he said, "I command each one of you to tell me a joke."

Nasser was nervous. He could not think of a single story of the kind Farouk wanted to hear, but fortunately before his turn came the royal whim changed and Farouk was off in search of greater excitement.

One by one other kings were losing their thrones. Since Farouk's ascension nine had abdicated: in England, the Netherlands, Belgium, Romania, Albania, Yugoslavia, Bulgaria, and two in Italy. One of Farouk's little jokes used to be: "Soon there will be only six kings left; the King of England, the King of Egypt, and the four kings on the playing cards."

Gradually his interest dwindled to gambling, expensive cars, and attractive women. His press agents wrote glowingly of his interest in more land for the landless, better education for the young, better housing for everybody. Although elaborate land-reform programs were drawn up, Farouk continued to hold onto all his own acres. Although three thousand new schools were built, the percentage of illiteracy was not decreasing. The corruption under Farouk extended from the palaces at Alexandria a thousand miles south to the frontier of the Sudan. Tax collectors were bribed by almost all the large landowners. City officials were bribed by anyone who wanted a passport, a building permit, a piece of paper of any kind bearing a government stamp and a signature. The greatest bribe-takers of all were in the Royal Palace. Even the law courts were corrupt.

But it was Farouk's treatment of his first wife that brought him into general disrepute inside Egypt, especially with the women. Farida was a popular queen, and few women in Egypt felt she should be blamed for giving birth to three girls. The marriage had been one of those royal idyls, pleasing to the sentimental. Then one day, while Nasser and the rest of the Army were fighting in Palestine, Farouk put away his wife by the simple device of issuing a royal decree.

Some time afterward as he was buying a small gift for a jewelry-loving friend he saw a young man and a seventeen-year-old girl happily choosing a wedding ring. He turned to an aide and ordered him to obtain the girl's name. A few months later every gossip in Cairo knew that the young man, a U.N. employee, had been sent back to the United States and that the girl, Narriman, was going to become Queen. Although the Groppi set savored scandal, they were not happy over the new romance.

The wedding was one of pomp and splendor, but coming so soon after the debacle in Palestine, it gave Nasser and his Free Officers a chance to make more propaganda. Farouk and Narriman sailed away on their honeymoon aboard one of the large royal yachts. Whenever they were on land they had a fleet of Cadillacs. They took entire floors in grand hotels. In the casinos Farouk tried to impress his bride by putting a thousand dollars, or sometimes even five thousand, on a single number or card.

Gamal Abdel Nasser was not antiroyalist at the start. Farouk was a symbol that neither he nor his Free Officers thought of attacking, at first. They had no share-the-wealth socialistic principles that Farouk was offending. His lavish expenditures actually were bolstering the morale of a people afflicted with an inferiority complex that had grown out of centuries of occupation and exploitation. He made them feel proud, as Egyptians, that they had so sumptuous a king, who could astound even Europeans with his wealth and extravagance.

Before the Palestinian war the only complaints against Farouk made by Nasser and the Free Officers were personal and limited in nature. Above all else they were professional soldiers, so they blamed the Palace clique because army promotions were slow, the pay low, the food poor. Because of Palace manipulations incompetents became generals. Prize assignments went to officers who merely knew the right people. Even the King's Italian barber could make or break any officer by whispering the right word at the right time into the royal ear. Once the son of a royal gardener was appointed captain without passing a single examination or taking a course.

After the war Farouk became more of a target. Nasser was certain that the King was responsible for the Army's receiving American equipment for which there were no available spare parts, British mortars for which there were no shells the right size, Italian hand grenades that exploded in the faces of the soldiers, Spanish weapons that had been made in 1912. One of the pamphlets the Free Officers distributed gave the names of three Farouk aides accused of sharing in the profits of the traffic in defective arms.

Corruption was not new in Egypt. Venality and greed had long been woven into the national fabric. Opposition politicians had been accusing those in power of nepotism, bribery, chicanery, and an excessive love of *bakshish* for generations. The people called it politics and were little moved, knowing that a change of administration would mean merely a change in the names of the bribe-takers. But Nasser decided that this time, if they blamed corruption for the loss of Egyptian lives and for Egypt's defeat in the Palestinian war, there was a chance of arousing public indignation. He was right.

The soldiers of the Faluja pocket had only a brief taste of being heroes. After a spate of parades, receptions, and awarding of medals (Nasser himself received a Military Cross), the High Command, suspicious of the Sixth Battalion's staff officer and his young associates, moved to break up the clique of malcontents. It was no secret to the

Palace or to the generals that Nasser was not a conventional military man. On file were reports of his attitude toward his superior officers in the field, sometimes even when a battle was in progress. The Palace and the generals were also aware that he had organized a secret society of rebels whose political direction was not yet clear, perhaps not even to the rebels themselves. So some of the Free Officers were transferred to Upper Egypt, others to Alexandria, the Western Desert, or the Canal Zone. Major Nasser himself was first sent to Ismailia, then he was stationed in Cairo, where he could be watched more easily, as an instructor in the Army School of Administration. The subject to be taught by this man who had been so critical of the way the army in Palestine had been supplied was logistics, the science of supplying an army.

The Free Officers had lost some of their best men in Palestine, therefore Nasser, as soon as he was established as a teacher again, began to look around for new recruits. Youth was a prerequisite. He trusted only men in his own age group. He was thirty-one when he came home from Faluja, and almost all the men he enrolled were between thirty and thirty-two. He made one notable exception. He and Amer had many talks about the general who wore the 3 on his chest. Mohamed Naguib was now almost fifty, which made him an old man from their point of view, but he had already proved himself a rebel in many ways and he was extremely popular.

"The day may come when we will need a man like him," Nasser said one evening to Amer. Together they decided that Amer, a member of Naguib's staff, would sound him out. Soon afterward the general became a recruit.

During his entire pre-revolutionary career Nasser was under constant pressure from the Communists as well as the Moslem Brotherhood. Each wanted him as a member. He met with both groups on many occasions, although their later claims that he had for a time actually been enrolled apparently are not true.

But they subjected him to a constant barrage of ideas, plots, and intrigues. The Communists, through Khaled Mohieddin, tried to convince him that what his group needed was an ideology, and sent him books in the hope that the reading matter would persuade him to adopt theirs. The Brotherhood appealed to his belief in the Koran, at the same time reminding him that the Brothers had a well-knit organization and a few lethal weapons hidden away. Abdul Moneim Abdul Raouf was the liaison man with the Brotherhood. Before Palestine, Nasser had often gone with him to hear the Supreme Guide speak.

"He can surely weave a spell with words!" Nasser once remarked. He was also impressed with the way El Banna mixed hatred, revenge, hope, and the promise of eternal reward into one propagandist concoction, which he fed to professors, lawyers, and doctors, as well as to poverty-stricken masses in the cities and in rural areas up and down the Nile.

But a few days after he returned home from the war the Brotherhood was made to pay for the murder of Prime Minister Nokrashy several weeks earlier. One day as he walked down a Cairo street Sheikh Hassan el Banna himself was murdered by men of the secret political police. Then the government moved to smash the organization for all time. After a few months most of the leaders were either dead, in prison, or in exile. But the membership was there, cell by secret cell, perhaps a million men, ready to be used if Nasser should ever decide to make common cause with them.

While he debated the Brotherhood question with Raouf, an event occurred that frightened him into a decision. At four o'clock one afternoon he was summoned to appear before the Commander in Chief of the Army.

"The Prime Minister wishes to see you," the general informed him. "I will accompany you."

Ibrahim Abdel Hadi Pasha was one of the King's favorites among the politicans on the extreme right. His chief of secret police sat beside him as he interrogated the young major.

"We have information that you have formed a secret society," he began.

Nasser shook his head.

"We know that you are training your members for armed rebellion."

"How can this possibly be true?" Nasser asked. "I went to Palestine more than a year ago. I have been back for only a few weeks."

"Do you know Mahmoud Labib?"

Nasser hesitated. Labib was an officer of the Brotherhood who had charge of initiating Free Officers desiring to take the Brotherhood vows.

"Yes."

"How do you know him?"

"We worked together organizing the Arabs of Palestine."

"Who introduced you to him?"

Nasser hesitated again. It was either Sadat or Raouf. But rather than mention the names of any Free Officers he said, "Captain Anwar el Seyahi."

The chief of the secret police wrote down the name, then demanded, "His address?"

"You will have to ask Allah. He died during the war."

Both Prime Minister Hadi and his police chief were indignant. They accused Nasser himself of being a member of the Brotherhood, of being the head of its terrorist section, of plotting to overthrow the government.

These were charges serious enough to cost a man his life, but Nasser, realizing by now that they had no real evidence against him, lost his temper, defied anyone to prove such charges, alternated between being angry and being hurt that he, who had just returned from fighting for his country, should be so unjustly accused. Finally the Prime Minister ordered the police chief to accompany Nasser to his home and make a thorough search for incriminating evidence. This was done. In their search the police almost tore his apartment apart. They found a small box of rifle bullets, nothing else. After five hours they left and he was free once more. He was never questioned again, but for the next two and a half years he felt that his movements were always being watched, that his telephone was tapped, that his mail was surveyed, that he was a marked man.

As the need for secrecy increased, key officers in the movement were given code names. Nasser became *Jim* or *Jimmy* the nickname he had been given in the Military Academy years ago.

On December 25, 1949, a son was born to Nasser and Tahia.

"Now we can have an Abdel-Hamid," she said happily.

But he answered hesitantly, "Let's call the *next* boy after your brother. Do you mind? This one—I had a friend in Palestine. He was an officer who served under me. He was killed. . . ." He did not tell her that the dead man had been more than just a friend; that he had been one of the first men to join the Free Officers. His name was Khaled, so that became the name of the Nassers' oldest son.

Toward the end of the year the Nassers also acquired their first automobile. It was a small and inexpensive black Austin, which almost immediately started to play a role in underground revolution, and eventually became almost as famous as any of Farouk's red Cadillacs.

Some of Nasser's fellow rebels, more organization-minded than he, wanted the Free Officers to become a formal body, with officers, committees, plans, and programs, but he rejected all their suggestions. Many of the officers, even some of those with whom he was in direct contact, were unaware that he was the founder and brain center of their movement, and because of all the secrecy, strange misconceptions about him were circulated. He remembers a conversation he had with one of the young rebels.

"Do you know the name of our chief?" the officer asked him.

"Why do you ask?" Nasser equivocated.

"I'm just curious. I know who he is, but I don't know his name."

"Who is he?"

"Don't you know? He's a very important and brilliant general close to the Palace. That's why he has to remain anonymous now. But when the big day arrives, he'll come into the open and lead the revolution."

Nasser smiled and said nothing. He decided that it would do no harm to let the man have this romantic notion.

Anwar el Sadat was out of prison again, looking even thinner, but with more revolutionary fire than ever in his deep brown eyes. He was one of those who wanted not only more action but more organization. As a concession to him and a few others, Nasser agreed to appoint an executive committee. Its members occasionally were changed. Their number fluctuated from nine to fourteen, but in the beginning it was called the Nine. There were no formal meetings. The only committee members who knew the names of all the Free Officers were Nasser and Amer. The others were not even certain how many Free Officers there were. Nasser liked it that way. Anwar el Sadat later wrote in a book that there were a thousand. Others of the Nine at various times guessed the total to be five hundred, four hundred, eight hundred. Actually, at the time of the revolution there were slightly fewer than three hundred Free Officers.

It was most difficult to persuade some of the men that the group needed no ideology, plans, or program.

"What if we someday overthrow the government? If we have no plans, no ideas, no convictions we'll be in for chaos!" Sadat and others complained.

Nasser's answer to them was that in trying to agree on a program they would dissipate their time and energy. Also, it would lead to endless disagreements over details.

Some of the officers even wanted him to create a shadow government such as the opposition party in a country like England has. This would enable them to prepare themselves to manage various departments of a government, long in advance of the revolution itself.

This idea he quickly and firmly vetoed. "I know what will happen if we do that," he said. "Instead of making a revolution we will be spending all our time trying to decide who should be Minister of the Interior."

The Free Officers finally did issue a six-point credo: *1.* Against colonialism; *2.* Against imperialism; *3.* Against monopolies; *4.* In favor of social justice; *5.* In favor of a strong army; *6.* In favor of a new democratic way of life.

It was as safe as a preacher being against sin, or a politician being in favor of marriage and babies.

Many traps were laid for the rebels. After his interrogation by Prime Minister Hadi, Nasser was always on his guard. One day a young army officer, Captain Mustafa Kamal Sedky, came to him and asked for a chance to talk in secrecy. They went for a ride in the Austin.

"I will be honest with you, Major Nasser," he began. "I am head of a secret organization specializing in murder."

Nasser already knew a great deal about Captain Sedky. He was the fourth husband of a famous Egyptian dancer and was a Palace favorite. He and his immediate followers were provided with champagne, caviar, attractive women, and other favors. This was what Sadat had reported. Sedky and his men were credited already with eliminating a number of prominent figures the Palace wanted out of the way.

"What I now propose, Major, is that we amalgamate, your secret organization and my secret organization," he continued.

Before Nasser could speak, Sedky began to point out the advantages. He knew Nasser had utopian aims, he said. But the best way to achieve these aims would be to gain the King's confidence; to use him as a tool. In this connection he, Sedky, could be very helpful.

At last Nasser had a chance to speak. "Captain," he said, "I appreciate all your compliments, but you must have me confused with someone else. This secret society you mention—what is the name of it? I haven't ever heard of such a thing. Who runs it?"

After this meeting he went to see Sadat and told him to find some Free Officer to join Sedky's group and keep an eye on it from inside. The man selected was so successful that before many months Sedky appointed him as one of five to assassinate an elderly politician who had been troubling the Palace.

"I will carry out any order the Free Officers give me," he reported in distress to Sadat, "but what am I to do?"

Sadat thought a few minutes and then told him to go through with the assignment, but to fire to miss.

The other members of the squad were not firing to miss, but they apparently were bad shots, for the victim received not a single mortal wound.

Gamal Abdel Nasser and Mohamed Hassanein Heikal finally met in 1949. The young reporter had come into possession of the complete file of the typewritten newspapers put out by Free Officer Ibrahim Baghdady in the Faluja pocket. They gave away no top secrets of the Free Officers, but Heikal, reading between the lines, discovered hints of what many Free Officers were not sure about until after the revolution: that Gamal Abdel Nasser was the real head of this secret band of malcontents.

"I remember you!" Nasser said when they were introduced.

"But we haven't met before," Heikal said.

"No," the major replied, "but I've had your name filed in my mind for quite a time. It was too bad no one took your advice about Palestine, wasn't it?"

At this time the Free Officers were not able to hold mass meetings, make speeches, or operate in the open, so they decided to become pamphleteers. Many of them took a hand at writing the propaganda sheets. Amer and Nasser wrote some. Khaled Mohieddin, the Communist, wrote a great many. The entire Committee often collaborated on them. The first pamphlet was entitled *The Army Gives a Warning*. It dealt with the scandal of defective arms in Palestine and named names. This was so popular that others followed in rapid succession, and before long Nasser even established an underground newspaper called *The Voice of the Free Officers*.

Because of the need for secrecy, many of the young officers worked on pamphlets like schoolboys reading dime novels behind geography books. One of them, a young lieutenant of infantry, was caught at it, taken before a military board of inquiry, and expelled from the Army.

It was dangerous to have the pamphlets printed, so at first they were mimeographed. This involved cutting a stencil on a typewriter. In those days a typewriter was not easy to get, but Free Officer Abdel Latif Baghdady owned one and agreed to sacrifice it to the cause. For some months it was kept in Nasser's apartment, and various Free Officers came at night and took turns as typists. But Nasser knew that a typewriter has almost as much individuality as a fingerprint. If the Palace police found the machine on which the stencils were made, the source of all these inflammatory pamphlets could be established. But he had a solution.

Ahmed Fouad, the young left-wing lawyer Nasser had met through Khaled Mohieddin, had moved into an apartment in a building just across the road from the Academy. No one would ever suspect him, because he was not even in the Army. When Nasser suggested that he take possession of the typewriter and make the stencils, Fouad spread his hands out in a helpless gesture and said, "But I don't even know how to use a typewriter!"

"The Free Officers will pay for a course of instruction," Nasser replied.

For weeks the young man, who was now a judge of minor criminal cases in Tanta, would drive home each evening the fifty-four miles from his courtroom, have a hurried supper, then go to a secretarial school to take his lessons. For the next two and a half years he spent most of his evenings making stencils of the subversive literature written by his friends. Nasser himself would then take the stencils to the home of a Free Officer who lived miles away in Giza and had a mimeograph machine in his cellar. They had chosen this man for the job because he was always laughing and joking, and no one would ever think that he was mixed up in anything serious, like a revolution.

Nasser devised a method of distributing the pamphlets. One of the Free Officers who worked in military headquarters had succeeded in stealing a list of the names and home addresses of the several thousand officers in the Egyptian Army. This became their free subscription list.

As soon as the Palace police discovered that the Free Officers had the arrogance to use the Egyptian Royal Mail to distribute antigovernment propaganda they concentrated on trying to stop it. But Nasser outwitted them. Each member was required to supply his cell leader with a batch of envelopes every week, no two of the same size or color. Every week there poured in from cell leaders and eventually up to Nasser himself a strange assortment: yellow, brown, white, gray; square, oblong. As many men as possible were assigned to do the addressing. Judge Fouad did a few on Baghdady's typewriter. Some Free Officers had their children write out the names and addresses for them. One day Nasser suggested to a group of volunteer envelope addressers, "Next week let's all try writing the addresses with our left hands."

Posting the envelopes called for both cleverness and intrigue. Nasser had this job so well organized that no two of them ever went into the same mailbox at the same time. This way a Colonel Mustafa Mohamed Mohamed of the King's Guard might get a pamphlet one week in a square yellow envelope addressed in a childish longhand and mailed from Abbassia on Monday night at eleven, while the next would come in an oblong gray envelope addressed by typewriter and mailed at seven o'clock on a Tuesday morning from a box in the Midan of Ismailia.

A few were distributed by hand, although Nasser discouraged this as involving too great a risk. Copies were even smuggled into the Royal Palace. Judge Fouad was acquainted with a Free Officer who had a friend on the staff of the chief of political police. One of the chief's jobs was to try to break up the Free Officers, or at least keep them from circulating their propaganda. The friend on the police staff saw to it that each morning when a new pamphlet was being distributed a copy was placed in the center of the chief's desk before he arrived at his office.

Wives turned out to be a troublesome problem for Nasser. When he first began his revolutionary movement he was a bachelor and so were most of his followers. Now he was married, and one by one the others were also taking wives. This new complication came when more secrecy than ever was needed. The shakier Egypt's internal situation became and the stronger the movement grew, the more vigorously palace police worked to break it.

Nasser's attitude toward women was a combination of the Moslem concept of the proper relationship between husband and wife, plus the typical attitude of a professional army man toward the female sex. He respected women, in a Middle Eastern manner, but he insisted that a wife or sister or mother was the last person a Free Officer should tell about his connection with the revolutionary movement. Especially not his wife. But many of the wives were as astute as their husbands, and several of them began to be suspicious.

The young wife of one Free Officer, now an important Minister in the United Arab Republic central government, described her own feelings:

"Before the revolution I got to hate the man they called Jim. I knew Jim was Major Nasser. And I knew that Major Nasser and my husband were up to something secret and probably dangerous. I also was very jealous of all the time my husband spent with Jim. We had been married only a short time, but night after night my husband would be away from home for hours. If Jim called, he would drop whatever he was doing and rush away. Always it was Jim. But I was an obedient wife, so I asked no questions."

Partly in the interest of secrecy the members of the Free Officers' Executive Committee became known as *Bikbashis,* the word for lieutenant colonels. If one talked about *the* Bikbashi, it meant Nasser himself.

After almost a year on the faculty of the Army School of Administration he had been given the rank of lieutenant colonel, and a few months later was appointed instructor in tactics, intelligence, and Middle Eastern history at the Staff College. Several of the Bikbashis were already teaching there, among them Zakaria Mohieddin.

One of Nasser's pupils in the Staff College was Hussein Shafei, a young cavalry major. He decided Shafei was good Free Officer material so he often called on him at his small villa within the military compound at Abbassia. There, in a quiet corner of the garden, they talked about revolution.

In enrolling Shafei in the movement Nasser told him that Zakaria Mohieddin would be one of his contacts. Also, as was his habit, he gave Shafei a long lecture on the need for absolute secrecy. Especially, he must not confide anything to his wife. And Mohieddin's name must never be mentioned.

Mrs. Shafei was very curious. She plagued her husband with questions about what he and "that man" were always discussing. She was never satisfied with his answers and frequently objected to Nasser's visits. "You'll never pass your examinations, Hussein," she said, "unless you spend your time studying instead of talking with that man."

One day, while shopping, she met a schoolgirl friend. After they had greeted each other, Mrs. Shafei said, "I've been married since I last saw you."

"So have I," her friend replied.

"My husband is a major in the Army," Mrs. Shafei went on.

Her friend laughed. "Isn't that curious? So is mine."

"My major's name is Shafei. Hussein Shafei."

"And mine is Zakaria Mohieddin."

That night as the Shafeis lay in bed, just after turning off the light, Mrs. Shafei suddenly said to her husband, "Hussein, do you happen to know Major Zakaria Mohieddin?"

He jumped up as if shot, snapped on the light, and turned to his wife, certain she had somehow learned the secret. "Why do you ask?"

"Is there any harm in such a simple question?"

"How do you know Zakaria Mohieddin?"

"Who said I knew him?"

"Then why——"

"What makes you so jealous all of a sudden?"

"I'm not jealous——"

"Is there any harm in just mentioning the name of a man?"

They lay in bed wrangling for more than an hour, she not wishing to give her husband the satisfaction of knowing how innocent her question was and he more suspicious than ever that his wife had somehow found out. When she finally told him of her meeting with Mrs. Mohieddin, he was somewhat reassured, but she was more mystified than ever when he refused to tell her what had made him so angry.

One night there was a film playing in Cairo that Colonel Nasser and Tahia both were eager to see, but on the way, as they were driving past an officer's house, he suddenly remembered that an important meeting of the Bikbashis was taking place there.

"I'm sorry, Tahia, but this is the home of a man I must see about something," he said. "I'll be as quick as I can."

Mrs. Nasser waited patiently for half an hour. Then another half hour went by. Gradually, as she grew sleepy, she readjusted the front seat of the Austin to have more leg room. As she did she brought into view a box that had been cached under the seat. With normal feminine curiosity she reached in to see what it contained. It was full of Free Officers' pamphlets. She knew about the Free Officers and their propaganda pamphlets. Everyone connected in any way with the Army, even the wives, knew about them by now. Free Officers' pamphlets were the talk of Cairo these days. Each army wife wondered whether her husband had anything to do with the movement, but few asked. If they did they received no satisfactory answers.

Tahia Nasser was the wife of the founder and the chief. But until after the revolution her husband set an example for others by not taking her into his confidence, even on the night of the coup. But now that she had found the leaflets the suspicions she already had were well confirmed.

When her husband finally left the meeting and returned to his car, she appeared to be sleeping and the box of pamphlets was safely under the seat, out of sight, so he did not suspect that his wife now had good reason to believe he belonged to the Free Officers.

Late in October 1951 a second son was born to the Nassers, and they named him Abdel-Hamid, after Tahia's brother.

Christmas Day, the birthday of their first son, was also the birthday of Sadat, who was stationed at El Arish, in the Sinai Peninsula. Amer was there, too. He and several other Free Officers were giving a birthday party for Sadat when the telephone rang. It was Nasser in Cairo, calling to say "Happy Birthday." But the real purpose of the call was contained in a sentence he wedged in, between the congratulations, in case anyone was listening in.

"Teytel will arrive tonight," he said. "Be ready to receive him."

Sadat understood. *Teytel* is an Arabic word for unicorn. The unicorn in this case was a powerful mine, which was to be assembled secretly in the desert and then transported to the Suez Canal and used to blow up the first large British ship that came along. Some of the Free Officers in Cairo had managed to steal it, one piece at a time. Nasser was sending it in four large cases. With it would come a mine expert to supervise the assembling.

The shipment arrived at El Arish in two planes "borrowed" for the occasion by two Free Officer pilots. When the work of assembling the mine began, it was discovered that one vital part was missing. While the officers waited for someone to steal this missing piece, Teytel was buried deep in the sand of the desert. It remained there for years, forgotten in the rush of other events, and was dug up only recently.

While the Free Officers worked diligently to stir discontent in the Army, they were greatly aided by the march of events. Their pamphlets about the arms scandal in Palestine had forced the government to investigate. As a result thirteen men were indicted, among them Prince Abbas Halim, cousin to the King, who was accused of pocketing nearly half a million dollars of secret government funds given to him to cover his expenses on a trip abroad to obtain arms during one of the Palestine cease-fire periods, in violation of a U.N. embargo. Another of the thirteen was a confidant of the King, who, while posing as an importer of American fountain pens, was reported to have collected several million dollars in bribes from munitions men who had been supplying Egypt with expensive, albeit defective, arms.

Then came the cotton-market scandal. Madame Zeinab Nahas, young and attractive wife of the aging Prime Minister, was accused of rigging the Alexandria cotton market and thereby making a fortune for herself and two intimate friends, both opulent pashas. The rich who had friends in the government were getting richer and richer. The government would impose severe restrictions on the export of certain commodities. The prices would fall and those who had been secretly advised of what was going to happen would corner the market. Then the Cabinet would suddenly abolish the controls, prices would skyrocket, and a few new fortunes would be made. Or a few old ones refurbished.

The poor were getting poorer and poorer. Unemployment and the cost of living were increasing. So was the birth rate. The few idealists in the Nahas government were leaving it, one by one. The Moslem Brotherhood was still outlawed, but its members filled the streets, shouting angry slogans. The fascist Misr el Fatat took a new name and also went to the streets. The Communists, too, were taking advantage of these ready-made ingredients for revolution.

Nahas met the situation with what looked for the moment like a stroke of political genius. He tried to channel all this seething unrest and hatred against some safe, non-Egyptian enemy. The street was shouting for blood, so he offered it blood: British blood. By abrogating the 1936 Treaty of Alliance and the Anglo-Egyptian condominium on the Sudan, he announced to the world that it was no longer either legal or right for British troops to remain on the Canal or in the Sudan.

The same mobs that had been shouting for the head of Nahas now began to surge through the streets with a half-new, half-old cry: *"Down with the British, long live Nahas!"*

A new generation of secondary school students joined in, with sticks and stones and banners flying, just as Nasser and his classmates had done sixteen years earlier. Schools were closed. Anti-British riots became commonplace. Men with British-sounding names were removed from government posts. Shops with British-sounding names were boycotted.

Nasser's own Anglophobia had reached such a point that every time he saw a British plane in the sky he would look up at it and say, "May disaster take you!"

In the Canal Zone bombs were thrown through the windows of officers' clubs. Almost every morning, the bodies of British citizens were found floating in the Canal. British soldiers were kidnaped. British installations were dynamited. British communication lines were destroyed. Pipelines were cut. Military depots were set on fire. Convoys were shot up. Bridges were blown. From Cairo well-armed young guerrillas streamed toward the Canal to kill and loot. Some were Communists, some Moslem Brothers, some members of the Wafd. Many were students. Doria Shawfik, the beautiful young wife of a Cairo lawyer, a feminist with a doctor's degree from the Sorbonne, organized a women's guerrilla unit.

Nasser and his Free Officers were secretly lending their support to the canal commandos. Teytel never went off, but many bullets they sent to the young terrorists did.

Finally the British decided to hit back. They poured in reinforcements from England by sea and air until there were eighty thousand soldiers along the Canal. In an effort to put an end to terror, they searched everyone who entered their zone, even Egyptian schoolteachers, journalists, and judges going about their peaceful business. When this news was published in Cairo papers, the nationalists decided that sufferance had reached its limit.

"Anything is likely to happen now," Nasser said to himself, "so we Free Officers must work harder than ever to be ready."

CHAPTER 7

BLACK SATURDAY

Two tall Egyptian peasants in white galabiyas started to push their cart of ripe oranges across the British-controlled bridge over the Sweetwater Canal near Ismailia. It was 3 P.M., Saturday, January 19, 1952.

A British traffic officer became suspicious when they hurriedly walked away, leaving their cart untended.

"Where are you going?" he demanded.

"To get some eggs," one of them answered. Then they started to run.

A moment later a bomb exploded under the oranges. Fragments hit a British radio van filled with antitank shells. This in turn was a signal for the nationalists to begin sniping from the Egyptian-held north bank of the canal. That same day, for the first time in broad daylight, Egyptian commandos made a mass attack on the largest British munitions depot in the Middle East.

On Sunday the British cordoned off Ismailia and started to round up guerrillas who had been shipped in from Cairo. One of them said he had come to collect the reward offered a few days earlier by the newspaper *Al Gamhour al Misr:* a thousand pounds to anyone killing the commander of British troops, Lieutenant General Sir George Erskine; a hundred pounds for any other dead British officer.

On Monday a pitched battle was fought in a Moslem cemetery at Ismailia. The Egyptians took refuge in tombs, and the British fired almost seven thousand rounds of ammunition into the tombs before they finally drove them out.

On Tuesday the British began to herd captured Egyptian terrorists into camps surrounded by barbed wire. On Wednesday, Egyptian guerrillas blew up a British munitions dump. On Friday, General Erskine decided to give the Egyptians a lesson they would never forget. He sent tanks to surround two barracks of the Buluq Nizam (Egyptian military police) at Ismailia, and delivered to the commander an ultimatum: By agreement the Buluq Nizam were supposed to be armed only with staves; he knew they had rifles and had been assisting the guerrillas; he

101

would give them exactly two hours to turn in their arms. The auxiliary police commander telephoned Cairo and asked what do. The Minister of the Interior himself gave the order, aware that he was inviting a massacre, "Resist to your last bullet!"

The battle lasted only a few hours. By 11 A.M. there were estimates of thirty to eighty dead Egyptians. Eight hundred others were taken prisoner. When the news reached Cairo, humiliation and indignation, which had become twin brothers in Egypt, approached the exploding point. Egyptians had been killed en masse, on Egyptian soil, by the hated foreigner. The thousands of years of subjugation, exploitation, and groveling were about to end in a burst of frightful revenge.

The youth division of the Wafd party met and planned a massive demonstration for the next day. Students from Al Azhar University also decided to march. By whispers from man to man a joint meeting of Communist, Wafdist, and Moslem Brotherhood students was called at Fouad University. Cairo headquarters of the Buluq Nizam ordered a strike of all volunteer police in the Cairo area. The Council of Ministers went into extraordinary session and came out with a decision to break off diplomatic relations with Great Britain and to arrest as hostages the one hundred most prominent members of the British colony. The British Consulate used its secret emergency communications scheme to advise all subjects of the Crown that danger was in the air. Many Egyptian servants cautioned their British employers against venturing into the streets the next day.

Black Saturday began at dawn on January 26, 1952.

King Farouk was concerned about a luncheon he was giving for six hundred army officers to announce officially that he was the father of a son.

Prime Minister Nahas had an appointment early in the afternoon with a manicurist.

The Minister of the Interior had arranged to meet an antique renovator to discuss what could be done with some of his old furniture.

Gamal Abdel Nasser was to deliver a lecture on tactics at the Staff College in the morning. In the afternoon he had arranged to pick up Salah Salem and drive with him to a meeting of the Bikbashis.

Abdel-Hakim Amer was to inspect troops in the afternoon at Rafah, close to the Israeli frontier.

At 7 A.M. three hundred striking Buluq Nizam left their barracks on the edge of Cairo and marched toward the university.

At 8 A.M. the Buluq Nizam and thousands of students converged on the home of the President of the Council, where they were met by a column of students from Al Azhar and crowds of secondary school boys.

"We want arms! We want arms!" they shouted. "Let us fight for the Canal!"

A heavy-set man with his red tarbush at an angry angle came onto a balcony. A cheer went up as some recognized him to be the Minister of Social Affairs.

"This is your day!" he shouted down to the strange mass below him, composed now of men and boys, galabiya-clad peasants and city people, students and workers, demonstrators and police, who for once were shouting with the demonstrators instead of beating them over the head.

From 8 until 11:30 A.M. they milled through the streets, with no fixed objective. They poured into the great square in front of Abdin Palace. Inside, servants were setting the tables for the King's luncheon party. No one in the palace seemed to pay any attention to the crowds, so they moved on.

At 11:32 A.M. a police officer in uniform was drinking a glass of whiskey at a table outside the Badia Cabaret, with one of its dancers.

"Aren't you ashamed? And when your brothers lie dead in Ismailia!" a man in the street shouted at him.

The policeman made an angry retort to the mob. The Egyptian dancer said something sharp under her breath. That was the first small spark. The man who had pointed out the policeman to the crowd gave his followers an order. They pushed aside waiters and busboys, charged into the cabaret, and soaked the tables and chairs with gasoline from cans they carried. In a few seconds the cabaret was ablaze. Someone telephoned the fire department. But before a drop of water could be turned onto the flames, the demonstrators cut the hose. Firemen appealed to police, but they shrugged their shoulders and looked the other way.

The Rivoli Cinema, a few hundred feet away, was next. The gasoline for this fire was brought in jeeps by men whose smoke-blackened faces were seen often during the rest of the day, always at the center of the trouble; cynical, hard-drawn faces; faces that, if identified, could have fixed the blame, but faces no one wanted to remember, when it was over.

At 12:30 P.M. the Chief of Police called the Minister of the Interior to say that the situation was out of hand. The Minister of the Interior called the Commander in Chief of the Army, who said it was unwise to resort to the use of troops.

After the Rivoli, the Metro Cinema, then the British Turf Club and other places in the foreign quarter patronized by people from abroad.

At the Turf Club four influential subjects of the British King were sitting at a table, discussing the measures the Cairo government was taking against them.

"It will turn out all right," the Canadian Chargé d'Affaires had just remarked to James Ireland Craig, a government adviser and Arabic scholar.

At that moment, the men with bottles and cans of gasoline burst through the door. They threw the gasoline over the clothing and the hands and the hair of the four men at the table, then over the furniture as well. As soon as the match was struck, there was fire everywhere. When the four flaming bodies staggered toward the door, men in the street, their faces warped with frenzy, forced them back into the burning building.

An Englishman in a third-story window was tying sheets together to make a rope. The crowd below watched, fascinated. When he had the rope long enough he started down. Lighted torches were thrown and the rope started to burn. The man fell. After his body hit the street, the crowd snuffed out any life left in him by beating and stoning him.

There were a hundred thousand foreigners in Cairo. How many would have to die this way to feed the mob's passion?

At 1:30 P.M. the Minister of the Interior telephoned the Commander in Chief of the Army and was told he was with the King and could not be disturbed.

By now every shopkeeper had locked his door, lowered his iron shutters, and sneaked away. But the men in the jeeps had tools to pry open the shutters, tools to break the locks, bricks to smash the windows. It was a simple thing to hurl a bottle of gasoline into a shop, then a flaming torch, and run on. Everywhere there were police, standing, watching. If firemen came, there were always hatchets and knives ready to slash their hoses.

About this time King Farouk's six hundred guests began to arrive at Abdin Palace, all in their dress uniforms. Among them there was a sprinkling of Free Officers. Also present were General Mohamed Naguib and his brother, General Ali Naguib, commander of the Cairo garrison.

Now the mob was setting fire to Groppi's tearoom. Trays of fresh pastries had just come from the kitchen. The demonstrators threw them into the street and trampled them.

They raced from café to cinema to automobile showroom, to any place that suggested the influence of the detested outsider. To some witnesses it seemed wild disorder, but the men in the jeeps with the cans of gasoline knew exactly what they were doing. Every movie house in downtown Cairo was now on fire.

Up one street, down the next they went. The pall of smoke was making Cairo seem a vast inferno. Now the five-story Jewish department store, Circurel's. The mob discovered that it made a lovely fire, so they went on and put the torch to the British-owned Robert Hughes department store. And to three others. Then the Ford showrooms, full of new models.

Down one street, up the next. Weinstein's stationery shop. Never mind that it was German rather than Jewish. The TWA office. Now the Twentieth Century French Art Gallery. Barclay's Bank. The Miami. The Cecil Bar. Kursaal's. The Ritz Café. The Hermitage. The St. James. The Parisian. All the famous restaurants and night clubs were on fire. The flames at these places had a peculiar color and smell. Every bottle containing alcohol was smashed. The contents made the fire burn brighter.

At 2:30 P.M. the Minister of the Interior went to the Royal Palace and saw the Chief of the Royal Cabinet, as well as the Commander in Chief, to demand why the Army had not been called out. He was told that some soldiers would soon be arriving from Abbassia.

The mob went through Opera Square many times. Some of them glanced questioningly at the opera house, which had been built especially for the first performance of *Aïda*, a foreign opera, and to impress a foreign visitor, Empress Eugénie, who came to see the opening of the same canal that was indirectly the cause of all today's trouble.

Several times they also passed a building that personified the foreigner for Cairo. Once it had been the palace of a Turkish princess. Then it became Shepheard's, a hotel all the world knew, a favorite of visitors from abroad. Its public rooms were dimly lighted and very Arabesque, filled with ivory-inlaid furniture and great sofas covered with luxurious cushions. In front of the hotel were dragomen in long blue coats, and men selling leather animals, imitation scarabs, fly switches, camel saddles. On the terrace, waiters in spotless galabiyas served tea in thin cups and the sort of gin drinks the British liked. But on this day the terrace was deserted, for Shepheard's had been warned.

The mob in the street had grown to terrifying proportions. By now it had attached to itself the worst elements of the population: beggars with diseased bodies, pimps, petty criminals, dope peddlers. Chanting *"There is none greater than Allah,"* they came pouring out of crumbling tenements on the edge of the Nile just beyond the old British barracks, from the anthills of buildings clustered around the base of the Citadel, from all the slums of Old Cairo. Among the rioters were many of the forty thousand Egyptians who a few months earlier had been forced or persuaded to give up their jobs in the Canal Zone in order to embarrass the British. They had all been promised work in government offices, but that many jobs were not available, even in the mushrooming civil service, so thousands of them were wandering the streets.

It was three o'clock when Shepheard's turn came. It almost seemed that the men in the jeeps had intentionally saved this place for the grand finale. The management had advised all guests to go to their rooms. There were only a few people in the lobby when the mob surged through the doors, yanked curtains from their fastenings, and added them to a pile of rugs and cushions and sofas. A woman screamed. A hand grenade went off. Reception clerks were hiding behind their desks. Then came the cans of gasoline. Next the match.

The guests who had taken the management's advice were trapped in their rooms as a coil of flame curled up the stairs to the roof. Several female Italian opera singers managed to escape by a rear door in their underclothes, clutching boxes of jewels to their breasts. A woman trapped on a fourth-floor balcony shouted to the crowd in the street for help. They laughed at her. Someone called up, "Get a ladder!" Someone else held up a rope and asked, "How much?" The woman jumped.

There were many who were never able to reach the windows.

In Abbassia, Gamal Abdel Nasser had finished his lecture, eaten lunch with Tahia, and was having his afternoon siesta. He had heard no reports of the trouble in Cairo.

At Abdin Palace, exactly thirteen hundred yards in a straight line from Shepheard's Hotel, the army officers were still at the tables. There had been many courses, and for those who were Copts, or for Moslems who were willing to overlook the Koran's injunction, there had been whiskey, a vintage wine, and cognac. Several times during the luncheon aides had come to the King and whispered in his ear. But what they said did not cause him to interrupt his celebration.

At 4 p.m. the looting began, almost as if by magic signal. Through streets filled with the charred remains of overturned American automobiles poured the poor and the ignorant, who had no understanding of what had happened. They knew only that here was chaos, with everything from rich pastries to priceless jewelry lying in the streets, and no police to lift a finger. They swarmed through the remains of department stores and the four hundred other establishments that had been smashed and burned. For some reason those who led them now concentrated on Jewish establishments, although what the Jews had to do with the Suez Canal no one explained.

At 5 P.M. the first Egyptian troops arrived in the general area of the disturbance, one hundred fifty foot soldiers to try to bring back order to a city ruled by tens of thousands of half-crazed people. The men in jeeps, whose identity and sponsorship were never fixed, disappeared as quietly as they had come.

At 6 P.M. Gamal Abdel Nasser drove his small black Austin to the home of Salem, where he heard the first reports that "something has happened in Cairo." About this time the last guests at the luncheon left Abdin Palace.

At 6:50 P.M. a meeting of the Council of Ministers was summoned and the Minister of the Interior urged that something be done to restore order. Reporters touring the city made a guess that the material damage would run to perhaps half a billion dollars.

At 8 P.M. the Cairo Chief of Police reported to the Minister of the Interior that the situation was steadily getting worse; that troops under General Ali Naguib were refusing to shoot, although the looting was increasing and fires were still being set.

After he had held a meeting of the Committee, Nasser drove in to the center of Cairo. Many buildings were on fire, and a blanket of heavy smoke hung over the city. Late that evening he heard by radio the announcement of a curfew and martial law.

That was Black Saturday in Cairo.

Gamal Abdel Nasser now had to decide whether the time had come for him and his Free Officers to strike. Were they ready? Did they have the strength to cope with the chaos of the present situation? His answer to both questions was *no*. Although he still had no real policy or program, by now he had a guiding principle. Years later he explained it by saying, "I never act. I only react."

In January 1952 he knew that the time had come to accelerate his activity but not to move into the open. One problem he had discussed long and earnestly with Amer and a few other intimates was the matter of someone who could be a figurehead.

"Remember, it must be a military man," he said. "Some senior officer, older than any of us; someone whose name will command the respect of the entire army, and later of the people. What we need is prestige."

"How about Masri?" a colleague asked.

"I love him," Nasser replied, "but isn't he too old?"

Someone else proposed General Fouad Sadek, respected by the Free Officers as one of the few honest generals, who had acquitted himself well in Palestine. Nasser sent Salah Salem to see him. During their conversation Sadek disclosed that he had a burning ambition to become Chief of Staff. Salem said that perhaps a group of young officers with whom he was associated could find a way, someday, to bring this about. While they were still talking, the telephone rang. Sadek took the call in another room. A few moments later he returned with a broad smile on his face.

"I have just been informed that the King has appointed me Chief of Staff," he announced. Salem congratulated him and departed.

This left only Naguib. Amer had already enrolled him as a member of the Free Officers, although revealing no secrets of the movement to him and mentioning nothing about Nasser's importance. But often Amer, now Naguib's aide-de-camp, would take his friend to call on the general at his home at night. Nasser was never as convinced as Amer that Naguib had all the qualities needed for the job. One essential was that he be content to remain a figurehead, for there was never any question in the mind of Gamal Abdel Nasser from the start about who was going to give the orders and pull the strings.

"I think we can control him," Amer said frequently.

Suddenly Naguib was replaced as commander of the Frontier Corps, the most important Egyptian command, by Major General Hussein Sirry Amir, one of Farouk's puppets and a man so detested by the Free Officers that they had long talked of assassinating him. Then a crisis occurred in the affairs of the Officers' Club on Gezira Island. The King was demanding that his man, General Amir, be elected president. Nasser, deciding the time had come to see who had the following of the officers, he or the King, had Amer persuade Naguib to stand as a candidate. Word was passed secretly to every Free Officer to start campaigning for the man with the 3 on his chest.

One stroke of Nasser genius was his idea of having the election meeting of the Officers' Club open with several minutes of silence in memory of a member of the Free Officers who had been killed by the secret police at Palace instigation. This set the mood for what was to follow. When the votes were counted, Naguib had eighty per cent of them. Two other Free Officers were elected to the Board of Governors. It was a bitter defeat for the King, who promptly declared the election null and void, withdrew funds he had allotted for a clubhouse, and threatened to send Naguib to some post in the desert.

One night a short time later someone brought Nasser what purported to be proof that General Sirry Amir was involved in a plot to sell munitions stolen from the Egyptian Army to smugglers in Gaza, who in turn would sell them to the Army of Israel. As fantastic as it sounded, Nasser ordered publication of a pamphlet narrating the story and demanding the general's prosecution.

When the pamphlet brought no results, he suggested that the others were probably right, that assassination was the only way to deal with the general. Until now he had hesitated to use violent methods, contending that while his own people were normally placid and not easily stirred to brutality, once their passions were aroused there was no limit to what they might do. Black Saturday had been proof. But in the case of General Sirry Amir he not only succumbed to the arguments of his associates but even agreed to go along as one of the actual killers.

They organized themselves into three squads, one to do the killing, one to guard the executioners, and the third to plan the escape. They studied his habits and daily routine, and plotted his demise in detail.

On the night chosen they hid in the darkness near the general's house, and as he was leaving they fired several shots. Quickly Nasser started the motor of his car and the assassins sped away from the scene. At that moment, a woman screamed and a child cried. The grief-stricken wailing continued as they fled, but long after they were too far away to hear it, the sound stayed with him. He could not seem to shake it.

Back home, he remained awake all night, lying on the bed, chain-smoking in the darkness, fearing to turn on the light.

"Have I done the right thing?" he asked himself. Self-righteously he answered, "My motives are patriotic." "But was that the only and inevitable means?" he again asked himself. Not so certain, he replied, "What else could we have done? Can the future of our country really be changed if we rid it of this or another individual, or is it a deeper problem?" In some confusion he said to himself, "I almost feel it is a deeper problem."

Gamal Abdel Nasser suffered that night, as many murderers or attempted murderers had suffered before him. There was the danger of getting caught, which would mean certain execution if they actually had succeeded in killing Farouk's favorite. Then there was his reaction to the screams, to the cry of the child. Second thoughts. Remorse. Fear. If Sirry Amir were dead . . . If they were caught . . . In the morning he reached out eagerly for the newspaper Tahia brought him. Sirry Amir was going to live. He was very much relieved.

The rest of the newspaper account was a little embarrassing to the army men involved. Some, like Nasser, were instructors in such subjects as tactics. All of them were supposed to be proficient in the use of fire-arms. The newspaper said that several dozen bullets had been fired by the aspiring assassins. Only fourteen had even entered the car. Only one had hit the chauffeur, who was seriously wounded. Not any had struck General Sirry Amir, the obvious object of the attack. He was "destined to live" for just one reason: because not a single member of the execution squad had been a good enough shot to hit him.

In the five-year plan agreed upon by Nasser and Amer in 1950, the date for the revolution had been fixed as 1955. But Black Saturday and the chaos that followed made them change their minds. The country was ripe for revolution.

One night early in July 1952 Nasser and Khaled Mohieddin dropped in on Colonel Sarwat Okasha, another inner circle member.

"Put on Rimski-Korsakov's *Scheherazade*," Mohieddin said.

Okasha wound the phonograph and put on the record.

Nasser sat listening and looking off into space. But as the last notes were played and Okasha lifted the needle, he jumped to his feet and suddenly announced, "We'll strike on August fifth."

He picked August fifth partly because some of the officers had suggested that it would be a good idea to wait until after they had all collected their July pay.

"It may be the last pay any of us will get for a long time," someone said.

Early in July, King Farouk, as was his habit, packed his trunks—two hundred four of them—and went off to his two palaces in Alexandria, where the sea breezes gave some relief from the desert heat. He was followed by his entire entourage: private barber, manicurist, personal physician, wife, children, nursemaids, the royal tailor, a small army of chauffeurs driving many of the royal cars, bodyguards, masseurs, and a hundred other supernumeraries.

The government also departed from steaming Cairo, taking along the more important clerks and aides, as well as many of the men whose only task was to sit outside offices beside their little portable stoves, waiting for some official to ring and say he wanted coffee for himself and his guests.

Most of the Free Officers went off on holidays, including Gamal Abdel

Nasser. Away from the heat and confusion of Cairo, he said, he would have a chance to plan for August 5. But on July 11 the Staff College sent him a message asking if he would like to return and correct a pile of examination papers. It was just the excuse he wanted. Farouk had dismissed another set of Ministers. Another government had fallen. The Free Officers should be in consultation with each other; the time for action was near.

He packed up his family and they all returned to Cairo, though Tahia and the children were not happy about it.

Unfortunately the Bikbashis were scattered. It was going to be difficult to plan a rebellion without a General Staff. Of the nine members of the Committee, four, including Amer, were in either Gaza, Rafah, or Alexandria. But then Amer suddenly came back on a short sick leave.

"After you get well you must still play sick and get your leave extended," Nasser told him. "I need you badly. Try to stay another five or six days."

The two friends conferred almost constantly, carefully drawing up plans.

On July 15 King Farouk dissolved the Board of Governors of the Officers' Club by royal decree and announced that henceforth no members of the Free Officers' Association would be eligible to hold office.

"The next move will be against us!" Nasser predicted.

"Yes, it's a race now to see who can strike first," Amer replied.

On July 16 Nasser called together his Committee for what he told them was the most important meeting they had ever held. After they had discussed the situation, he announced, "In my opinion, a revolution is now impossible. Our forces are too scattered. Military units are being shifted from one part of the country to another, and there is great confusion in the Army. Most Free Officers are away on leave."

There was no disagreement. These were facts. But someone asked, "So what do we do, go out of business?"

Nasser raised his head and protruded his jaw a little more than usual. "No," he replied. "I think the solution is a wave of assassinations."

Some of the men, knowing how emotionally he had reacted to the attempt they had made on the life of General Sirry Amir, were surprised by this answer.

"We must organize at least thirty assassination squads," he continued.

They sat around late that night, drawing up plans for the killings; making and revising lists of their intended victims, working out the details.

Two days later, on July 18, Nasser called his Committee into session again and said he had decided the assassination plan was too risky. He was afraid they would fall into the hands of Farouk's secret agents, even if they succeeded in killing all the men on their list and outwitting the regular police.

It was a practical, pragmatic decision. Instead of assassinations he had decided that they should attempt a *coup d'état*, even with the skeleton force they had, and the next day he said to Amer, "You must see Naguib tonight, just as soon as you can. Don't tell him any details of the coup. Just ask him, in case there was to be a coup by the Free Officers, of which he is a member, what would he think."

Amer reported that Naguib seemed receptive, so he had told him he would return "with some of my colleagues." That same night, Nasser and Amer drove in the black Austin to Naguib's house to invest him with nominal leadership of a revolution. But Naguib had several visitors. One was a young army officer. Another was Mohamed Heikal, the newspaperman. Nasser and Amer did not want to have their conversation with Naguib in the presence of a reporter, however much Nasser was inclined to trust Heikal. Yet they were reluctant to arouse suspicion by asking Naguib's guests to leave. After making small talk for a few moments, they were about to go when Heikal turned on them angrily and demanded, "Why are you and your Free Officers taking this latest insult from the King so meekly?"

Nasser smiled. "We are not going to take it," he said. "We have plans."

"Plans? What kind of plans?"

"We have decided on action."

"What sort of action?"

Nasser was enjoying himself. "We have made an important decision."

"To do what?"

"To take the case of the Officers' Club to the courts," he said finally. Then he reached into his pocket, pulled out a small roll of bills, and handed six Egyptian pounds to Naguib's officer friend. "Here," he said. "This is my contribution to the legal costs of the case."

Then they left, and there was no further opportunity before R Day for Amer and Nasser to call on Naguib again.

From seven to nine o'clock that night, Nasser corrected examination papers. Then Amer and Kamal Hussein, another of the Bikbashis, arrived and they formed themselves into a General Staff to draw up detailed plans for the coup, which they had by now decided should take place in forty-eight hours, at midnight on Monday, July 21. They conferred around Nasser's golden oak dining-room table.

"My idea is to use a small force," he told them. "We have only one battalion out of the ten that we can really count on."

"It's a big gamble," Hussein declared.

"But few of our Free Officers know we are as weak as we really are," he pointed out.

"We don't have any tank outfit we can count on," Amer said.

"And we have only ten officers in the Air Force," Nasser added. "Therefore our success will depend on careful planning. We must isolate the entire army area on the edge of Cairo and stop any contact with the outside until we have it all under firm control. To do this we must have someone who can cut all the communication lines."

"Anwar el Sadat is the man for that," Amer volunteered.

"He's in Gaza," Hussein replied.

"Then be sure someone sends a plane for him tomorrow, without fail," Nasser ordered. "Get Ibrahim to steal a plane if necessary."

So it went, for most of the night, as the three rebel leaders laid their plans. The next day, Sunday, R Day minus one, Nasser sent urgent word to the Free Officers he trusted most that they must be in Cairo without fail on Monday; that the *coup d'état* was about to take place; that they must remain at their homes from 3 P.M. on, to receive instructions.

On what was to have been R Day, Monday, July 21, final details had not yet been worked out, so the revolution was postponed for twenty-four hours.

With all this activity Nasser had been getting little sleep. His wife pretended to be curious, but he smiled and shook his head every time she asked a question. Nevertheless, Tahia Nasser knew more than her husband realized. Not only had she found the box of pamphlets under the seat of the Austin, but a few nights ago something else had happened.

Gamal had been away most of the evening at a meeting. When he came home he thought she was asleep, but she had one eye half open and saw him put an orange crate under the bed. She thought nothing of it, assuming it was more citrus fruit, which an artillery officer often gave him for the family. The next morning, while Gamal was still sleeping, she got up to prepare breakfast and decided to surprise him with the juice of some of the oranges. She tried to pull the box from under the bed without waking him. It was extremely heavy, so she just reached in her hand and pulled out an orange. It was the oddest orange she had ever seen. Then she realized that the box was not full of fruit at all, but hand grenades.

When Gamal awoke and came to breakfast, she merely said, "You must be very tired with all your work of planning—whatever it is that you are planning."

CHAPTER 8

OPERATION BEGINS TONIGHT

On Tuesday, July 22, 1952, King Farouk had a swimming party at his Arabesque palace, called Montazah, on the edge of the Mediterranean, surrounded by some of the most beautiful gardens in the Middle East. Queen Narriman spent an hour in the morning playing with Fouad, the six-month-old heir to the throne. Later she had a fitting for a new evening gown. The King's brother-in-law, now Minister of War, went over a plan for a wholesale transfer of army officers, to break up any possibility of trouble from the malcontents. Jefferson Caffery, the American Ambassador, entertained at a small luncheon party at his summer embassy by the sea.

In Alexandria there was a slight breeze. In Cairo the temperature was 98 by noon.

In a four-room apartment on the third floor of a building on Galali Street, in a middle-class neighborhood of Cairo not far from Abbassia, Gamal Abdel Nasser slept later than usual. Mona and Huda, now five and six, wondered if he was ill. His sons, Khaled and Abdel-Hamid, were too small to notice.

Early in the afternoon a final meeting of the Committee was held at the home of Communist Khaled Mohieddin. They went over the plan for the last time. The revolution would be carried out in two stages: first by seizing control of the Army; second by eliminating Farouk. The password for the night would be *Nasr* (Victory). The slogan already adopted was *"Resolution and boldness."* Zero hour would be 1 A.M.

Nasser had drawn up his own list of the Free Officers to be trusted with the secret. Of the three hundred members there were only ninety he felt it would be safe to have participate in the plot. He informed only those he felt he could trust completely; men he was sure did not drink, had no other weaknesses, and could keep a secret.

This selectivity led to complications later. Some of the other two hundred ten never forgave him. As soon as they found they had been left out they asked him, "How can I ever explain to my children that I

115

spent the most precious night in the history of our country in bed with my wife?"

Ninety men to make a revolution in a country of twenty-one million. Seldom have so few men tried to seize a nation.

Nasser had already seen most of the ninety officers and given them verbal orders about their night's duties, but there were some still to be visited. Of the twenty-eight generals in the Army, twelve were on the list of those to be picked up by specially delegated squads. The prisoners would be taken quickly to the Military Academy and locked up, one man to a room. Because the real enemies of the revolution were the high-ranking officers, no one with the rank of colonel or higher should be permitted free movement after zero hour.

Target No. 1, G.H.Q.; Target No. 2, Army Communications Center. Anwar el Sadat would be responsible for cutting all communications, so that if any of the generals slipped through their fingers and tried to call troops into Cairo from the outside they would have no way of doing it. The First Infantry Division at Rafah was the responsibility of Salah Salem, who was already there. Hassan Ibrahim had taken a plane— without permission—to go to Rafah and Gaza to tell the Free Officers there that no attempt would be made to communicate with them until after the coup had succeeded.

That afternoon, Nasser was worried about one missing link, as he called it: Alexandria. There seemed to be no way to get final orders to the garrison in that city, now swollen with Ministers, Ambassadors, minor diplomats, the King and all the King's entourage.

"I told our men up there I would send them final orders today," he said, "but now I don't know how to do it. I have no one to send."

He finally decided to use his brother, Az el-Arab, as messenger. Az el-Arab was not a military officer, not even a soldier, but at least he could be trusted.

After the meeting Nasser drove to Sadat's home and found that his old friend had taken his wife and daughter to a cinema. This was the revolution's first small reverse. Sadat the rebel had dreamed for years of such a night as this; now that it had come and there was so important a role for him to play, he was watching make-believe drama on a movie screen. The apartment-house doorman had no idea at which cinema he was or when he would return. So Nasser wrote a note: ANWAR, OPERATION BEGINS TONIGHT. COME TO AMER'S HOUSE AT 11.

"You are to give this to Mr. Anwar el Sadat, understand?" The doorman nodded. "Mister, I said. Not Mrs. Sadat. *Mister* Sadat. Understand?"

He knew how jealous the wives were of him. Besides, he did not want any wife to know their secret. He had not even told Tahia, and did not intend to.

After that he made a check of Free Officers to whom he had given critical assignments. Going from house to house, he tried to convince each man how great the chances of success were, and as he talked he actually convinced himself.

Then he joined a group of cavalry officers at the home of Sarwat Okasha. They were sitting in the kitchen, having a buffet supper. As he ate a sandwich with them, one of the cavalry officers remarked that they needed machine guns. "I'll go and get you some right away," he said, and got up to leave. Okasha followed him to the door, and Nasser put his hand on the younger man's shoulder. "Sarwat, I know how sentimental a man you are," he said. "What is going to happen tonight will be in some ways like a movie, but there is going to be no room for sentiment." He paused, then added in English, "Remember, no room for sentiment tonight!"

Then he drove to the home of a Free Officer who had charge of a cache of weapons. There were no lights in the apartment and no one answered his pounding. This was the second blow of the evening. The third was right around the corner. He got back into his car and was on his way to the home of another Free Officer when a motorcycle policeman ordered him to pull over to the curb. "Don't you know the law?" he demanded gruffly.

"What's the matter, Officer?" Nasser asked.

"You haven't any taillight!"

They both went around to the back of the car and looked. The taillight was not burning.

"You weren't running away from anything, were you? Scene of a crime, or something like that?" the policeman asked.

The worst thing that could possibly happen at this moment would be for him to get arrested, even for something so minor as this. He tried to explain. Time was precious. He was afraid to annoy the policeman further by looking at his watch. But at last, with one more reprimand, the man got onto his motorcycle and drove off, unaware that for a few moments he had had the fate of a revolution in his hands.

After calling at the homes of those of the ninety he had not already seen that night, Nasser went back to his apartment on Galali Street. He was very tired, but was afraid to lie down.

Tahia and the children were asleep, but two of his brothers, Leisy and Shawky, both schoolteachers, were there, listening to the radio. He took a bath, then began to dress. It was now eleven-five. As he was putting on his jacket, there was a sharp knock on the door. From the sound of it he could tell it was an army man. The visitor was Captain Sa'ad Tewfik, a Free Officer who worked in intelligence. That was why he had not been one of the ninety. Nasser had been afraid to involve him. He was in civilian clothes, and looked quite distraught.

"What's going on tonight, sir?"

Nasser shook his head and asked the man in.

"There's something going on tonight, isn't there?"

Again Nasser denied it.

"Then why do you have on your uniform?"

Nasser threw up his hands, then said angrily, "Did you come to cross-examine me?"

"No, sir, I came to tell you that you must call it off."

"Call what off?"

"Whatever it is you are doing."

"Why?"

"Because they know."

"Who knows?"

"Farouk has been informed that a *coup d'état* has been prepared, and he's been in touch with the Chief of Staff."

"Yes. What else? Quickly! Tell me!" Nasser was holding him tightly by the arm. This was the fourth and worst blow of the evening.

"The Chief of Staff has ordered all divisional and brigade commanders to report at once to G.H.Q. at Kubri el Kubba [a suburb adjacent to Abbassia]. Please, Colonel, if you're planning something for tonight, call it off!"

"How do you know all this?" Nasser demanded.

"I'm duty officer in intelligence tonight. I just slipped away from my post for a few minutes to come and tell you. You *will* postpone it, won't you?" begged Tewfik.

"No, that's impossible. The wheel has already begun to turn. We must go through with it. Now you get back to your post."

The panic on the young man's face disappeared. "No, I think I'll desert," he said. "I want to be in on it. That's why I am a Free Officer."

Nasser told him to hurry home, change into his uniform, get his revolver, and wait at the end of his street. He would be picked up there
later by the black Austin.

After Tewfik left, he turned to his brothers and said, "I've got two
hundred pounds here. I'm going to save one pound for myself and give
you the rest. If anything happens to me tonight, give the money to
Tahia. With this added to her own income, she'll be all right. But you
keep an eye on her and the children." He paused. "That is, if anything
happens," he added slowly. Then he ran out to his car.

He drove directly to Amer's house, where he found blow number five
waiting for him. There was no sight of Sadat yet, so they agreed on a
substitute to take over his job of cutting communications. Then they
discussed what to do about the General Staff meeting.

"It may be a break for us," Nasser said, "if we can catch them all
while they are there together."

"Zero hour isn't until 1 A.M."

They looked at their watches. It was exactly eleven forty-two.

"We must go to the barracks and try to get some troops to help us,"
Amer said. "We can't capture the General Staff singlehanded."

They drove to the first large gate of the military compound. It was
closed, and in front of it stood an extraordinary number of M.P.s. As
they reached the second gate, it was just being closed.

"Is it our men who are doing this or theirs?" Nasser asked.

"I don't know," Amer replied, "but we had better drive around
quickly and try to get in from the rear of the compound."

Just then Nasser remembered that he was supposed to pick up Tewfik.
It was now eleven-fifty. They used up valuable minutes detouring so
Nasser could keep his promise to the intelligence officer, who was waiting
at the appointed place. It was now after midnight. They were driving
through the center of Heliopolis when, suddenly, as they turned a
corner, they stared into at least fifty sets of headlights coming from the
direction of the Huckstep barracks.

"Our enemies are working fast," Nasser said as he jammed on the
brakes.

"I think it's some of our own crazy people," Amer replied.

"But they were told zero hour was 1 A.M."

"They may have got ambitious and jumped the gun."

"Well, let's just park here quietly and see."

The column approached rapidly. As the first few khaki-colored
vehicles passed, Nasser and Amer realized they were from the Thir-

teenth Machine Gun Battalion. Suddenly one of the cars screeched to a stop, forcing the entire parade to halt. A young lieutenant jumped out, ordered his men, who were carrying tommy guns, to surround the Austin, and said to Amer, "You there, you're a major. You can go. But you"—he nudged Nasser with his revolver—"you're a colonel. No colonels are doing any circulating tonight. You're under military arrest."

This was one more backfire of their plans. Minutes counted now. The generals might be breaking up their meeting and going home at this very moment. Or, worse, they might be sounding an alarm, calling out troops.

"I happen to know your commander," Nasser said.

"You don't know anybody," the lieutenant shouted. "You don't know anything. You don't know what a night you live in tonight!"

Just then a jeep pulled up and out of the darkness came a voice: "Gamal, what in hell are you doing here?"

Nasser recognized it as the voice of Colonel Youssef Mansour Sadik, one of his staunchest Free Officers and a member of the machine-gun battalion. That morning he had called on Sadik and extracted a promise from him not to take part in the coup because he was suffering from an advanced case of tuberculosis. Looking at him now, Nasser saw that he was bleeding profusely from the mouth, yet he grinned as he asked again, "What in hell are you doing here?"

"We're under arrest."

"Speaking of arrests," Sadik said, "we've arrested the commander of our division. We've got him in one of the jeeps up ahead. And we've got a full company here, ready for action. Most of the officers are just out of the Academy. Some of your own pupils, Gamal."

Nasser smiled. Then hurriedly he explained about the leak and the meeting at G.H.Q. "Let's use your company to capture the generals," he suggested.

Sadik and Amer agreed, so the order was flashed down the line and the column began to move on Kubri el Kubba.

Amer took charge of the operation at the plain yellow building just off the main Cairo–Heliopolis road that housed G.H.Q. The General Staff meeting was still in progress. The Free Officers surrounded the building and then tried to force their way in. Guards on a stairway resisted and opened fire. The shooting lasted about ten minutes. When it ended, two men were dead, two wounded. All four were guards. Soon twenty generals were being marched out of the building, their hands above their heads.

"That's eight more than I had on my list," Nasser said with a laugh.

Suddenly there was a great commotion. Some officer trying to get into G.H.Q. had been arrested and was bellowing loudly enough to be heard in Alexandria that he was a friend, a Free Officer. Nasser recognized the voice of Anwar el Sadat and ordered him released. This was one example of the confusion that resulted from all the Free Officers not knowing who all the other Free Officers were.

Sadat relieved the tenseness for a moment by telling how, when he and his wife and daughter arrived home from the cinema, the doorkeeper had said, "I have a note, but I am not supposed to give it to anyone but *Mrs.* Sadat."

Mrs. Sadat read it and then with an expression of disgust handed it to her husband, saying, "I've always been suspicious of that man Nasser. What does he mean, 'Operation begins tonight'? Besides, it's after midnight already. It's morning."

By 1:30 A.M. Gamal Abdel Nasser, who had created a revolution with ninety men, was sitting behind the Chief of Staff's desk on the second floor of G.H.Q., in charge of a nation, although the nation was not yet aware of it. And might not be for a long time. Reports were flowing in from Free Officers. General Ali Naguib, brother of General Mohamed and commander of the Cairo garrison, had been taken prisoner. One of the security teams had gone to the home of the chief of political police and placed him under arrest.

"That should be good news to Sadat," Nasser said with a laugh.

The order to cut communications had not been executed. This turned out to be fortunate, instead of disastrous, for now the Free Officers could reach their own people around the country. Calls to Alexandria disclosed that the Free Officers up there had taken no revolutionary action. They had received the message through brother Az el-Arab but had not believed it to be authentic.

At Nasser's elbow were several telephones. One did not go through any switchboard and the number (60–005) was known by only a select group of high-ranking officers. Each time this phone rang, Nasser answered it himself. One call was from a man who demanded, "Who's there?"

"This is headquarters," Nasser replied evasively.

"Good, this is General Mohamed Naguib. What's going on?"

"Why do you ask?"

"I have just received a telephone call from the Minister of the Interior in Alexandria. He says Farouk's Palace woke him up to inquire whether there's any truth in reports that there's been some trouble in Cairo. The Minister asked me to try to find out something for him."

Nasser thought quickly, then said, "General Naguib, this is Colonel Gamal Abdel Nasser. Our boys have occupied G.H.Q. Wouldn't you like to come down and join us?" When Naguib agreed, he added, "Are you alone?"

"No. There's a young newspaperman here, Mohamed Heikal."

"Yes, I know," Nasser replied cryptically.

"How am I to get there?" Naguib asked.

"We have the city cordoned off, but we'll send two armored cars for you. You get as far as the bridge near the Metro station and our cars will pick you up there. And bring Heikal with you."

When the phone rang a short time later, Nasser, beginning to feel exhausted by now, lifted the receiver and without thinking said, "Hello, this is Gamal Abdel Nasser."

There was a long, significant silence. Then a voice asked, "And what are you doing there?"

"Who is this?" Nasser asked.

"This is the adjutant general!" was the indignant reply. He had been one of Nasser's teachers in Staff College.

"General," said his former pupil, "I think the best thing in the world for you to do at this moment would be to ask no more questions but just quietly go back to bed."

The phone at the other end was hung up with a bang. A short time later ordnance troops arrived at G.H.Q. with the announcement that they had been dispatched by the adjutant general to make an attack on whatever forces were in possession of G.H.Q. Instead, their commander said, they would like to join the insurgents.

While the Committee waited for Naguib, someone explained how the leak had occurred. One of the ninety Free Officers who had been alerted went home during the evening to change into his uniform. His mother, suspicious, asked an older son who was in the Air Force and was not a Free Officer to stop his brother from whatever he was about to do. The brothers had an argument that ended when the Free Officer left to carry out his night's assignment. His brother then telephoned the palace in Alexandria and gave the alarm.

At 3 A.M. General Naguib arrived. As he entered the room, there was a broad smile on his dark, wrinkled face. *"Mabrouk!"* he said. Literally it means "May it be blessed," but it is the expression all Egyptians use when they want to say "Congratulations!" He shook hands with Nasser, then sat down to discuss the role he would assume as the figurehead of the revolution.

One of the Free Officers ordered to report to G.H.Q. after its capture was Ali Sabri, chief of air intelligence and brother of Zulficar Sabry, who had gone to prison for trying to fly General Masri to the Nazis. (The brothers are such individualists that they spell their last names differently.) When Sabri arrived at G.H.Q., Nasser said to him, "You have a connection with the American Embassy, don't you?"

"I know the Assistant Air Attaché, Lieutenant Colonel David Evans," Sabri replied.

"Good! Go to him at once. Wake him up. Tell him there has been a coup, that it was virtually bloodless. You needn't mention my name at all. Tell him that General Mohamed Naguib is the leader of the Free Officers and that he will soon be issuing an announcement to the world. Tell him the revolution is not directed against any foreign powers."

"Is that all?" Sabri asked.

"No. Tell your American friend to have the American Ambassador pass all this information on to the British Ambassador—unless you have some good contacts at the British Embassy, too."

Sabri reported a little later by telephone that he had found Evans awake; that the news was being transmitted at once to Washington; that Ambassador Caffery was informing the British; that the Egyptian generals were not the only ones who had been taken by surprise, for several top British diplomats and the chief of British intelligence were in London on leave.

From scouts sent out along the road to Suez there were comforting reports: no sign of any British military movements from the Canal Zone toward Cairo. Many of the young Free Officers thought the time had come to start congratulating themselves. The plan had misfired in many ways, there had been one serious leak, yet not any of the ninety men Nasser decided to trust had proved unfaithful.

The officers who came and went brought reports from which Nasser was able to piece together a story of what had really happened. Several times that night he turned to one or another of his officers and said, "We have been very lucky!" No one denied it.

At 4 A.M. a tired, dust-covered cavalry officer, Colonel Hussein Shafei, appeared in the doorway. "Mabrouk!" he said to Nasser, then recounted how, quite by accident, they had captured the commander of the Armored Brigade.

"The Chief of Staff sent him to make an inspection and be sure nothing was going on. He walked right into our arms. After my men surrounded him with fixed bayonets, he sent for me. First he threatened me. Then he said we were playing with foolishness. Then he tried to appeal to my sentimentality. We locked him up in my office, after giving him some tea and coffee. I guess he's still there. It was a little bit embarrassing because, as you know, he was my first commander in the Army."

Shafei said his tanks, in accordance with Nasser's orders, had occupied strategic points in the city, including the broadcasting buildings, telephone exchange, railroad station, and airports.

For Nasser there was only one serious disappointment that morning. General Sirry Amir, whom he had once tried to kill, was not among those rounded up. He had escaped again. As long as he was at liberty he could be a source of trouble. Another disturbing thought stayed with him, the omnipresent possibility of counterrevolution.

"Every revolution faces the danger of counterrevolution," he told himself. "The makers of every coup must watch out for a countercoup. There are always jealousies that can be exploited."

At 4:30 A.M. a call came through from Sinai. Salah Salem and his brother Gamal had taken over G.H.Q. at El Arish and were in control of the garrison.

At 5 A.M. there was a call from Prime Minister Hilaly. Nasser gave the phone to Mohamed Naguib. It was a long, complicated, and thoroughly unsatisfactory conversation for everyone. The Prime Minister said something. Naguib listened, then replied, "Wait a minute." He relayed Hilaly's words to Nasser and Amer. They discussed them. Then they told Naguib what to answer.

The Prime Minister offered to re-form his Cabinet. He offered to dispense with the King's brother-in-law. He offered to make General Naguib Minister of War if he would call off the coup. Naguib was told to answer *no*. He did. After half an hour the attempt to reach an agreement was abandoned.

At 6 A.M. messengers were sent to the newspapers with copies of a proclamation. Early in the evening Amer had scribbled it on several pieces of copybook paper while he was waiting in his home for Nasser, but it was put out under Naguib's name. There had been a short discussion between Nasser and the Committee as to what title Naguib should be given.

"Let's say 'Commander in Chief of the Armed Forces of Egypt,' " Nasser suggested.

There was no disagreement. They were feeling their way slowly, as if through some no man's land that might be sown with mines.

At 7 A.M. Sadat went by army jeep to a studio of the Egyptian State Broadcasting system and read, in the name of General Naguib, Amer's proclamation. The rich baritone voice of this specialist in terror was pleasant and cheerful as he addressed a city just starting a new day: "People of Egypt! Our country has lived through one of the darkest periods of its history."

Amer had not spared words in writing about the generals locked up at the Military Academy. "Led by fools, traitors, and incompetents, the Army was incapable of defending Egypt...."

Only a few newspapermen besides Heikal had found their way to G.H.Q., but the broadcast brought reporters and photographers in droves. At Naguib's first informal press conference questions were put to him in machine-gun style:

"General, how did you organize this revolt?"

"Will you tell us, General Naguib, who is going to be Prime Minister?"

"General, have you any plans for the King?"

Nasser stood in a corner of the room, listening to the answers. Naguib was charming and generally evasive. The reporters stared at the other men clustered around the table, noting the names of those they recognized. All of them passed over Nasser.

After the press had been dismissed, Nasser thought of a personal matter. He called his sentimental friend, Sarwat Okasha, into a corner and said, "Go to my home and tell Tahia what's happened. I don't want her to worry. But tell her I've made a promise to myself not to return home until Farouk is out of the country. I don't know when that will be."

When Okasha came back he was smiling. "She woke up during the night when she heard the shooting," he reported. "You had told her you were going to attend a meeting at the Staff College and would be home late. She asked your brothers, when she heard the shooting, what kind of a meeting it was. But I think she knew."

During the early morning hours the Committee held a conference and made some decisions. Phase one of the revolution was over. The Free Officers were in indisputable control of the Army. The next problem was the formation of a government. Nasser proposed the name of Aly Maher, who had become Prime Minister after Black Saturday and had managed to restore some degree of order out of that chaos. One of the others said, "He hates the British as much as we do, and he's old, and he's respectable——"

Nasser interrupted. "What is most important," he pointed out, "is that he may have enough influence over Farouk to convince him that he must abdicate quickly."

Sadat was then ordered to go and see Maher on behalf of the revolution. He came back a little later to say that he had found Maher in his bath, that he had given the old man a rather fiery speech against the King "to make him realize that a real revolution had occurred and what type of man he was dealing with," and that Maher had said he would think over the suggestion of heading a government.

Wednesday in Cairo was hotter than Tuesday, but people didn't seem to mind. There was plenty to divert them from the oppressive heat. Some heard it first from the radio. Some suspected it first upon seeing the tanks. Then the newspapers appeared with huge headlines in red ink, the size that usually proclaimed an assassination. Overhead, Egyptian fighters and bombers were zooming, power-diving, making a spectacular show.

Correspondents for newspapers abroad were caught off guard. Before long New York and London editors were sending urgent cables asking who this man Naguib was, and what would be the attitude toward Britain, and was Farouk to stay? No one asked about Gamal Abdel Nasser, for only the ninety men who had made the revolution knew him. That day, his name appeared in no newspaper in America, Europe, or the Middle East, not even in the paper that employed Mohamed Heikal.

General Naguib was sent into the city during the day to show himself to the public. Wherever he went, people who had been without dignity since before they could remember and without hope for a long time cheered him tumultuously. They had heard his name on the radio before breakfast. They had read it in the morning papers. They knew him as the man who had planned and plotted their deliverance. So they cheered him wildly wherever he went.

On Thursday, Nasser heard rumors that Farouk was planning a countercoup, and he decided to move quickly against him. He ordered two armored columns to start for Alexandria during the evening, one over the desert, one up through the Delta. Several members of the Executive Committee would take a plane the next morning for the summer capital. Before he lay down on a cot to sleep a few hours he received what for him was the best report of the week. Troops going across the desert had stumbled onto General Sirry Amir in full flight. He was being sent back to Cairo under heavy guard.

The next morning, Nasser took Sadat aside and said, "Naguib wants to go, too, so take him in the same plane with you."

Sadat nodded. Nasser took a long, deep puff on his cigarette, a habit he had when he was about to make an especially serious remark. "Remember," he warned, "Farouk must be out of the country within twenty-four hours; forty-eight at the very most."

A few hours later he received his first phone call that day from Free Officers in Alexandria. The message said Naguib had been given a roaring welcome from crowds at the airport and all the way into the city. A digest of the day's other phone calls showed the rapid movement of events toward a new climax:

Alexandria: It is uncertain where Farouk is. Some say at Montazah Palace, some say Ras-el-Tin, some say he's hiding in a hospital.

Nasser: Your intelligence men must locate him quickly.

Alexandria: A Palace tipster insists Farouk has been in conversation again with the British, asking for military assistance from the Canal.

Nasser: We should begin military operations as quickly as possible.

Alexandria: Wire tap shows Farouk to be in his Montazah Palace.

Nasser: Keep a watch on Ras-el-Tin anyway.

Alexandria: Commanding officer of armored columns advises that we wait until tomorrow to begin operations. His men have had no sleep for three nights. Also, some of his tanks broke down on the desert road.

Nasser: Zakaria Mohieddin is in charge. His decision is final.

Alexandria: We have reason to believe that Farouk has gone to Ras-el-Tin Palace, at the other end of the city, to be able to escape to the open sea more easily.

Nasser: Both palaces must be attacked tomorrow.

Alexandria: Sadat has prepared the ultimatum for Prime Minister Maher to deliver to the King tomorrow. It ends, "And whereas you have thereby damaged the reputation of Egypt in the eyes of other countries; and whereas you have condoned the bribery and treachery revealed in consequence of our defeat in the Palestinian war; I, Mohamed Naguib, in the name of the Army, which represents the will of the people, have been authorized to demand that you abdicate in favor of your son, Prince Ahmed Fouad II, before 1200 and that you leave the country forever before 1800 today. If you refuse to comply with this ultimatum, you will be held responsible for the consequences."

Nasser: Tell Sadat to deliver the ultimatum to the Prime Minister as early as possible in the morning, for transmission to the King.

Alexandria: Gamal Salem is in disagreement with the plan for tomorrow. He thinks Farouk should not be allowed to escape but should receive the maximum punishment as quickly as possible.

Nasser: He thinks we should hang him?

Alexandria: Yes. Sadat insists that your orders for tomorrow be carried out. Zakaria Mohieddin is remaining neutral. He's on the floor of headquarters, working on maps, preparing tomorrow's siege of the two palaces. Naguib is not taking part in the disagreement.

Nasser: Farouk must be sent into exile.

About 6 A.M. an orderly awoke Colonel Nasser at G.H.Q. Gamal Salem had arrived by plane from Alexandria to argue for Farouk's death. Nasser listened quietly. When Salem had finished, he said, "I have an idea. I'll go and see General Masri. It's a shame to wake up the old man so early in the morning, but let's find out what he says."

He dressed quickly and called for a car.

The old man sided with Salem. "A head like Farouk's interests me only after it has fallen," he snorted.

Nasser warned there might be no way to stop the flow of blood, once started.

"You must kill, and kill, and kill," Masri replied. "You must slay thousands in order to purge the country."

A short time later five members of the Committee were assembled at G.H.Q. Gamal Salem made an eloquent plea to them. Then Nasser spoke. "If we hang Farouk, the next day the mob will murder at least three hundred of his entourage," he told them solemnly. "That will lead to other killings. There will be no way to stop it."

Several others spoke. Then a vote was taken. The majority were on Nasser's side.

Several hours later messages began to come in from Alexandria again.

Alexandria: We are in constant communication with our men at both palaces and at Bulkeley, by wireless. Meteor and Vampire jets are flying back and forth over the two palaces. Above them are flights of four-engine bombers carrying demolition bombs. We have a flight of Hawker Furies alerted for interception in case the King tries to slip away by air. Shots have been fired on our men from a turret at Ras-el-Tin. The fire is being returned . . . The fire on both sides has now ceased . . . The Royal Guard has surrendered . . . Six men have been wounded . . . General Naguib and Anwar el Sadat have gone to the government's summer headquarters at Bulkeley to present the ultimatum . . . Farouk has finally agreed to abdicate on seven conditions.

Nasser: What are they?

Alexandria: First, that the act of abdication should be drawn up in a dignified manner.

Nasser: There is no reason it should not be dignified.

Alexandria: Second, that he be permitted to go to Naples on the royal yacht, the *Mahroussa.*

Nasser: That yacht cost the Egyptian people a great deal of money. He may sail away in it, but it must be returned after it has put him ashore in Naples.

Alexandria: Third, that he be given a salute of twenty-one guns.

Nasser: The salute is okay.

Alexandria: Fourth, that Naguib should attend his departure in order to assure his safety right up to the last minute.

Nasser: Okay.

Alexandria: Fifth, that Antonio Pulli, his former court electrician, who usually accompanies him on his adventures at night, and Mohamed Hassan, his valet, be permitted to sail with him.

Nasser: Request denied.

Alexandria: Sixth, that he be permitted to take his stamp and coin collections with him.

Nasser: Those stamps and coins are worth millions of Egyptian pounds and they were bought with the people's money. Request denied.

Alexandria: His final desire is that the fortune within Egypt belonging to himself and his sisters should be administered on their behalf.

Nasser: We can make no such promise as this.

Alexandria: The King has agreed to sign the abdication agreement at twelve noon.

Nasser: That will give him just six hours to pack and say good-by.

Alexandria: Yes.

Nasser: Who is writing the abdication agreement?

Alexandria: Supreme Court Justices Hafez and Sanhouri. They have just finished it.

Nasser: Read it to me.

Alexandria: "We, Farouk Fouad I, desiring the welfare, happiness, and advancement of our country, and wishing to help it overcome the difficulties with which it is faced in the present delicate circumstances, have decided to abdicate in favor of our son, Crown Prince Ahmed Fouad II. We hereby authorize His Excellency, Aly Maher, President of the Council of Ministers, to proceed in accordance with this act."

Nasser: That is not satisfactory. You must insert somewhere in the first sentence something about the will of the people.

Alexandria: The two judges are discussing this matter.... They are inserting the words "in accordance with the will of the people" after the word "decided." Farouk is now reading the revised version.... He has been persuaded to sign it.... His hand was trembling so badly the signature was hardly legible. He has apologized and now has signed it again.

Nasser: Instruct all the Free Officers you have available to station themselves on the principal warships in the harbor, to be sure the situation remains under control.

Alexandria: We have counted two hundred and four trunks which have already gone aboard the *Mahroussa*. Also some cases of champagne and wine from the royal cellars. Farouk has changed into the white dress uniform of an Admiral in the Egyptian Navy. He is saying good-by to people in the grand salon of the Palace. Two of his five sisters and their husbands are here. Farouk is saying good-by to them. The King has sent Queen Narriman and his three daughters and the baby boy to the yacht. Also the baby's English nursemaid, three Albanian guards, and a dog trainer. The Prime Minister and American Ambassador Caffery are here. They are having a final conversation with the King. Now Farouk is leaving the Palace by a staircase leading to a landing stage. Now he has gone out by tender to the *Mahroussa*.

Nasser: Where is General Naguib?

Alexandria: He had difficulty getting through the crowd, but now he is going out in another small boat. Farouk is standing on the deck of the *Mahroussa*, waiting for him. On the deck now are General Naguib, his aide, Gamal Salem, Hussein Shafei, and Colonel Ahmed Shawki.... Now the Free Officers have shaken hands and left the yacht.

Nasser: What were Farouk's last words?

Alexandria: He said to Naguib, "What you have done to me I was getting ready to do to you." Then he said, "Your task will be difficult. It is not easy to govern Egypt." Now the guns are giving the salute. The *Mahroussa* has begun to move out to sea.

Nasser: Thanks to Allah!

CHAPTER 9

THE RELUCTANT DICTATOR

Rarely, anywhere, has a man worked so diligently to achieve anonymity as Gamal Abdel Nasser did in the summer of 1952. Many reasons have been advanced. His own explanation is simple:

"I ordered that no name be given any publicity except Naguib's. I wanted all the light cast on him. I gave this order principally to avoid a split in the Free Officers. We were all of us either thirty-two, thirty-three, or thirty-four years old, except Khaled Mohieddin, who was a little younger. We were all about equal in rank. I knew how the British and our internal enemies would try to pit us one against the other, if we gave them a chance. But if we had the sense to let an older man like Naguib be the figurehead, we could retain our unity."

Free Officers were instructed not to talk for publication, not to mention names, not to take or give credit. Strict censorship was imposed, internally and on dispatches, broadcasts, photographs, and newsreels sent abroad.

But for weeks censorship was not necessary to keep the name of Gamal Abdel Nasser out of print. At first few men in the world except the three hundred Free Officers knew the truth. And not all of them. General Mohamed Naguib had been portrayed by the press of the world as the man who had engineered the revolt from the start. His picture appeared on the front cover of news magazines. Every chapter of his life was ransacked for details that would make him an exciting personality. An American book publisher signed a contract for a biography of him.

One day, several weeks after the revolution, a British journalist with a reputation for keen powers of perception appeared in Cairo to find out how the revolution had been executed. He met Mohamed Heikal, and Heikal took him to see Nasser, without saying why. It was the first interview Nasser ever gave. But it was never printed.

"He talks like a Communist," the Englishman said as he and Heikal left G.H.Q. "He doesn't sound a bit important. Can't you get me in to see General Naguib?"

131

About the same time, Naguib, in answer to a delicate question put to him by an American radio commentator and a reporter for an American weekly magazine, said, "You had better ask El Bikbashi."

"Who is El Bikbashi?" they wanted to know.

Late that night, Naguib's secretary took the two men to the apartment on Galali Street, where Nasser gave them a six-hour interview on the purposes of the revolution. Little if any of it was used. To editors in New York, "Nasser" meant nothing in the summer of 1952.

His name first appeared in Cairo papers three weeks after the revolt, when he lost his temper with Prime Minister Maher and paid a formal call to demand why no more progress was being made with the land-reform scheme Maher had been ordered to put into effect. The newspaper articles that day referred to him as "Colonel Gamal Abdel Nasser, one of the revolutionary leaders." It was not until September that the first hint of his real importance was given—by Mustafa Amin, the publisher of the daily newspaper on which Heikal worked. From Heikal he learned that Nasser had really created the revolution. Amin himself took a photograph of Nasser and used it to illustrate the first of a series of articles entitled, *The Story of the Nine,* in which Nasser was referred to as "the leader." El Bikbashi was very angry, and had a word with his censors. The other articles never appeared.

All this time it was Mohamed Naguib who toured the city in open cars, kissed babies, gave newspaper, radio, and television interviews to foreign correspondents, spoke over the Egyptian wave lengths. He made speeches to immense audiences and issued long decrees, written for him by members of the Committee. His warm, pleasant personality made him popular wherever he went. One day a Free Officer complained to Nasser that he should not permit Naguib to have all this acclaim, which actually belonged to him.

"Why should I be jealous?" Nasser replied. He was happy as long as he could sit behind the scenes, directing the action, issuing the orders. But reporters in Cairo began to be suspicious when an Associated Press dispatch that had been cleared by Naguib himself was held up.

"Why?" the correspondent demanded.

"El Bikbashi disapproved," was the answer.

By now the AP man knew who El Bikbashi was. The title was being used more and more. And more and more he and his colleagues heard, "I must see El Bikbashi before I can tell you." "El Bikbashi has not yet given his decision." Eventually Nasser's love of anonymity won him, in certain quarters, the sobriquet "the reluctant dictator."

At first Naguib was embarrassed over getting full credit not only for all the decisions being made exclusively by Nasser and the Committee but also for the years of planning and plotting with which he had had almost no connection. It was difficult to face reporters and try to answer questions such as: "When, General, did you first get the idea of organizing the Free Officers movement?"

One day he said to a friend, "I'm robbing the glory from these young men. It isn't fair."

But his frank and amiable manner during this period won him the deep respect of the younger men. Abdel Latif Baghdady, a member of the Committee, said to Sadat one day, "Anwar, I love that man as much as I do my own father. Maybe more."

Gradually the myth of Naguib's leadership was repeated over and over again, so often, so convincingly, that the general himself began to believe it. In this country, which has little of the Western attitude toward precise fact, myth and truth were soon being completely tangled.

One day Mustafa Amin was jailed because of an article on the Sudan that offended the general, but Amin felt certain he was really being punished for giving that first bit of publicity to Nasser.

Then an American news magazine printed an article that began: "There is a man named Nasser . . ."

This annoyed both Nasser and Naguib; the one because he still wanted to remain anonymous; the other because he was beginning to be jealous.

Then somehow a cartoon slipped by the censor showing Nasser as "The Second Man of the Revolution." Naguib asked for an investigation of how it happened to be passed.

Some saw in Nasser's desire for anonymity a deep astuteness. "He had read history," said a friend. "He had learned that revolutions nearly always turn cannibalistic and eat their own creators. He wanted to avoid for himself the fate of a Kerensky."

He also knew his own country, knew the truth of the old Arab proverb "When the calf is thrown, the knives appear." At this moment the country was more united than ever before in its reaction to Farouk's departure, but now that he was gone, how would the Moslem Brotherhood, the Communists, the Wafd, the British, and all the other forces up and down the Nile and in the Delta react? Against whom would the knives be turned? How could three hundred young army officers and one amiable general hold onto the power they had seized, with twenty-one million possible enemies? There was need for a man to sit in the shadows, plotting, planning, watching for counterintrigue, quickly nipping any sign of opposition, figuring and refiguring every day how to hold the good will of the people, how to keep the street under control, how to get some quick and spectacular results to convince all Egyptians that the revolution had been made for them, and not just for the benefit of a few army officers.

Nasser was free of any inhibiting policies or doctrinaire plans. Until now he had promised nobody anything specific. Yet the lack of an *idée fixe* was also a handicap. Playing it continuously by ear meant the ear always had to be cocked. The revolution had been against Farouk, the British, and corruption, and in favor of something very vague, "a better life for everyone." Everyone included fellahin, capitalists, shopkeepers, army officers, even old-line generals, if they would agree to reform themselves. The only exceptions to "everyone" were the King and owners of more than two or three hundred acres of land.

Farouk was gone, but the British and corruption were still a plague. So was poverty. Until the revolution could eliminate all three, the minds of the people would have to be diverted.

Nasser decided he could satisfy the people for a time by continuing to attack the paunchy Farouk, now resident in Naples. So the Egyptian newspapers received the suggestion and began to tear at the shabby remains of Farouk's reputation. Vilification was the order of the day. "Lecherous" was one of the more polite terms they used. The papers told how he had once lost $140,000 in a single night of gambling in Europe. They chuckled because, when he fled, he left behind in one of the palaces twenty-four golden cups encrusted with precious jewels, just one of which would have kept a man in champagne and caviar for almost a year.

Nasser arranged for one of his Free Officers to be given the title Controller General of the Confiscated Property of the Mohamed Aly Dynasty and of the Royal Palaces of King Farouk. He made a catalogue, like the catalogue for an auction sale of paintings in London or New York. Then bids were invited.

One day on Nasser's order the great wrought-iron gates of Kubbah Palace were swung open to admit the press, domestic and foreign alike. The reporters filed from room to room, staring, poking, and exclaiming, amazed at what they saw. The girl Queen, Narriman, had left *Lady Chatterly's Lover* on her bedside table, and they noted that Farouk's bedroom was "heaped high with a weird mixture of pornography, childishness, and sentimentality." One of the Free Officers showed them a box full to the brim with diamonds, emeralds, rubies, and platinum brooches.

At this same time Egyptian fathers were encouraged to change the names of any of their sons whom they had unfortunately called Farouk. One father who ignored the suggestion was Naguib, who had named his eldest son after the King in a moment of royalist enthusiasm fourteen years earlier.

All afternoon and sometimes during most of the night the Committee sat around its conference table on the second floor at G.H.Q. and made decisions. Naguib and three young Free Officers were added to the inner circle, making it thirteen now, except that thirteen rarely sat down at the table. Naguib understood that he was an ex-officio member of this body of young men, so he attended meetings only when specifically invited. The next morning he was always informed of the decisions that had been arrived at and the orders he must issue.

Nasser let the others argue, object, and equivocate, but when he finally called for a vote the matter was usually decided as he had originally suggested.

They changed the name of Fouad University, called after Farouk's father, to Cairo University. They released all but three of the generals, and even went so far as to name Major General Ali Naguib Under Secretary in the Foreign Ministry.

Most of Farouk's old cronies were ordered arrested. It was decided to abandon the practice of moving the government up to Alexandria each summer, Nasser considering it undemocratic for government officials to enjoy the cool of the seaside while the rest of Cairo had to stay and suffer the summer heat.

The honorary titles *pasha* and *bey* were abolished. In the days of the Turks they had been given only to men of considerable distinction, but by 1952 there were so many pashas and beys that there was little snob appeal left to the titles. (Naguib had automatically become a bey when he received his rank of general.)

Three regents were appointed to serve until Fouad II came of age. One was Colonel Rashid Mehanna. Nasser's insistence on naming him was considered at the time a sample of his genius. Mehanna was an imposing aristocrat, closely associated with the Moslem Brotherhood and never a very certain friend of the Free Officers, but he had a following in the artillery, so now he would be in a high but empty position, and out of the way. That was Nasser's theory.

The most serious decision was taken at the first meeting after Farouk sailed away and the committee members came back from Alexandria. There were nine on the Committee then, but Khaled Mohieddin was absent. Nasser himself began the discussions.

"The King has gone," he said. "Now we are running the country. We have a great responsibility. We must decide at once what philosophy of government we are going to follow. There is no time for intellectual argument. We must reach a decision tonight."

The other seven, some of whom had read little except military manuals and novels of adventure, were suddenly being asked to answer, in a few hours, a very profound question. The result was that the discussion turned at once to a facet of the problem about which they could all be articulate: how to deal with past, present, and future enemies of the government.

"Maybe it was all right to let Farouk go, but now we must start being harsh," one of them said.

"I am in favor of building gallows immediately in front of Abdin Palace and in the Midan of Ismailia," the next man added.

Nasser sat at the head of the table, listening for a long time to his colleagues demand quick trials and public executions. Then he held up his hand.

"I have heard your speeches. Now let me remind you that we have told the people we came to relieve them of tyranny; the tyranny of Farouk and the old politicians. How can we start this same week applying an even worse tyranny? If we hang a hundred men this week, what shall we do next week, when we find a hundred who are more deserving of such a death? And if we hang the second hundred, what about the following week, and the next, and the next? Where will it stop? And what will happen to us? There are only three hundred of us. Think how many enemies we make when we hang a hundred men. Think how many relatives and friends a hundred men have."

Each of the seven had something to say in rebuttal.

"We must not give the masses an excuse to take to the street," Nasser warned. He reminded them that the Egyptian revolution of 1919 against the British failed partly because the leaders lost control over the people, who in one village went so far as to cut Englishmen into small pieces and run through the streets, carrying chunks of bleeding flesh and shouting, "British meat for sale." In another village they stopped a train, murdered eight British soldiers who were passengers, carved their faces grotesquely with knives, then propped the bodies up in the windows so they could be seen and jeered at as the train continued its journey through the Delta.

"This is a time for caution," he went on. "If there are disorders, the British may march in. Perhaps even the Americans."

After more discussion a vote was taken. His oratory and logic had had no effect. The vote was seven to one against him. He began to gather his papers. The others sat watching him. He put the papers into his brief case, then stood.

"Comrades," he said firmly, "I give you my resignation as head of the Committee and as a member of the Free Officers. I shall also resign immediately my commission in the Army. I cannot take responsibility for what you have just voted to do."

Then he turned on his heel and strode from the room. They all began to talk at once. One after another pointed out that they would be lost without his guidance. There was no one to take his place. Even if he was wrong, it would be wiser to let him have his way. It was after midnight when they passed a unanimous vote of confidence in him and appointed a committee to inform him that he could do whatever he liked if he would return to the head of the table.

The next day, he was back at his desk in G.H.Q. The color of the revolution would continue to be khaki. The Committee would continue to operate on the democratic principle that all decisions must be made by majority vote. But after the debate was over, it would be Nasser's opinion that prevailed.

Communist Khaled Mohieddin suggested to Nasser that experts in various fields be called in to make plans for revising Egypt's political and economic life. Their mutual friend, Judge Ahmed Fouad, helped make up the list of names. Men of many different professions were invited: professors, lawyers, engineers, doctors, educators, others who might be useful. They were offered no remuneration, no titles, no promise of future position, although today many have well-paid posts.

They assembled late each afternoon in an army building in Abbassia, after their normal work was finished. At the front of the room was the Committee, with Nasser always leading the discussion, asking questions, seeking advice, searching for ideas to incorporate into government plans. They were an odd assortment of men, these experts. Some had been violently antimonarchial. Others had an intense dislike of the British. Some were Communists, some socialists, some politically uncommitted. Often they sat around the barracks until three or four o'clock in the morning, trying to help the young army officers understand the complex new matters with which they now had to concern themselves.

One of the immediate post-revolutionary problems faced by both the Free Officers and the Moslem Brotherhood was what attitude to take toward each other. El Banna was dead. His successor was Hassan el Hodeiby, a mouse-gray, mild-looking judge with steel-rimmed glasses. Yet it was no secret that the Brotherhood had been growing, not only in numbers but in its interest in terrorism. Hodeiby discovered that at least a hundred of Nasser's Free Officers had now, or had had at one time, some connection with the Brotherhood, including some officers at the very top. So the Brothers were told to say prayers in the mosques for the success of the revolution. Flags were flown from headquarters. Thousands of the Brothers were sent into the streets to guard embassies, legations, consulates, and even foreign businesses against attacks by mobs and to organize "spontaneous" demonstrations whenever Naguib appeared in public. The brethren, who thought they might get their theocratic state through Nasser, took credit for the complete lack of opposition to the revolution at the start, and probably deserved it.

Nasser, on his side, also decided on a course of action. As a student in the Staff College years ago he had learned a military principle that was always called Rule No. 1: If you are exposed on many fronts, you must make every possible effort to isolate all but the front on which you are currently making your attack. As soon as the revolution was over, he discovered that this was a good principle to apply in internal as well as in foreign affairs. He would, he decided, always make temporary peace with all enemies but the one he was about to attack. Following Rule No. 1, he came to the conclusion that this was not the time to antagonize the million members of the Brotherhood, and he sent word to Hodeiby that he would be pleased to see him.

The Supreme Guide, vacationing in Alexandria, sent back word that when he had time he would consider dropping in. Then he set to work writing a paper giving his ideas about a theocratic state, while his aides made up a list of the cabinet posts to which they felt the Brothers were entitled.

The committee members now thought they should have a name, so they decided to call themselves the Revolutionary Command Council, and they moved from the cramped quarters at G.H.Q. on the edge of the city to a three-story gray stone building Farouk had had the government build for him on Gezira Island. It was a mooring station for his many personal river boats, but in the royal manner. The grounds were landscaped by the palace gardener. The building itself, surrounded by immense palm trees, contained enough bedrooms, bathrooms, and dressing rooms to accommodate a yachtful of guests. There also were offices for all the men who occupied themselves with the personal navigational matters of His Royal Highness. There were electric refrigerators from the U.S., *bidets* from France, automatic elevators from Switzerland. Nasser chose the building because it offered seclusion in the very center of the city. Here, on an island, while Naguib was meeting the crowds a mile or two away, the R.C.C. could try to come to grips with Egypt's problems.

They usually met at night, for the days are hot in Cairo most of the year. Nasser himself had discovered that he did his best thinking after the sun had set, regardless of the season. Often the men would sit all night around a large table on the top floor, arguing and planning. One servant was kept busy in a kitchenette making Turkish coffee and another running in and out of the conference room with a brass tray and small china cups. Sometimes the officers wore khaki, more often mufti. There was no formality about the meetings. They interrupted each other's speeches to borrow a cigarette or ask for a match. Sometimes Nasser would get up and stare at the lights in the hotels and embassies across the river. Many of the discussions were heated, with considerable pounding of the table and loud talk, but because they were army men, when Nasser rapped for order, order was always quickly restored.

At the top of the Council's list of problems was trying to get Aly Maher, the Prime Minister they had chosen, to take action on the first and only reform they had in mind: seizure of the royal estates and confiscation, with adequate indemnity, of all large private agricultural holdings. The plan they had drawn up was to permit no one to own more than two hundred feddan. Maher had argued for five hundred. Nasser had agreed to a small compromise. Owners of large estates would be permitted to hold two hundred and transfer another one hundred to their children. Still Maher hesitated.

Nasser waited seven weeks, then acted. One day in September, the people of Cairo heard on the 7:15 A.M. news broadcast that General Mohamed Naguib had replaced the politician Maher as Prime Minister. Several London papers, reporting the news, said that General Naguib had made himself a military dictator. Nowhere in the world, neither in London, New York, nor even in Cairo, did the people yet know anything about the man who was actually pulling the strings and issuing the orders.

CHAPTER 10

THE GENERAL AND THE COLONEL

Mohamed Naguib and Gamal Abdel Nasser are both professional army men; both had graduated from the Royal Military Academy and the Staff College, like to play chess, learned English as children, early in life became admirers of Egyptian nationalist Mustafa Kamel, and their fathers each sired ten children. But these two men, who jointly dominated post-revolutionary Egypt for two years, are distinctly diverse personalities, with different backgrounds, different viewpoints.

Mohamed Naguib came from a long line of distinguished officers. His maternal grandfather had been an acting brigadier. His father served as a captain with Kitchener and Wingate.

Naguib was a scholar from youth. He was the highest in his class at the Staff College. He learned to read and speak French, Italian, German, and even some Hebrew, as well as English, his second language.

Once in a schoolroom Mohamed's teacher in English dictated a statement from a book for the pupils to write: "Egypt is governed by the British."

Mohamed jumped up and shouted, "No, sir, not governed, occupied!"

For that outburst he received ten lashes, which apparently discouraged him from any further displays of anti-British feeling.

His boyhood hero was Napoleon, and because Napoleon liked to sleep on the floor young Naguib also liked to sleep on the floor. Because Napoleon ate dark bread, young Naguib would not eat any other kind. His desire to become an Egyptian army officer was so strong that at the age of fifteen he ran away from home, traveled a thousand miles alone by foot, train, boat, and bus, part of the time disguised as a Sudanese servant to a teacher, smuggled himself across the Sudanese-Egyptian frontier, and when he got to Cairo begged admission to the Military Academy. When the officials measured him they found he was only five feet three, one inch shorter than the admissible minimum. He went back to the Sudan, bought a stretching machine, and took up fencing and gymnastics, but managed to increase his stature by only half an inch. He was admitted anyway. Eventually he became a member of the King's Guard, but his inherent antiroyalism was aroused when Farouk's father ordered a guard flogged for stealing a few dates from one of the royal palms.

The year young Gamal finished his first grade in primary school, Mohamed received the first of two master's degrees.

The first time Naguib ever tried to kill a man was during a chase across the Eastern Desert one day in the thirties, when he was a captain in the Frontier Corps. He and an elderly guide were pursuing five smugglers leading four camels loaded with nearly ten thousand bundles of hashish. Naguib apparently was a better shot than Nasser. His own comment on the slaying was, "Fortunately I killed one of our five opponents with a lucky shot."

The casualness of the comment is in marked contrast to Nasser's statement of remorse after his own attempt at manslaughter.

Naguib has never forgotten three drunken British soldiers who in a Cairo suburban train during World War II struck him over the head with a beer bottle and stole his wallet. However, just before the war he had gone on a two-month tour of England and France with a group of other Egyptian officers. This gave him a new perspective and tempered his hatred of the British.

At the time of the abdication Nasser had had only his one slight contact with Farouk at the Officers' Club, but Naguib had actually been the King's guest in Montazah Palace for six days. It had happened in 1938 when he was a major, temporarily in charge of the Military Museum in Cairo. Farouk, eighteen, was starting a private arms collection of his own. Naguib, twice the King's age, took two truckloads of historically valuable guns up to Alexandria to give to Farouk, who was so pleased that he asked the major to stay awhile and explain the ancient weapons to him.

Both Nasser and Naguib lived modestly in the days before the revolution, the general in a small house in suburban Zeitun. Nasser's small Austin was matched by Naguib's small German Opel, which still was not completely paid for at the time of the revolution.

Nasser had been married once, Naguib twice. He had divorced his first wife, who was childless, and married an infantry colonel's daughter, who bore him three sons.

Nasser smoked interminable numbers of cigarettes. Naguib puffed constantly on a pipe in which he used crushed Tuscan cigars.

The war in Palestine, in which both men served, made Naguib a national hero. One of Egypt's military classics was the story of how during the fight for Hill 86 a tank under his command stalled and was caught in the crossfire of two Israeli machine guns; Naguib, although a brigadier, crawled five hundred yards under heavy fire and tried to rescue a wounded gunner trapped inside. It was then that he received his third and almost mortal wound of the war.

The people in the street called him the Man with the Pipe and shouted *"Long live Naguib!"* He smiled back at them with genuine warmth and they cheered even louder. He seemed like a kind father to them, even to people older than he. He exuded self-confidence. Wherever he went he behaved like an American politician in October of election year, yet he seemed to do it naturally. He smiled into the cameras, presided at charity functions, and even adopted an orphan child.

Unlike Nasser, Naguib always sprinkled his conversation, his writings, and his speeches with religious references. In one of his most successful appearances before a crowd he recited a long prayer to Allah, which he composed on the spot and which he asked the thousands in his audience to recite after him, sentence by sentence. Nasser had never gone on a pilgrimage to Mecca before the revolution, but Naguib had made the long trip in 1950 to pray for a dying daughter.

During an interview with a reporter from New York whom he knew to be Jewish, Naguib pulled open the drawer of his desk and extracted a Torah. "A gift from the Egyptian Jewish community," he said as he showed it to his visitor. "I regard all Egyptians, whatever their color or creed, to be equal. On my wall at home I have, hanging beside several quotations from the Koran, a Christian religious picture given to me by a Coptic priest."

Once on Yom Kippur he astonished the Jews of Cairo by going to the Ismailia synagogue to attend a service. He also dropped in occasionally during Greek and Armenian Orthodox, Maronite, and Roman Catholic services. He even remembered what some Christians overlooked: that there were Protestants, too, in Egypt. One Christmas Eve the Reverend Ibrahim Said looked down from the pulpit in his Protestant church and almost lost his power of speech, for there was the general striding up the aisle.

Such a man was Mohamed Naguib when the struggle for power among the revolutionaries began.

Nasser stood only three or four inches taller than the general (Naguib had added a little height since his cadet days) but he seemed to tower over Naguib. Nasser's physique is that of a professional football player. He gives the impression of being a "big man" even in a country where men as a rule are tall and stalwart, and six feet seems shorter than the average.

Anwar el Sadat, who has a penchant for picturesque language, says, "Gamal always reminds me of a wonderful desert animal, a black panther."

In those days he kept in trim playing tennis with some of his R.C.C. associates. (At the Academy, tennis and boxing had both been compulsory.) Whenever he had the opportunity he also went swimming. His favorite form of recreation in pre-revolutionary days was chess, which he began to play when he was still in secondary school.

He was always losing, so without telling anyone he went to the Cairo library and found they had many books in English on chess. He studied them and soon was not losing nearly so often.

His strongest and most noticeable physical feature is his jaw. Normally it is square and determined, but when he wishes to emphasize a point he throws his head back a little, the jaw comes forward, and no one can possibly question that he means what he is saying.

His eyebrows are heavy. His hair is a mass of small black curls. His mustache is always closely trimmed. His hands are large but not unattractive, and on a finger of his left hand he wears a gold wedding band. His eyes are the gray brown of Beni Mor. They are restless eyes. Sometimes they light up with sudden interest or excitement. When he is amused, they crinkle at the corners. There is nothing hard about either his eyes or their expression. This is his greatest asset when he is dealing with skeptics or critics. His physical charm, a latent hypnotic power, begins with the first pleasant glance of the eyes and lasts until he has graciously shown his guest to the door. It disarms almost everyone.

He walks with the healthy masculine stride of a country boy, or an army officer leading his men on the start of a cross-country hike. He has a frank and open manner, and seems to be holding nothing back, yet even his close associates complain that he is not a "giving" man.

"It's very odd," one of them says. "When you are with him you are convinced he is being completely frank and telling you everything. But after you have left him you realize you have no idea what actually is in his mind."

Nearly all of Nasser's R.C.C. colleagues have developed a nervous habit of cracking their knuckle joints while sitting in a meeting or taking part in a conversation. Many Egyptians carry Moslem prayer beads, which they use to count and recount the divine attributes of Allah. But in Cairo they are called "nervous beads" because many Moslems buy them and play with them the way a smoker toys with his lighted cigarette. Gamal Abdel Nasser neither cracks his knuckles in public nor carries prayer beads, although he has a nervous habit of his own: when someone is talking, he sits with his right leg crossed over his left, jiggling it constantly. Otherwise he rarely displays any nervousness and seems to have himself under perfect control most of the time.

He speaks English with just enough of a Middle Eastern intonation to make you always aware that you are listening to a man whose mother tongue is another language. From the many Hollywood films he has seen he has acquired an American accent. When a guest is talking he listens with his head bent slightly to one side, as if he were weighing every thought, deciding the truth or falsity of every statement. When he speaks himself, it is in a well-modulated voice.

In conversations with friends or strangers, in Arabic or English, he seldom uses his hands to gesture, but he uses them constantly to pictorialize. If he is telling a story about one man being here, and another just across the road, he will draw a map of the scene with his right index finger on the palm of his left hand. During a conversation he sits up straight most of the time or even bends forward to show his interest. Whenever he hesitates about answering a question, looking for just the right word or weighing what he plans to say, he tilts his head back, looks at the ceiling, and takes several long breaths or, if he is smoking, inhales deeply. Then, finally, he speaks.

He chain-smokes much of the time, but he likes to have a servant empty his ash tray frequently so as not to be reminded of how greatly he is violating his own doctor's orders.

When he meets someone, whether an old friend or a new acquaintance, a man coming to ask a favor or someone bearing a gift, he is reluctant to get down to business. He will even discuss his caller's weight, or the state of the weather, if he sees no other way to sidetrack the main conversation.

He labors to avoid the issue. "Are you still taking insulin for your diabetes?" he may ask. He once thought he had diabetes himself. Many tests were taken before it was determined that this was not his trouble. However, he has always retained an interest in the malady.

He seldom decides anything quickly. Despite the pressure of events, he always seems willing to let anyone who is able to get past the barriers erected by his aides say what he came to say, no matter how long it may take. He likes to hear men with conflicting views give their reasons. But when he has made up his own mind, it is difficult for anyone to change it.

In many ways he is not a typical Egyptian. He is more reserved than most, less turbulent. He is an intense man, yet in a quiet, unbombastic way. One of his characteristics typical of Egyptians is his love of intrigue, of the Baron Münchhausen type of story, of complicated conspiracies with just a touch of horror. This has long been the synthetic alcohol for a people denied real alcohol by their religion.

Arrogance in any form is to him the unforgivable discourtesy. He also reacts strongly against people who use long words, sprinkle an English conversation with French or other foreign expressions, or exhibit any degree of self-importance.

He has a sense of humor, but by 1960 Western standards he is a puritan in what amuses him. One of his favorite jokes, which he tells anyone who professes not to have heard it before, is an old Turkish story about a British ship that entered the harbor of Constantinople and failed to receive the usual courtesy of a twenty-one-salvo salute. The captain, upset, went ashore, called on the commander of the garrison and asked, "Why didn't we get a salute?"

"There are one hundred and thirteen reasons," the commander said.

"One hundred and thirteen? What are they?" the captain demanded.

"The first," said the commander, "is that we have no ammunition, and——"

The captain held up his hand. "Never mind the other hundred and twelve. You don't need any more."

Nasser is disappointed if his telling of this story is not greeted with prolonged laughter.

Just as Naguib was secretly convinced during the war in Palestine that he had the special blessing of Allah that spared him from death in order to accomplish some divine purpose, so Nasser feels he has been "a lucky man." His favorite line in any article ever published about him is: "When he stumbles he always falls forward; even when he falls he seems to land on all fours, like a cat."

Nasser's self-control is phenomenal in Cairo, a city of men who blow up like angry volcanos over the slightest grievance. When he does get angry, the first sign is a narrowing of his eyes. One thing that annoys him is for his friends to use strong words to him. He rarely reacts spontaneously. He is a sentimentalist, although he is such a lone man that he has few intimate friends. He is touched by small things: a gift from someone who had no reason to bring him a gift, someone remembering something he said long ago. He is an introvert, a man with great self-discipline; sensitive, in many ways shy, and easily hurt.

But of all the characteristics that come out in long hours spent talking with him and trying to analyze him, visiting him in his office, sitting with him in his home, seeing him on holiday away from Cairo, relaxed, in a sport shirt, the most striking is his pride. He is determined to obtain some degree of dignity for his own people, no matter the price non-Egyptians or non-Moslem Egyptians may have to pay. He is resolved to end the long centuries of humiliation, whatever the cost.

CHAPTER 11

WE DON'T KISS HANDS

They argued all night long, sitting around the big table on the top floor of Farouk's old mooring house. General Naguib was at home in bed. Most of the people of Cairo were asleep. But Gamal Abdel Nasser and his Council had a grave problem to solve, the first of its kind since the revolution. At a town in the Delta close to Alexandria, one Saturday afternoon less than three weeks after Farouk had sailed away into exile, hundreds of cotton-mill workers held a demonstration against their employers, who had refused their demands for higher wages.

"Hurrah for Mohamed Naguib!" they shouted. "Long live the people's revolution!" "Praise Allah that at last we have an army!"

Company guards swung their clubs. The workers fought back. Police were called in and began shooting. In their rage the workers set fire to two buildings. The next morning, units of the same army they had been cheering arrived and opened fire on five or six hundred of the demonstrators who had locked themselves in a factory building. By the time the rebels surrendered, nine men were dead, thirty wounded, and two hundred had been arrested.

Strangely enough, the trouble occurred at one of the few model factories in the Middle East. It boasted a free clinic, cafeteria, athletic fields, and a shop where workers could buy food and clothing at cost. It also had a labor union that the management said was Communist-directed. This led to the accusation in Cairo that the strike was inspired by "enemies of the revolution."

Gamal Abdel Nasser and his R.C.C. acted quickly. They appointed one of their own members to fly to Alexandria and preside over a court-martial. "You must make an example out of those responsible," Nasser told the chief judge.

The trial was held on the factory grounds. It took only five days for the R.C.C. man from Cairo and his associates on the bench to decide that two of the workers were guilty of a grave crime against the state.

147

"I can see heads ripe for the plucking!" the prosecutor shouted. "I demand them. They are mine." The R.C.C. colonel and his associates acquiesced. The two strikers were ordered to be hanged by the neck until dead. Twelve others were sentenced to spend long terms in prison. Then the colonel ordered all the factory employees drawn up in line and the sentence read to them over loudspeakers.

While the loudspeakers blared forth their warning, the two men condemned to death shouted over and over again, "Long live the revolution!" "Hurrah for Naguib!"

Nasser and the Council were meeting now to make the final decision: should they, as the highest authority in post-revolutionary Egypt, show mercy? Until now it had not in any sense been a red revolution—neither in its political orientation nor because of spilled blood. A regime had been overthrown and a King sent into exile at a cost of only two dead, two wounded, and this in a part of the world where those in power, or those seeking power, had always held life cheaply—at least the lives of others. If the death sentences were permitted to stand, the record would begin to be spattered with blood. "I feel we are making a tactical error," Nasser told the Council.

If the death sentences were permitted to stand, the new regime would, in effect, be declaring war on the political left.

"This, also, would be a tactical error," Khaled Mohieddin told them.

They argued until the first light of morning. Then they took a vote. Nasser, Mohieddin, and one other member voted *no*. The rest were for death. So the two men were hanged in the courtyard of the prison at Alexandria. First blood had now been splotched on the record.

Immediately pamphlets appeared denouncing the "military dictatorship" that had permitted an evil and corrupt King to sail away on a yacht with his two hundred four trunks, his champagne, his dog trainer, his wife and her choice pieces of jewelry, and so far had not made a single serious move against the court favorites who had been bleeding the people of Egypt for generations, yet would hang two simple workers who had been demonstrating for higher wages.

Just two days after the executions Nasser and the R.C.C. had another grave problem to face, this time from the right. Adli Lamlum was a character out of a western movie, and his performance that day in September was in true Hollywood style. He was the eldest son of one of the wealthiest landowners in Egypt, who had two thousand acres of some of the best land along the Nile that produced an annual income of about half a million dollars. Adli was twenty-four but was already a bey. His mustachios were long and flowing, and his penchant for hunting (animals or girls) was well known up and down the Nile.

On this Wednesday in September, Adli Lamlum galloped into the village of Maghaha, not far from Beni Mor, followed by about thirty other horsemen. All were well armed. They rounded up the villagers and announced that this land-reform business was "Cairo talk," "Communist foolishness." There would be no land reform in Maghaha. Anyone trying to divide the Lamlum estate would be murdered on the spot.

After they had left, local officials assured the peasants that the land-reform law would go through, whatever the Lamlums thought of it. Hearing about this, Adli and some of his horsemen returned the next day. Soldiers and policemen were waiting. Shots were fired. A policeman and a woman were wounded. The young bey and some of his men were arrested.

"Proceed as in the cotton-mill case," Nasser ordered, so a member of the R.C.C. went to Upper Egypt and presided at a military trial. Three of Adli's followers were acquitted. The other five were given light prison terms. The young bey who had defied the government was sentenced to hard labor for the rest of his life, but after a few weeks the hard labor part of the sentence was dropped, then he was provided with facilities to study, and after several years he would quietly be given his freedom, when the case had been forgotten.

While Naguib and the others concerned themselves with new housing, land reform, water systems, and other constructive matters, Gamal Abdel Nasser, still sitting in the shadows, concentrated on what to him was a matter of transcendent importance. "Beware the counterrevolution!" Those words burned brightly in his mind. The Communists were not the only ones he feared. The Brotherhood, too, was a constant danger. Farouk's friends were waiting for a chance to restore the King. There were also army officers, jealous because they had not been part of the plot. All had to be watched. But how? As yet he had no private espionage service. Who could be trusted on his side? There were only ninety Free Officers who had helped in the coup. Many of the others were disgruntled because he had not shared the secret of the revolution with them. Almost all three hundred of them were interested, now, in what high places in government they would be given. Already there were jealousies among the inner circle. Even if he could keep them all loyal, how could such a small group watch over the machinations of all the various political enemies who threatened them? He was in a dangerous and delicate situation, but he relished it. In his dreams he had been living in situations like this one since boyhood.

Naguib, now that he was Prime Minister, was more popular than ever. Wherever he went, the crowds strained their voices cheering him, lost their tarbushes, tore their galabiyas, trampled on each other trying to get near him. Nasser suggested that he go on a tour of the Delta. When he got there, people fought with each other trying to kiss his hand. "This is the new Egypt," he shouted to them. "We don't kiss hands any more. Every man is now the same."

The Jews of Egypt pointed out that he had come to their synagogues. The Copts decided that perhaps they had nothing to fear. Even the British thought that maybe they could come to terms with this moderate man.

While "the Naguib," as the correspondents affectionately began to call him, was taking all the applause, R.C.C. members were making plans for a better Egypt. Nasser gave them his blessing. Parks, bridges, better housing, more schools, community centers, medicine for the sick, pure water, an end to the ugly bureaucracy. All these benefits would come, they said, as quickly as they could arrange for them. Meanwhile there was the feeling of freedom. You could spit at Abdin Palace and call the British curs, and any man in Egypt could have a red automobile or a telephone painted green.

A few foreigners, sensing the coming xenophobia, packed their bags and quietly departed. Each day a few more went. This left vacancies in business houses, offices, apartment buildings, and on the sidewalks of Kasr el Nil that could be filled by the men in galabiyas.

The Council organized a Liberation Province. With the money obtained from selling Farouk's stamp collection, jewels, and other possessions they created a settlement on the desert where peasants could live in dignity, drink pure water pumped from the earth, and have separate houses for animals and humans. All the men would wear trousers and all the women blue skirts and blouses. No more veils, tarbushes, or galabiyas. No one would go hungry, or have bilharzia, and unless there was too much protest from religious elements they would enforce a rule that no family could continue to live in Liberation Province unless the number of children was kept to three. The constitution of the province would forbid polygamy, divorce, and a mother-in-law living with a man's family.

Much more important was land reform. Farouk's regime had had the idea first, but like Farouk's plans for education, housing, and everything else, it was mostly on paper, the proof being that Farouk himself was still the greatest feudal landowner in Egypt, and the following twenty names on the list were his next of kin.

Full credit for land reform (or full blame, depending upon whether one is a once-rich landowner or a fellah beneficiary) belongs to Nasser and his close associates. In a hospital in the United States, while recovering from injuries received in an airplane accident, Gamal Salem had studied economics. He was the one who made the first draft of the law. The magic figure was always two hundred. The figure on which the opposition was willing to compromise was five hundred. The law that was finally approved by Nasser and the R.C.C.—after sitting around the table in the house on the Nile for almost ten hours one night, without recess—allowed a man to give fifty feddan to each of two children, while retaining two hundred for himself.

Three hundred feddan are slightly more than three hundred acres. An acre of land that produces two crops a year, and much of Egypt's land does, can be worth up to two thousand dollars and bring in an annual profit of as much as three hundred dollars. So the Nasser regime was stripping each feudal landowner down to his last half million dollars' worth of land and leaving him an income of up to ninety thousand dollars a year. It would have been difficult to organize a national day of mourning for the men who would have to suffer such privation in a country where the average fellah has an income of forty dollars a year. Furthermore, the owners of the land to be expropriated would be paid a price ten times the annual tax bill. This would have been a fair figure if all the land had been fairly assessed. But in the days of Farouk a few large bank notes passed under a table here and there could cause amazing tricks to be performed in subtraction and division, and when the basis for reimbursement of seized land was announced it was possible to tell who had bribed the tax assessors most by who shouted the loudest. The land would be paid for by issuing to the former owner government bonds redeemable in thirty years, bearing interest at three per cent, but neither transferable nor negotiable on the Stock Exchange. (A post-factum decision taken several years later cut the interest rate to one per cent and extended the maturity date to forty years.)

The land was then sold to half a million fellahin who until now had had no land at all, or not enough to sustain a family. They would pay for the land from their crops, in thirty annual installments, at ten times the tax rate, plus the interest, plus a handling fee for the government.

Agrarian reform had another purpose even more important than trying to assuage some of the fellahin's land hunger. Its principal aim was to destroy Egyptian feudalism. Most of the expropriated land was taken from two thousand families who owned extensive estates. They lived in Cairo and Alexandria during the winter, but when the weather turned unpleasant were off to Europe. They could discuss the latest play in London, the smartest shop in Paris, the choicest gossip from the Riviera. They spoke foreign languages well, although many had to talk to their Egyptian tenant farmers through interpreters. They did see that the fellahin had seeds for planting, tools that were often expensive, mud brick houses, and credit when they needed it—at interest rates that would not bear explaining.

Beside the reforms, other changes were occurring in post-revolutionary Egypt that at first did not much affect the average man. The strictest censorship Egypt had ever known was quietly imposed. Before, to get a passport meant slipping the right small sum to the right petty bureaucrat under the table. Now few Egyptians were being permitted to go abroad at all, even if they slipped big bundles of bills to important people across a desk. The men of the R.C.C. were suspicious that anyone interested in travel must be trying to get money out of the country, and therefore must be an enemy of the new state. And for the most part they were right. Telephones by the thousands were being tapped. Publishers, editors, reporters were arrested as "enemies of the state" or as friends of the old politicians. The newspapers were told not only what they must not print, but also what they must print. The many Egyptian dailies, whether in English, French, Italian, or Arabic, began to look exactly alike. The same headlines appeared over the same stories in the same columns of the same pages. If a man was arrested now, he might disappear for months. No one would know where he was. There was seldom a trial. He would merely be held "on suspicion."

These were all part of the defenses that Nasser felt he had to order, to protect what he had fought for so long and now, having won, was reluctant to let slip away.

There were hints of other activities that disturbed many people, inside and outside Egypt. Naguib had quietly appointed one of Adolf Hitler's economic experts, Dr. Wilhelm Voss, head of the Egyptian Central Planning Board and chief adviser to the War Ministry. Dr. Johann von Leers, who had been one of Goebbels' most trusted anti-Semitic rabble-rousers, was named political adviser to the Information Department. He had escaped from Germany to Argentina, where he had been publisher of a notorious German monthly, *Der Weg*, dedicated to perpetuating Hitler's ideas about Jews. The former Grand Mufti of Jerusalem had obtained the position in Cairo for him, and when he arrived, greeted him publicly, adding, "We thank you for venturing to take up the battle against the power of darkness that has become incarnate in world Jewry."

Voss and Von Leers were only two. Every day additional names were whispered. Other foreigners might be trying to get out of Egypt, but the ex-Nazis were pouring in. There were hundreds of them, who saw in post-revolutionary Egypt a place they could fish in troubled waters. They changed their names so as not to embarrass their hosts. Von Leers became Sidi Mohamed Ali. Bernard Bender was known in the police circles in which he worked as Lieutenant Colonel Ben Salem. L. Moser, who helped organize an Egyptian youth movement, was called Colonel Hassan Suleiman. In the security force there was a Colonel al-Nahar, but his real name was Gleim. An adviser on publications was listed as Hassan al-Maan, although his passport said Buhle. Many of these men had been brought in by Farouk, but they were not unpopular with Free Officers like Anwar el Sadat, who had seen nothing wrong with Hitler except that he lost.

Nasser was watching for counterrevolution. He went first after a man he himself had agreed should be named one of the three regents, to act for the baby Fouad II, who was now in Europe.

Colonel Rashid Mehanna was a plotter in his own right, having led in 1947 a revolution that failed, so he was jealous of the success of the Free Officers. He was too closely enmeshed with the Moslem Brotherhood to please Nasser, who asked for daily reports on his movements and conversations. This was the first big post-revolutionary cat-mouse game, and Nasser was enjoying it. After a few months he pounced. He told Naguib and the Council he had evidence Mehanna was opposing most of their policies, and he insisted the colonel be charged with treason. Naguib argued for moderation. He persuaded Nasser that it would be enough to dismiss Mehanna from the Council of Regents and place him under house arrest.

Several days later Naguib, on his own authority, went to call on Mehanna. The suave officer apologized for having caused the R.C.C. any trouble. Nasser must have misunderstood, but of course, General Naguib, being an older man, would not. Naguib went back and persuaded the Council to let Mehanna have his full freedom. Nasser warned against it, but he was outvoted.

As soon as Mehanna was released he began a virulent campaign against land reform—"a Communist trick"—and against the "antireligious policies" of the R.C.C., which was "trying to destroy Islam." Nasser kept a closer eye than ever on him. Several months later he pounced again, but this time he had his evidence ready to bring into court. Members of the Council decided to try Mehanna themselves, in secret, with Nasser presiding as both judge and prosecutor. After a short trial he was sentenced to life imprisonment. But in a few years, after he had been forgotten and no longer had a following, his cell door would one day open and he would be permitted to go home, under house arrest at first. Then, if the eyes and ears of the government reported that he was behaving, he could go to the Gezira Sporting Club, or have tea at Groppi's and would be completely free, so long as he had learned his lesson. But he would be constantly watched by unseen eyes and what he said would be carefully listened to by unseen ears, and at the first small mistake he would find himself back in prison again. This was Nasser's way of dealing with his opponents.

Besides watching for his internal enemies, Nasser had another burning interest—the British. It had been his hatred of them as a boy that had led him into the paths of revolution, not an interest in social welfare, better housing, clean water, or higher wages for Egyptians. Before facing the problem of the Suez Canal he decided to try to force the British out of the Sudan, the land that controlled the water Egyptians needed to live.

Almost all the revolutionaries had some personal interest in the Sudan. Naguib and the Salem brothers had been born there. Many of the others had served military hitches in the Sudan. The Council adopted the general principle of permitting the Sudanese to choose whether they wanted to continue to be aligned with the British, or with Egypt, or have complete independence.

Salah Salem was sent there to do some political organizing and propaganda work. This now sophisticated man from the city went so far as to take part in a native dance in the primitive southernmost region of the Sudan, where dancing is a wild and exhausting test of fortitude. Not wishing to appear overdressed by local standards, Salem stripped to his underwear. Someone snapped a picture that was printed in magazines all over the world, so wherever he goes he is still known as "the dancing major." But when he left the Sudan, the pro-Egyptian Sudanese were banded together in their first national front, the Unionist party.

Most of the foreign correspondents and diplomats agreed that Nasser,

Naguib, Salem, and the others were supreme negotiators when they obtained signatures on an Anglo-Egyptian-Sudanese agreement providing for the election of a Sudanese legislative assembly in a few months and a referendum in three years. At that time the Sudanese would decide whether they wanted to join a union with Egypt or have complete independence. Either way Britain lost. Nasser considered it his first victory.

Now he could turn to his real concern, those tens of thousands of British soldiers over on the Canal, whose presence, even so far away from Cairo, was like many sharp steel goads in the hide of a bull, a painful and infuriating reminder of humiliation. Israel was forgotten, a problem of minor importance now. The real goal of the revolution was to get the British out. The Free Officers had tried the methods Captain Cohen told Nasser had been so successful in Palestine. The Free Officers had given more aid than most people realized to the commandos along the Canal. But the methods of the Israeli underground armies when used in Egypt made the British seem more determined than ever to stay. Nasser decided to try to outnegotiate them. The British prided themselves on their brilliance around a green baize table even more than on their ability with gun and sword. And this was a field in which none of the R.C.C. members had had a single hour of experience before the revolution. But Nasser began the attack as if it were an everyday tussle he knew he could win. Because world opinion was involved, he had to become a propagandist as well as a negotiator, so he decided gradually to come out of the shadows. In November 1952 he issued a statement over his own name:

"Hand grenades will be thrown in the night and British soldiers slain in the streets unless the seventy-year-old occupation of our beloved land is brought to an end."

If Naguib had said it, it would have been front-page news around the world, but most foreign correspondents ignored the statement until months later.

In the spring of 1953 a correspondent for the London *Observer*, Tom Little, had the first interview with Nasser that ever saw print. He wrote: "Recognized as the second man in Egypt's revolutionary council and a dominant figure in the new regime, [Nasser] said Egypt would be willing to begin discussions tomorrow with Britain for a just and practical solution of the Suez problem." The British Foreign Office cabled its Cairo Embassy asking whether Nasser spoke for the regime. The reply, in essence: Nasser, more than any one man, *is* the regime.

The next day, *The New York Times,* commenting on the *Observer* interview, described Nasser as "the man whose leadership of the army revolutionary movement actually antedated Prime Minister Naguib's entry on the scene." Now it was out. The secret had been kept for eight months and eighteen days.

As the negotiations with the British were about to begin, it was announced that the Egyptians would be represented by Prime Minister Naguib, Foreign Minister Fawzi, and four men of the R.C.C. The British Ambassador cabled London that the most important man at the table would be Gamal Abdel Nasser, a thirty-five-year-old infantry officer who did not even hold a cabinet post. Toward the end of 1953 correspondents started to write of Naguib as "titular head of the government" and foreign diplomats began to call on Nasser rather than the general.

At first Nasser used Naguib as the Egyptian spokesman with the British, but the general was gentle and mild, and before long El Bikbashi lost patience. One day Naguib came back from a meeting with the British Ambassador bearing the suggestion that the United States participate in the projected talks over the Canal. Nasser called the Council into session at once and denounced "this piece of stupidity." "If we were about to fight a war on a battlefield with the British, would we agree in advance that it would be all right for them to have the assistance of America?" he asked. After that he did most of the negotiating, gradually losing his shyness and his embarrassment over not knowing all the rules of protocol that his British counterparts were so insistent on following.

One of his early domestic decisions was that all key members of the R.C.C. should live within a military compound. He set the example himself by choosing a modest five-room, sand-colored house just a little beyond the main Abbassia military buildings, in a suburb called Manchiet el Bakry. It was protected from the curious public by a seven-foot stone wall, as was all the rest of the compound. Behind the house was open desert. It was even more modest than the home Naguib mentioned in his speeches as the place he loved better than any of Farouk's palaces.

The old political parties were a problem. Nasser kept getting secret reports that his overthrow was being planned by some of them, so an order was issued to dissolve them. In their place an organization called the Liberation Rally was formed, the government party in a one-party state—with Colonel Nasser as Secretary-General. It had some of the trappings of fascism, and a youth organization whose members were taught by men who had once been Nazis.

Young army officers were being placed in all departments of the government, some in important positions. They knew more about taking a machine gun apart than dictating to a stenographer, but no one questioned that they would be less venal than the officials whose places they took. Each young army officer added a telephone or two to the battery already beside the desk on a revolving stand, and a few extra buzzers. Some of the new government officials had eight phones and even more buzzers. The number of men in galabiyas outside office doors, squatting over kerosene stoves, making thick sugary coffee for the new bureaucrats grew greater and greater.

One day in the spring of 1953 revolutionary Egypt received her first important foreign visitor from the West. Secretary of State John Foster Dulles was on a good-will tour of the Middle East. The Egyptians were happy that he had decided to spend three days in Cairo and eight in other parts of the Arab world, yet only two in Israel. He brought with him his wife, his counselor, the Mutual Security Director and his wife, the Assistant Secretary of State, and aides. Also a pistol.

That morning, the Cairo newspaper *Al Misri* ran an open letter to Mr. Dulles in which it said, "You should know, Mr. Dulles, that the Arab world detests and distrusts the United States of America."

Mr. Dulles received a three-hour briefing from the American Ambassador, then went to see Naguib. It was the first conference the general had ever held with so important a personage, and he was a little taken aback when Mr. Dulles opened it by pulling from his pocket a .32-caliber automatic revolver and placing it on the conference table. But then the Secretary of State explained: "A gift from President Eisenhower."

The American general and the Egyptian general had never met, yet the pearl-handled weapon was inscribed: "To General Mohamed Naguib from his friend, Eisenhower."

(Several days later in Tel Aviv, Prime Minister Ben-Gurion gave Mr. Dulles a Bible.)

Nasser did not attend the pistol presentation, but he and a few other government leaders were invited by Ambassador Caffery to a dinner party for Dulles at the Embassy, and he and Amer had a private conference with the Secretary of State. It was the first and last personal contact Nasser and Dulles ever had. Discussing it afterward, Nasser said, "It was not easy for me to form any impression of him, because we were together only forty-five minutes and I did all the talking. I told him Egypt would not tolerate any more outside interference; that we would not welcome America trying to take the place of Great Britain in the Middle East. Then I said that if any Arab rulers told him on his trip that they would tolerate American influence as a substitute for British influence those Arab leaders were deceiving him."

On a Wednesday night in June the men of the R.C.C. met for the most important session they had ever held. Nasser's jaw seemed squarer and more determined than ever as he opened the discussion with the announcement: "The time has come to abolish the monarchy and declare a republic."

There were some monarchist plots brewing, he said. Prince Mohamed Aly in Paris, Farouk's debonair but aging uncle who had been heir apparent until Fouad was born, was talking as if he might like to overthrow the Bikbashis and become King. The British, with whom little progress had been made in the negotiations over Suez, needed to be impressed with some sign of the legitimacy of the men who faced them across the conference table. Third, the mind of the people must be taken off the failure of the Bikbashis to achieve paradise on earth in eleven months. The street was restive. He had heard rumblings. The people needed something new to cheer about.

There was little disagreement among the men of the Council over the idea, but they argued for twelve hours, with no recess, about details. Nasser himself suggested that Naguib be declared President as well as Prime Minister. Some of the others demurred. Secretly they were worried about putting so much authority into the hands of the general. They noticed that he was beginning to change under the daily dose of adulation. After much discussion Nasser agreed to leave the shadows and accept the role of Deputy Prime Minister, with Naguib continuing to make the speeches, review the parades, tour the country, kiss the babies, and be the revolution's gift to the people.

Most of the twelve hours was taken up with an argument over who should be Commander in Chief of the Army. "This is one point on which I am adamant," Nasser declared. "Abdel-Hakim Amer is going to be Commander in Chief." Naguib objected. Amer had been his aide-de-camp, was the one who had brought him into the Free Officers, and was the one who had persuaded Nasser to choose him for the leading role. Still, Naguib wanted to be Commander in Chief, as well as everything else. But Nasser would not give in.

There was another matter about which he was stubborn. He insisted on the portfolio of Minister of the Interior for himself. Prestige had nothing to do with it. The Minister of the Interior in Egypt, as in most other countries, is responsible for internal security. For almost a year, he said, he and he alone had been watching the machinations, the plotting, of the opposition. He could do it better if he had the machinery of security under his direct control.

Nasser was ill that night. He was so ill that several times he stopped talking in the middle of a sentence and clutched his side. Some of the officers wanted to send for a doctor, but he brushed the suggestion aside, lit another cigarette, and went on with what he had been saying.

The people of Cairo were on their way to work when the meeting ended. Amer was now Commander in Chief. Egypt was about to become a republic. Gamal Abdel Nasser, the new Deputy Prime Minister and Minister of the Interior, went first to a doctor's office, then to a hospital. He had an acute case of appendicitis that would keep him confined to hospital and home for the next seventeen days.

Early that evening, while Prince Fouad, eighteen months old, slept in a crib in a villa near Rome, an announcer on Cairo Radio excitedly told the Egyptian people that the baby would never be a king. The monarchy had been abolished, he said. So the dynasty founded by a tobacco merchant from Albania was ended, for better or for worse. Egypt now was a republic run by a handful of army officers, all but one of them young; all very inexperienced.

That summer, Prime Ministers Jawaharlal Nehru of India and Mohamed Ali Jinnah of Pakistan came to Cairo. Between them they represented half a billion people. It was exceedingly hot, so a river steamer was turned over to them, and after they had had their discussions with each other they met with Naguib, Nasser, and the rest of the Council and talked about world politics and neutrality. These were subjects that had not crossed the ken of the young army officers. Until now they had left foreign affairs to Mahmoud Fawzi, the only important member of Farouk's entourage who had been retained; the slightly bald, middle-aged Foreign Minister who once had represented Egypt in Washington and Tokyo. The R.C.C. men were aware that he had a reputation for being able to outtalk and outmaneuver even suave men from Downing Street and the Quai d'Orsay, and that he was respected personally by rulers in most of the capitals of the world. He seemed to have no political philosophy of his own, and when the Free Officers called him in for consultation he agreed to serve them as loyally as he had tried to serve others. So, until they could develop some Free Officer who could approach Mahmoud Fawzi in this field, they decided to let him handle foreign affairs.

But that day aboard the boat on the Nile, Nehru convinced them their future lay in not committing Egypt to either side in the Cold War. The next day, a statement was issued by "an anonymous government spokesman" that began:

"We must remember that there is in the world today a great force which aims at goodness and which will not permit itself to be an instrument of evil. This force is headed by India and Pakistan ... This great force, representing one third of the world, which has been used in past wars as an instrument of death in the hands of the imperialist powers, will no longer allow itself to be used as cannon fodder in the service of imperialism in any future war."

There was a literary quality to the statement unlike any that had ever appeared in a Free Officers' pamphlet. It was the first small step, gingerly taken with outside guidance, toward formulating a new foreign policy for Egypt.

Toward the end of the year the R.C.C. gave prison terms to a few old-regime men for "corruption," ruled that Queen Narriman could have the clothes she had left behind but not her jewels, ordered confiscation of the property of a hundred or more descendants of Mohamed Aly the Great, and hanged four men because there was evidence they were friendly to the British and had given them certain "aid and comfort." Four more small red stains on the record.

The big court case was the trial of Ibrahim Abdel Hadi, the Prime Minister who had subjected Gamal Abdel Nasser to such an ordeal of questioning about being a Moslem Brotherhood terrorist. The indictment against Hadi accused him of treason, corruption, terrorism, graft, and complicity in murders. The trial took place not in a courtroom before a judge and jury but on the second floor of the island house. The judges were the officers of the R.C.C., with Nasser presiding.

In a very short time the tables had been completely reversed. Now it was the young army officer who was putting the questions and the friend of Farouk who had to answer.

"Is it true that you sent troops you knew were unprepared into the Palestine war?" Nasser asked. "Is it true that you wasted a million and a half dollars having just one of the King's yachts repaired? ... Tell us about the paved road you had built with government funds to your country home."

For many long nights the men of the R.C.C. listened to the evidence. Finally they passed judgment: "You shall be hanged by the neck until dead." They had voted unanimously. Days later, after Egypt and the rest of the world had been sufficiently impressed, they commuted the sentence to life imprisonment at hard labor. After six months they pardoned Ibrahim Abdel Hadi and permitted him to go his way, broken. Other military juntas had done worse. Others to come would do much worse. The color of the revolution was still khaki, only slightly splattered with drops of red.

Late in the year King Ibn Saud of Saudi Arabia died. The R.C.C. voted that a delegation headed by Nasser should go to pay its respects. Some of the others had already been abroad, but until now Colonel Nasser had never traveled farther than the Sudan for military duty and a few miles across the frontier into Palestine to take part in an invasion. He never forgot this first real trip abroad. He had heard about Mecca since his youth. Now, at last, he was seeing it. He saw the place where the Prophet Mohamed had tended sheep as a boy and the caves in which he had prayed when he was offended by the idolatry and murder of his own people. For the first time also, Nasser met a man he would deal with often in the future, H. M. Saud, the new King of Saudi Arabia, a tall, strange man with sick eyes that were hidden by dark glasses.

Soon afterward, back in Cairo, Nasser and Naguib began to eye each other with jealousy and suspicion. Before 1953 ended, the outside world heard the first guarded whispers that these two dominant personalities of the new regime were in conflict. Late in the year Naguib said he would like to make another pilgrimage to Mecca and wanted to take with him Colonel Ahmed Shawki. The colonel was not the typical Free Officer. He was the son of a wealthy pasha, had a fondness for some things prohibited to Moslems by the Koran, but had disliked Farouk. His friend Naguib had induced him to join the revolutionary movement, and Nasser accepted him only a few hours before the time set for the coup.

When Naguib's pilgrimage plans came up for discussion, Nasser suggested that two other members of the Council go along, ostensibly just for the trip, but actually to keep an eye on both Naguib and Shawki. He did not trust either of them. After the pilgrims left, those who stayed behind debated whether Naguib's motives had been strictly religious or whether he was making a gesture to please the Moslem Brotherhood, which had grown greatly in strength during recent months. When the party returned, the ears of the committee reported to Nasser that Naguib had had several intimate conversations with the new King of Saudi Arabia. Then Shawki, who had been named head of a military court to try Communists, resigned and let the rumor slip out that the real reason was his many disagreements with Nasser. He thought the Army should go back to its job of being an army. He thought the country should be run by a Parliament. He especially was concerned over rumors that the tall colonel would like to strip his friend the general of some of his offices.

The next day, the Council ordered Naguib to broadcast a speech calling people who spread rumors "worse than cockroaches." The stage was being well set for the struggle over who was to run Egypt.

CHAPTER 12

THE GENERAL IS TRAPPED

With an old-fashioned pen that had to be dipped into an inkwell, Mohamed Naguib wrote out the words himself, in precise Arabic letters: "In the name of Allah the Merciful, I address myself to the gentlemen of the Revolutionary Command Council."

The general puffed on his pipe and chose the words that followed with exceeding care. He wanted to put nothing on paper they could use against him.

I present my compliments and regret to announce that I can no longer carry out my duties in the manner best calculated to serve the national interests, for reasons you will excuse me for not mentioning here. I must therefore ask you to accept my resignation from all the posts I occupy, and I give you my thanks for the co-operation each of you has given me during my term of office.

After he had affixed his signature he asked his aide-de-camp to deliver the note. When Gamal Abdel Nasser received it at headquarters he immediately called the R.C.C. into session. No one was much surprised. The fight had been brewing for months. Naguib did not need to apologize for leaving his reasons unexpressed. He had stated them over and over, in this same room, sitting at this same table.

Every man of the Council had heard both sides of the story. Again and again Naguib had told them Egypt was being run by committees: the Cabinet, the R.C.C., and a joint committee composed of the Cabinet and the R.C.C. meeting together. Theoretically he was head of all three. Actually he was still no more than a figurehead. They knew it. So did he. He and Nasser disagreed about many matters. Amer, as Commander in Chief, ignored him when issuing orders. The Cabinet made decisions without bothering to get his approval. The R.C.C. failed even to inform him when it was going to meet. He agreed with Colonel Shawki that an army's business was fighting and not politics. The militarization of the government was ridiculous and dangerous. He was against giving inexperienced young army officers important cabinet posts. The Army

163

had made the revolution, but now it should get back to its barracks. The old political parties should be permitted to function again. There should be elections and an end to censorship. They should stop throwing so many people into prison. Egypt, he said, should begin to act like a modern, democratic state. He felt that the Free Officers owed him a debt for using his popularity in the early days to win the support of the people.

On many occasions, after Naguib had made his complaints and left for home, Nasser had given his version. The general was too old, too attached to the past, too involved with reactionary elements, he said. At heart he was a man of the old regime. He had been a bey and he still had the mentality of a bey. He had friends like Shawki, who was not even a good Moslem. His fight with Farouk had been superficial, merely over his own appointment. He even had a son still named Farouk. Of course he was in favor of free elections, because he thought he had acquired such popularity that he could run for President and beat anyone else. What Naguib really wanted was veto power over the R.C.C. He was the one who wanted to be a dictator. If they went slowly, as Naguib demanded, the revolution would accomplish nothing. On the personal level, it was the revolution that had made Naguib popular, not the other way around.

It was difficult for these hot-tempered young men to be patient with the easygoing Naguib. There was little in common between him and a man like Anwar el Sadat, whose specialty had always been violent action. There was not even much in common between Naguib, who believed in conventional, democratic methods, and Nasser, who had once engaged in an assassination attempt himself and only a few days before the revolution had seriously considered the murder of a long list of opponents as a legitimate way to power.

But now here they were, with the resignation on the table before them. Was this what they wanted? Salah Salem spoke up first. He and Naguib had once been close friends, but now he accused the general of making speeches on the Sudan without consulting him. "I say, let's accept it," he ended firmly.

The others looked at Nasser. El Bikbashi bent his head slightly to one side, as if cocking an ear, then advised that they reject it. The timing was not right. In one week Naguib and Salem were to go to the Sudan as Egypt's delegates to the opening of the first Sudanese Parliament. "I suggest we send a delegation to call on the general and urge him to reconsider," he said. The meeting lasted many hours. At one point tempers were so out of control that Sadat pulled a revolver from his pocket and banged it down on the conference table without explanation.

Finally Gamal Salem and Hussein Shafei were chosen to carry out Nasser's suggestion. They returned several hours later. Instead of an agreement with Naguib, they brought with them Naguib himself. He was adamant, but after a discussion that was at times bitter they reached a compromise. Naguib's resignation would be kept secret until after the trip to the Sudan. Then the R.C.C. would discuss the matter for another two weeks and decide if there was any possible solution.

The next day was Wednesday, the day Naguib normally presided over a formal meeting of the Cabinet, in which there were six members of the R.C.C. besides himself. When he banged his gavel he noticed that Nasser and Salah Salem were absent. After a few minutes Gamal Salem and Baghdady got up and unceremoniously left. In another few minutes Kamal Hussein yawned, stretched several times, then rose and walked out. Zakaria Mohieddin was the last Bikbashi to go.

Afterward Naguib was surrounded in the hallway by reporters who wanted to know what was happening. Was the general aware that the R.C.C. was meeting in the island house without him? Naguib smiled as if he knew all about it, then had his driver take him home.

Meanwhile, on the top floor of headquarters the R.C.C. was holding another of its all-night meetings. Through the open windows reporters heard the sound of excited voices. Salah Salem was later reported to have become so angry that the others were afraid he was going to have a heart attack.

When General Mohamed Naguib turned on the radio at 6 A.M. in his suburban home he learned that two hours earlier the R.C.C. had decided to accept his resignation. Gamal Abdel Nasser would assume the position of Prime Minister; the office of President would remain temporarily vacant.

When Naguib tried to telephone he discovered the wires had been cut. He looked out his windows and saw that a mixed detachment of infantry and military police with fixed bayonets surrounded his house. His servants were not permitted to leave to buy kerosene to make his breakfast. Then over the radio came a communiqué announcing that he had not been arrested; he was merely being asked to stay in his house for a month or two. He was accused of pouting like a child; of absenting himself from meetings unless the R.C.C. acceded to his prior demands; of being obsessed by a psychological complex. He had demanded dictatorial rights. He had tasted popularity, now he wanted power.

It was extremely confusing to the outside world, for during the past year and a half Naguib had been pictured universally as a hero, not a villain. It was more than confusing for the Egyptian people, for they desperately needed someone and something to believe in, and the amiable general had come to fill that need.

Nasser and the rest of the R.C.C. mistook the general confusion for approval, so the next day they gave sharp-tongued Salah Salem the privilege of speaking to the press. He said this man who seemed so good and gentle was actually a conceited, dictatorial, power-hungry old man. (Naguib was fifty-three.) He might have a kindly face but he was an autocrat at heart. No one should be sorry for him, whatever happened to him. He asked the correspondents to tell their readers that Naguib had been Machiavellian, despite his appearance of simple innocence. Nevertheless, he explained, "We decided to deal with him mildly, although it would have been easy to prepare a dirty solution: that is, to have killed him."

"You mean you considered killing Naguib?" one correspondent asked.

There was no reply. Privately to a correspondent he said, "I would rather go to prison for a year and live on bread and water than work one more day with that man!"

The next day, Salem went even further. Over the radio he said that Nasser and his committee had been forced to accept Naguib's resignation "by their responsiveness to the will of the majority of Free Officers." (The majority of Free Officers had not even been consulted.) "Do you know what would have happened if we had refused to listen to the majority?" he asked dramatically. "Those army officers would have killed Naguib and then gone to our homes and pulled us out of bed by force and handed us back the administration, even against our wills."

It was now Friday. That evening, Khaled Mohieddin decided to break with his long-time friend Nasser. He went to the cavalry officers' mess and sat around for hours extolling Naguib's character and his ideas about running the country. Someone hurried to Nasser with news that a coup was brewing, and hot-headed Salah Salem was sent over to straighten out the trouble. But the cavalrymen were not impressed by the sort of bombast Salem was accustomed to use over the radio and told him so. By now there were more than a hundred officers in the room and the trouble looked serious, so someone went back for Nasser himself.

It was his first experience facing a thoroughly hostile audience of Free Officers. He stood before them, arguing, pleading, answering questions, for more than seven hours. In that time he smoked three packages of cigarettes, in his nervousness sometimes crushing one out almost as soon as he had lighted it. He felt that there was at stake not only the position he had worked unceasingly for so many years to achieve for himself, but the future of the country. At one point a supporter whispered to him that the building was surrounded with mounted machine guns. It was like revolution night, except that this time he was the one who was trapped.

At 2 A.M., exhausted, he finally gave up. "Call back Naguib, if that's what you want. I'm finished!" he told them. Then he went back to R.C.C. headquarters. The Council was waiting for him. The discussion that followed turned into a debate between him and Mohieddin, with the rest listening. Mainly the argument was about the kind of government they were to give Egypt: the return to unregimented parliamentary democracy suggested by Naguib or the tight military dictatorship suggested by Nasser.

"I cannot possibly afford to give you the sort of government you want," Nasser said to Mohieddin. "If I do, Egypt will go back to what it was a year and a half ago. And what, then, will the revolution have profited us?" His voice was husky now, and his eyes were bloodshot. These men who had been his General Staff for years were divided. Several were inclined to side with Mohieddin; at last he turned to the young cavalry officer and said, "All right, you take over as Prime Minister, with Naguib as President, and see if you can run the country."

The others protested, but Mohieddin jumped to his feet. "Okay. I accept that offer. I'll go out and see what the general says."

At 5:30 A.M. Naguib was awakened by a tapping on his bedroom window. "It's Mohieddin. Khaled Mohieddin, General." Naguib put on trousers and opened the door. There were seven other cavalry officers with the young major. Mohieddin announced that the R.C.C. had just agreed on a solution: Naguib as President, he himself as Prime Minister. Naguib was not enthusiastic about so young a man as Mohieddin —then thirty-one—in so high an office, but in his early morning bewilderment he said he would abide by whatever the R.C.C. decided.

One hour later, while the R.C.C. back in the island house was still debating what actually should be done, a bizarre incident occurred. Who ordered it was never publicly disclosed, but at 6:30 A.M. Naguib had visitors again, this time two military policemen who gruffly told him to get dressed and then abducted him. He was taken to artillery head-quarters, some distance from Cairo, and then driven out onto the open desert. He was certain they were about to murder him, but after a few hours he was driven back to his home without any explanation.

By that time the R.C.C. members had finished their all-night meeting, taken a vote, and gone home to bed. They had decided that Naguib would be restored as President. Nasser would retain the office of Prime Minister and continue to head the R.C.C. Once during the early morn-ing hours there had been a suggestion that Mohieddin, who was blamed for the entire trouble, be sent into exile. Nasser vetoed it. "Not now. Not yet. The timing is not exactly right," he replied. "Later, maybe."

The news of Naguib's restoration was announced that afternoon. The street, which had never quite understood the demotion, despite all of Salah Salem's speeches, knew what this new communiqué meant. Their favorite, Naguib, was back as President again. They went wild with excitement.

"Mabrouk!" they shouted. "Long live Naguib!"

In many streets all automobile traffic had to stop as the crowds took over. They sang, shouted, marched in a long line holding hands, kissed each other on the cheek, threw their tarbushes in the air. The demon-stration was too boisterous, too frenzied not to be sincere. When Nasser heard about it he realized his carefully attuned ear had deceived him. He knew the general had street appeal but he had been misled about the extent of his popularity. Still, perhaps, it was not too late. He had reached a low point in his own career. He was being forced, publicly, to admit that he had made a grave misjudgment, but by yielding a little now he might ultimately win. Naguib and his friends might bring about their own downfall, eventually, if he only made no more miscalcula-tions. One report he received that day was that many of the men who seemed to be whipping up the crowds wore fuzzy short beards and car-ried yellow prayer beads. He pigeonholed the implication.

Naguib was in his modest stucco home, going over a document the R.C.C. had sent him to sign. This time it had not been necessary for him to write it out himself. The Council had done that for him. The note lavished praise on the R.C.C. members, those wise men who were working so diligently to advance the national interests. It spoke of "sacred goals" and appealed to "sincere patriots" not to "use my name in vain," whatever that meant. While he was reading it he heard the noise of the crowd down the street. Coils of barbed wire were still around the house. The guards remained there, some of them not sure whether they were watching over an enemy of the state or the victim of a small error who was about to become a hero again. But the crowd seemed to know. They broke through the police cordon and came surging toward the house. It was long after midnight before they dispersed.

The next day, a mass of people began assembling in the great square in front of Abdin Palace even before the first light of morning. By 9:30 A.M., when the genial Naguib, pipe in hand, stepped onto the balcony, the crowd was the largest ever seen in the square. The general made a forgive-and-forget speech. He said certain elements were using his differences with the R.C.C. to exploit their own ends. He mentioned something many did not yet know: already that morning several students had been killed and many wounded on the campus of Cairo University. And as a result of a riot in front of the Semiramis Hotel one student had been taken to a morgue and many more to hospitals. Mentioning these deaths was a mistake. A shout went up from the crowd. Suddenly a giant of a man with a great black beard appeared directly in front of the balcony holding a blood-soaked handkerchief. He turned to the crowd, waved it, and shouted, "This belonged to one of our Brothers!" Then he wheeled on Naguib and asked why no investigation had been ordered yet. Naguib recognized him as the Moslem Brotherhood's Deputy Supreme Guide. To quiet him, he invited him up onto the balcony, another tactical error. Towering over the general, the black-bearded man kept waving the stained handkerchief and shouting for revenge. Without any authorization from anyone, Naguib announced, "We are going to call on the people to elect a Parliament." The cheering and shouting were tumultuous.

That afternoon, the two revolutionary leaders had a reconciliation as they met for a cabinet session. "Mabrouk, my old friend!" Naguib said in greeting the younger man. Then, for the benefit of news cameras, they embraced, wept, put their arms around each other again, and shook hands affectionately. "There is no grudge in my heart," Naguib said.

To the photographers who had been called in to record the scene, the protestations of affection seemed sincere, but some members of the R.C.C. knew how indignant Nasser actually was over Naguib's announcement of elections. He considered it a stab in the back.

By far the oddest meeting that day was between Naguib and Salah Salem. As Naguib amiably shook hands with the dancing major he said,

"Don't forget, my friend, we are going to the Sudan together tomorrow."

Naguib had lost some ground as a result of the week's events. He no longer was Prime Minister or chairman of the Council. But political gymnastics had given him the power, he thought, to get anything he might demand in the future, just by threatening to resign.

Neither side trusted the other now. A Minister of Republican Affairs was appointed to assist the President, but Naguib soon discovered the man's real functions were to screen his visitors, his telephone calls, and even his mail.

Blood was splashed over the record again on Monday. Three students who had been shot by police in Cairo died, and in Khartoum the arrival of Salem and Naguib touched off a demonstration of thousands of primitive Sudanese tribesmen in long white robes and tight-twisted turbans, shouting against Egypt as well as Britain. They charged the Governor-General's palace, where Naguib was staying, some waving spears, clubs, and knives that glistened in the sun, others carrying crudely lettered banners. When police tried to disperse them with tear gas, they began a grand melee that ended with thirty-one dead, including the British chief of police.

During the several days Naguib was out of the way, Nasser began turning the screws sharply, trying to tighten the controls that had almost slipped out of his grasp. His boldest move was to order a number of officers court-martialed for supporting Naguib and helping to make him President again. Naguib had been the victor, yet one by one the men who had helped him win were now going to be punished.

When Salem and Naguib disembarked from their plane at Cairo they learned that Nasser had also ordered more than a hundred men arrested for "fomenting disorders," mainly for organizing celebrations of Naguib's return to power. A majority were Moslem Brotherhood members.

Soon after the Sudan trip the general demanded that in addition to being President he be permitted to resume his posts as Prime Minister and chairman of the R.C.C. The Council voted to grant his request. Even his title of Military Governor of Egypt was restored. Several days later he held his first press conference since his return and caused more embarrassment to the Council.

"Mr. President, is it true that you were kidnaped from your home the morning of the cavalry coup?" a reporter asked.

Naguib smiled, puffed on his pipe several times, and nodded his head.

"Is it true they threatened your life?"

"Yes," he replied.

"Was this done by artillery officers supporting Colonel Nasser?"

"Yes."

By now, late March 1954, Nasser was at the low ebb of his popularity, his strength, and his influence. The month-old tussle for power seemed over. The tough-minded young revolutionary apparently had lost completely to the advocate of traditional methods. He had lost more than just his titles. Those he had never really wanted. He had also lost the support of many of his Free Officers. Even the R.C.C. was split. Khaled Mohieddin, on whom he had often leaned heavily, was alienated. He still had against him the Moslem Brotherhood, growing stronger than ever, the Communists, and the old political parties. The mass, the street, was with Naguib. Large landowners seemed to trust the general while they detested him. Foreign governments were more favorably disposed to Naguib. Worst of all, he was having to give in to his opponent on matters of basic principle.

One evening he took Tahia to see a film version of *Julius Caesar,* which was being shown in a Cairo cinema. As he watched the story unfold he felt again that some of Caesar's words seemed to be pertinent to what had been happening in Cairo: "Such men as he be never at heart's ease whiles they behold a greater than themselves; and therefore are they very dangerous."

The next day, he had an idea for bringing about the fall of Naguib. It was bold, reckless, and cunning.

During a meeting that took place the following week, the Council conferred until Naguib was too tired to continue. Then they announced what looked like a victory for the general. All the old political parties would be permitted to resume their activities. Elections would be held in three months. A new Parliament would convene a month after that. All forms of press control were to be lifted. The R.C.C. would go out of existence. The Bikbashis would return to the Army. Civilians would run the country.

"We want the Army to be divorced from politics." It was an amazing statement to come from Nasser, who had spent months infiltrating every government department with bright young officers.

It was he who drew up the communiqué of March 25, 1954, but it bore the signature of General Mohamed Naguib. It clearly implied that Nasser, Naguib, and all the rest of them would soon vanish completely from public life. Naguib came from the meeting at the island house, grinning broadly. "Good news!" he told reporters. "We are going to have a Parliament." He realized later, too late, that he had been trapped. On the surface it was just what he had been demanding. But Nasser knew the effect it would have on the public.

Just in case the street was as blind as Naguib, Nasser issued a statement saying that he and some of his colleagues had been compelled to give in to the forces of reaction. The result? "Everything will return to its former state," he declared. He went so far as to say that in the new nonmilitary era he would not even be a candidate for election to any public office. "I am a revolutionary, not a politician."

His next move was to seek and obtain control of the most powerful Egyptian labor union, the Federation of Cairo Transport Workers. This gave him his first mass following. The conductors and motormen of buses and trams were tough characters; men who could take a great deal of pushing around by police and push back, if ordered. They could be put into the street and become part of it. They could shout as loudly as Communists or Moslem Brothers. To get them all away from work at the same time and on the street, plans were made for a strike to be called the moment Nasser, relying on his well-tuned ear, decided that the psychological moment had come. Every day, in the meantime, crowds were parading and chanting, "We want the revolution!"

Nasser, appearing to ignore the street, started playing chess with the Army. Naguib's men were dismissed, demoted, transferred. Army officers whose loyalty he doubted but thought he could win were given promotions and choice assignments.

Now a new voice began to be heard. Major Amin Shaker, whom Nasser had enrolled as a Free Officer in Gaza and who had recently been appointed one of his personal aides, began to test public reaction by sniping at Naguib. "A tool of reactionary elements, conspiring to deliver the country to dishonest politicians," he said of the general.

President, Prime Minister, R.C.C. Chairman, and Military Governor Naguib, still unaware that he was in a many-sided trap with the walls slowly closing in, daily made mistakes. One afternoon he set free hundreds of political prisoners, including the Supreme Guide of the Moslem Brotherhood. The next day, he ordered the release of Mustafa Nahas, the eight-time Prime Minister whose young wife only a few days earlier had been found guilty of crimes for which the government had confiscated a quarter of a million dollars' worth of her property.

As the situation mounted toward its inevitable climax, King Saud of Saudi Arabia dropped in for a week's visit. He could not have come at a worse time. He arrived in his private plane, the *Flying Palace,* complete with revolving throne and a hundred thousand dollars' worth of interior plushwork. Nineteen of his sons accompanied him. Naguib met him at the airport and later presented him with the Grand Collar of the Order of the Nile, Egypt's highest decoration.

In London, Anthony Eden did not improve Anglo-Egyptian relations by issuing a statement that there was "too much cox and box" going on in Cairo, a British expression few Egyptians understood.

In Moscow the Soviet Government announced that it was raising its Cairo legation to the status of an embassy.

Naguib now made another error. He ordered the release of five hundred Moslem Brothers. Nasser did not interfere. He was gambling on a certain amount of planned chaos.

King Saud, an embarrassed guest, tried to act as peacemaker between the general and the colonel, but without much success. They were now openly hostile to each other. One day late in March, Nasser decided the time had come, so an order was issued for the transport workers to begin their hunger and sit-down strike. Slow paralysis began to grip Cairo. At midnight King Saud succeeded in getting Nasser and Naguib to face each other across a small table. They argued until two-thirty in the morning, with no tangible results. Men who should have been driving buses and trams milled through the city shouting for Nasser, for the revolution, against Naguib.

The next day, the Cabinet and the R.C.C. were supposed to hold a joint meeting. General Naguib and his bodyguard arrived to find the street outside the building packed with demonstrators. Most of them looked like union men, perhaps transport workers. The bodyguard said it would be dangerous to try to go in by the front entrance. He knew a side way. He suggested that he and the general both proceed with drawn revolvers. Once inside the building they were surprised that there was no sign of Nasser or any of his faction.

An hour later, after the crowd had grown larger and even more boisterous, Nasser and Amer arrived—carried on the shoulders of the demonstrators to the entrance of the building. They informed Naguib they had declared a state of emergency and ordered all troops to remain in their barracks. The meeting had to be recessed four times so Nasser or Amer could go out onto the balcony and assure the crowds below that the revolution would go on, despite President Naguib's proclamation of March 25. The meeting lasted nine hours. There was no communiqué, no announcement to the waiting reporters except one significant sentence: "The revolution will continue." It was now finally clear to Naguib that he was in a trap; that the purpose of the proclamation he had signed was only to snare him.

The next day, King Saud departed. Nasser, Naguib, and several car-loads of other dignitaries went to the airport to bid him good-by. As the King was about to enter the plane, General Naguib stood at the top of the stairway, shaking hands with him. Some of Nasser's men, suddenly deciding that the general might try to fly away on the royal plane, rushed up the stairs and surrounded him, then edged him down to the tarmac and stood guard over him until the *Flying Palace* was on its way. A moment later Naguib clasped his hand over his heart and fell to the ground, moaning, "I feel that I am about to die!" Nasser helped him to his feet and then to his car. The general was driven to his home and put to bed.

Back in Cairo improvised sound trucks manned by men shouting against Naguib filled the air left quiet by the absence of the rattling buses and trams. Early in the afternoon a mob besieged the Supreme Court building looking for the presiding judge, Abdel Razek el Sanhouri, the distinguished elder statesman who had helped write Farouk's abdication proclamation. He was a friend of Naguib and might, if the military dictatorship ended, become an important figure in a new regime. While the demonstrators beat him over the head, the judge shouted his denial that he was a traitor, but the mob would not listen, so he pulled out a revolver from the drawer of his desk and shot two of his attackers. A crisis was averted by the fortuitous arrival of Salah Salem in an army truck. Wearing dark glasses and a beret, he mounted to the roof of the truck and gave the crowd a tongue-lashing. "Stop acting like fools!" he ordered. "Do you want the British to come marching in?"

On street corners and in public squares orators who did not hesitate to identify themselves as Communists, Brotherhood members, socialists, and even fascists harangued the crowds. On the campus of Cairo University thousands of students ignored the appeal of their dean to return to classes. Amer, at Nasser's suggestion, sent an armored column into the city, to prevent a repetition of Black Saturday.

Shopkeepers who had not been sure these last few days whose picture they should be displaying in their windows quietly began to remove the wrinkled face of the general and replace it with the tight-lipped young colonel with the confident expression. But most of them did not destroy Naguib's pictures. They might be needed again.

Late in the day the R.C.C. held a meeting and announced that a return to a civilian, parliamentary, democratic way of life for Egypt would be postponed indefinitely. The military would retain power. The R.C.C. would not go out of business "until we have freed the Suez and won social justice for workers and peasants." Censorship would be reimposed. There would be no elections in the immediate future. Political enemies of the regime would be dealt with severely. No more demonstrations would be permitted. The struggle for power was over.

Three weeks later the ailing and unhappy general put his name to a document that had been prepared for him. It stated that he had voluntarily relinquished the title of Prime Minister. For a second time Gamal Abdel Nasser would take over that position from him. Only this time the power went with it. The military dictatorship was back to stay. If Mohamed Naguib escaped with his life he would be lucky.

CHAPTER 13

MY LIFE IS YOURS

It was a Tuesday in October 1954. Prime Minister Nasser was on his way by train to Alexandria, where that evening he was to address what might be the largest crowd that had ever assembled anywhere on Egyptian soil.

It was six months since the R.C.C. had ordered Naguib to invite him to become Prime Minister and form a Cabinet. After that there had been no more trouble with the general. He had rheumatism badly now and spent most of his time at home. He seemed content to hold the empty title of President, make an occasional speech, sign documents, confer a decoration now and then, and not interfere with the important business of running a state. He had not even protested when the leadership of the Liberation Rally had been taken from him.

As he sat looking out the window of his private car, Nasser thought back over these six months. He had the reins tightly in his hands now. For the first time he felt completely in control. There had been several counterrevolutionary plots, but every one of them had been nipped before it could grow into even a bud. The Army would always have to be watched, but at the moment it seemed free of intrigue.

The press had been a worry, but it, too, was finally under control. Censorship was so tight that not a single word could be put into print by any of the several hundred daily, weekly, and monthly publications until it had been read and approved by army intelligence men. The Fath brothers, the most powerful newspaper publishers in Egypt, had been broken. Though they had been subtle in their criticism, they had been against the revolution. They owned *Al Misri*, one of Cairo's largest dailies, as well as two papers in French and one in English. It had been a clever move to revoke the permit for *Al Misri* and suddenly put it out of business, then to swear out warrants for the arrest of the Fath brothers. The elder, Mahmud, had fled to Switzerland and was given a ten-year prison sentence in absentia. Then the pair was fined over a million dollars. That took care of them. News sent abroad was also be-

176

ing watched by alert men who had orders that if they ever were in doubt they were to say *no*. To be sure they made no mistakes, late every night Nasser received at home a copy of every dispatch sent out of the country and read them all before he went to bed. The Egyptian papers had been ordered to print no more pictures of Naguib and of course they obeyed. The censors struck out almost any reference to Naguib in dispatches going abroad, so the outside world, too, would soon forget him.

Inside the revolutionary junta there had been a few troubles, but now they were straightened out. It had been necessary to discipline Salah Salem. He had held a sensitive post as Minister of National Guidance and was probably better known to the public than anyone else except the Prime Minister and the President. It had been a problem how to discipline him without shaking public confidence in the regime, but finally it was announced that he had been granted "a leave of unspecified duration." That night, he had come to Manchiet el Bakry and for four hours they had talked things over. Before he left he made some promises. The next day, his leave was terminated. Now he was back at work, guiding propaganda again in his usual bombastic manner.

Khaled Mohieddin was out of the way, probably for good. Instead of arresting and trying him, making a martyr of him, Nasser had sent him into exile. But nicely, on a government mission. He would remain at least two years in Rome representing the National Production Council.

The R.C.C. had been purged, quietly, of several other troublemakers. Those who remained were the hard core of officers who really could be trusted, and they were in control of the Cabinet now. Before, under Maher and then Naguib, the majority had been civilians. By putting Amer in as Minister of War and Sadat as Minister of State he had raised the number of officers in the Cabinet to ten, against nine civilians. And everyone knew who controlled the votes of the ten.

During the summer there had been trouble from an unexpected source. Sermons critical of the regime were preached in many mosques. The climax came in the Delta city of Tanta, where a Moslem priest called members of the government "heretics who do not comply with the teachings of the Koran." This led to a battle with knives inside the mosque. But now the situation was under control. An order had been issued forbidding sermons in mosques unless they were written by the Minister for Religious Affairs or someone in his office.

The universities had also been a source of trouble. He knew from his own experience how opposition forces counted on the university students to join in subversive activities. An R.C.C. member, Major Kamal Hussein, was made Minister of Education, with orders to clean up the schools and universities. He had done so. Forty professors were dismissed in a single day. A permanent cordon of police was thrown around Cairo University, and henceforth every student who came or went would have to show an identification card.

Then there were the trade unions—now all under the regime's control. One of the Bikbashis was made Minister of Social Affairs and Labor and regimented the entire labor movement. Enough Communists were arrested to keep that group quiet. Even the police department had been cleaned up, with more than a hundred officers receiving permanent vacations.

To give the street an outlet for its emotions, a full-scale, front-page attack had been ordered against France. Her Premier, Mendès-France, was described as "this little Zionist, imperialist Jew," an attack so vituperative that it disturbed many Egyptians who felt it violated Egypt's long-standing practice of religious tolerance.

Land reform had not yet revolutionized the lives of the eighteen million fellahin, but a start had been made. He himself had presided at the first ceremony at which deeds were handed out to nearly a thousand peasants, each of whom received about four acres.

The big accomplishment of these six months was the agreement with the British, signed just six days ago. The British would be out in another twenty months, out to stay, leaving Egyptians masters of all Egypt, even the Canal. The day the preliminary agreement was initialed, the papers printed the word EVACUATION! in red ink across their front pages. That morning, a crowd of two thousand had milled around in front of his house in Manchiet el Bakry until he came out and made a front-porch speech. All along the route to his office the crowds blocked his way. This was what he would talk about tonight. The British. The evacuation. The victory.

The celebration had begun two days ago, with parades and demonstrations. In several impromptu speeches he had promised that he and the government would now turn their attention to "eliminating poverty, disease, and ignorance."

Having done a great deal of speaking in these six months, he felt surer of himself on a platform. Of course he did not begin to match Naguib. People listened to him, but he knew he lacked the oratorical facility the general had. He was always too busy thinking of just the right words to concern himself with gestures, voice modulation, and all the other tricks his aides had tried to teach him. Perhaps he made his speeches too long. He was planning to talk tonight for at least three hours.

But everything was going well. His *baraka*—his luck—was holding out. Great Britain was lifting its prohibition against arms shipments to Egypt. The United States promised to start giving economic aid at once. Still, there was something missing to make it all perfect. He was the leader now. No one disputed it. Not even Naguib. But there was nothing spectacular about it. He had come to power six months ago by back-room intrigue. Now he needed something to dramatize his position, something to help him win the acclaim of the masses. He also needed an excuse to be rid of Naguib, once and for all. There was, besides, a third and much more vital need. While tightening his hold on the country he had one great worry: the Brothers. He had played cat-and-mouse with Hodeiby and his followers ever since the revolution. Hodeiby had been in and out of prison several times. There had been a number of riots involving the Brothers. In one, ten policemen were wounded. Whispers had reached him that the Brotherhood's arms caches were getting larger and larger. The Brotherhood was incensed over the agreement with London. They called it surrender. He must find a way to break the back of the Brotherhood for all time. The problem was that it had its roots in Islam and most Egyptians were followers of Islam. So were all the R.C.C. So was he himself. Trying to crush a religious movement was dangerous, even if it was a counterrevolutionary threat. What he needed was something spectacular. As he thought about these things he noticed that the fountain pen in his left breast pocket had leaked and made a small dark stain directly over his heart.

In the five-room, sand-colored house at Manchiet el Bakry on the edge of Cairo, Tahia Nasser turned on her radio early in the evening, to be sure she would not miss any of her husband's speech. This was probably the only way she would ever hear him, since he did not approve of her attending meetings.

In the great square called the *Midan el Tahrir* (Place of the Liberation) the crowd had already gathered by the time he arrived. Police officials told him there were a quarter of a million people in the square and under loudspeakers in streets leading into it.

Emile Karem, a photographer for the Cairo newspaper *Akhar Sa'a* and for AP, found a good seat in the press section up front and began taking pictures of the crowd. Then he focused his camera on the spot where he knew Nasser would be standing when he spoke. At the back of the square is the Alexandria Stock Exchange, which begins as a one-story building, then steps back before rising to its full height of several more stories. The roof of the one-story part forms a large terrace. On it fifty chairs had been placed. At the front of the terrace were the microphones of the Egyptian Broadcasting station and the amplifying system that would carry the Prime Minister's voice into all the streets leading to the square. In the front row, close to the microphones, sat Mirghani Hamza, the Sudan's Minister of Agriculture and Commerce, who was in Egypt on a visit. Near him was Ahmed Moursi Badr, an Alexandria lawyer.

At 7:31 P.M. Nasser began to speak—slowly and quietly at first, but soon he grew excited, trying to work up the crowd. He waved his right hand in a sweeping gesture and cried:

"My countrymen, in this same square—only then it was called Mohamed Aly Square—in this same square as a small boy I participated in my first demonstration. It was against the British. In this square for the first time I saw men being hit over the head. I saw Egyptians shooting down their fellow Egyptians. But I am alive today. I am alive and helping to free my country."

He gave his voice that rising inflection that almost demands applause. The crowd responded. "I am alive today," he repeated, "and . . ."

At this moment in the press section photographer Karem raised his camera, readjusted the focus slightly, and put his finger on the button.

And at this same moment down below, in the eighth row of chairs, a round-faced man with a shock of black hair hanging down over his forehead raised a .36-caliber Italian revolver, aimed it at the speaker, and began firing. His first bullet went wild. The second hit an electric light globe just over Nasser's head. Several others also missed their mark. After the sound of the shots and breaking glass, there was an instant of complete silence, then pandemonium. The people in distant parts of the square had no idea what had occurred. Those on the platform looked at each other to see who had been killed. The only victims were the Sudanese Minister and the Alexandria lawyer, who were slightly cut by the flying glass. Nasser blinked, brushed pieces of the light globe from his shoulders, then looked down to see what was happening below. The assassin was being manhandled, punched, pummeled by all who could get their hands on him. It was some time before police could rescue him.

Nasser returned to the microphones. "O free men, let everyone stay in his place!" he shouted to the excited crowd. "This is Gamal Abdel Nasser speaking to you." Again and again he repeated it. "My blood is your blood. My life is yours. You are all Gamal Abdel Nassers. If I had been killed, it would have made no difference, for you would carry on the struggle. You are all Gamal Abdel Nassers."

In Manchiet el Bakry, Tahia Nasser, now that she knew her husband was safe, called a servant to make her a cup of coffee.

Late in the evening, after the meeting had ended and the Prime Minister was being entertained in the Alexandria Lawyers' Club, one of his friends suddenly pointed to his left breast and exclaimed, "My God, you *have* been hit!"

Nasser smiled. "Ink!" he said, pulling out the defective pen.

The next day, on the way back to Cairo by train, he noticed a man sitting dejectedly in an aisle seat with a camera hanging from a leather strap around his neck. "Weren't you sitting in the front row of the press section last night?" he asked.

"Yes," replied Emile Karem.

"Just before the shots were fired I saw you aiming your camera at me. You must have gotten a fine shot of me just as the gun went off."

Karem, embarrassed, hesitated a moment, then said, "I am ashamed to admit it, but I was so frightened I dropped the camera and forgot to press the button."

When the train made its first stop, Nasser discovered that a religious fanatic had done for him what months of propaganda and "national guidance" had failed to do. He was a hero now, someone to be wildly cheered and loudly applauded. Every time the train stopped, so many people swarmed around that it was difficult to get it under way again. In Cairo there were masses of people milling around the railroad depot, shouting his name and fighting to get a look at him. It took his car two hours to make the ten-minute drive to his office. When he finally reached his desk he discovered that he was not just a national but an international hero. Among the cables of congratulation there was even one from Winston Churchill.

No two reports agreed as to whether Mahmoud Abdul Latif, the would-be assassin, was a tinsmith, a carpenter, or a plumber. But they did agree that he was thirty-two years old, a Cairene, and had been a Moslem Brother for sixteen years. Two months earlier the terrorist branch of the Brotherhood had picked him to kill Nasser. They had given him the Italian gun, several months of target practice, and $5.79 for his round-trip railroad fare, third class. He had been accompanied to the meeting by three friends. All were Brothers. This was the excuse Nasser needed to declare full-scale war against the Brotherhood. Within a few hours after the attempt on his life a plan for breaking the organization was put into effect. From Alexandria down to the Sudanese frontier Brotherhood leaders were arrested. Hundreds of them were led off to jail, Supreme Guide Hodeiby and four members of his Supreme Guidance Council among them. All were accused of plotting the overthrow of the regime. One by one, the hidden caches of arms were uncovered, in mosques, graveyards, underground hide-outs, caves. Soon enough dynamite was in hand to have blown up most of Cairo and all the British installations along the Canal. Then a spectacular assassination plot came to light. Two men had been assigned to kill each member of the R.C.C. If the first assassin failed, his alter ego must do the killing. After that 116 other Free Officers were going to be put to death. The only exception was Naguib. He was to be spared.

While the mass arrests were being made, a street mob stormed the Brotherhood's Cairo headquarters and burned it to the ground. The arrested men were all questioned in secret, but occasionally Salah Salem called in the press to give them a little guidance. Each time, Naguib's name somehow came into the story. At first Salem merely said the Brothers were going to spare the general in the wave of killings. Then he said the Brothers admitted they had been indirectly in touch with Naguib. Day by day the accusations became graver. After Nasser and half the Free Officers had been killed, the Brothers intended to make Naguib Prime Minister again. At first Salem said that maybe the general himself was unaware of the plan. But as the net tightened, he implied that Naguib had been a plotter with the Brotherhood from the start.

On the second Sunday of November the R.C.C. met for three hours. As usual, Naguib was not invited, but at 11 A.M. he received a telephone call at his office in Abdin Palace: "Minister of War Amer and Minister of Republican Affairs Ibrahim will be calling upon you at noon."

He suspected what they were going to do. He went through his desk, taking the few small personal things he could put in his pockets. At exactly twelve o'clock Amer, the man who had once been his aide, who had enrolled him as a Free Officer and afterward persuaded Nasser to make him the chief, walked through the door, followed by Ibrahim.

Half an hour later an emaciated, tired, sad-looking general, surrounded by guards, descended the palace stairs and entered a military car. He seemed to be having difficulty controlling his emotions.

Salah Salem was the one who announced that General Naguib would spend an indefinite time under house arrest on the expropriated private estate of Madame Nahas. The official communiqué was simple: "General Mohamed Naguib was today relieved of his position as head of the Egyptian Government."

Everyone knew what it meant, yet no demonstrations took place in the street. Not a voice was raised. Not a murmur was heard. The man who so short a time ago had been the idol of Egypt's millions had lost the battle to a shrewd, calculating, and clever opponent.

The treason trial of the Brothers was held on the top floor of the island house. Three R.C.C. men served as judges and jury. There were so many defendants that no one of them had much chance to make a case for himself, but there were two principals: Latif and Hodeiby. The trial was *in camera*, with Salem at the end of each day telling the reporters what they could write. By now more than a thousand Brothers were in prison, he said, and the organization had been permanently banned.

On the first Sunday of December, shortly after midnight, the three-man People's Court gave its verdict. The following would be hanged by the neck: Supreme Guide Hodeiby; Latif, who had fired the shots; a thirty-year-old Cairo lawyer who had given the gun to Latif; a *mullah* (Moslem preacher) who was spiritual adviser to the terrorists; and the man who had given Latif target practice.

Now it was up to the R.C.C. to decide whether these sentences should stand. They had a new system. After a case had been reviewed, each man would write on a slip of paper what he thought the verdict should be. After the slips were all in, Nasser would open them, one by one, and read aloud what they said. The rule was that the final verdict would be the mildest punishment written on any of the slips. This meant that the death sentence could never be imposed unless the Council voted unanimously for it.

Nasser's R.C.C. associates liked to tell of the time when seven of them sat around the table in the Nileside house arguing about a verdict for seventeen hours. Then it came time to write out the slips. Nasser opened them slowly. On each was written: "Death." Then he picked up his own slip and read what it said: "Ten years." The others stormed at him until he agreed to compromise for twenty-five years. But less than a year later he set the prisoner free. In this case the discussion took little time. All agreed that Hodeiby's life should be spared. He was old and ill. But the slips in the other six cases all read: "Death."

Three days later, at eight o'clock in the morning, the six who were to die were dressed in red caps and loose-fitting black smocks. One by one they were taken to a corner of Cairo prison, fitted with a brown hood, and put to death at the end of a rope.

One man said to his executioners, quietly, "Be careful with the rope. They've broken both my arms." Another shouted as he passed a huddle of reporters, "We were judged by our enemies." A third said, "I die a martyr." The others were mumbling prayers to Allah. Not one of them had been accused of murder. The worst that any had done was to fire a revolver and miss. The record was now badly splattered with blood.

News of the executions was published in Cairo papers that same afternoon. What was not announced for either domestic or foreign consumption was that a trial had been held of another man accused of treason. He had been found guilty, but his death sentence had been commuted to ten years' imprisonment, then to permanent isolation under heavy guard on the Nahas estate in suburban Cairo.

No one would be permitted to call on him. No newspaper would be permitted to print his name. His judges were afraid to put him to death. But they were also almost afraid to let him live.

CHAPTER 14

A HERO TO LEAD THEM

It was a calculated risk, and Gamal Abdel Nasser violated all his own principles and ignored all his own theories by taking it. It was he who had warned the other Bikbashis, "If we start killing, there will be no end to it. . . ." It was he who had been so determined not to use the gallows as an instrument of the revolution that he had resigned from the movement rather than accede to the vote of the R.C.C. to deal out capital punishment to enemies of the new regime. Yet he permitted the six Brotherhood men to be put to death. Was it personal revenge because one of them had tried to kill him?

In the autumn of 1954 Nasser felt that he was in danger of losing power. His spies convinced him that Naguib and the Brotherhood were in communication with each other. If the million or more Brothers, with their network of cells, their caches of arms, and their fanatic willingness to die for a cause, were to acquire one more asset, the personal popularity of the general, what chance would a small group of army officers have against such a combination? The Brotherhood was a serious threat to his personal power and it must be broken, whatever the consequences. So six men were hanged and the world saw the soundness of the theories Nasser had preached but did not have the wisdom to practice: "If one enemy is executed, ten new and even more bitter enemies may be created among the immediate survivors."

In this case the immediate survivors refused to claim the bodies. Everyone in Egypt knew what this meant. A vendetta, a curse on the executioners, vengeance for the dead. But it was not just the families of the dead. A thousand Brothers had been imprisoned and were being held without trial until someone decided it was safe to let them loose again. In Egypt if a thousand healthy young males are taken away, it means that perhaps ten thousand wives and children, fathers and mothers, aged uncles and aunts will go hungry. There were also the million who were still free. Bitter men. Talking men. Greater enemies than ever. Men full of stories—true or not—about how this one had been tortured

185

and that one had had his feet slashed. Because these people were already fanatics and believed that they were engaged in a jihad, a holy war, and therefore would ascend directly to heaven if they died for the cause, the execution of six Brothers did not serve as a great deterrent. Some of the arrested brethren later admitted they had taken a holy oath at the time of the hangings to sacrifice anything, even their lives, to avenge the wrong. They raised a secret fund for the families of the men Nasser had killed and for the neediest families of those in prison. All these things Nasser thought over, after it was too late.

The old political parties were shocked by his ruthlessness. So was the street, the people who worshiped Naguib. Internally and externally at the end of 1954, the situation was critical. Up to this time, except for the vague midsummer declaration of admiration for cold-war neutrality, Nasser and his regime had not concerned themselves much with foreign affairs; but now, suddenly, the Moslem world was aflame with antagonism. Syria, Lebanon, Jordan, the Sudan, even distant Pakistan were denouncing this blow to Islam by a man who himself was a follower of Mohamed. The Moslem Brotherhood was not exclusively an Egyptian organization. It had branches in other Arab countries that reacted violently.

Relations with the Sudanese, which Nasser had carefully cultivated, were now strained, not only because of the executions of the brethren but because of what had been done to their native son, Naguib. Sudanese delegations came to Cairo to add oratory to logic. The President of the Islamic Congress sent a cable. In Damascus fifteen thousand students walked out of their classes in a mass demonstration. These were all the voices of Arabs, his own people.

To make matters worse, Salah Salem's idea for casting further disrepute on Naguib had boomeranged. He called the press together and announced that he had a sensation for them. Before the general's dismissal three Sudanese Ministers had made a trip to Cairo and offered him their support if he would prepare a coup against Nasser. If it failed, they proposed to kidnap the general, take him to the Sudan, and set him up there as President of a republic. Salem even named the three men. After the story had been cabled abroad, Nasser heard about it and suggested to Salem that this was hardly a way to win the good will of the Sudanese, who had not yet decided whether to amalgamate with Egypt or become independent. It was too late to stop publication abroad, but that night Cairo newspapers received instructions to eliminate the word "kidnap" and not to disclose the source of the story.

Gamal Abdel Nasser was now in an unenviable position. It looked as if his baraka had run out. Was the calculated risk he had taken too great? Was there yet a way to silence the clamor, to prove that he was a good Moslem, to give his Arab critics some other outlet for their emotion? He knew it would have to be something dramatic. Hate has a strange ability to unite diverse people. History is full of proof. In 1948 the Arab world had been as divided as ever: monarchies, republics, sheikhdoms, protectorates, colonies; semimodern and primitive states; places as diverse as feudal Yemen and cosmopolitan Alexandria. Yet a mutual hatred had welded six Arab nations together long enough for them to wage a brief war in a common cause. Perhaps it was the memory of Palestine that gave Nasser and the R.C.C. the idea of making a *cause célèbre* out of what should have been a minor court case.

Twelve men and a girl, all Jews, had been arrested in Cairo. Most of them were young. Some had lived all their lives in Egypt, some had only recently come from Europe. But they had in common a warm feeling for the new Jewish state. That made them Zionists, and in post-revolutionary Egypt, while no especial stigma was attached to being a Jew, being a Zionist was as bad as being an advocate of colonialism.

The case of the thirteen Jews was carefully timed. Four days after the Brothers were hanged, with the clamor over the executions growing ever louder, Nasser ordered the trial of the thirteen young people to begin. They were accused of being spies and *agents provocateurs*. The court was told they had placed fire bombs in U.S.I.S. libraries in Cairo and Alexandria to discredit Egypt in American eyes. Also in cinema houses and mailboxes. Reporters representing papers in other parts of the Arab world were given unusual facilities to cover the trial. The state kept promising sensations. The prosecution charged that the State of Israel had trained most of the defendants in the use of firearms, wireless instruments, and secret codes. For days Cairo papers made it their principal story.

But there were three sensations not planned by the prosecution. First, it became known that one of the defendants, Moshe Cremona, had died while being beaten. Then, on the third day of the trial, a French-born girl, Marcelle Victorine Nino, told the court she had been tortured in an attempt to force her to confess to crimes she had never committed.

As the tenth day's session of the trial was about to begin, Max Bennett, accused as the ringleader, committed suicide in his cell.

On a bleak Thursday in January 1955 the court gave its decision. Dr. Moussa Marzook, French surgeon on the staff of the Jewish Hospital,

Cairo, and Samuel Azaar, teacher, would be hanged by the neck. Five other men and the French girl would spend years, perhaps life, at hard labor. "Prime Minister Nasser has already approved the sentences," reporters were told.

Protests came from all over the non-Arab world, pleas for mercy, appeals for reconsideration. On the fourth day, while the messages were still pouring in, a black flag was suddenly raised over Cairo prison and the warden announced that the young surgeon had just been hanged. Half an hour later the Jewish teacher went to his death in the same way.

The Prime Ministers of most of the Arab states were meeting that day in Cairo, and this may have had a connection with the timing of the executions. Perhaps the other Arab states would believe that Gamal Abdel Nasser was a good Moslem after all.

The record of the new regime was now covered with red, but the outcry in the Arab world immediately began to subside. For Nasser, a pragmatic man, this may have been justification, although in other places abroad he had lost good will he could never regain.

For the first two post-revolutionary years the frontier between Egypt and Israel had been relatively quiet, but now something began to happen that seemed to be part of a plan. Up to the spring of 1955 Israel had filed more than a thousand complaints against Egypt with the U.N. Mixed Armistice Commission. In that period 257 Israelis had been killed or wounded by infiltrators from the Egyptian side of the line. The damage to Israeli property had been in the hundreds of thousands of dollars. After the Moslem Brotherhood attempt on Nasser's life this activity was suddenly intensified. Houses were dynamited. A school was bombed. A bridge on the road to Elath was blown up. Roads used daily by settlers were mined. Most disrupting were organized Egyptian raids on water lines leading to Negev settlements. The Armistice Commission repeatedly condemned Egypt, but night after night the killings and the sabotage continued.

This frontier situation could not have been unknown to Nasser, for he had control over the Egyptian representatives on the Armistice Commission, who read every complaint Israel filed. Indeed, the saboteurs and infiltrators could find encouragement in words that Nasser and his Ministers now began to use.

"If we go to battle again we can retrieve all that we lost," Nasser told a group of new officers on March 4, 1954. "The time for action and not for words is approaching."

Four days later Egyptian commandos presented a revolver to him, and in thanking them he said, "You must be ready for the great battle of Palestine. Make yourselves ready for the jihad in Palestine."

In December, Minister of Social Affairs Hussein Shafei, at a memorial service for those who had died in the war of 1948, said, "We are about to embark on a second round."

In Israel, David Ben-Gurion returned from his retirement in the desert and once more took the portfolio of Minister of Defense.

February 28, 1955, was a Monday. Gamal Abdel Nasser went to bed early that night. He had had a busy day, and was tired. Shortly after midnight the telephone on the table beside his bed rang. It was Ali Sabri, one of his closest aides. "I have bad news, Gamal," he said. "Are you awake enough to understand?" Nasser asked for a moment to slip on his robe and pick up a pencil.

"The Jews have made an attack in the Gaza Strip, two miles inside our lines," Sabri informed him. "They seized a Taggart Fort and blew up a pumping station northeast of Gaza. One of our trucks carrying re-inforcements hit a mine and blew up. The first report says thirty-seven of our men are dead and thirty or more wounded."

Nasser did not go back to bed that night. He was on the phone for hours with his military advisers, with men in the Foreign Office, and with his Minister of National Guidance, Salem.

The next day, the death total was raised to thirty-eight. Nasser called on the Security Council to hold a special meeting. In Jerusalem, Israel's Prime Minister Sharett said the attacking party had been chasing in-filtrators back across the frontier and had attacked only a military strong point; that if Egypt insisted on maintaining a technical state of war with Israel she would have to face the consequences.

The day after that Nasser presented a flag to cheering cadets at the Military Academy and told them, "I hear that Israel threatened us yesterday. If they want a battle, we will give them a hard lesson."

Early in 1955 something else happened that he felt was even more important to Egypt's future than the frontier incidents with Israel. In Baghdad the Turkish and Iraqi Prime Ministers had drawn up a treaty that came to be known as the Baghdad Pact. Later Pakistan, Iran, and Great Britain also signed, while the United States gave its moral sup-port. The West was now trying to induce other Arab countries to join this cold-war alliance.

Nasser took the Baghdad Pact as a personal insult. It colored all his thinking. It influenced almost every political move he made for years. From his schooldays on, he had had only one motivation. All these

years he had been ruled by his hatred of those who for centuries had
governed and exploited Egypt, especially the British, because they were
still there. He had preached that it was better to starve and be free than
to prosper and be the slaves of the detested outsider. From his study of
history he had concluded that pacts, alliances, and treaties were clever
devices by which great powers manipulated small countries for their own
selfish ends. Therefore he was against them in principle, whatever their
avowed purpose. Although he himself had done nothing so far to bring
about any degree of Arab unity, this was one of his future plans, and he
saw in the Baghdad Pact a furtherance of the Western practice of keeping the Arab world divided and playing one small country against another. Besides, his pride was hurt because Iraq had been chosen as the
foundation stone of the pact. Egypt had not yet even been approached
to join.

February 1955 was international visitors' month for Nasser. First,
Marshal Tito of Yugoslavia arrived by ship at Ismailia on his way
home from a journey to the Far East. Nasser went aboard and sailed as
far as Port Said, a trip of six and a half hours. He and Tito talked in
English, although the Yugoslav spoke it brokenly and with much less
assurance than Nasser. They talked briefly, then had lunch, and afterward both took a short siesta.

"I was very much impressed with him," Nasser said later. "He was
quite different than I had imagined. We quickly became good friends.
He seemed to me to be a simple man and a reasonable one. He had no
pretensions. He did not try to impress me that he was a more important
person than I was, or a better soldier, or knew more than I did about
anything. We got along well together."

One of the subjects they discussed was the Baghdad Pact. Tito had
no direct interest in it, but he agreed with Nasser that it was "a device
of Western imperialism" and that Egypt should stay out of it. That
led to a brief discussion of the Cold War and neutrality.

"I want to keep Egypt uncommitted," Nasser said.

"I think you are making a wise judgment," Tito answered.

At Port Said they issued a joint communiqué stating that Marshal
Tito had accepted an invitation to pay Egypt an official visit in the fall.

Ten days after Tito's visit Prime Minister Nehru arrived. This time
he came alone and stayed for two days. Nasser went to the airport to
greet him. They had three separate conferences and a long luncheon at
the Indian Embassy.

They talked mostly about their common desire to remain uncommitted in the Cold War. Of course, they had no language problem, for Mr. Nehru's English is naturally perfect. They had no ideological problems, either, because they saw eye to eye. During that visit, Nasser developed a great respect for this Indian statesman.

Three days after Nehru left, Anthony Eden, the British Foreign Minister, stopped in Cairo overnight on his way to a conference in Bangkok. The British Ambassador gave a dinner party in his honor, and Nasser was the principal outside guest. The men were all invited to bring their wives, but Nasser came alone. Tahia had never yet appeared in public with him. At one end of the long banquet table was the British Ambassador, with Lady Eden at his right. At the other end was the Ambassador's wife, with Eden on her one hand and Nasser on the other. That put Eden and Nasser facing each other.

For Nasser, unaccustomed to much formality, it was the most uncomfortable evening he had ever spent. Afterward he said with a laugh, "If I had known I was ever going to have to go through anything like that I don't think I would have made the revolution."

They had cocktails before dinner, several kinds of wine, champagne with dessert, and after that whiskey and soda. As a practicing Moslem, Nasser drank nothing but fruit juice, water, and coffee.

Sometimes there was laughter, but what the Britons laughed at seemed very unfunny to this army officer only one generation removed from the gray brown of Beni Mor. Occasionally Eden or the Ambassador's wife would turn to him, after everyone else had expressed an opinion about something, and say, "And what do *you* think about it, Mr. Prime Minister?"

When he tried to tell them, no one seemed to pay any attention. Once during the evening he and Eden had a short, serious talk. But he deeply resented what he felt was Eden's superior attitude. When he presented arguments that later turned out to be perfectly valid, Eden raised his eyebrows, shrugged his shoulders, and made him feel as if he had uttered a series of absurdities. The only thing that saved the evening for him was that Amer was there. When he glanced down the table at his friend for moral support, Amer gave him a look that said, "Bear up, it will soon be over."

Two days later the nineteen-year-old King of Jordan, Hussein I, arrived. Nasser felt like an old man in the young King's presence, but they had many things in common. They were Arabs. They spoke the same language. At the moment, each was the undisputed ruler of his country. They had a common enemy, Israel, against which their countries were still technically at war. Both Egypt and Jordan had quietly annexed pieces of Palestine that, by United Nations decision, were supposed to have been formed into a new Arab state. Yet despite all this their relationship during the King's official visit was strictly formal. Hussein stayed at Kubbah Palace, where Egypt always housed visiting heads of state. Nasser invested him with Egypt's highest decoration, the Grand Collar of the Order of the Nile, which could be given only to the head of a nation. There were formal banquets, and the King received all the honors due a man in his position. Although there was no antagonism between them, there was also none of the rapport Nasser had had with Tito and Nehru, both non-Arabs.

By now the colonel with the small scar on his forehead was beginning to be known around the world. His first television appearance was over the CBS network. Correspondent Frank Kearns conducted the interview in the garden of the house at Manchiet el Bakry. Nasser was in a summer uniform, his shirt open at the neck, and he sat in a wicker chair behind the table bearing the microphones. The equipment was a 16-mm. sound camera Kearns had borrowed from the Cairo police department. While they were rehearsing, Nasser turned to him and said, "You know, Mr. Kearns, I have no desire to be a professional actor."

At another point he asked one of his aides, "Do you really think there is any value to my doing this?" It was a terrible ordeal for him. Later he said he was more nervous than he ever had been under fire. After it was finally over, he felt that he never wanted to appear on television again.

One day about this time the Minister of Education proposed at a cabinet meeting that the Director of the National Library be discharged because of alleged mismanagement of the library's affairs.

"What did you say his name is?" Nasser asked.

"Tewfik Hakim," the Minister replied.

"Tewfik Hakim? You mean the author who wrote *The Soul Regained?*"

When the Minister said that was the person, Nasser banged the table with his fist and exclaimed, "That man had a great effect on my early thinking! I read *The Soul Regained* twice. It was a fine novel. I wish I had written it myself."

So instead of leaving his post in disgrace, Tewfik Hakim was named, on Nasser's order, to the Egyptian Academy of Arts and Letters.

In principle Nasser trusted, liked, and associated with only young, revolutionary-minded army officers. These were the men he understood, wanted in key government positions, liked to have around him socially as well as professionally. Mohamed Hassanein Heikal was the one exception. By 1955 he had become one of Egypt's most important editors. First he had been made editor in chief of the weekly magazine on which he worked; then, in addition, editor of a new daily paper, *Al Akbar*.

All the machinery of propaganda, control of the press, handling of foreign correspondents was in the hands of army men. Few if any of them had had practical experience in the field of journalism, and they made innumerable mistakes. But they would have made even more if Nasser had not had the unofficial advice of Mohamed Heikal. He was the only civilian who could lift a phone and get through immediately to El Bikbashi, the only one who could drop in to the house at Manchiet el Bakry and be sure he would be welcome, whatever the hour of the day or night. He was one of the few experts in any field whose opinions Nasser would accept as if they were proven fact. Heikal was a handsome young bachelor then, smoked small black cigars, could do with less sleep than Nasser, had a better command of English, and kept up with the books published in New York and London. A stream of subeditors, foreign correspondents, top army officers, and even an occasional Minister flowed through his office all day long.

He had persuaded Nasser to let him ghostwrite the Nasser memoirs of the Palestinian war; five articles had been published under Nasser's by-line in the magazine Heikal edited. In 1953 they collaborated on what came to be known as *The Philosophy of the Revolution*. It began as a series of three articles in the magazine. Nasser wrote the first one, but after Heikal read it he suggested some drastic revisions.

"You rewrite it yourself, Mohamed," Nasser told him.

He did, and it was published as rewritten. They used a different system on the second and third. Heikal had a series of conferences with Nasser, who talked while the young editor took notes. This went on for many hours, night after night. From that monologue came the second and third articles, which Nasser corrected and approved before they were published.

In 1954 *The Philosophy of the Revolution* was reprinted as a booklet in Arabic by the Liberation Rally, whose members sold copies to raise funds for their political organization. In the spring of 1955 a publisher in Washington, D.C., put out an American edition, with an introduction by Dorothy Thompson. It was Miss Thompson's idea to change the title in the American edition to *Egypt's Liberation,* which pleased neither Heikal nor Nasser, but that was the title used. The editor, in a foreword to the second printing a year and a half later, said, "When *Egypt's Liberation* made its appearance in the spring of 1955 it was all but ignored."

A few years ago an American correspondent during a discussion with Heikal contended that Nasser was wrong in a certain matter.

"How do you know what Nasser thinks about it?" Heikal asked.

"I know very well what he thinks," the correspondent replied. "I can prove what he thinks about it."

Thereupon he pulled from his pocket a copy of *The Philosophy of the Revolution,* found the passage, and then, gloating, said, "There it is, in black and white. In Nasser's own words."

"Nasser's own words?" Heikal asked with a smile.

"Yes, Nasser's own words. This is his book, *The Philosophy of the Revolution.* Surely you've read it?"

"Read it? Yes, I've read it, my friend. In fact, I wrote it."

While the Western world was ignoring *The Philosophy of the Revolution,* several printers in Cairo were putting out new editions. The government issued it in many languages to send abroad as propaganda. By the end of 1959 nearly a million copies had been distributed. It became the bible of the Nasser revolution.

The most sensational of the three articles making up the book was the second, in which Nasser admitted that he had once contemplated assassinating King Farouk and some of his entourage, and then told the story of the one assassination attempt in which he did take part, the plot to kill General Sirry Amir. But the name of the intended victim was not given, nor the date, and it was made to appear that the shooting occurred when Nasser was young and somewhat irresponsible, rather than in 1952, only a few months before the revolution that eventually made him a head of state.

A passage in the third article entitled "A Role in Search of a Hero" eventually caused the most comment. After recalling Luigi Pirandello's *Six Characters in Search of an Author,"* Nasser and/or Heikal wrote: "The pages of history are also full of heroic and glorious roles which never found heroes to perform them. For some reason it seems to me that within the Arab circle there is a role, wandering aimlessly in search of a hero. And I do not know why it seems to me that this role, exhausted by its wanderings, has at last settled down, tired and weary, near the borders of our country and is beckoning for us to move, to take up its lines, to put on its costume, since no one else is qualified to play it."

After describing the Arab circle of fifty-five million inhabitants, the author then tells of two other circles crying for a hero to lead them: Africa, population two hundred twenty-four million; the Islamic world, population four hundred twenty million.

"Sometimes I sit in my study reflecting on the subject, asking myself: What is our positive role in this troubled world and where is the place in which we should fulfill that role?

"I review our circumstances and discover a number of circles within which our activities inescapably must be confined and in which we must try to move.

"Fate does not jest and events are not a matter of chance—there is no existence out of nothing. We cannot look at the map of the world without seeing our own place upon it, and that our role is dictated by that place."

This article ends on a note of optimism:

When I consider the eighty million Moslems in Indonesia, and the fifty million in China, and the millions in Malaya, Siam and Burma, and the nearly one hundred million in Pakistan, and the more than one hundred million in the Middle East, and the forty million in the Soviet Union, together with the other millions in far-flung parts of the world—when I consider these hundreds of millions united by a single creed, I emerge with a sense of the tremendous possibilities which we might realize through the co-operation of all these Moslems, a co-operation going not beyond the bounds of their natural loyalty to their own countries, but nonetheless enabling them and their brothers in faith to wield power wisely and without limit.

And now I go back to that wandering mission in search of a hero to play it. Here is the role. Here are the lines, and here is the stage. We alone, by virtue of our place, can perform the role.

Heikal is indisputably one of Nasser's greatest admirers and strongest champions. Perhaps as he wrote that last line he was thinking of his friend as the leader of all the hundreds of millions of people in the three circles: Arabs, Africans, and Moslems all together.

Did Gamal Abdel Nasser have the same thought as he approved those last eleven words?

CHAPTER 15

CHOU PRESENTS HIS COMPLIMENTS

One day early in April 1955 Prime Minister Nasser stepped into an Indian commercial plane at Cairo International Airport to take off on his first long flight. For the first time, he was going out of the Arab world; he was also going to take part in an international conference. Twenty-nine nations would be represented at Bandung, all of them non-Western, most of them more important than Egypt. At the conference there would be powerful figures, some of them with years of experience in international affairs. There would be a thousand small problems that might embarrass him. He would have to make speeches, give impromptu answers to unexpected questions, state national policies, formulate international ones overnight. But he also was aware that he had certain advantages. Of the twenty-nine nations taking part in the first Asian-African Conference, the largest bloc would be the nine Arab countries. Because Egypt had a greater population than any other three Arab countries together, she naturally should be the leader. Twelve of the countries would be Islamic. Also, Egypt had received considerable publicity lately because of her success in persuading the British to sign the evacuation agreement.

He glanced around the plane after take-off. There were fifteen in his party. He had brought along the Egyptian Ambassador to Washington and Foreign Minister Fawzi to help with questions and protocol, Salah Salem to direct public relations, and Ali Sabri, on whom he leaned more and more these days. Also Machmud el Gayar, a handsome young major, the grandson of Mobarek el Gayar, on whose farm at Khatatba Gamal and his father used to go hunting for birds. Nasser liked the young man's good nature. A head of government, with so many occupational worries, needed a little cheer and brightness around. Now, as he watched the young major's happy expression, he said teasingly, "Machmud, when didn't you smile?"

The plane took them first to Pakistan, where they stayed for three days as guests of Prime Minister Mohamed Ali Jinnah. Then to New

196

Delhi, where they remained another three days. Then they flew to Rangoon, accompanied by Nehru and the Deputy Prime Minister of Afghanistan. As soon as the plane's wheels touched earth, they could see from the windows that they were to get an extraordinary welcome. The reception committee was led by Chou En-lai, who had been sitting at the airport for half an hour, waiting for them. He and Nehru greeted each other first, then Nasser was presented. Chou welcomed him with such warmth that the newspapermen watching made note of it. After that Nasser and U Nu, Prime Minister of Burma, were presented to each other. Nasser knew that only last year U Nu had been a guest of David Ben-Gurion at his retreat in the desert of Israel, yet he and the Burmese were soon on a friendly basis. U Nu impressed him as being a "good and simple man."

Nehru and U Nu spoke English, but conversation with Chou had to be conducted through an interpreter. Five minutes after they had met, however, they were getting along well. From the very start Nasser "found Chou polite, willing to listen, and very patient."

While they were having fruit juice at the airport pavilion the Chinese leader said to Nasser, "You must take advantage of this trip and visit all the Asian countries." He smiled as he emphasized the word *all*. Nasser smiled back, but did not commit himself. He knew that such a visit would be impossible unless Egypt accorded diplomatic recognition to Communist China.

That afternoon, they attended a Burmese New Year's festival. During the climax the wives of several Burmese Ministers, following an ancient custom, conferred good luck on the four Prime Ministers by dousing them with water. The visitors entered into the spirit of the festival and turned silver bowls of water upside down on top of each other's head.

In the evening there was a banquet. Nasser felt both proud and humble:

"I had to keep telling myself that I really was at such an important gathering with such important people. As I looked across the table at Chou En-lai and Nehru I could not help thinking that these two men represented more than one third of the entire population of the world."

His ego was further inflated when Chou said to him, "My government and my people have the greatest respect for Egypt."

He smiled and said, "Thank you."

"I would like to repeat what I said at the airport. I think you should visit China before you return home."

Nasser smiled again and repeated the noncommittal "Thank you."

From Rangoon they flew to Bandung. They were greeted at the airport by Dr. Ali Sastroamidjojo, the Indonesian Prime Minister, and young Prince Silhanouk of Cambodia. Bandung, a mountain city, was in bright attire for the conference. Buildings had been redecorated and painted gleaming white. Thousands of workmen had been repaving streets, stringing up flags of the represented nations, preparing for the greatest event in the city's history. The two luxury hotels were bulging with guests. One of the finest villas in the city had been vacated by its owners so that Nasser could stay there.

The Egyptians spent part of Sunday sight-seeing. All that day planes bearing dignitaries came in from the four points of the compass. The streets began to fill up with a diverse crowd: American reporters and a few delegates in Western clothes; U Nu with a bandana tied around his hat in the Burmese fashion; a man from the Gold Coast in a gaudy red, green, and yellow Kenti cloth; men wearing long white garments like nightshirts; men in flowing burnooses; men with white turbans wound around their heads.

Nasser was younger than nearly all the other delegates, handsomer than most. He was also the only delegate in a military uniform, so the crowds recognized him from a distance. He was loudly cheered wherever he went, a not unflattering experience. Looking over the other delegates, he realized they had very little in common. They represented monarchies, republics, feudal states, Communist and anti-Communist states, countries on every economic level. But there were three powerful bonds that tied them together and would make the conference a success, whatever happened. None of these men had white skins. They ranged in pigmentation from the black of the Gold Coast delegates to the sunburn color of Nasser. Almost all of them had been under colonial domination at some time. And they had all recently drunk deeply of the intoxicant called nationalism. In the past decade ten of their countries had gained independence.

On Sunday afternoon leaders of the five sponsoring nations met to make plans for the opening session. Nasser, with the support of Iraq and Jordan, proposed that Palestine be placed on the agenda. U Nu objected, saying that his country was friendly with both Israel and Egypt and an embarrassing situation would result if the subject were to be brought to the conference floor. He was supported by Nehru.

The conference was held in the auditorium of Independence Hall, which in colonial days had been a Dutch club. A speech by Indonesian President Sukarno opened the first session. Nasser applauded vigorously when he said, "The nations of Africa and Asia are no longer the tools and the playthings of forces they cannot influence."

A short time later there was some embarrassment in the hall when the Iraqi Minister of State, waving a finger in the direction of Chou En-lai, denounced communism as a new form of colonialism. He also called on the conference to brand Israel an illegitimate state.

There was discussion about whether a representative of each country should have an opportunity to make an opening speech. Nehru, aware of the many issues to be settled, argued against too much speechmaking, but he was voted down. Many of these delegates had come a long way to make a speech, and most of them had never had a forum like this before. One of the longest opening speeches was made by Nasser. In it he attacked the United Nations on both the North African and Palestinian issues.

The next day, there was an expectant silence as Chou arose to deliver his opening address. "My country desires friendly co-existence with all the world," he said.

It was a moderate speech, and Nasser later told members of his delegation that it convinced him the Chinese Premier was not as dangerous a man as he had been pictured by the West.

On the second day of the conference some of the reporters discovered that Nasser was the best-guarded man in Bandung: he had brought eight personal bodyguards with him to supplement the white-helmeted Indonesian military police who guarded his villa and patrolled the street in front of it in jeeps.

Salah Salem, facing his first public relations crisis of the conference, explained this to the reporters: "We were informed before we left Cairo that a number of Moslem Brotherhood members who somehow escaped the net when we rounded up the terrorists were planning to come here to Bandung and create a sensation by assassinating our beloved Prime Minister. As you know, they tried to kill him in Alexandria some months ago. Also, there is, as you may not know, an Indonesian counterpart of the Moslem Brotherhood, *Darul Islam*. Besides, we heard there are armed bandits in the mountains around Bandung who might cause trouble. We are taking no chances."

On Wednesday, Chou En-lai renewed his campaign to win Egypt's friendship by announcing that his delegation would support a resolution on Palestine demanding territorial revisions and recognition of the rights of Arab refugees.

Nehru answered him, "I have great sympathy for refugees, but when you discuss Palestine I think of the five and a half million Jews who met a tragic death at the hands of the Nazis." He said the Palestine problem demanded an early settlement, but, he added, "How can there be a settlement as long as the Arab nations refuse to negotiate with Israel?"

Both he and U Nu spoke in favor of a negotiated settlement, which had long been advocated by Israel.

Privately Nasser and the others of his delegation agreed that regardless of what sort of resolution was adopted they had won a strategic victory, for the propaganda effect of getting the Palestine issue discussed at all was great.

The next day, Salah Salem delivered to the press a violent attack on the United States for even considering a subsidy of American cotton exports. In the same statement he hinted that Egypt might accord diplomatic recognition to Communist China. That night, Nasser was host at a dinner party for Chou.

Halfway through the conference, Nasser—now beginning to enjoy the important role he was playing—announced that he had a seven-point program he would like to have adopted. Away from the Middle East for the first time in his life, he had suddenly begun to think in global terms, but his seven points were vague and hardly debatable. They called, principally, for an end to power politics, a cessation of the practice of using small nations as tools of large nations, adherence to the letter and spirit of the United Nations Charter.

Two days before the end of the conference a messenger arrived at the Nasser villa with an invitation from Chou En-lai for dinner that night.

"I am very sorry but I cannot possibly accept because I am giving a dinner party myself tonight," he replied.

Soon the messenger was back. Prime Minister Chou En-lai presented his compliments again and said he thoroughly understood the problem. However, the Egyptian Prime Minister really should taste Chinese food. The Chinese Prime Minister would be happy to postpone the commencement of his dinner until 11 P.M. Surely at that hour the Egyptian Prime Minister could excuse himself from his guests. But please, would he not eat very much at his own dinner, because at 11 P.M. he would be served with a very elaborate Chinese dinner, and at Chinese dinners there are always very many courses, so he must not spoil his appetite.

Nasser agreed. At 11 P.M., when he appeared at the Chinese villa, he found that the host was not present. Then he learned that Chou also had two dinner engagements and had not yet returned from the first. However, after the dinner finally was served he decided he liked Chinese food very much—what he was able to eat of it.

One of Egypt's strongest supporters at Bandung was Afghanistan, non-Arabic but Moslem. The Afghanistan delegates introduced the most favorable resolution—from Nasser's point of view—and invited the entire Egyptian delegation to visit Kabul on their way home.

The final communiqué adopted by the conference mentioned Palestine, although it was intentionally vague. It declared support of the rights of the Arab peoples of Palestine, called for the implementation of the U.N. resolutions on Palestine, and favored a peaceful solution of the entire problem.

Nehru made the final speech. He spoke of people in ferment, people desirous of change, people on the march. He gave them a new motto to take home: in place of co-existence, "living in peace."

The final dinner, at which the main figures of Bandung came together for the last time, was given by President Sukarno, with Chou, Nehru, and Nasser all present.

During the evening Sukarno mentioned to Nasser that Indonesia is made up of three thousand islands and that on this one alone, Java, there were fifty million people. "Do you realize that we have here one of the greatest densities of human beings in the world?" he said.

"How many per square mile?" Nasser asked.

"More than one thousand!" Sukarno answered impressively.

Nasser smiled, then after a moment said, "Mr. President, where I come from, Upper Egypt, the density in most places is more than two thousand per square mile."

As he packed for the trip home by way of Calcutta, New Delhi, Kabul, and Bahrein, he felt content with himself. Like a shrewd traveling salesman, he had not only won the good will of Chou En-lai, but had persuaded him to place a definite order: fifty thousand pounds of cotton in exchange for Chinese goods that Egypt might not need but could resell elsewhere. Also, Chou had agreed to send a Chinese purchasing mission to Cairo. What he had wanted in return was Nasser's promise to recognize the Peiping government. This Nasser evaded. He decided recognition was worth more than an order for twenty-five tons of cotton, as much as Egypt needed new cotton customers. Recognition could be used as a bargaining point later on.

In this initial venture into the international field he had given his first but not his last demonstration that he could look in two directions at once. The closest friend he had made at Bandung was the representative of the most populous Communist country in the world, and in his conversations, off the record and on, there had been hints that Egypt and Communist China would do some collaborating in the future. At the same time, he had supported the West on two important matters. He had voted to condemn Communist colonialism and he had favored a Western-sponsored resolution to link prohibition of atomic weapons and effective international control with a reduction in conventional armaments.

Before it was all over, he had created for himself a position as one of the Big Four of the world of color. Exactly how he had done it, others on the Egyptian delegation had some difficulty explaining after they returned to Cairo. It was not that he had made a speech so scintillating that it had attracted world attention, or that he had advanced a new and brilliant idea. It was not that he represented great masses of people, as Nehru and Chou did, or that he had performed any astounding political tricks. He could not even claim control of any large bloc of countries. It may have been partly the same personal charm that visitors to the house in Manchiet el Bakry were unable to resist. Whatever it was, when he left Egypt for Bandung early in April he was nervous, a little fearful of the mistakes he might make. In less than a month he returned home with a well-established world reputation. His name might still be anathema in parts of London and in certain other places, but he was respected now by the representatives of the forgotten people, five eighths of the world's population.

CHAPTER 16

ARMS FROM THE REDS

His plan had been to keep it a secret as long as he could, for he suspected that when it became known the repercussions would echo around the world. But on an afternoon in late September 1955, Nasser received a telephone call that the British were planning to reveal the news in a day or two in London. That made him change his mind.

He was scheduled to open an army exhibition on the Gezira Island fairgrounds that evening with a few remarks. Now he decided that an army exhibition would be the perfect place to drop the bombshell. He called in his aides and began to issue instructions: "Tell the foreign correspondents I will be delivering an address of worldwide importance at the exhibition tonight.... Be sure announcements are made by Cairo Radio that all listeners should stand by.... I must have two stenographers right away to take down notes of what I wish to say."

A few hours later, just as dusk was settling over the island, he began his speech to a crowd well sprinkled with army officers. In the middle of the address he made the announcement:

"We received an offer from Czechoslovakia showing readiness to supply us with as many weapons as our Army required, on a purely commercial basis, in return for Egyptian products such as cotton and rice, which I accepted with thanks. An agreement was concluded to this effect between Egypt and Czechoslovakia last week."

Reporters made a dash for telephones, typewriters, and the cable office. In a few hours the news was on front pages around the world: COMMUNISTS TO ARM EGYPT. But it had not happened so casually as the Prime Minister intimated. The reasons for it, the way he had manipulated it, are worth studying.

Long after the fact an attempt was made to place entire responsibility for the Czech contract on the deterioration in the previous seven months of the situation on the Egyptian–Israeli frontier. This was intentional oversimplification. From the hour that the Free Officers occupied

G.H.Q. at Abbassia that night in July 1952, the one matter that had concerned Nasser most was the attitude of the young Egyptian army officers toward him and the revolution. This was even more vital than getting British soldiers off Egyptian soil. His only safe, sure following was the Army, not the fellahin soldiers but the officers who controlled them. For more than three years he had been putting young captains, majors, and colonels into high government positions, doing everything that came to his mind to keep the officers loyal to him. But the Army kept clamoring for more and newer weapons. Even without a potential enemy the officers would have demanded the modern arms available in other parts of the world. Perhaps it was too much to expect Colonel Nasser to get hydrogen bombs for them, but the Egyptian Army should have at least the newest types of jet planes, high-velocity tank guns, and other 1955 weapons.

Israel's existence was not the primary reason, but it gave the Egyptian Army an excuse for seeking arms. As long as a peace conference could be avoided, Egyptian officers could point out that a technical state of war still existed, and a country at war naturally needs all the weapons it can get.

Nasser was aware that his army officers were still suffering from a sense of humiliation greater than that felt by any other group of Egyptians. All the insults of invaders and occupiers through the ages had been fatalistically accepted by the fellahin and even by more sophisticated city people. But a professional army—any professional army— needs to be nourished on a continuous recital of its own glorious achievements. The Egyptian Army could remember only that it had failed to protect its King when the British Ambassador arrived at Abdin Palace with a few tanks to make a *coup d'état,* and its 1948 defeat by a small group of Jews, very young and poorly equipped. Since then Egyptians had been told that this could never happen again. Yet such words often had a hollow ring, especially if they were uttered by Nasser after an Israeli force had once more embarrassed the Egyptian Army by crossing the frontier and seizing a Taggart Fort (supposed to be invincible) without meeting any effective resistance. Each time a new military fiasco like the latest Gaza raid occurred, the Army's High Command, starting with Amer, would come to Nasser with demands that he obtain for them the equipment they needed. So to keep the Army happy he had been trying to get new military equipment wherever he could. He had sent military missions to the capital cities of the great powers. But there were two stumbling blocks in dealing with the West.

Britain, France, and the United States had signed a treaty under which they agreed to try to maintain peace in the Middle East by keeping military power there in delicate balance, on the theory that nations equal in strength would not attack each other. This required Washington, London, and Paris to decide how much military equipment to let Egypt and the other countries buy, and all three seemed to agree that Egypt already had enough to balance the strength of her potential Middle Eastern enemies.

The other problem was that the United States Congress had passed a law forbidding the shipment of American weapons to any country that would not permit a certain amount of American control over their use. The purpose was to deter anyone from fomenting aggression and capitalizing on national animosities around the world. But Nasser called these restrictions "strings," and in his fierce desire for complete independence he would sign no agreement with any conditions attached to it, even when it was pointed out to him that there are conditional clauses in almost any contract ever drawn, governmental or commercial.

Members of at least one military mission sent to Washington came back raging over the affronts they felt they had suffered in the Pentagon. They said American army leaders might be ballistics experts but they were inept amateurs at dealing with foreigners. These young Egyptians shared their chief's almost fanatical desire to be regarded as equals by everyone. The mission that returned from Paris was even more choleric. The French, they complained, wanted them to drop all Egyptian interest in freedom for North African Arabs as one of the prices for arms. This they had refused to do.

There was also the Baghdad Pact. The West seemed determined to build Iraq into the strongest of all the Arab nations. Nasser felt he must react to this, or his dream of someday dominating the first of his three circles would fade away before he could even begin to achieve it.

A secret stenographic report of a meeting he called in Cairo of the Prime Ministers of all Arab states to solicit their united opposition to the Baghdad Pact disclosed that in his address to them he made the flat statement: "Egypt alone is superior in strength to Israel." But he knew better. If his statement was true, Amer's strongest argument for needing vast imports of new weapons—an argument that he himself used later in justifying his action—was not valid. If his statement was false, then he was deceiving his fellow Prime Ministers and through them the people of the Arab world.

Nasser was still trying to look both ways at once. Others might be confused by the performance, but he was not. He knew exactly what he was doing. He was playing it by ear, getting ready to take one more calculated risk. Once more he would count on his baraka, his ability to fall and land on his feet.

This was the state of affairs that day in April when the Egyptian delegation boarded an Indian plane for the East. At the third stop, Rangoon, something happened that even men high in the Egyptian Government did not know about until months later. At Rangoon, almost as soon as Nasser met Chou En-lai, he made a decision. Through an interpreter, when no one else was listening, he said, "Mr. Prime Minister, do you think the Russians would agree to sell me arms if I asked them to?"

Chou smiled and replied quickly, "With your permission, Mr. Prime Minister, I will take their pulse on the subject. I do not believe they will refuse."

Upon his return home from Bandung, Nasser found himself the darling of the left. Cairo was full of new pictures: Chou and Nasser, side by side, smiling. Whether he wanted it or not, he had a new source of enthusiastic support.

The Russian Ambassador at Cairo was Daniel Solod, who had lived for years in Lebanon and knew a few tricks of Oriental bargaining. Months before, he had succeeded in pushing the door open a little by negotiating a barter agreement with the Egyptians: machinery and chemicals for cotton and wheat. It is likely he also had something to do with a sizable East German contract—and with the note Moscow had issued early in the year announcing that Russia would not "remain indifferent" if military bases were set up in Arab lands under the Baghdad Pact.

Soon after his return from Bandung, Nasser attended a diplomatic reception at which Solod was present. As soon as he saw the Prime Minister the Russian hurried across the room, greeted him warmly, led him into an empty corner, and said, "Would you be interested in the purchase of arms from the Soviet Union? If so, I would like to inform Moscow at once."

Nasser smiled and thought to himself, "Chou has been busy." Aloud he said, "The suggestion appears to me to be of the greatest interest. I am ready to begin talks with that end in view."

Solod informed Moscow, and the negotiations began, but there were hesitations on each side. Nasser ordered his Ambassadors in both London and Washington to make a final attempt to get arms from the West.

He even authorized them to drop broad hints that such help was available from another source. But neither Washington nor London appeared to believe that it could happen.

Early in July, Nehru stopped off for a few hours in Cairo on a tour of seven countries. He and Nasser issued a joint communiqué against military alliances. Nasser felt this strengthened his hand a little in what he was about to do.

Then Dmitri Shepilov, tall, gangling editor in chief of *Pravda,* arrived in Cairo to attend the third anniversary celebration of the revolution. For five days he was treated as if he were the editor in chief of an important foreign newspaper, but nothing more. He sat in a good seat in the press box one evening, listening to a two-and-a-half-hour speech by the Prime Minister, not one word of which he understood, and the next day he watched a five-hour parade of British, French, and American military equipment that did not seem to impress him. Three days later he went to Alexandria to witness the celebration of the anniversary of Farouk's departure into exile. There he met Ali Sabri, to whom he complained bitterly about his treatment, implying that he had come not to witness parades and listen to speeches, but to deliver an important message to Egypt's head of government, to whom no one had yet introduced him.

Finally, on July 27, he met Nasser. "What I came to tell you," he said, "is that the Soviet Union is ready to give you arms. All the arms you wish."

Day after day there were hints of the surprise Nasser was preparing for the West. In mid-August it was announced that in a few months he would visit Moscow. The same day, it was confirmed that China had placed a "multi-million-dollar order" for cotton.

In August, Cyrus Sulzberger of *The New York Times* had an interview with Nasser, who made some extremely frank statements. Without qualification he declared, "Throughout my life I have had faith in militarism."

A little later he said, "I have read much about socialism, communism, democracy, and fascism. Our revolution will not be labeled by any of these names. We seek to meet the needs and requirements of our own people and we are not trying to copy anybody else's ideology."

About this time he began to be overwhelmed with troubles. Peppery Salah Salem danced his way out of the official family, resigning—or being discharged from—the Cabinet. He had antagonized almost everyone connected with the press. Worse, during the summer he had insulted the Prime Minister of the Sudan, thus making it almost certain that Nasser would fail in his first attempt to create an Egyptian-dominated Arab empire by forming a union of Egypt and the Sudan.

Salah's brother Gamal was on an extended tour of the Far East, and there were reports he might not return.

One day Minister Abdel Latif Baghdady complained, "Why aren't we doing something about keeping our promise to give the people a Constitution?" Nasser rebuked him sharply.

Three other members of the R.C.C. besides Naguib had been dropped, and there were rumors that an anti-Nasser bloc had been formed in several branches of the Army.

Then late in the summer came an Israeli attack on Khan Yunis, in the Gaza Strip, a bloody episode in the bloodiest chapter of the Egyptian-Israeli story.

At the start of the year Nasser, in consultation with Amer, had approved the organization of terrorist bands called *fedayeen* (self-sacrificers). At first there was great secrecy about them, but before long Cairo Radio was instructed to advertise their exploits, for two purposes: to give Egyptians some quasimilitary victories to cheer, and to undermine Israeli morale. Volunteer terrorists were recruited from among the two hundred thousand Arabs crowded together in the Gaza Strip, trained by Egyptian army officers, and sent into action. At first they entered Israel only from the Gaza Strip, but later they were shipped to Jordan, Lebanon, and Syria, so they could infiltrate Israel from all sides. Their aim was to strike deeply into Israeli territory, inflict the maximum possible damage and casualties, stay as long as their ammunition held out, then return with any military information they could obtain.

Early in the year one fedayeen band made an attack within ten miles of Tel Aviv, which gave Cairo Radio the opportunity to broadcast: "Weep, O Israel, because Egypt's Arabs have already found their way to Tel Aviv. The day of extermination draws near. There shall be no more complaints or protests to the United Nations or the Armistice Commission."

In one five-day period there were sixty-four attacks, with twenty-four Israeli citizens killed or wounded. In Egyptian military circles it was hoped that these will-o'-the-wisp raids might succeed in doing what the formal war of 1948 had failed to do: unnerve the Israelis and persuade them to leave the Middle East. Cairo Radio put it bluntly: "There will be no peace on the borders because we demand the death of Israel." Even Nasser himself visited fedayeen headquarters at Khan Yunis several times and addressed the terrorists.

The situation came to a climax at midnight on the last day of August, when Nasser received a telephone call from Amer. The general's voice was tense. "Gamal, the Jews are in Khan Yunis," he said.

Nasser was aware that the fedayeen headquarters were a full five miles inside the frontier.

"I am ready to move the Army in an all-out attack," Amer said.

Nasser hesitated only a second. "Not now, Abdel. Hold it until daylight, and then call me again."

By daylight the attacking force had turned the Taggart Fort into a mass of rubble and killed thirty-five of the Arab defenders. But when Amer called again, Nasser once more vetoed his suggestion for all-out war on Israel. He felt it would be better to wait until they had real superiority of equipment.

But the time had come to give the world a sensation, so he decided to take the final step. First, he gave the American Ambassador one last chance. Calling him personally by telephone, he said, "Either you get action on my request for arms from Washington or I am going to sign a contract with the Russians."

A few days later, just so no one could say there had not been adequate warning, Sabri told reporters, "If in the course of the coming week the Americans do not agree to give us what we are asking for yet again, we shall have to buy armaments from the Communist countries."

The contract was actually signed secretly on Saturday, September 24, 1955. On Monday, Nasser made a telephone call to the American Ambassador and told him what he had done. Later that day, the British Ambassador asked if he could see the Prime Minister, urgently. When he arrived, somewhat distraught, he said he had been told the news by the Americans. "Is it really true?" he asked.

"We have made a purely commercial agreement," Nasser replied.

On Tuesday, he made the public announcement at the military exhibition. Washington reacted quickly. George V. Allen, Deputy Secretary of State for Middle Eastern Affairs, was put on the first available plane for Cairo. When this news was published, Cairo chortled with pleasure. One Egyptian newspaperman said, "In the old days we had to crawl on our bellies to Washington. Now Washington crawls on its belly to us."

While Allen was on his way, Washington listed what it had heard would be in the Czech shipment: two or three hundred MIG-15 jet fighters, twenty-five medium bombers, one to two hundred Stalin tanks, six submarines, and shipload after shipload of smaller matériel.

When Allen arrived he was taken at once to the American Embassy for a briefing. An audience with Nasser was arranged for the next morning. Allen, accompanied by the American Ambassador, arrived a little before the appointed time. They waited half an hour and then asked if the Prime Minister had been told they were there. He had been. They waited an hour and asked a secretary if some error had been made. No error had been made. "The Prime Minister is aware that you are here," he said.

It was an hour and a half before they were admitted. Several different accounts were later given to reporters to explain the delay. The Embassy said the Prime Minister had been waiting for clarification from his own representative at the United Nations in New York of some point involved in the controversy. Allen later explained that his trip was not about the Czech arms shipments at all. Others said the delayed appointment had been due to "a misunderstanding."

Four years afterward the Egyptian official who had handled the situation for the Prime Minister declared, "This is one subject on which we and we alone are competent to comment, for no one else in the world knows why we did something except we ourselves. We kept Mr. Allen waiting because we had heard he was bringing from Washington an indignant letter and that he intended to bang the table and give us a lecture. We kept him waiting to cool him off. We kept him waiting until he agreed not to present the note he had been sent to deliver."

Whatever the reason, the result was that the personal representative of the President of the United States was held up to embarrassment in the eyes of the world. Egypt had waited many centuries to humiliate so powerful a nation publicly. The Czech contract was signed now, and she could be supremely and even arrogantly independent, if she pleased. Or so she thought. The Allen trip convinced Nasser, his advisers, and the Arab public that the West was panicky. This caused delight in a large part of the Middle East.

Nasser was the hero of the Arab world now. People were paying hard-earned money for copies of his picture in the shops of Amman, Beirut, Damascus, even Baghdad. This almost universal Arab reaction demonstrated the hunger of these people for what Nasser kept calling "dignity." Perhaps that is not exactly the correct word. They seemed to want to hit back at whoever had made them feel inferior.

In their excitement they convinced themselves that shortly all their problems would vanish. Palestine would be reoccupied by Arabs. The Jews would disappear. The simpler Arabs even believed that somehow this would mean more food, better housing, good clothes, and salvation for everyone. So they loudly cheered Gamal Abdel Nasser and Czecho-slovakia, a country few of them had ever heard of.

What actually happened was that the Russians decided to take quick advantage of the fact that the door to the Middle East was now partly open. Through it they began to pour not only experts to supervise the use of Czech weapons, but all the aids needed for an economic, cultural, and political penetration.

East Germany, Poland, Czechoslovakia, Romania, Hungary, Bulgaria, China, and Russia began to compete for the favors of Egypt and the rest of the Middle East. They sent ballet troupes, folk dancers, opera companies, and vocalists to give the Middle East a taste of European culture. They filled bookshops with volumes in Arabic, English, French, and Italian, beautifully illustrated and selling for a fraction of the cost of production; everything from a Chinese version of "Cinderella" to Gorki, Hemingway, and Jack London. They sent feature-length films and documentaries for use, without cost, by groups interested in self-education.

East Germany won a contract to build a bridge over the Nile. Russia would build Egypt's first nuclear laboratory. China became the largest purchaser of cotton. Almost every day there was an announcement of another commercial contract signed with an Eastern European nation or China, at prices generally only three quarters of the competing Western bids. Before this there had been only the local Communist parties, neither large nor effectual, and compelled to operate *sub rosa*. But now it was all right to have a Communist bookshop on Kasr el Nil, to show Russian films in the Rialto, and put up Skoda signs in the Midan el Tahrir.

The fever began to spread. Crown Prince Faisal of Saudi Arabia announced that Russia had offered arms to his country, too. The Prime Minister of Lebanon said he hoped to trade citrus fruit for Czech guns. Each day in Cairo Ambassador Solod was seeing the ambassador of some Arab country with outstretched hands. The Secretary of the Arab League said he saw no difference between oranges and ammunition. "Oranges are purchased where the price is right and the taste is the best."

But Nasser himself was not entirely pleased with the consequences of his action. He was worried. This was hardly the neutralism Nehru had advised. Actually, he had never intended opening the door so wide. Also, he had underestimated the anger with which the West would react.

His arms-exhibition speech had not been specific about the kind of equipment Egypt was getting, but before many weeks ships began to arrive at Alexandria with the first consignments, carefully concealed in wooden crates. One day a reporter from New York asked him about 138 immense boxes he had seen at Alexandria.

"Everybody wants to know what's in those hundred and thirty-eight boxes," Nasser said, enjoying himself. "But only a few of us know, and nobody else is going to know. For the first time in history the Egyptian Army has secrets."

About this time four members of the U.S. Senate Appropriations Committee on a junket arrived in Cairo and had an hour-and-a-half talk with the Prime Minister. As they were leaving his office, accompanied by the American Ambassador, a dwarf, Sheikh Ahmed Salem, who had the reputation of being the smallest sheikh in the world, accosted them and shook a money box in their faces. The four Senators made contributions. The Ambassador turned his pockets inside out to prove that he was temporarily without cash funds.

The next day, the Cairo papers had a field day. They thanked the Americans for their generosity and this unmistakable proof that they really did support Prime Minister Nasser's military plans, for this was Armament Week and Egypt was raising by voluntary contributions, such as the four Senators had just made, a million dollars to pay to the Czech Government as the first installment on the armament bill.

The American Embassy in Cairo called a hasty press conference to explain that the Senators thought they were contributing to the support of the dwarf's family, that they were not even aware this was Armament Week. Privately Nasser was amused.

One evening during this period a government announcer over Cairo Radio said, "American democracy leaves the capitalists free to rule the country, while the masses chase dollars and watch baseball. The Soviet Union is a true democracy, in which the rulers are chosen by the people through the Communist party."

CHAPTER 17

APPOINTMENT WITH DESTINY

Hours before the train from Suez was due to arrive, workmen in the Cairo railroad depot began to spread an immense red carpet along the platform and all the way out to the street. Nasser had ordered that no expense be spared, no courtesy overlooked to show Egypt's distinguished visitor the country's friendly feeling for him.

At Suez, Marshal Tito, on his way home from a visit to Haile Selassie in Abyssinia, left the Yugoslav naval vessel on which he had been traveling and boarded the train for Cairo. Waiting to meet him at the capital depot were his wife Jovanka, who had arrived several days earlier with a Yugoslav team for an international basketball tournament, and Nasser, who greeted him with an enthusiastic embrace. They drove in an open car through streets lined with men, women, and children waving small Yugoslav and Egyptian flags, throwing confetti that had been given to them for that purpose, and shouting Tito's name almost as excitedly as Nasser's.

During the next nine days the marshal and the colonel talked together for innumerable hours. Their countries had one important mutual problem: how to remain uncommitted to either East or West while collecting all the material help they could from whoever would give it. There was an ironic aspect to the friendship that was developing between them. Tito, though he might disagree with Moscow's Cominform tactics, was a doctrinaire Communist. Nasser, who was still successfully avoiding the adoption of any specific ideology, rarely let a week go by without ordering the arrest, imprisonment, and sometimes severe punishment of Egyptian Communist party members. At the time of Tito's visit a list was being compiled by the government, on Nasser's order, of 150 newspapermen—from reporters to editors in chief—who would be deprived of their right ever to work again as journalists because they were suspected of harboring sympathy for either communism or, equally *lèse-majesté*, the democratic political parties that had been outlawed. Yet for Tito, one of the most thoroughgoing Communists in the world, Nasser had ordered the unrolling of the largest red carpet in Egypt.

213

They flew together to Aswan, the Communist who wanted to stay clear of the East's domination and the anti-Communist who wanted to stay clear of the West's domination. There they inspected the site of the dam that Nasser told Tito was going to be for him what the Great Pyramid was for Cheops. "This is my dream," he said, and they both stared at the spot in the river that might someday be filled with millions of tons of concrete. The Yugoslav seemed impressed.

The idea of constructing a barrage across the Nile many times larger than the one the British had built years ago, just a few miles away, was not his own, Nasser said. This new dam, the Aswan High Dam, had been planned in the days of Farouk. But it would be built in the days of Nasser. About this he was determined. His publicity advisers had suggested a slogan: *Seventeen times larger than the greatest pyramid.* Figured in some ways, this was not an exaggeration. It was a slogan to make anyone proud: the actual builders, the head of state who would someday get credit for it, or the people who might have to go hungrier than usual for years to pay for it. Seventeen times larger than the greatest pyramid! That would assure a man his place in history for perhaps another five thousand years.

He admitted to Tito that it would cost a fortune, even for a wealthy country. It would cost each Egyptian fellah and his family all of their income for ten years. But it would not have to be paid for in ten years. There were two countries in the world rich enough to do the financing over a long period at bargain rates of interest, if they wished: the Soviet Union and the United States. At the moment, both seemed willing. But Nasser and Tito agreed that the Russian offer ought to be used only as a bargaining device, for the money should come from America; Egypt was already committed enough in the other direction. It would be poor strategy to permit Russia to get control of the country's principal economic development, after making the Egyptian Army dependent upon her for spare parts for most of its new weapons.

Some of his advisers, Nasser said, had been afraid that acceptance of the Czech-Russian arms would so antagonize the West that Egypt would be forced into a marriage with the East instead of a spring flirtation. His own premonition had been sounder. As he had expected, the West now was ready to prove that the democracies could provide cheaper, better assistance than the people's republics of the East. It looked as if an infallible formula had been evolved. Egypt could probably play the United States against Russia indefinitely.

The hot, dusty town of Aswan was festooned with eucalyptus leaves and crossed Egyptian and Yugoslav flags. There were triumphal arches, set up for the occasion, and the crowds, well coached, were chanting a few Yugoslav words. Tito seemed to be enjoying himself.

When the visit was over, at the end of ten days, Nasser went to Alexandria to see his guest off. As Tito said good-by he reminded his host, "Do not forget to follow the example of India, Burma, and Yugoslavia." Nasser said he would remember.

Tito left Egypt with a favorable opinion of her young leader. He said so in a radio broadcast after his ship was well out on the Mediterranean, praising Nasser especially for his independence.

The next day, Soviet Ambassador Solod came to say good-by. He had been recalled to Moscow. For two hours he talked to Nasser about how the Soviet Union and Egypt together would eliminate every trace of Western influence from this part of the world. When reporters asked him on his way out what he and Nasser had discussed for so long, he smiled and said enigmatically, "Time has no value when friends meet."

Little more than a week later, on the evening of January 17, 1956, Republic Square was packed with a waiting throng. Three years before that day, with the approval of the R.C.C., Nasser had suspended the old Constitution. Since then Egypt had been ruled by an undisguised dictatorship. Now, to this great mass of people, he announced that the legal minds of the R.C.C. regime had written a new Constitution for them. Voters would be called upon to approve it or reject it by secret ballot in June. At the same time, a President would be elected for the next six years.

"The true revolution begins today," Nasser proclaimed. "The whole people will constitute a supreme council for the revolution."

"Long live Gamal!" shouted the crowd.

The new Constitution declared that Egypt would be a welfare state, with a one-party political system. Elections for a national legislature would take place at an unspecified future date. Meanwhile the new President would rule the country. All parties except the government-sponsored National Union were still banned. The Constitution stated that the new Egypt would be an Islamic, Arab state. This was a hint that the Egyptians might soon, under the leadership of Nasser, set out to dominate the first circle he had described in *The Philosophy of the Revolution:* the conglomerate world of the Arabs.

The new Constitution led to fresh trouble with Doria Shawfik, the feminist. She was not satisfied with the prospect of Egyptian women voting for the first time in June. "Why is there no provision for women to hold government positions?" she demanded. Then she threatened that her organization, the Daughters of the Nile, would cause trouble unless the Constitution was amended.

Some British and American reporters were using Doria Shawfik in an attempt to embarrass him and the regime, and Nasser knew it. The official government newspaper called her "the perfumed and soft feminist, motivated exclusively by an interest in self-glorification and not at all interested in the ordinary women of Egypt," and the censors had orders that none of her criticism of the government was to be published inside the country.

But minor annoyances were forgotten in the surge of important events. For weeks Eugene Black, President of the International Bank for Reconstruction and Development, conferred in Cairo with Nasser. The American banker indicated that his country would lend two hundred million dollars to start building the dam. This would be only one sixth the total cost, but it would commit the United States.

There had also been two visits by Selwyn Lloyd, the British Foreign Secretary. He arrived the first time soon after the Czech arms deal became known, to promise that British arms would start flowing at once to Egypt again, and then he suggested a compromise on the Baghdad Pact: Britain would not attempt to enlist additional Arab members, while in turn Egypt would cease her anti-British propaganda. To this both he and Nasser agreed.

However, a few weeks later a British general appeared in Amman, the capital of Jordan, on an important mission: to negotiate Jordan's adherence to the Baghdad Pact.

But Nasser got even. Months passed, then Lloyd came to Cairo again. He was treated with stiff politeness. A formal dinner party was given for him at Abdin Palace, during which he offended many of the Egyptians present because they felt he was lecturing them as if they were schoolboys. At one point the question of Britain's strength in the Middle East arose.

"Remember," Lloyd admonished them, with what the Egyptians interpreted as pomposity, "we still have Glubb Pasha in Jordan."

There was a long silence, finally broken by the quiet voice of Nasser saying, "You *had* Glubb Pasha, Mr. Secretary. May I inform you that Glubb was removed from office just before we came in to dinner."

It was true. Lieutenant General Sir John Bagot Glubb was an English army officer who spoke Arabic fluently, dressed like a Bedouin tribesman, had organized the Arab Legion, and liked to be called by his acquired title, Glubb Pasha. That afternoon, he had been called in by King Hussein's Prime Minister and given two hours to leave the country he loved perhaps as well as his own.

Glubb's removal pleased Nasser. Although he gave Glubb credit for certain military victories against the Israelis in 1948 he blamed him for losing the New City of Jerusalem and for not coming to the Egyptians' assistance when they were hard pressed in the Negev.

After Lloyd left, an Arab Big Three Conference was held: King Saud of Saudia Arabia, President Shukri el Kuwatly of Syria, and Nasser, who presided. The three leaders and their advisers sat around a massive octagonal table at Kubbah Palace for eight hours a day, six days in a row, discussing mutual defense problems and hammering out agreements that were carefully lettered and then bound into a great green leather book and affixed with many red seals and signatures. Nasser persuaded Kuwatly and Saud to sign a pledge with him: "We hereby declare our determination to safeguard the Arab world against the evils of the Cold War by keeping away from its diverse currents and also by adopting an unbiased policy toward it."

This was a victory for the neutralism that he was convinced was the key to a happy future for Egypt and her neighbors. It was also a personal triumph for him. He was emerging as the leader of neutralist Arabia.

Several days later French Foreign Minister Christian Pineau arrived in Cairo. Even this meeting was fruitful, for Pineau agreed that France would never join the Baghdad Pact, promised elections in Algeria, and made some concessions about reducing the supply of arms to Israel.

Every day new and favorable developments proved to Nasser that he was wise to play East against West. From Moscow suddenly came an offer to set up an atomic reactor on Egyptian soil, supply the required uranium, and introduce young Egyptian scientists to the nuclear age.

In April, during an interview with a New York reporter, Nasser said, "I have in my pocket a Soviet offer to help finance the Aswan Dam and I will consider accepting it if there is any breakdown in negotiations with Washington." He was operating from strength now, and wanted the American people to know it. He also used the interview as an excuse to lecture the West.

"You Americans are concentrating on military bases. With atomic and hydrogen bombs these bases will be useless. . . . You can have your military bases but around each one of them there are thousands of nationalistic bases and the Communists are winning them one by one.

Do you not look at the map of the world and wonder why the Soviets are winning this war . . . ? The Russians are very clever. They know what I want to say and they please me by saying what I want to say before I say it myself. . . . They have taken all the nationalists' slogans and made them their own."

In the middle of May he persuaded the R.C.C. to approve a bold step, which he was cautioned might have serious international complications: recognition of Communist China. At the same time, he announced a spectacular barter agreement: forty-five thousand tons of Egyptian cotton for sixty thousand tons of Chinese steel.

It took six days for any real reaction from Washington, then Secretary Dulles issued a rebuff, but a much milder one than Nasser had expected. It was quickly followed by a conciliatory statement from President Eisenhower: "We think Egypt is mistaken in recognizing Communist China, but a single unwelcome act by another nation should not destroy friendship for that nation any more than spats within a family should lead to the divorce court."

He answered Eisenhower by announcing that he would soon visit Peiping, that he had invited Chou En-lai to attend the revolution's third anniversary celebration, and that he had accepted an invitation to send Defense Minister Amer to China for military conferences.

Several days later he permitted publication of the real secret of the recognition of China under the by-line of his friend, Major Shaker, now director general of *Al Gomhouria,* the government-owned daily newspaper. It had been a step to outwit British Prime Minister Anthony Eden, who had obtained agreement in principle from the Soviet Union for setting up machinery to stop a Middle East arms race. This, Shaker wrote, would be like "tying a noose around the neck of the Arab states." But now "Nasser has put Eden's noose around Eden's own neck. People's China is the biggest producer of armaments at present, and can supply the Arabs with all the war matériel they need," he declared.

Because she was not a member of the United Nations, Communist China would not be bound by any embargo agreement. Thus Egypt, by recognizing the Peiping government, was assured a free flow of arms, whatever happened. This was playing a third side of the street, and it caused some sharp outcries. French Defense Minister Bourgès-Maunoury said, "Nasser is a dictator desirous of camouflaging the misery of his people by launching an expansionist venture composed of fanaticism and obscurantism."

No one had ever used such strong words about him before, but Nasser was not perturbed, for he felt that they were indirectly a tribute to the success of his diplomatic maneuver.

About a week later he turned his attention to domestic affairs again. In a three-hour speech he tried to generate enthusiasm for the new Constitution. He reiterated to the crowd that no trace of military rule would be left after the Constitution went into effect. The R.C.C. would vanish. All its members but one would go back to being army officers. The crowd knew who the exception would be and cheered. He made it clear that he would have no opposition for the presidency. Voting would be compulsory for all males over eighteen, with a heavy fine for any man who failed to cast a ballot. For all females over eighteen voting would be possible for the first time in Egypt's history, but optional.

Early in June 1956 Dmitri Shepilov, who had been merely the editor of *Pravda* when he first visited Egypt the year before, suddenly was named Soviet Foreign Minister. He was received with high honors when he arrived two weeks later at Cairo airport with his twenty-year-old daughter and three aides to attend one of the most important celebrations the Egyptians had ever held. On his arrival he issued a statement meant to flatter Egypt and his host personally: "The Soviet Union looks on the people of the Arab countries as brothers."

Nasser and Shepilov held one conference after another for two days. On Saturday it was arranged for word to leak out that they were talking chiefly about the Aswan Dam. Also that Shepilov had discussed with the Minister of Trade and Commerce a great catalogue of goods Russia was willing to supply in return for more Egyptian cotton. The Saturday conference continued until almost dawn Sunday. After a short nap they began again. When Sunday's four-hour session terminated, reporters were told unofficially that the Soviet Union had offered to lend Egypt almost the entire billion and a quarter dollars the dam would cost, at a very low rate of interest, for many years.

Early on Monday, Nasser took the big Russian to visit a model village on the Nile built with some of the confiscated Farouk fortune. That day, as a gesture to impress Shepilov, six hundred political prisoners, including many Communists, were ordered released.

Later in the morning the two men flew to Port Said, where Egyptians were preparing to celebrate the departure of the last British soldier from their soil. The Russian Foreign Minister had been invited to join in cheering this defeat of Western colonialism. But the British had found a way to avoid the embarrassment of departing with the taunts of Egyptian mobs ringing in their ears. Instead of turning over the keys of their headquarters to Prime Minister Nasser or Defense Minister Amer at this public ceremony on Monday, June 18, the announced date of departure, they had shipped out their last soldier five days ahead of schedule. Quietly, without any ceremony that might have lionized Nasser, they turned over the keys to an Egyptian second lieutenant. They did it too suddenly for Cairo to change the celebration plans, so for a few days Egypt had been free, while pretending that she wasn't. But now, on Monday, the formal thanksgiving was under way.

By the time Nasser and Shepilov, in an open car, had traveled through the hysterical crowds packing the streets between the airport and the center of town, the Russian, perspiring under the blistering sun, looked somewhat disheveled. "It is worse for me than you," he shouted to his host above the din of the mob. "I'm not accustomed to such heat."

But Nasser was exultant. When they arrived at Navy House, he kissed the Egyptian flag and raised it over this building that had been head-quarters of the powerful British naval base at Suez.

"Oh, compatriots, this is the most memorable moment of a lifetime," he cried. "This generation of Egyptian people has an appointment with destiny. This generation is privileged to see with its own eyes the remnants of the foreign invaders sneak out, back to where they came from."

The next day, Cairo had its celebration. Instead of looking down into tens of thousands of perspiring faces, as at Port Said, Nasser was look-ing at hundreds of thousands of people who seemed oblivious to the suffocating heat as they wedged themselves tighter and tighter into the square outside Abdin Palace. They stood with upturned faces for two hours listening to him speak.

"Today," he told them, "not a single foreign flag flies over Egyptian soil. For the first time in centuries we are completely free to fight for our own destiny. Today marks the start of a new era. . . ."

He announced that martial law, in effect since the revolution, was now finally lifted. The crowd applauded wildly. He declared that all political prisoners held on a charge of plotting against the revolution had been freed. He even admitted that at one time there had been as many as three thousand such enemies of the regime in prison.

"Our policy is frank," he declared. "We shall co-operate with anybody or any country ready to co-operate with us . . ." And he smiled at Shepilov, sitting in the front row on the platform.

On Wednesday, the last of the three new legal holidays, Nasser stood in a green-canopied reviewing stand and took the salute of the Army.

For four hours war machines rumbled past: new Stalin tanks, MIG jet fighters, Iluyshin twin bombers, six-wheel Russian troop carriers, flame-throwers, light and heavy artillery, Czech T-36 tanks, chewing up the asphalt, filling the sky with thunder, making the air seem even more stifling. Collars were wilted. A man in the reviewing stand fainted. But for four hours Nasser and Amer stood side by side, most of the time stiffly at attention.

Interspersed with all the war matériel from the East were token forces from each of the neighboring Arab countries except Iraq. Jordan had sent a detachment of its Arab Legion; Lebanon some ski troops; Yemen a group of cadets; Libya, the Sudan, Saudi Arabia, and Syria regular army units.

Everyone seemed impressed by the display of Egypt's new military strength, correspondents and diplomats, Egyptians and foreigners alike. It was intoxicating, especially for men whose business had always been soldiering. Even more intoxicating was the knowledge that Egypt was free and that powerful nations were competing for her favor.

Apparently he could have as much as he wanted of anything from the East. A three-year contract had been signed with East Germany: heavy goods in exchange for cotton. Russia and many of the other Communist countries were willing to send him all the technicians he needed. One hundred tons of small arms had arrived from China. Four minesweepers made in Poland had been delivered. Czech military matériel was coming in by the shipload. Nineteen torpedo boats had been received. Poland had agreed to train five hundred Egyptian naval officers. Czechoslovakia was to build rubber and cement plants; Hungary seven bridges; East Germany a shipyard, chemical plant, sugar refinery, automobile factory, and power stations; Bulgaria plants to process oil and preserve food.

In the West, Sweden had decided to resume arms shipments to Egypt, although not to Israel. France was delivering machine guns, artillery pieces, mortars, tanks, and jet fighters again, on a ten-million-dollar order, despite the fear of French politicians that some of the weapons might find their way to Algeria and be used against France herself some-day. Nearly two hundred Valentine tanks had arrived from Britain by way of Belgium, with more reconditioned British war machinery on the way. Canada had lifted her arms embargo and begun shipping trainer planes in quantity. The United States had already given Egypt more than sixty million dollars' worth of economic and technical aid, but through the Egyptian Embassy, Washington was informed that this was not much, compared with what the East was doing.

There had been other, less material triumphs. The Aga Khan had made a small but symbolically important contribution to the armament fund. Invitations had been received for official visits to fourteen foreign countries, including most of the Eastern bloc. There was even a plan to travel to Rome to have an audience with the Pope. The Soviet Union was opening in Port Said its first consulate outside Cairo. One day Czechoslovakia sent him a personal gift of a two-engine, five-place plane, and a short time later from Moscow came an Iluyshin-14, exactly the type of plane Khrushchev used.

Tomorrow Shepilov would be leaving. But almost immediately someone else would take his place at the conference table. Eugene Black would be landing in Cairo again in a few hours, and he urgently wanted to see the Prime Minister. The system of noncommittal was working better and better.

The day after tomorrow Egypt would go to the polls, and if all went well only a tiny fraction of the population would vote against him for President, or against the adoption of the Constitution.

Then, next month, he would go off to Yugoslavia for a conference with Nehru and Tito.

There was nothing that hot June afternoon to disturb the thoughts of an Egyptian nationalist.

CHAPTER 18

FLOWER POTS AND TRICYCLES

On June 23, 1956, more than five million Egyptians went to the polls to elect a President—for the first time in the country's long history. There was only one candidate, Gamal Abdel Nasser. Voters were permitted to indicate merely whether they approved of him (by marking a red circle) or disapproved (by marking a black circle). They were also given the privilege of indicating whether they accepted or rejected the Constitution. There was no other alternative here, either. That night when the ballots were counted, it was found that Nasser had received 99.948 per cent of the votes. Only about two thousand men and women had marked the black circle. The Constitution did not fare so well. The percentage in favor of it was only 99.8.

The Arabic expression for President is *El Rayis*. From now on Gamal Abdel Nasser would be formally addressed as El Rayis, Mr. President, the highest title in the land. But in colloquial Arabic this same word, given a slightly different intonation, *El Rayiis,* is the equivalent of "boss." It is used for the foreman of a gang of laborers, the headwaiter in a restaurant, the editor of a newspaper, the desk sergeant in a police station, the conductor of an orchestra—generally with affection. An Egyptian wife will call her husband the Boss, behind his back as well as to his face. So Nasser now became both El Rayis and El Rayiis. When Tahia talks about him to a stranger she refers to him as Mr. President, but to Heikal, Amer, or some other intimate friend of the family she speaks of him not as Gamal but as the Boss.

Egypt's boss is unlike any other military dictator the world has ever known. His foreign critics often compare him to Hitler or Mussolini, yet he has none of the personal qualities of either. He and his family live in the house at Manchiet el Bakry with almost no ostentation. They have a gardener, a nursemaid, and a combination cook, butler, and upstairs maid. This is normal for a middle-class family of seven people in Egypt. There are two other servants, government-paid, who serve in the rooms the President uses in his official capacity. When Nasser travels on government business he rides in one of the two black government-owned Cadillacs available to him. He never uses them for personal trips. His small black Austin fell apart two years after the revolution, and he bought, on time, a pistachio-colored Ford.

Because Farouk spent so much of his life in public places of amusement, Nasser avoids them. The Semiramis Hotel has a roof garden, with potted palms, flower boxes, soft music, and a splendid view of the Nile. It is one of the pleasantest places in Cairo to relax on a hot summer night, and a corner of it was always reserved for the King. Years after Farouk was exiled, a reception was held there for Archbishop Makarios. Nasser, in his eagerness to pay his respects to the leader of Cypriot nationalism, overlooked his own rule and accepted an invitation. Upon his arrival, as he stepped out of the elevator and walked onto the roof garden he exclaimed, "Why didn't anyone ever tell me how beautiful it is up here?"

On the road to the pyramids are many night clubs, some expensive. Ministers and top officials avoid such places, unless they wish to incur the wrath of El Rayis. He is even stricter about the wives of his colleagues, for he remembers the gossip about the wives of government leaders in previous regimes. Accordingly, Tahia and Ministers' wives avoid tearooms like Groppi's and the salons of the large hotels, and entertain simply in their own homes.

Nasser is unrelenting in his insistence that top government officials be scrupulously honest. They may have as many phones and buzzers as they wish in their homes and offices, as well as air conditioning and Cadillacs to ride to work in, and they may go abroad on official junkets, but their bank accounts must be open for inspection and they must avoid any suspicion of engaging in the sort of corruption that made the Egyptian people so cynical about pre-revolutionary politicians. He has several times dismissed top officials who violated these rules.

His house at Manchiet el Bakry has been enlarged twice, partly because there are five children (the youngest, Hakim, named after Amer, was born in January 1955) and partly because it has become the place where he does all his work and receives official visitors. After the two additions and some expert landscaping it is still no more pretentious than the suburban home of the vice-president of a small bank almost anywhere in America. The house is guarded day and night by six soldiers in uniform. Inside are two aides in civilian clothes, on duty during all of his waking hours. There are also several plain-clothes guards, who are seldom seen.

The visitor goes through a gate into a small courtyard. To the left is a private tennis court, and to the right a newly built stone structure housing Nasser's archives and library. The front of the main house is banked with three hundred pots of flowering plants, in three rows of varying heights. The pots are changed as fast as the flowers stop blooming.

Stories have been published that the house is floodlighted as a protection against possible assassins. This is not true. Scattered around the grounds are six concrete pedestals, each fitted with an ornamental light. These are kept lighted as long as guests are present, which is often until 3 or 4 A.M.

Behind the house is an extensive lawn lined with trees. In a far corner under the largest tree are several chairs, a table, and a stone pedestal. Here on pleasant summer days Nasser often works, with a portable telephone plugged into a connection in the pedestal.

One of the government-paid servants takes the visitor's hat as he enters the hall and shows him into a salon almost twenty feet square. At the far side is a red brick and black marble fireplace. On the mantel are eight autographed photographs in heavy silver frames, of former President Shukri el Kuwatly of Syria, President Sukarno of Indonesia, Prime Minister Nehru of India, Haile Selassie, Tito, Chou En-lai, President Romulo Betancourt of Venezuela, and President Rajendra Prasad of India. To the right, on a marble-top commode, stands a framed photograph of Prime Minister Nkrumah of Ghana, too large to fit on the mantel. These nine men are Nasser's favorite political personages in the outside world. On the wall over the fireplace hangs a four-by-five-foot oil painting of two peasant children, presented to him by the Spanish Government. On another wall is a conventional painting of a flock of chickens.

The furniture is arranged with mathematical precision. In front of the fireplace are two large baroque chairs facing each other, with a small coffee table between them. Here Nasser has his formal conversations with visiting foreign dignitaries. At the opposite end of the room is a suite of imitation Louis XIV gilded furniture: a sofa and half a dozen fragile chairs upholstered in heavy, flowered brocade, and three small tables. Several years ago El Rayis lost his temper over an article in an American magazine that said the gilded furniture had come out of one of Farouk's palaces. As head of state he had a right to occupy one of the palaces, or to move as much furniture as he wished into his government-owned house, but he actually had paid for this gilded suite himself. On his order every page of the offending article was cut with scissors from every copy of the magazine that arrived in Egypt. Hanging from the salon ceiling is a large crystal chandelier. Like gilded furniture, this is a symbol of elegance that most middle-class Cairo housewives hope their husbands will someday be rich enough to buy for them. There are two large Oriental rugs on the floor and a prayer rug of rich blues and reds in front of the fireplace. The walls are pale gray, the ceiling white. The windows are screened, unusual in Egypt even in homes of the wealthy, and the entire house is equipped with central heating and air conditioning.

In the salon the President receives Ambassadors, Ministers, foreign correspondents, and other visitors from abroad. Some bring their own interpreters. They come with gifts, questions, demands, or offers of help. Many arrive with a polite skepticism about their host and his ideas, but his charm generally disarms them. Photographs of him and his guests are always taken in front of the fireplace, so the Spanish painting has become one of the most frequently photographed works of art in the world.

Several of his associates from R.C.C. days who are still members of the Cabinet have built homes in suburban Cairo that look like intentional replicas of the home of El Rayis: the same gilded furniture, Oriental rugs, porcelain angels, cupids and bric-a-brac, except that in their homes there is always a three- or four-foot-square color photograph or painting of Nasser, and on the opposite salon wall, of equal size, a color photograph or painting of the aide.

Two windows of Nasser's salon look out onto a stone-paved terrace, where there is a ping-pong table, now covered with an American electric train. On the lawn are two red tricycles on their sides, close together, as if their owners had just met in a head-on collision and left to have their injuries bandaged.

At the opposite end of the hall from the salon is Nasser's office. This is a restricted area, where servants, guests, members of the family, and even close friends are rarely permitted. The far wall is of glass brick. In front of it is a seven-foot desk covered with piles of letters, government reports, magazines, and newspapers in well-arranged disorder. On one corner is a pile of notebooks in which, over the years, he has recorded his impressions of people, events, and issues. Beside the desk is an all-white switchboard with eleven outlets. By half turning in his chair and flicking a button he can connect himself with an operator or with the ten most important men in the country. If their offices are closed, their telephones ring at home. Also within reach of the desk are a seven-foot safe, an American dictating machine, and the most powerful radio receiver in Egypt. Office decorations include a Swiss clock showing the time anywhere in the world, a picture of him made from mother-of-pearl, the original painting for a 1955 cover of *Time* by Giro. Near the desk is a large sofa. Here he sits when he confers with close associates. Within his reach are three buttons. One calls a servant, the second his secretary. Few except Nasser himself know the purpose of the third buzzer.

The family's bedrooms originally were behind the hall and office. When a second story was added, they were converted into a library, a ladies' salon where Tahia can entertain her friends, and a dining room. In Nasser's upstairs sleeping room there are three telephones and a powerful radio.

He normally gets up at 7 A.M., bathes and shaves, then breakfasts alone on tea, white cheese, a bowl of bread and milk, and a dish of *ful,* the native peasant dish of beans. He lingers a long time over the meal because this is when he reads three Cairo morning newspapers, partly to find out what has been happening, partly to decide whether the editors and censors did their job well. If not, they will soon hear about it. Then he walks the few feet from dining room to office, where he spends the next four hours reading his Ministers' reports, his Ambassadors' cables, and whatever mail his private secretary thinks he should see. While he is on the telephone he has a habit of making designs on his calendar pad. A scrutiny of these pads for four years shows certain ones repeated over and over again:

During the morning his aides do a great deal of running back and forth between his office and a two-story secretariat building across the road. This is headquarters for his two private secretaries; each works a ten-hour shift, so that there are only a few hours just before daylight when neither is on duty. They are assisted by four stenographers. All six are male. Ordinary letters from abroad are routed directly to the former R.C.C. headquarters on Gezira Island. Two or three thousand letters addressed to President Nasser personally are received each day, about half from the United States and many from Communist countries. They are answered by a staff of sixty-two men, mostly ex-army officers, and two women, who can read and write almost every language in the world. In the island house a former army sergeant sits at a desk for ten hours a day writing Nasser's name on Nasser photographs, sometimes a thousand in a single day. He was chosen because his handwriting resembles the President's. The staff also mails out biographies of Nasser, free copies of *The Philosophy of the Revolution,* postage stamps to philatelists, and even dolls requested by collectors. The stationery used is embossed in one corner with a seal of the country and bears across the top in flowing red Arabic letters the words "In the Name of Allah the Merciful."

Colonel Amin Shaker, in charge of the letter-answerers, selects about ten communications a day to show to Nasser, either because they are amusing, difficult to answer, or significant. In 1959 a woman teacher in Upper Egypt who was having a feud with the female principal wrote:

> She is giving me the hardest time, because she very much wants to get married and I have a relative, a man, who is also unmarried, and the principal asked me to arrange it so he would marry her. I asked him but he was not interested. Because of my failure she has moved my class into a narrow corridor, which is very humiliating to me, so I am writing to you, El Rayis, to come to my help before I go crazy.

Nasser never dictates letters. He gives a secretary verbally in Arabic a general idea of what he wants to say. The secretary then writes the letter in the language of the addressee.

At noon lunch is announced. During the next hour and a half Tahia has her husband to herself. Telephone calls are forbidden, the children are having their lunch at school, and the house is deserted except for servants. The midday meal consists mainly of vegetables and cheese, seldom any meat. If they linger over it long enough, the children may come bouncing home from school and say hello to their father before going out to play.

After lunch Nasser reads the day's batch of newspapers from other cities of the Arab world. This may take two hours. Then he sleeps until 5 P.M., when his real workday begins. For the next eight or nine hours he holds one conference after another, with his Ministers, with diplomats stationed in Cairo, with domestic and foreign reporters. He likes to put off interviews with foreigners until as late in the day as possible, because the later the hour the better able he feels to match his wits with theirs. At 8 P.M. Tahia has dinner with the children, who may, if their father has no guests, quietly steal in to say good night. Nasser himself has his final meal at midnight: highly salted white cheese and bread, served on a tray in his office.

Many foreigners arrive in Cairo with the assurance of some Egyptian Ambassador that they will be able to see President Nasser. Often they are kept waiting in their hotel rooms for weeks or months. The theory is that the majority will become discouraged and leave. Those with enough fortitude to remain are often rewarded. H. V. Kaltenborn played tennis in Cairo for six weeks before he was given an interview. Others have waited longer.

During the first few minutes of a visitor's conference a servant appears with two cups of sirupy Turkish coffee. If the conference lasts more than fifteen minutes, which is unusual, fruit juice is served. Nasser may drink ten to twenty cups of coffee and a few glasses of fruit juice in an evening.

Guests find him a patient listener. He often leans forward as if eager not to miss a word of the conversation. His normal expression in the presence of visitors is compounded of timidity, restlessness, surprise, youthful frankness, disarming innocence. Dominating all other emotions is his almost fanatical determination not to be humiliated or victimized. He has an uncanny ability to get his guests to speak their minds, even when they would rather not. He not only allows but encourages them to ask embarrassing questions. A former American Ambassador who took many people to see him reported that on the way back to the Embassy they would often say, as if surprised by their daring, "Did you hear what I said to him?"

From all the films he watches, the vast amount of periodical reading he does, and the variety of people he sees, he picks up a great welter of information, which he seems able to sort out, catalogue, and file away in the orderly manner of a military man into mental pigeonholes.

He has little interest in discussing either artistic or purely intellectual matters, although once he answered a question about his religion by saying, "In my youth I refused to be a Moslem just because my father was. When I was young I tried to ask questions. By 1947 I felt I knew all the answers. I do not believe in the outward forms of religion, but I do believe in something deep within my heart. My main argument against communism is its antireligious nature. I would find it impossible to decide what is right or wrong without my religion. But I believe that all religions are basically the same."

At nine o'clock each evening a messenger arrives from Cairo with the first copy from the press of a daily journal edited and published for

Nasser and his top ninety-nine aides by a staff of writers, editors, and researchers in the Department of Information. Only a hundred copies are printed, then the type is distributed. Each is labeled, in large letters, HIGHLY CONFIDENTIAL. Only Ministers and other important officials are permitted to see it because it contains reprints of all the attacks on the regime made anywhere in the world during the past twenty-four hours. In a typical issue the first three pages are devoted to quotations from articles and editorials from the world press about Egypt; page 4 is always reserved for news and comment about Israel; page 5, the Sudan; page 6, Asia; page 7, the East-West Cold War; pages 8 and 9, digests of world-wide radio broadcasts; page 10, a summary of a new book. In addition to this daily digest, the Information Department prepares a twenty-page summary of every book published in any major language that it considers important. At least one of these summaries a day is sent to Nasser.

Twice daily he gets a sheaf of news dispatches from the printer machines. If a bulletin of special interest to Egypt arrives it is rushed to him at once, no matter what he is doing. When aides have a message for him they never whisper it. It is always written on a small piece of paper and handed to him without comment.

After the last guest has gone, the last report has been read, the last phone call answered, he goes to his bedroom with an armload of American, British, European, and Arabic newspapers and magazines, undresses, turns on his bedside radio, and spends the next hour or two reading.

"Much of it is a repetition of what was in the digest, but I like to see it in the original," he says. "I consider the digest a duty, the papers and magazines a pleasure. This is my real hobby. Often I see things in the papers the digest missed, minor stories, but of interest to me. If I did not read the papers themselves I would never have known about the British birdman. Such stories link me with the world. I enjoy magazines like *Time* and *Life* for the advertising. I like the cartoons and illustrations in French magazines."

Some of his associates privately criticize him for reading too much. Some days he spends five or six hours turning the pages of periodicals. They feel he could use this time to better advantage. But he likes to see his name in print and always wants to read the original of any article about himself. He also takes to his bedroom the sheaf of dispatches foreign reporters cabled to their papers during the day. He reads them even more carefully than the censors do, and he is rather sensitive to comments about the way he handles this task:

"Once a New York newspaper said I read the dispatches at breakfast and got into such a rage it spoiled my appetite and sent my blood pressure up for the day. Not true. My staff has orders to let me see everything written against us, because I personally plan our propaganda and I must know what the opposition is saying."

Since he has become President, his schedule has left him little time for sports or recreation. As a result, he has gained weight, a point on which he is sensitive, partly because Egyptians think of Farouk when they see a corpulent male. When one visitor asked him his weight he replied, "I now weigh ninety kilos [198 pounds]," then quickly added, "But remember I am 182 centimeters [five feet eleven inches] tall!"

Since his appendectomy, his only serious physical trouble has been violent sinus attacks, caused by dust and desert sand in the air. They give him almost unbearable headaches, plunging him into black moods that disappear only when the sinus attacks end.

Chess remains his favorite indoor game, and he has taught his two daughters and his eldest son to play, but he has found that watching American films is more relaxing than anything else. Until the revolution he took Tahia to a cinema once or twice a week. When his security officers advised him to stop, he bought a projector and set up a screen on the tennis court. During periods of crisis he sometimes watches two or three feature-length films in a single evening, to take his mind off his problem. He was once asked if he applied the Nasser principle of positive neutrality to the selection of films.

"If I did," he replied, "I would have to see bad as well as good. I am not interested in bad films, even for the sake of a principle. What I like are cowboy pictures and musicals. I do not like dramas and heavy films."

On Friday, the Moslem holy day, the Nasser children do not have to go to school, so they may stay up late Thursday night and watch a film. By family custom they are allowed to choose it. But, their father says, "Their taste is not the same as mine. They like heavier pictures than I do, especially war films. So after they go to bed I usually put on the film I wanted."

He is very much interested in clothes. Even when he was in the Army he wore mufti as often as possible. But he is quick to point out that he does not have the kind of wardrobe Farouk had:

"My policy has always been to have one new suit made each year by my Cairo tailor, but I skipped 1959."

Ties are his weakness, and because most of his friends know it he receives hundreds as gifts. The Crown Prince of Morocco sent him the fifty most expensive ties he could find in Paris. But Nasser has definite ideas about what makes a good tie. "I do not like the modern ones covered with things like hearts and flowers," he says.

For him the perfect tie has wide, varicolored stripes, but the stripes must run from northeast to southwest as he looks at them in a mirror. All the ties that don't please him are given to his brothers or his aides.

He has never counted the number he has kept, but there are several hundred. Once he had his picture in Cairo papers for forty-seven consecutive days wearing a different tie each time. He has been given gifts ranging from half-million-dollar planes to autographed books, but his eyes light up brightest when someone brings him a tie with the stripes running in the right direction. He does not own either a tuxedo or tails, for he feels that "such clothes are not in keeping with the new Egypt."

He says his favorite colors are blue and pale gray, but the color combinations he wears prove his own statement that "colors are actually of no importance to me." His ties are gaudy and his socks, pocket handkerchief, tie, shirt, and suit seldom blend into a well-thought-out ensemble.

He wears a gold wedding band and a heavy gold wrist watch. Most of his Ministers have similar watches, which in the summer they wear over the left shirt cuff to prevent perspiration from ruining the strap. Nasser wears his on his wrist in the usual manner.

He has often described himself as a "family man," and he is happiest when he, Tahia, the children, and an aide or two drive to what is commonly called the Barrage, thirteen miles down the Nile from Cairo. In Farouk's day a three-story resthouse was built there by the government. For years it was used by Prime Ministers. When the Nassers go there, for a few days every month or two, it is heavily guarded and not even government officials are admitted unless El Rayis has sent for them. This allows the Nassers to live momentarily like a normal middle-class family. Whenever word spreads that "Nasser has gone to the Barrage" everyone knows he is the victim of fatigue or that some crisis is in the offing which he suspects will demand an excessive expenditure of nervous energy and so he must prepare for it.

Although he sees his children less than most fathers, he has a typical father's pride in them. He insists they learn to speak and read French as well as English and Arabic. He has no particular ambition for his sons.

"Children should be permitted to choose their own vocations," he says. "One boy now thinks he wants to be a pilot; the other, a naval officer."

Although neither son has any political interest, Khaled often goes around the house pretending to be making a public speech and mimicking all his father's oratorical mannerisms.

Tahia has been called the least known and least publicized wife of any chief of state in the world. This is as her husband wishes it. During the first four post-revolutionary years she never granted a press interview, had her photograph taken for the newspapers, attended an official reception, met any of her husband's state visitors, or left the country. When she goes shopping, no one ever recognizes her. All her social activity is with the wives of Cabinet Ministers and with Hidayat Heikal, the young wife of editor Mohamed. She has never planned a formal dinner party. When her husband entertains kings, presidents, crown princes, and other important visitors from abroad, he does so in Kubbah Palace, almost as elegantly as Farouk did, and with some of the same servants. Tahia seldom attends even these events. Occasionally she gives informal dinners at Manchiet el Bakry for her husband's intimate friends, former army officers and their wives.

Nasser has an interest in music, which began when he was living in Alexandria with his grandparents, who had a gramophone. Listening to their records, he became acquainted with the voice of a young woman named Ohm Kalthoum, who sang Egyptian songs in a throaty, syncopated style. Tahia, who plays the piano, has tried to broaden his musical taste, leading him gradually from light foreign tunes to classical music. She even persuaded him to begin a collection of serious recordings. Now if he is asked who his favorite composers are he will say Rachmaninoff and Chopin, but Ohm Kalthoum still sings for three hours every Thursday night in some Cairo theater and over Cairo Radio, and during those three hours most radios in the Arab world, in palaces, apartments, and mud huts, are tuned in to hear her, and as often as he is able El Rayis is among her listeners. One evening in 1959 the Hilton Hotel lobby in Cairo was crowded for several hours with people who had heard that President Nasser was scheduled to be there for an Army Day reception, but he did not appear. Later it was learned he had been listening to Ohm Kalthoum. She has even been given an army medal, at his suggestion.

Whenever he is asked to name his favorite American author he says,

"Mark Twain." In recent years he has had little time to read anything except periodicals and government reports, but in his younger days his literary interest ranged from Dale Carnegie's *How to Win Friends and Influence People* to Prown's *War and Psychological Conditions of Peace*.

Few except his most intimate associates realize his capacity for anger. With rare exceptions, he has kept it well hidden. Once a Pakistan paper reported that as a young man he had consulted a gipsy fortune teller who predicted that he would marry her daughter, and that he had. Because there was not the slightest basis for the story, he lost his temper when he read it in a second and a third publication.

Under his personal command are four separate intelligence systems, dealing with espionage and counterespionage, internal and external. Their agents operate independently of the Army and the Ministry of the Interior, their identity is known only to El Rayis, and they report personally to him. One of their minor chores is to collect any antiregime stories they hear. Nasser enjoys passing them on to his aides. Many are revivals of jokes told against Hitler, Mussolini, or Stalin, such as the one about the unemployed Egyptian who caught a fish and rushed home with it, only to be told by his wife she had no oil in which to fry it.

"Then boil it!" the husband ordered.

"There is no fuel for the stove," the wife replied.

Despondently the man took the fish back to the sea and threw it in. As it hit the water it raised its head and shouted, "Hurrah for Nasser!"

Another story told on him is about how he and twelve members of his Cabinet were in a plane, and as they flew low over Cairo he said to the pilot, "Do you suppose if I tore a hundred-pound note into a dozen pieces and threw them from the window to those people down there it would make some of them happy?" to which the pilot replied, "If you want to make all of them happy, throw yourself and your dozen friends out the window."

When Nasser's eldest son, Khaled, was six, a London newspaper carried a picture of a British woman who claimed to be "the fiancée of Nasser's son." A British correspondent later asked the President if he was angry. He replied, "Not at all. I've been looking at the picture of the young lady and it makes me jealous of Khaled."

A short time after the revolution he appointed an obscure professor, Dr. Hassan Abou el Seoud of Alexandria University, Under Secretary in the Ministry of National Guidance. Café gossips spread the rumor that he was chosen because he was "the husband of Nasser's sister." During one of the President's rare press conferences Egyptian reporters subjected him to a barrage of oblique questions about the case. For almost an hour he parried with them, then at last said with a smile, "And I would like to conclude by telling you that I do not have a sister!"

He has strong feelings about nepotism, more of a custom than a crime in pre-revolutionary Egypt. He insists on severely punishing anyone caught engaging in it.

Several years ago he telephoned Mustafa Amin, publisher of the Cairo daily, *Al Akhbar*. "Did you see the back page?" he asked. "Yes," Amin replied, "you mean the picture of your father. What's wrong?" Nasser answered slowly and deliberately, "I don't like my father to get publicity. I'm afraid it will go to his head. I want my father and my brothers to live like ordinary people. I don't want my position to spoil them." Since then pictures of his relatives have seldom been printed.

Several weeks after the revolution he said to a friend, "Did you read the statement Mohieddin made today that there is no one left in jail who has committed a crime against the revolution? Well, it isn't true." Then he disclosed a story that has never been published. A wealthy Frenchwoman in Alexandria, in trouble for violating the regulations of some government bureau, asked a brother of Nasser's mother, whom she knew, to intercede for her. When he did, the head of the government bureau communicated with Nasser and asked for instructions. It was a difficult decision for Nasser to make. His feeling about his mother was still strong. This was her brother. But on his orders his uncle was arrested and imprisoned.

He is acutely aware of the frustrations of young army officers in the government because he shares many of them. They were frustrated about land because their families owned little if any acreage; about education, because they had so little of it; about languages, because most of them spoke only Arabic and English; about travel, because few had ever been outside Egypt and the Sudan; about culture, because they knew little about literature, art, and music. But soon after the revolution most of them seized any excuse to go abroad on government junkets. They studied foreign languages. They began to acquire libraries of serious books. Five of the original R.C.C. members have obtained or are in the process of obtaining university degrees, in some cases by mail from such reputable institutions as the London School of Economics. Since the revolution twenty new magazines have been started, most with the backing of Nasser himself or his close associates. There is even a new magazine especially for bodyguards. Nasser has encouraged this semi-intellectual activity.

The sensitivity that he and his colleagues have about their background has resulted in many complexes. Nasser himself never feels relaxed with a group of foreigners. This is one reason he shuns any form of social life and spends most of his time within the four walls of the house at Manchiet el Bakry. With such individuals as Nehru, Tito, and Chou En-lai he can talk as an equal, but with half a dozen Europeans, even though they may be only first lieutenants in the British Army or salesmen of nuts and bolts, he immediately feels defensive and uncomfortable. The attitude of envy and resentment that most Egyptians have toward foreigners grows out of their deep-seated feeling of inferiority. Two Cairenes were overheard discussing their President. One said to the other, "That Nasser is an able chap. He must have a drop of Turkish blood somewhere." It may take three or four generations for them to lose this attitude.

After a parade in 1953 one of Nasser's advisers brought him a photograph taken of the reviewing stand. Naguib, still in office, was smiling agreeably; Nasser was scowling. "You must learn to be like the general," the adviser said. "The public will like you better if you seem relaxed and happy. Why do you frown so much?"

"I can't help it," Nasser replied. "I am thinking of all the problems we have."

Soon after Naguib's disappearance Nasser's public relations men made a concentrated effort to win the people's affection for him. One scheme was to plaster the fences and walls of Egypt with two-foot-square pictures of him. He himself chose the photograph to be reproduced. In it his lips were tightly closed and he looked serious and determined. The results were not good, so another picture was chosen, and soon Egyptians found themselves staring into a face that smiled pleasantly at them. A year or so later the public relations men went a step further and ordered millions of new posters showing Nasser grinning so broadly that the American correspondents named it "the toothpaste poster." On some walls in Cairo there are as many as fifty of these heroic-sized faces in a line, one after another. They are pasted on the front of most buildings. They hang, framed, on the walls of almost every government and nongovernment office in the country. They are part of the window dressing of almost every shop. Smaller pictures are glued onto the windshields of taxis, buses, and even private cars. For years it has been difficult to go anywhere without looking into the smiling face of El Rayis. In the Alexandria office of his brother Az el-Arab there are six pictures of Nasser in the waiting room, three on the walls of a corridor, and seven more in his private office, in addition to a paperweight made in Nasser's image. Many government functionaries try to outdo one another in the number of likenesses of El Rayis on their walls. An American once remarked to a minor official whose office was especially well decorated, "You forgot one place." "Where?" the official asked eagerly. "The ceiling," the American replied.

Nasser's advisers have made certain that the only other leader whose picture is ever displayed is Amer, the logical successor to the presidency in the event of assassination or fatal accident.

At the time of the revolution Nasser was one of the world's worst public speakers. He had neither personal nor political magnetism. But each year he has improved. He is at his best when speaking extemporaneously, but he is aware that every word of the speeches he delivers is read critically by his political enemies at home and abroad, so he usually speaks from a carefully prepared text. He also knows that when hundreds of thousands of men and women pack a public square and stand for three hours under a hot sun listening to him, most of the words he utters are of no significance to them. The fact that he, an Egyptian, one of them, can string so many words together is more important than what they mean. The people look more than they listen. He is the mirror in which they see their own reflection; the reflection of themselves as they would like to be. Many of them have bodies wracked by illness. His is straight and strong. They have eye diseases. His eyes are bright and clear. They are dressed in rags: El Rayis is as handsome and well groomed as most foreigners who step from a plane. They have no power; El Rayis can make foreign villains tremble. Kings and Prime Ministers come thousands of miles to see him. He is the symbol of the new Egypt, which no longer bends its knee to anyone.

Nasser has never lost the literary ambition he had as a boy. He told an author who was interviewing him, "I envy you more than you can imagine. I have twenty-five notebooks full of reactions to what I have heard and read and seen, but I am always too busy to do anything with all this material. I wish I could have a month to do nothing but write." Sometimes he indulges his literary inclinations in strange ways. Once the Foreign Office sent him a fifteen-line routine memorandum. When it was returned it contained his handwritten comments under the fifteen lines, in both margins, on the back, and then on a separate piece of paper, in a flowing Arabic literary style.

Asked by an American to name the five greatest figures of all times, Nasser hesitated, then replied, "I look on Lincoln as a great man. Also

Washington. I read about him only lately. When the Communists were trying to get me to join their party, I read about Lenin. I consider him a great man, too. Also Gandhi. Mustafa Kamel, who struggled alone against the British, was a really important figure. Ataturk impressed me but he hanged too many of his friends. Of course, Christ and Mohamed must be included in the list." If he had been making the list for someone other than an American the names might have been different, for he has the desire found in many Egyptians of wanting to give a questioner the answers the questioner seems to wish.

One of the weaknesses in Nasser's character is his tendency to blame someone else when things go wrong. It began in childhood when he complained about his parents and teachers. It was most evident during the Palestinian war, when he blamed Farouk, the Egyptian High Command, and even his immediate superiors for defeats. Later he blamed England, then the West in general, for Egypt's difficulties. He has a quality of inconsistency not uncommon in the Middle East. He sees nothing odd about his frequent public attacks on birth control while advertisements for contraceptives appear on the screens of movie houses and in government-controlled newspapers, and birth control advice is dispensed in government-run clinics up and down the Nile.

He has an imagination that has been nurtured on spy stories, adventure films, and his own frequently stated conception of himself as an actor in a thriller. Sometimes this imagination causes him temporarily to distrust everyone.

Just before the Suez crisis a friend said to him, "Gamal, we've been the closest of friends for years, yet to be honest I don't feel I really know you." Nasser smiled a little sadly and replied, "Nobody does. Perhaps it's because I'm suspicious of everyone. I can't help it. This is why I can't open my heart to anyone."

He is at his best in moments of crisis. Several times his excitable friend Amer has demanded permission to launch full-scale war on Israel in retaliation for some military move. Each time, Nasser has remained calm and said *no,* just as before the revolution he frequently said *no* to Sadat's plans for violence.

When anyone asks him face to face whether he considers himself a dictator he replies that Westerners in general and Americans in particular are too inclined to equate military rule with ruthless, inhumane totalitarianism. He insists, as many another totalitarian ruler before him has, that he acts only in the interests of the people. He says the individual in Egypt enjoyed less democracy before the revolution than after the R.C.C. abolished Parliament, imposed almost perpetual censorship, restricted freedom of movement and assembly, limited the right of free speech, abolished opposition political parties, and put the country under military rule. The reason, he says, is that colonialism has now been abolished, so Egyptians are free men.

Those who know him well say his close associates do him a disservice by being afraid to give him any adverse criticism, a trouble many a leader before him has suffered. He also is handicapped by never having visited a Western country. He knows the West only through motion pictures, magazines, newspapers, the radio, and the diplomats, businessmen, and correspondents who come to call. He has no conception of what a free press means. For him the press is an instrument of government, to be used to advance a cause. Under his personal direction one of the most unpredictable censorship systems in the world has been set up in Cairo. Before a foreign radio reporter can make a broadcast he must submit seven copies of his script to the censor, who can delay approval until the foreigner has missed his air appointment or eliminate certain words and make the broadcaster say the opposite of what he intended, and it is forbidden to mention on the air that the script has been censored. Censorship of newspaper dispatches is blind: the correspondent does not know what has been excised until he gets back a copy of his paper, perhaps weeks later.

When Nasser gives an interview to a foreign correspondent, the dispatch is taken to the President for his approval before transmission. Often he blue-pencils words he uttered only a few hours earlier but which, on reconsideration, he decides would not look well in print abroad. Sometimes whole paragraphs considered by him and his censors proper for foreign consumption are deleted before the interview is published domestically. This is invariably true of any moderate statements he may make about Israel.

All newspaper and radio correspondents from abroad are closely watched, on his orders. Their telephones are tapped, their mail is opened, and they are often followed.

Sometimes the entire Middle East section is ripped from incoming American news magazines before they are permitted on the stands. Every shop that makes microfilms is required to submit secretly to the censor anything a customer brings in, before photographing it.

Even books used at the American Cairo College, opened several years ago for children of foreigners, are censored. The language of the curriculum is English, and many of the teachers are wives of American government officials. The pupils include children of nearly thirty nationalities, among them sons and daughters of some families from Communist countries. Care was taken by the school authorities to select books that contained no favorable mention of Israel. However, one day during school hours a delegation of four censors arrived, scrutinized all the books being used, and decided that ten pages of a history book should be removed. "But there is nothing on those pages but factual information," the principal complained. The ten pages, nevertheless, were torn from every copy of the book in the school.

The American Ambassador's automobile is followed wherever it goes, and the American Embassy has a daily ritual known as "decontaminating" its offices. This is to prevent Egyptian officials' eavesdropping by electronic devices. All incoming mail for American employees stationed in Egypt arrives by diplomatic pouch, a precaution taken only in countries where censorship is so thorough that mail is not safe.

At frequent intervals, without either domestic or foreign publicity, huge bonfires are built at remote spots on the desert to burn books confiscated because the censors disapproved of them.

Nasser sees nothing incompatible between this system of thought control and what he terms "the new freedom."

CHAPTER 19

N DAY

As the wheels of his Vickers Viscount touched the ground at Belgrade's military airport, twenty-four guns boomed a salute for the Egyptian convert to positive neutrality. When he stepped from the plane, Marshal Tito greeted him with an affectionate embrace and the crowd of Yugoslavs let loose a noisy cheer. Both leaders were in military uniform. For once Tito was almost outdone in sartorial splendor, for his guest was bedecked with at least as much gold braid as he. After Egypt's June 1956 election the Revolutionary Command Council had been dissolved and all its members who remained in the government, except General Amer, had been divested of their military rank. Nasser had set the example by announcing he was no longer a lieutenant colonel; that he would never wear khaki again. But here at Belgrade in July he was already reneging. In place of a lieutenant colonel's insignia he had on his shoulders the red tabs of commander in chief. Both he and Tito were elegant-looking, but both needed to take setting-up exercises to reduce their girth.

They rode in an open Rolls Royce the twelve miles to town. All government offices had been closed at noon to assure that there would be crowds in the streets. Newsboys held up copies of *Borba,* the morning paper, bearing an enormous headline in Arabic script: *Welcome, El Rayis!* The streets of Belgrade looked somewhat like the streets of Cairo: everywhere were immense pictures of Nasser, reproductions of the photograph with all teeth showing.

As they rode into the city, waving to the crowds, Tito explained to his guest that during his visit he would stay at Dedinske Dvor Palace, former home of the boy king, Peter, who had fled when the Nazis struck and was never invited to return. They joked about it; how each of them had replaced a king; how they had scorned the opportunity to move into a palace, preferring simple quarters, but how, when they visited each other, they were housed in royal style.

With Nasser had come a planeload of advisers, for this was being called a summit meeting of the neutrals, a little big three meeting. Prime Minister Nehru was scheduled to arrive next week, and they would start planning how to remain independent of both East and West. Meanwhile there were festivities. They began that night with a many-course dinner, at which Nasser was made an honorary citizen of Belgrade. The next morning, he decided to see what his new city really was like, so he rose early, put on a blue business suit, and went for a walk, incognito. But when he smiled he resembled so closely the man whose face was glued on walls and fences everywhere and displayed in all the shop windows that people swarmed around him, clapped him on the back in rugged Serb fashion, and shouted *"Zdravo!"* When he went into a coffee shop to order a dish of ice cream for breakfast, they followed him and nearly wrecked the place. At a formal luncheon that day, he and Tito exchanged toasts and talked about the problems of industrializing their nations and catching up with the rest of the world.

In the evening the Egyptian delegation faced a grave sartorial problem. When the trip was being planned, the Egyptian protocol officer had suggested that something would have to be done about formal clothes. There would be banquets and receptions, at which business suits would look out of place. Nasser was opposed to wearing a tuxedo or tails. Neither he nor the other members of his entourage, with the exception of Foreign Minister Fawzi, possessed them, and as a matter of principle, he did not think they should order dress clothes just for the Yugoslav trip. After much discussion a compromise was reached. A Cairo tailor designed what he called a *frac* or pea jacket, with a formal cut and satin lapels, but no tails. One was made for each member of the delegation. But that first evening in Belgrade, Nasser reversed himself and decided against the frac. Instead he put on his fanciest uniform, while the others wore their business suits. The fracs were never seen.

On the third day, Tito staged a parade to show off the military equipment he had received from the United States. Nasser admitted that at least some of it looked as good as what he had been getting from the East. While they were waiting for Nehru, he visited the Bosnian city of Sarajevo, spiritual center of Yugoslavia's million and a half Moslems, who greeted him with flowers and cheers. When Nehru arrived, they all went to the Adriatic island of Vanga, five minutes by motor launch from Brioni, a larger island where Tito had a summer home of white marble. There they talked for several days in secrecy. The daily communiqués implied complete agreement about everything, but actually their mutual interest in not being dominated by either Russia or the United States was all that held them together. Even here they were not in perfectly harmonious accord. Tito and Nehru felt—and they told him so—that Nasser was leaning too far in the direction of the East for safety. The little big three situation was complicated further by the close religious ties between Egypt and her Moslem sister, Pakistan. There was also the matter of Israel. India and Yugoslavia had both recognized the Jewish state and developed normal trade relations with her that neither one, despite all Nasser said, had any intention of dropping. But it was on Algeria that they had their most serious disagreement. Nasser had come with the hope of convincing the others they should support the rebels. Neither Tito nor Nehru was receptive. This piqued him. He was put in a bad mood also by news cabled from Lille, France, about an outburst by French Premier Guy Mollet: "I denounce the megalomania of Colonel Nasser. He hopes to line up behind him not only the Arabs but the entire Moslem world. I would think myself back in the Middle Ages." And he was irritated by a bulletin that the Egyptian military attaché to Jordan, a friend, had been fatally wounded by a bomb sent through the mail to him from some Jordanian as yet uncaptured. Also, the Soviet Union had signed a commercial agreement with Israel, promising more oil.

The Egyptians were scheduled to fly home at three o'clock on the afternoon of July 20, but at dinnertime the three leaders were still arguing over the wording of their final communiqué. Nehru insisted on many moderate statements, and he persuaded them to avoid all mention of Cyprus, then in the midst of its struggle for freedom. The communiqué was also weak, Nasser felt, on Palestinian refugees and Algeria. It was eight-twenty before they finally climbed into the plane. "Come back soon!" Tito shouted, then they were off. There was an extra passenger on the return trip, for Nehru had decided to visit Egypt again before returning home. But he and Nasser did little talking. Both were so tired they dozed most of the way. The plane landed at Cairo at 3 A.M. and was met by several members of the Cabinet. As soon as they came close enough for him to see their faces, Nasser could tell that something was wrong.

"Dulles has withdrawn the dam offer," one of them told him at once.

Nehru was taken to Tahar Palace. Nasser went directly home and summoned his full Cabinet for an emergency meeting. There was no time for sleep, no time for food. This was a crisis that might change the course of Egyptian history. Nasser began to chain smoke. The news had put him in one of his coldly angry moods. There had been vague warnings for weeks that this might happen, but he had gambled it would not. It was obviously Dulles's answer to his recognition of Communist China. But he was furious about the way it had been made. It was almost in a class with Sir Miles Lampson's ultimatum to Farouk. The diplomatic cables on his desk described exactly what had happened. Ambassador Hussein had called on Secretary Dulles in Washington that morning to announce that President Nasser had decided to accept the American offer of a fifty-six-million-dollar grant, the British grant of fourteen million, and a two-hundred-million-dollar loan from the International Bank to finance the first stage of the Aswan High Dam construction. Dulles announced curtly, "It is not feasible in the present circumstances for the United States to participate in this project." The Ambassador remained for fifty minutes, arguing. What irked Nasser most was an attack Dulles had made on the soundness of Egypt's economy. He told the Ambassador that Washington now knew the Czech arms purchase came to a quarter of a billion dollars, much more than originally suspected; that even the interest payments would put a tremendous burden on Egypt's economy; that he, Dulles, doubted Egypt's ability to pay the East and at the same time to build the dam. Because Dulles permitted the American press to quote him indirectly, Nasser felt a world-wide attack had been made on Egypt's financial standing. He was even more enraged when his secretary showed him wire-service dispatches from Washington. Without quoting Dulles, they said Egypt was being punished for working against the interests of the West in Jordan, Saudi Arabia, Cyprus, North Africa.

"What right has America to try to punish us for anything?" he shouted in anger to one of his Ministers.

Less than twenty-four hours later he was given additional cause for an outburst of temper. Great Britain canceled, too, and did it in what he felt was an even more insulting fashion. Three and a half hours before the Egyptian Ambassador to the Court of St. James's was notified by the Foreign Office, the story was handed to newspaper reporters. Nasser's first inkling of this new blow came over his news ticker, which also brought a dispatch from Tel Aviv saying Hammarskjold and Ben-Gurion had just held "fruitful talks on how to achieve peace in the Middle East." On the ticker, too, were dispatches from Belgrade reporting that Nehru had succeeded so well in his attempt to curb the extremism of Tito and Nasser that the Egyptian "dictator" for the first time in years had been forced to take a back seat. There were still other news stories, which said Washington officials had been convinced Egypt was planning to use its new weapons for a full-scale invasion of Israel, and that the dam cancellation was Dulles's way of trying to discourage such a move. Other reports, privately circulated, then publicly printed, said Washington was purposely insulting him in order to weaken his leadership in the Arab world. Each dispatch raised his blood pressure a little more.

The worst blow of all came from Moscow. Shepilov was quoted as declaring the Soviet Union had never considered helping Egypt build the dam. This was tantamount to calling him a liar, for in an interview with a New York reporter just a few weeks ago he had said, "I have a Soviet offer to build the dam right in my pocket and I am considering accepting it if there is a breakdown in negotiations with the United States." Shepilov went even further and said he felt new industries were more important than the dam anyway. Finally there was a dispatch from Washington that Nasser called "brutal." It flatly stated that the dam cancellation was designed to bring about the downfall of Gamal Abdel Nasser; that it was time to show other Arab leaders it did not pay to try to play Washington and Moscow against each other.

In his anger Nasser called in his friend and public relations adviser, Mohamed Heikal. The next morning, Cairo papers carried an article that concluded: "Britain and America have once more unmasked themselves and have frankly told the whole world that their policy is based on destroying people's free will and that their aid in all forms is merely intended to buy peoples, enslave them, rob them of their sovereignty and independence. But we still have the last word to say . . ."

After four days of official silence Nasser himself spoke publicly. He used the opening of a new refinery on the edge of Cairo as an excuse to deliver the most vitriolic speech of his career. He spared Britain, and concentrated on the United States. The veins on his neck and forehead stood out more prominently than ever and his voice was high-pitched and almost hysterical as he shouted to the crowd, "We Egyptians will not permit any imperialists or oppressors to rule us, militarily, politically, or economically. We will not submit to the dollar or to force. You Americans may issue statements from Washington and you may put out lies from Washington. If these statements are the result of wrong information, it is a tragedy. If they are deliberately made to mislead, then the tragedy is worse, seeing that America claims to lead the world."

Then, leaning forward toward the battery of microphones that were sending his voice to all corners of Egypt, to far parts of the Arab world, and thousands of miles into Africa, he cried, "I look at the Americans and I say, 'May you choke to death on your fury!' "

Cairo editors took their lead from El Rayis and the next day began a campaign of verbal violence against America. One article claimed that United States Technical Assistance was only a thinly disguised organization of spies and saboteurs. Another said the free chickens, goats, and bulls sent from America to help improve the strains of Egyptian livestock were all diseased, intentionally. A third paper referred to "poisoned methods of espionage and intrigue" practiced by Americans in Egypt.

The Soviet Union promptly rewarded Egypt for this attitude by dispatching two economic experts by plane to Cairo and announcing, "We are ready to finance the dam if Egypt wishes it." Soviet Ambassador Evgeny Kiselev was in conference with Nasser several times each day.

On Thursday, July 26, 1956, Gamal Abdel Nasser made a three-hour speech in Liberation Square, Alexandria. He indicated how important he felt it was going to be historically by arranging for his two daughters, his three sons, and his wife to be present, for the first time in all his years of speechmaking, although no one in the crowd knew they were there, for they had seats on the obscure balcony of a nearby building. The speech started calmly, but soon, speaking of events leading to cancellation of the dam offer, he said, "The American financial expert, Mr. Black, came to my office. When he sat across the desk from me, I could visualize Mr. Lesseps, the Frenchman who had charge of building the Canal, when he visited the Khedive. Mr. Lesseps." There was something peculiar about the way he repeated the name. But then he went on.

What the crowd in the square at Alexandria did not know was that the word *Lesseps* was a signal. At Port Said, Mohamed Riad, Egyptian Governor of the Suez Canal, and three army officers were at a radio listening for it. In Suez and Ismailia other men were huddled around radios, waiting for the chosen word. On a side street in the Garden City section of Cairo a stout, broad-shouldered former army engineer named Mahmoud Yunes was sitting in his car with the radio on. The moment he heard *Lesseps* he turned the ignition key. The moment those in Port Said, Suez, and Ismailia heard it they, too, began to act on detailed instructions they had received the previous day from Egypt's master intriguer, Gamal Abdel Nasser.

Governor Riad, supported by a squad of policemen, took possession of Navy House, Port Said headquarters of the Suez Canal Company. Those at Ismailia and Suez seized canal installations. Riad marched into the Cairo offices of the canal company, near the American Embassy, followed by policemen in uniform, and announced that in the name of the revolutionary government of President Nasser they were taking possession of all assets of the company. To the stunned officials Riad said, "If you have a radio, turn it on." They tuned in just in time to hear Nasser say, "The Cabinet and the Council of Ministers have ordered the dissolution of the Compagnie Universelle du Canal Maritime de Suez and all other foreign bodies connected with the Canal. Stockholders will be repaid at the prevailing price on the Cairo stock market. The Ministry of Commerce of the sovereign state of Egypt will run the Canal. The Suez Canal belongs to us. The income will be ours in the future. The Canal was built by Egyptians. One hundred and twenty thousand Egyptians died digging it. A new Suez Canal company will be formed. From now on we will rely on our own strength, our own muscle. The Canal will be run by Egyptians, Egyptians, Egyptians! Do you hear me? Egyptians!"

The crowd heard and went wild. Fezzes were thrown into the air. Men embraced and kissed. Some put their arms around each other and began to dance. Tahia smiled down at her children. One of them looked at her and asked, "Mother, what does it all mean?" In London, while Nasser was finishing the rest of his speech, a messenger handed a slip of paper to Anthony Eden, who was host at a dinner party for King Faisal of Iraq. Eden excused himself for a few minutes to consult the Foreign Office by phone. When he returned, his face wore an exceedingly grave expression.

Nasser went on. "Britain and the United States offered us seventy million dollars to help build the dam. The Suez Canal Company's annual income is a hundred million dollars. In five years we will have half a billion dollars from the Canal to use in building the dam." Most of the figures he used were open to question. There had been only several hundred deaths from all causes among all nationalities working on the Canal (the average annual mortality was 1.7 per thousand and the average labor force twenty thousand during the ten years of building), and the hundred million dollars was annual gross income, not profit, but no one was in a mood to quibble. Twelve years before Egypt was due to get the Canal for her own, under the terms of the original lease, Nasser was seizing it. First he had rid Egyptian soil of the de-

tested foreigner. Now he was freeing Egypt from the economic domination of the outsider. That was what the people thought. That was what
he told them. That was why they cheered and cheered.

In the days to come, diplomats and students of the Middle East
would debate whether Nasser's act had been spontaneous, sparked by
events, or had been long planned. His close associates knew the answer.
Soon after coming to power he had appointed experts to draw up a plan
for nationalization and another for Egyptian operation of the Canal.
Every detail was carefully worked out. He had no intention of waiting
twelve more years, until the concession ran out, but neither had he
fixed, even vaguely, a date on which he would give the signal. It de-
pended on others. His policy was still to react rather than to act. His
own reaction to the prod from Dulles was emotional, but others had
made practical plans, so ships continued to move through the Canal, to
the amazement of many who believed the stories they heard about
Egyptian incompetence.

On Nationalization Day plus one, Great Britain lodged a formal protest in Cairo, France indicated she favored military occupation, Secretary Dulles called nationalization "a grievous blow to international
confidence," the Soviet Union heartily supported what Nasser had done,
and martial law was declared in the Canal Zone.

On N Day plus two Nasser tried to get home from Alexandria. His
way was blocked by deliriously happy crowds. The French were calling
it treachery and plunder, but the Egyptians cheered him wildly. When
at last he arrived in Cairo he addressed the mass of humanity that had
converged on the depot. To many he seemed a changed man. He seemed
to be saying whatever words came to mind, without weighing them.
He lashed out angrily, almost hysterically, at "Egypt's enemies."

In his office he found a mound of congratulatory telegrams and cables.
Apparently he had become a hero to Arab masses and Arab leaders
everywhere. Village and city people alike, Moslems and Copts, the
Brothers and agnostics, Egyptians and their neighbors, all seemed to be
elated that he had dared talk back to foreigners in high places. He was
confounding men like Eden and Dulles. The ultimate consequences?
They did not seem to be worrying. There is an old Arab proverb that
says, "Tomorrow must care for its own dead cats." One Egyptian explained his countrymen's attitude with the remark, "If Nasser built
the High Dam at Aswan he would gain some additional popularity, but
if after building it he dared to blow it up in order to spite the West,
Arabs everywhere would treat him like a god."

CHAPTER 20

TAKE REVENGE, MY BROTHERS

Although he had sown only a breeze, he was about to reap a whirlwind. This was clear from the diplomatic messages that poured in during August 1956, and from the newspapers that he read in bed each night before he went to sleep. Nationalization had made him the world's most controversial figure. In Arab papers he read about parades held in his honor, but *Le Soir* in Beirut said, "It appears rather unlikely to us that a man conscious of his responsibilities and preoccupied with his own future, the future of the country, and the peace of the world could carry out under the influence of bad temper a gesture so heavy in consequences." *The New York Times* commented on his "increasing self-confidence and insolence." In England, Glubb Pasha, now signing himself Sir John Bagot, wrote, "If the governments of the world acquiesce in Nasser's claim that the Suez Canal is the private property of the Egyptian Government, they will be acquiescing in the right of this or any subsequent Egyptian government to hold up a great part of the world for ransom whenever they feel so inclined." French Premier Guy Mollet said, "Nasser is imitating Hitler in addressing the democracies in insulting language."

But there were more serious developments to worry him. The British Treasury suddenly blocked all Egyptian accounts. A British cruiser was ordered to break off its courtesy call at Alexandria. The American State Department sent a sharp protest against his "intemperate, inaccurate, and misleading statements." Most disturbing, *Tass*, the official Soviet news agency, cut from a report of his speech the implication that the Soviet Union might help finance the dam. If Moscow reneged, too, his policy of playing East against West might come a cropper.

The week he returned from Alexandria, a messenger brought him a report that several clandestine radio stations had gone into operation just beyond Egypt's frontiers. One, broadcasting only two kilocycles away from the wave length of Cairo's Voice of the Arabs, was openly trying to foment counterrevolution. Predicting that the Nasser regime would be overthrown in a few weeks, it began sending out enigmatic messages. "Ali asks Salah el-Din to wake up the seven sleepers in the magic cave," said one. A few days later another said: "There are forty camels in a caravan proceeding quietly toward the oasis." His secret service advisers disagreed about whether these were coded instructions to counterrevolutionary agents inside Egypt or just propaganda designed to make the Arab world believe there were agents in the country. Then came a third broadcast: "The moon shines on the Nile water." Nasser's reaction was to order a tightening of all security regulations. Then the clandestine station accused him and his Free Officers of "ruling by steel and fire, fattening their own fortunes on the Egyptian Treasury, failing to achieve any reforms, and besmirching the reputation of Egypt before the world by the Suez seizure." The broadcast ended: "The salvation of Egypt depends on ousting the mad tyrant, Gamal Abdel Nasser. The sane people of Egypt are consulting on this matter, and you will hear a report soon on his removal."

If he had not had three espionage and counterespionage agencies operating independently of each other, and if all three had not reported to him that there was less internal opposition than at any time since the revolution, he might have been more worried. His chief concern now was with what was happening in the capitals of the West. The French National Assembly passed a resolution branding him a "menace to peace" and accusing him of aiming to establish his hegemony over all the Arab world. Secretary Dulles charged him with "an angry act of retaliation against fancied grievances." Queen Elizabeth issued a proclamation calling up a half million British reserves. Whitehall ordered all British subjects in Egypt to quit the country unless duty demanded they remain.

Early in August 1956, very weary, he tried to get away from the enervating temperature of Cairo and the heat of his critics' accusations by going with Tahia and the children to the seaside, near Alexandria, but he was there only a few hours when fresh reports from Paris, London, and Washington forced him to return home for emergency meetings with Amer and Fawzi. He told them he had a premonition that Egypt faced grave military trouble, and he directed Amer to prepare for it by converting every sports club and social center in the country into a military training post. He postponed indefinitely the trip to Moscow he had been planning. He summoned the American Ambassador to his house almost every day for a long conference. He repeatedly probed at the Soviet Ambassador, trying to find how much support he could expect from the East. Even his critics seemed to agree that the seizure of the Canal had been a masterfully planned operation, but he had underestimated the fury it would create in the West. To what extent would this fury now go? That was the question he and Amer discussed most often after he returned to Cairo.

The same day a message reached him that a conference on Suez of all nations using the Canal had been called to meet in London, he received a coded cable from an Egyptian naval attaché that three British aircraft carriers loaded with men and machines had started for the Mediterranean.

Reporters and photographers from all over the world were pouring into Cairo, so the Ministry of National Guidance announced that on Sunday, August 12, the President would hold one of his rare press conferences and give the British his answer to their invitation to join the twenty-two other nations invited to London. Meanwhile he was busy eighteen or nineteen hours a day. To the house at Manchiet el Bakry came envoys, aides, and military men, as well as Ambassadors and Ministers from all over the globe, but especially from the Bandung Conference and Communist countries.

Several days before the press conference he sat in his office with his short-wave radio tuned in to London and heard Anthony Eden deliver a broadcast that poured fuel instead of oil on the troubled waters. "Our quarrel is not with Egypt, still less with the Arab world," Eden said. "It is with Colonel Nasser." He smiled wryly at several aides who sat in front of the radio with him while Eden pictured him as "a plunderer whose appetite grows with feeding and whose words are worthless." When the Briton spoke of using force as a last resort, he turned to his aides and said, "I warn you that this is just what he is likely to do."

Now Eden was attacking him even more personally: "When he gained power we felt no hostility toward him. We even made agreements with him. We hoped he wanted to improve the conditions of life for his people and be friends with this country . . . but instead of meeting us with friendship Colonel Nasser conducted a vicious propaganda campaign against our country. He has shown he is not a man who can be trusted to keep an agreement. We all know how fascist governments behave and we all remember too well what the cost can be of giving in to fascism."

Nasser snapped off the radio and turned back to his desk. His jaw seemed to protrude more than usual and his lips were set tight. That night, he ordered Egypt's small-arms factory to go on twenty-four-hour shifts and authorized the formation of a National Liberation Army of men, women, and boys under the command of Minister of Education Hussein.

The day of the press conference he put on a conservative blue suit, but chose to wear one of his most flamboyant striped ties. As he stepped to the rostrum in the room where Parliament formerly met, he looked down on three hundred reporters and photographers. Every important magazine and newspaper in the world was represented. There were dark circles under his eyes, and he looked tired. Slowly, in English, he read a twelve-page statement into a battery of microphones. "Egypt will not attend the London Conference," he said. He spoke calmly, yet some of his sentences had a sarcastic bite, especially: "The Egyptian Government considers the proposal for creation of an international authority but a mild word for what should be called collective colonialism." He accused the United States as well as Great Britain and France of "a planned conspiracy aimed at threatening and starving the Egyptian people."

That evening, in a broadcast to his own people in Arabic, he stated without qualification that the International Bank for Reconstruction and Development had offered him a billion-dollar loan to improve the Canal or build another. "I rejected it," he added. A few hours later in Washington bank officials said the statement was an invention; there had not even been any discussion of the subject with Nasser or with any other Egyptian.

The next day, tired and oppressed by Cairo's heat, he went on a picnic with his family, his first relaxation in several weeks.

Early on the night that the London Conference was to issue a communiqué making known its decision about the Suez Canal, Heikal telephoned Nasser from his newspaper office. "Amer and Mohieddin and I are just leaving for the cinema," Nasser told him.

Heikal was incredulous. "On a night like this, when the very future of Egypt may be at stake?" he asked.

"It will probably be three hours before the communiqué is issued," Nasser replied. "What should I do, stay here and pace the floor for three hours?"

So, while the communiqué was being prepared in London, the three top figures in Egypt's government sat in a Cairo movie house. They returned to Manchiet el Bakry just as the first bulletin came over the news wires announcing that eighteen nations had agreed to London's proposal for international control of the Canal. Nasser's reaction was to order a general strike as a protest. The next day, Cairo became a dead city as every wheel of industry and traffic stopped. Sympathy strikes at least partially halted city life in such scattered places as Tripoli, Tunis, Baghdad, Beirut, Damascus, and Karachi. In Amman, Jordanian crowds stoned British and French embassies.

Late in August silver-haired Robert Menzies, the Australian Prime Minister, arrived as head of a committee to acquaint Nasser with details of the plan the user nations had drawn up at London. The same day, Amer announced that mobilization of all the armed forces of Egypt had been completed. Even the women and boys in the Liberation Front were in possession of guns. With Nasser's approval he said, "My confidence in the soundness of our position has no limits. I can now say we are ready. I assure you we shall never be taken by surprise."

The meetings of the Menzies committee began amicably enough, with a party given by Nasser on an island in the Nile in a palace that had once belonged to Prince Mohamed Aly. El Rayis himself led the Australian and his colleagues through the rococo rooms of the sprawling building that his regime had converted into a museum, then through the most exotic tropical gardens in the Middle East. Host and guests seemed relaxed and convivial, but within a few days the spirit changed. Menzies tried to persuade Nasser that Egypt should act merely as a landlord and permit an international users body to run the Canal as a tenant. Nasser answered that he wanted no foreigners running anything in Egypt, not even if they were called tenants. In a bitter statement he castigated the West for hostile acts while he and Menzies were conferring. The conflict reached a climax one afternoon when he decided that Menzies was threatening him.

"This I refused to tolerate," he explained later, "so I brought the whole conference to an end. I was so angry that I even decided to cancel a dinner party I was supposed to give for the committee that night, but Loy Henderson, the American on the committee, and the Ethiopian Foreign Minister, who was in Cairo at the time, persuaded me to reconsider."

After the committee left, Cairo Radio, always following by a few hours the path charted by Nasser, turned its fury on the chairman: "Menzies did not speak as an Australian Prime Minister, but as an Australian mule. . . . He bucked, reared, plunged, and kicked up his hind legs. . . . He trampled on all the principles by which the twentieth century lives."

With the London Conference thus a failure because of his refusal to co-operate, Britain and France turned a new weapon on him. From its old headquarters in Paris the Suez Company announced that at midnight, September 14, its five hundred non-Egyptian employees in the Canal Zone would leave their jobs in a mass walkout, on company orders. It was expected that with only a handful of technicians and pilots left, such a log jam of ships would be created that the Canal would virtually go out of business. Nasser bit his lip, then issued an order: "See that those who wish to go get exit visas at once. Tell the airlines to give them priority reservations."

One of his aides gasped and said, "Is that all you're going to do?"

"No," he replied with a smile. "One thing more. Have the army band play the 'Marseillaise' and 'God Save the Queen' when they go." Then he changed his tone. "We'll show the world we can run the Canal ourselves." It was a reckless boast. Pilots were paid twenty thousand dollars a year because they were highly skilled in guiding ships through a waterway that narrowed at some points to little over a hundred feet and was plagued by tricky winds and sandstorms. While a pilot was on board he was complete master of the ship; all responsibility was his. It took twelve hours to make the run, but the work was so exacting that a pilot worked only six hours at a stretch, and thus it took two of them to guide each ship through the Canal. To induce the pilots to leave, the old company was giving each man a bonus of several years' pay and a guarantee of a job elsewhere.

Late in the evening of September 14, Yunes, the new managing director of the Canal, issued a batch of emergency orders with Nasser's approval. Pilots would work twelve hours instead of six. Each would take a ship all the way through the Canal. Days off, holidays, vacations were canceled. Half an hour before twelve o'clock of that crucial night Antoli Chikov, the Soviet Consul, appeared at Ismailia and said to Yunes, "I have fifteen Russian pilots outside for you." At midnight the southbound convoy dropped anchor at Lake Timsah, the halfway point on the Canal, and the British and French pilots clambered down the rope ladders and were gone. But Egyptian pilots in launches were ready to take over. Then the northbound convoy arrived and the same thing happened. Before long Yunes had only seventy-two of his 205 pilots left; sixty Egyptians and twelve foreigners who had refused to walk out. Later in the day the Russian volunteers were joined by some Iranians, Greeks, South Africans, Indians, and even a few Americans, who came in answer to advertisements placed in newspapers in many parts of the world.

Day by day the crisis moved more rapidly toward its explosive climax.

On Nasser's invitation the Foreign Ministers of nine Arab countries and their deputies came to Cairo to meet with him. Communist China's Mao Tse-tung joined the Soviet Union in a pledge of support to Egypt. The Ulemas, all-powerful high priests of the Moslem world, met at Al Azhar and declared a political, economic, and cultural boycott of "the Western imperialist countries." Because the bulk of Saudi Arabian oil moved through the Canal and King Saud wanted nothing to interfere with the million-dollar-a-day flow of royalties into his pockets, he sent three messages to Nasser urging moderation and compromise. These so worried Nasser that one day late in September he and President Kuwatly of Syria took a plane for Dhahran. King Saud treated them lavishly, assured them that he still considered valid the military alliance he had signed six months earlier with Syria and Egypt, and then sent them home in his private plane. Nasser arrived in Cairo to find that Western attacks against him were growing more and more vituperative. Mollet used the words "apprentice dictator," while Pineau called him "a congenital liar." These were pin pricks. He was more disturbed by the activity on the Israeli–Jordanian frontier. Half a dozen hit-run attacks had been made inside Israeli territory. One night four Israeli civilians were killed. The next day, a tractor driver was kidnaped. A meeting of Israeli archaeologists was broken up by Jordanian gunfire and sudden death. Thirty-six Israelis in all had been killed. The day after his return from Dhahran units of the Israeli Army, in retaliation, surged across the frontier and blew up a Jordanian police station, killing at least fifty soldiers and civilians.

Early in October he gave an interview to an old friend turned enemy, purged, punished, now a friend again, Major Khaled Mohieddin, the Communist, who had become publisher of a new Cairo newspaper, *Al Messaa*. The article predicted that the United Nations would collapse, as the League of Nations had, unless it supported Egypt on Suez.

The next day, October 11, a long Arab-Jewish artillery duel was followed by another Israeli attack on a Jordanian police station; nine dead. A few hours later the Jordanian Foreign Minister, Awni Abdulkadi, called on Nasser to beg for military aid. He said there was evidence Israel was getting ready for a massive invasion. While discussions were going on, word of another retaliation raid was received: the dead, forty-eight Jordanians, eighteen Israelis. Nasser promised to do what he could. Secretly he was angry over intelligence reports that great numbers of Iraqi troops were poised on Jordan's frontier, ready for a quick entry if the situation worsened. After Abdulkadi left, he called in Salah Salem, now publisher of the newspaper *Al Shaab,* and ordered him to write an editorial accusing Prime Minister Nuri as-Said of Iraq of plotting with Britain to take over Jordan, mainly in order to destroy the prestige of the Egyptian regime.

Cairo Radio and the secret stations began vying with each other in the use of slander. Dulles and Eden were Cairo Radio's pet targets. One broadcaster told the Arab world, "In Dulles's view everything has a price, even honor and the freedom of people. . . . Eden is only a British aristocrat who thrives on the exploitation and humiliation of other people. He fills his belly while others go hungry, and dresses fastidiously while others wear tattered rags."

Problem piled upon problem. Every hour seemed to bring a new crisis, the necessity for another major political decision. There was no time for consultations and cabinet meetings. Orders had to be issued quickly, often without sufficient consideration. He was smoking far too many cigarettes. The circles under his eyes were growing darker. At the U.N., Britain and France were insisting on international control of the Canal. The Soviet Union was opposing it, yet her deputy Prime Minister, Mikoyan, took Israel's side by stating that all countries, including the Jewish state, should have an equal right to send ships through the Canal. This annoyed Nasser. He was further piqued by another of Eden's outbursts. "Peace at any price in dealing with dictatorships means to increase step by step the dangers of universal war," Eden said. Ben-Gurion made the same point when he told the Knesset, "The gravest danger Israel faces is an attack by the Egyptian fascist dictator who rules by force, suppresses by violence all who oppose him, aspires to dominate all the Arab countries, and who does not conceal his intention to liquidate the State of Israel."

One night about the middle of October, Nasser received a visit from Hanson Baldwin, writer on military affairs for *The New York Times,* who, among other questions, asked if he considered himself a dictator. At first he just shrugged his shoulders, but then he suddenly leaned forward and said, "As long as the people of the country support me, it is not a dictatorship. If the majority are against me, I must quit, for that is what the revolution was for, the people." He did not explain how the majority, if they were against him, could express themselves now that he had outlawed political parties and parliamentary elections were no longer being held.

Each time Amer came to Manchiet el Bakry to discuss the military situation he presented more evidence that Israel would soon attack

Jordan. On Sunday, October 21, Jordan held a parliamentary election. A majority of winners were anti-Western and pro-Nasser, so King Hussein decided to ask Cairo for help. Nasser promptly sent Amer to Amman to confer with both the Jordanians and the Syrians about how to defend Jordan when the inevitable attack came. Amer took with him two planeloads of military assistants and Egyptian reporters. On Wednesday, October 24, he sent back word that King Hussein and his General Staff had agreed to drop their defense treaty with Britain and accept the idea of an over-all Egyptian command in the event of war. Nasser was delighted. This would crowd out the Iraqis. The price was that Egypt and Saudi Arabia between them would have to make up the thirty million dollars a year in financial aid that until now Great Britain had been supplying. In his report Amer said he and his mission would stop in Damascus to pay a courtesy call on their way home.

On Sunday, October 28, Israel announced mobilization, stressing the Jordanian situation. It was a day of crisis everywhere. In Hungary, Soviet tanks sealed off a section of the capital city called Buda. In the Jordanian part of Jerusalem a mob burned and sacked the French Consulate in anger over the execution of five rebels in Algiers. Syrians rioted in Damascus.

On Monday, Nasser was at the Barrage with Tahia and the children, enjoying a short relaxation from the strain of the past few weeks. He was sitting under the trees in the garden, looking over a file of reports, when a secretary brought him a message. As he read the first sentence, an expression almost of terror crossed his face. Amer's own plane had been shot down as it was passing Israel, well out to sea, on its way from Damascus to Cairo. Twenty-three men had been aboard. There were no survivors. His first concern was over the loss of Amer. It would be almost impossible to carry on without his closest friend. But then he read the rest of the message. Just before take-off Amer had transferred from his own plane to the other one. This second plane had arrived safely at Cairo. "Allah be praised!" he said half aloud, then ordered his secretary to start packing. He must return home at once. At his office he found urgent diplomatic cables pouring in from around the world. In Washington, President Eisenhower had issued an order for all Americans to quit Jordan, Syria, Egypt, and Israel immediately, unless their presence was vitally necessary. In Amman preparations were being stepped up to meet the inevitable invasion.

That evening, at Manchiet el Bakry, there was a birthday party for Abdel Hamid, who was now five. Nasser had promised that he would turn his back on government business long enough to take part in the celebration. But he had been with the children for only a few minutes when Major Machmud el Gayar, his aide, rushed in with a piece of paper. Everyone could tell from the expression on the major's face that something serious had happened. Nasser read the words in silence, then asked in an icy voice, "When did we get this news?"

"Just a few minutes ago," Gayar replied.

Nasser read the message a second time. The Israeli Army was attacking, just as everyone had predicted. Instead of another retaliation raid it was full-scale invasion. Amer had been correct all along in his estimate of the situation—except that the country invaded was not Jordan. It was Egypt. Several powerfully armed Israeli columns were already deep in the Sinai desert. He left the party quickly and went to his office. There he began pressing the keys of his white switchboard, one after another. His first call was to Amer. Each fresh report he received made the situation seem worse. The first invaders had crossed over in the area of Kuntilla and knifed their way sixty miles in the direction of the Canal without meeting resistance. At the same time, thousands of Israeli troops were dropped by parachute at Mitla Pass, only twenty-five miles from the Suez Canal. This was twentieth-century airborne warfare. The surprise had been so complete that the Israeli planes had the sky to themselves. Egypt's vast air force had been caught napping. The hundreds of jet-propelled Russian planes were still on the ground. Later reports said five thousand Egyptian soldiers had been taken prisoner already. Most of the military equipment received from the Communist countries and stockpiled in the Sinai desert was being lost without a fight. Thousands of Egyptian soldiers were fleeing toward the Canal, leaving everything behind: giant tanks, light and heavy artillery, flame-throwers, even the shoes they needed to save their feet from the blistering heat of the sand.

There was little sleep for any of them that first night. "We must order our army to make a stand at some point," Nasser declared. The desert village of Abou Aweigila was chosen, but meanwhile some units of the Israeli Army that had advanced far into the desert cut back and took many Egyptian strong points along the Israeli frontier by surprise from the rear, among them Kuntilla Kuseima, a town that had been the jumping-off spot for many of the fedayeen raids on Israel.

Nasser and his General Staff were not in complete agreement about whether the British were getting ready to join the attack. Nasser did not believe they were, and explained later:

"My opinion was that any British military move, especially in alliance with the French and Israelis, would only produce catastrophe for Britain, no matter what the results of the military operation. Britain had tremendous interests in the Middle East which any foolish military move would destroy.... I considered it most improbable that any responsible Briton would take any such action."

On Tuesday he and Amer agreed they should send a limited number of Egyptian planes into action, although no attempt would be made to bomb any Israeli cities. In dogfights over Sinai three of the MIG supersonic jet fighters were lost. Late Tuesday front-line reports indicated that the enemy had captured Ras en Nakb, near the Gulf of Elath, and several strong points on the way to the Canal. During the afternoon he received an urgent coded message from his own Ambassador in London. He was so stunned when he read it that he sent for the decoding officer to be sure no mistake had been made. The cable said that at noon Mollet and Pineau had arrived in the British capital. Four hours later the Egyptian and Israeli Ambassadors had been handed a joint British-French ultimatum. It demanded that both Egypt and Israel stop military operations within twelve hours, that they withdraw all their military units to a point ten miles away from the Suez Canal and permit the armed forces of Britain and France to occupy the three key cities on the Canal: Suez, Ismailia, and Port Said.

He could hardly believe it. Withdraw Egyptian forces from the Suez Canal? Why? Egypt had been invaded, yet London and Paris were telling him he had to withdraw Egyptian troops from Egyptian territory. He was angry because his own theory about the improbability of British intervention had proved to be fallacious. He was even angrier because he suspected that England, France, and Israel had secretly planned this action together and his own espionage agents had been unaware of it.

Without waiting to consult Amer or anyone else he made up his mind. "Send for the British, French, American, and Soviet Ambassadors," he told his secretary. When Sir Humphrey Trevelyan and French Chargé Guy Dorget arrived, he told them, "Your demand is categorically rejected. Egypt will defend her dignity." He handed Soviet Ambassador Kiselev a note for Premier Bulganin and American Ambassador Raymond Hare a note for President Eisenhower. "Please dispatch the contents with the greatest possible speed," he told each of them. The notes asked for the support and assistance of the two powers.

That evening, dozens of official automobiles were parked around the house at Manchiet el Bakry. First an emergency cabinet meeting was called. It was delayed half an hour because of an air-raid alert. Blacked-out Cairo heard the crackling of antiaircraft fire, but no bombs were dropped.

All this time, on Nasser's own instructions, the Egyptian people were being told by press and radio—and the people of surrounding countries by the Voice of the Arabs—an account of what had happened in Sinai that would be repeated so many times, day after day, then year after year, that the very authors of the fable would gradually begin to believe it themselves. The story was that a small Israeli force crossed the frontier at a point guarded only by a narcotics patrol mounted on camels; that the Israeli soldiers were chopped down as fast as they came in contact with the Egyptian Army; that most of the Israeli Air Force was destroyed in the first twenty-four hours; that everywhere the Egyptian Army was victorious until the French-British ultimatum made Nasser decide to order a retreat so he could use the bulk of his army to defend the heart of Egypt; that even then the retirement was in good order; that there was little loss of equipment. Eight years earlier, when he was a young officer in Palestine and saw the Egyptian Army suffering disastrous defeats at the hands of the Israelis, he had cursed his own high command for broadcasting reports of victories that had never occurred —for not telling the people the cold truth—yet now that he was in supreme command himself, he went far beyond Farouk and Farouk's officers in trying to keep up Egyptian morale with battle-front reports that bore almost no resemblance to reality.

In other Arab capitals voices were raised in denunciation of Israel. All of Egypt's allies made loud protestations of solidarity and vague offers of military support, but actually not a single soldier, tank, plane, or ship went to Egypt's aid during those first critical days. President Kuwatly of Syria had been invited to Moscow for a two-week visit and left on Tuesday, even though on that day his ally was faced with the possibility of imminent annihilation. Phone calls were received from King Hussein, who was much relieved that Jordan had been merely the diversionary objective, and from King Saud, who was more worried than ever about how Saudi Arabian oil would get to market.

There was little sleep for anyone on Tuesday night, either. The twelve hours of grace were to expire at 6:30 A.M. Wednesday, Cairo time. Early that morning, he was holding a conference with the Indonesian Minister for Foreign Affairs when Cairo's air-raid sirens went off. "Do you mind if we continue to talk?" he asked. The Indonesian smiled his assent. A few moments later there was the deafening noise of exploding bombs not far away. "Go to the roof and see what you can see," he said to Major Gayar. Two or three minutes later the ordinarily jovial major returned, greatly agitated. "It's the airport, El Rayis!" Nasser and the Indonesian climbed to the roof and watched billows of smoke and flame rising from the military airport, only a mile or two away.

This was the fiery start of the destruction of Egypt's Air Force, its runways, and its airdromes by British and French planes. It was a bombardment without precedent. An Arabic voice broadcasting over the Cyprus radio station told Egyptians exactly what targets were about to be attacked, advising them to stay away at such and such an hour from this or that airport, radio station, railway depot, or army barracks. "We shall do all in our power to spare your lives," the announcer kept saying, "but you must do your part. Seek shelter from air attacks and keep away from military installations so you may escape death and injury." At the end of seventy-two hours London and Paris claimed that the Egyptian Air Force had been "virtually annihilated." Cairo Radio gave its listeners a different story: the smoke and fire resulted from enemy bombs igniting imitation cardboard planes that the Egyptian Air Force had hastily constructed and scattered around its airfields to fool the attackers; the real planes had all been flown off to safe airports in Saudi Arabia. President Nasser himself still tells that story when visitors from the West ask questions about the 1956 attack. Except in Moscow, where he later sought replacements of the losses, he has never admitted there were any.

During the first airport raid Major Gayar suggested that he move Tahia and the children to the Gayar farm at Khatatba. "Your house is surrounded by military targets," he said. "But at Khatatba your family would be safe." Nasser shook his head. "It would set a bad example," he replied.

The most mortifying piece of news he received on Wednesday was a report about the *Ibrahim el Awal,* an old Egyptian destroyer. She had been sent to shell Haifa, but almost all her one hundred sixty shots had fallen short, into the water. Then she was chased by an Israeli destroyer of identical vintage, hit, and set afire by several shells. When the crew attempted to scuttle her they were unable to find keys to fit most of the seacocks, and the valves were so rusty no one could turn them. So the captain surrendered and now the *Ibrahim el Awal* was being towed to Haifa, an Israeli prize of war.

This news was balanced by reports from London of the stormiest parliamentary debate in years, with British Socialists and even some

Conservatives denouncing Eden in terms almost as acrimonious as Cairo Radio's.

That night, he decided to move his personal headquarters from Manchiet el Bakry to the old R.C.C. building on Gezira Island. There he could sleep, eat, and run a war without any domestic problems. Amer would operate out of an underground G.H.Q. at Abbassia, but they would be in constant communication with each other. Tahia was nervous when she saw him packing. She began to cry when he told her bluntly he would not be back until the crisis was over. "How long will that be?" she asked. "I hope only a few days," he replied. Her last words to him were a warning to conserve his voice. He had a bad case of laryngitis. His doctor had advised him to stop smoking and talking, or at least to cut down on both, but as soon as the doctor left the room he lit another cigarette and reached for the telephone.

On Thursday, as the round-the-clock British-French bombing continued, he sent for Fawzi and ordered him to go through the formalities of breaking diplomatic relations with Britain and France. While they talked in his office, they could see smoke curling up from the grounds of the British Embassy, just across the Nile. "They're burning secret documents in the center of the embassy courtyard," Gayar explained. Later that afternoon, he issued an order for the seizure of all British and French property in Egypt, and for the closing of the Suez Canal to shipping. Then he went to a studio of Cairo Radio and read over the air a message addressed to "my dear brothers." His voice was quiet as he began, "I am speaking to each of you personally." Soon his words were tumbling out in an angry cascade. "Egypt is faced with the choice of living a free and honorable life, a dignified and good life, or a life of tyranny. . . . Each of you, my brothers, is a soldier in the National Liberation Army. Orders have been issued to distribute arms to everyone, and we have plenty of arms. We shall fight a bitter battle. We shall fight from village to village, from house to house. . . . We shall fight, fight, fight, and never surrender. I promise you I shall fight with you until the last drop of my blood."

When he returned to his office he was so hoarse he could barely speak above a whisper. Gayar sprayed his throat with an atomizer.

Friday, November 2, was a day neither Nasser nor anyone else in Cairo would ever forget. For the first time two of the British jets flew low over downtown Cairo. One was hit by ack-ack fire and fell to earth on the outskirts of the city. There were fifty-five separate alerts during the day. The people were in a constant state of agitation; therefore,

despite the soreness of his throat, he went to Al Azhar at the time of
Friday prayers and talked to the crowd that sat cross-legged on the
vast rug-covered floor, and to twenty thousand who stood outside in
the streets, listening to his voice coming over loudspeakers. There was
one air-raid alert while he was driving to the mosque and another in
the middle of his four-hour talk, but he ignored them both. Many of
those in the streets leading to the mosque looked up nervously at the
sky, but they all remained in their places to hear what their leader had
to say. "Egypt has always been a tomb for its invaders," he told them.
"All empires have vanished and crumbled when they attacked Egypt."
This was an oversimplification of history, but the crowd cheered wildly.

Most of Friday's news was bad. The holding action he had ordered
at Abou Aweigila collapsed. Units of the Israeli Army had sealed off the
Gaza Strip. Just ninety hours after the beginning of the invasion Tel
Aviv was claiming that all Sinai was under Israeli control, with thirty
thousand Egyptian soldiers killed, captured, or put to flight.

From the start Nasser had taken personal command, directing troop
movements, strategy, and even the general line that Egyptian propaganda should follow. He was gambling as he had never gambled before.
He knew the truth about the Sinai debacle and how impossible it would
be for the remnants of his army to hold off the British and French for
long, after they started landing operations. But he was gambling that
a diplomatic victory would annul all the military gains his enemies had
made, or would make. He was certain that the United States and the
Soviet Union would support him. Amer, not so certain, said to him,
"Gamal, we must have an alternate plan if you turn out to be wrong."
He agreed, so between them they decided that if the invaders succeeded
in seizing the Canal, and then if they marched on the capital and Cairo
fell, the key figures of the revolutionary government and the military
units that could be saved would make for Mankabad, the military camp
in Upper Egypt, across the river from Beni Mor. There, hundreds of
miles from Cairo, they would hold out as long as possible, and if
Mankabad eventually was also overwhelmed they would fly off to Saudi
Arabia and constitute themselves a government in exile.

But in his speech at Al Azhar he admitted no possibility of defeat.
His obvious optimism, his apparent fearlessness, his claim that Egyptians would die to the last man before surrendering any of their country
seemed to intoxicate the crowd. As he left the mosque, they mobbed
him, tried to touch him, to embrace him, to kiss him on the cheeks. He
reached his automobile with difficulty. The driver was forced to stop

the car every few feet because of the press of humanity that refused to open a path.

The British and French were about to land troops on Egyptian soil in the belief that the people of Egypt were ready to turn on him, but after his experience at Al Azhar he knew that he had no cause for worry. The street was with him. The people were his.

On Friday afternoon Major Gayar handed him a bulletin from the news wires. The U.N. had passed an American resolution calling for an immediate cease fire. The Soviet Union, the United States, and sixty-two other nations had been opposed only by Australia, New Zealand, and the three belligerents. He was elated. This was the kind of diplomatic victory, he told Amer, that would make the Mankabad plan unnecessary.

That same day, strings of fifty-pound bombs were dropped on the transmitters of Cairo Radio from Canberra light bombers, until the station finally went off the air. This gave a clear field to the British station on Cyprus, now calling itself Radio Free Egypt. Broadcasting in Arabic on a frequency close to that of Cairo Radio, it announced that landings would soon take place in the Canal Zone. While Nasser and Amer were in almost constant consultation over the defense of the zone against such landings, the announcer on Cyprus kept saying, "We only want to help you Egyptians rid yourselves of that traitor Nasser, who has almost delivered your country into Moscow's clutches."

By Friday, too, seven ships were lying at the bottom of the Suez Canal. This had been his own idea. He has admitted, "I ordered the ships prepared with cement for sinking immediately after I received the ultimatum from the British and French."

On Saturday, as more and more Egyptian soldiers and civilian volunteers arrived in the zone to prepare its defense, Nasser sat in his office on Gezira Island and listened to a news broadcast from London announcing the resignation of Anthony Nutting, Minister of State in the Foreign Office, as a protest against Eden's policies. He grinned as he turned away from the radio and said to Gayar, "England seems to be as divided as they hoped we would be."

Early Sunday the radio and news wires announced the creation by the U.N. of the world's first international police force, the United Nations Emergency Force. Its task would be to take over frontier areas after Israeli troops withdrew. At first he was suspicious of it, but eventually he gave permission for the force to come to Egypt on the understanding that he could say where it would be stationed and order it to leave whenever he wished. Later in the day he heard a live broadcast from

Trafalgar Square, London, where tens of thousands of Englishmen were demonstrating against Eden. "I hope Eden is listening, too," he said.

Cairo Radio, back on the air again, spent Sunday broadcasting one victorious communiqué after another. Three British warships had been sunk. Also a French cruiser. A total of eighty-seven British, French, and Israeli planes had been shot down. These were Cairo Radio's claims. Its listeners believed because they wanted to believe. As zero hour for the inevitable invasion approached, he decided he should make a personal inspection of the Canal Zone. An hour before midnight, accompanied by Major Gayar and some General Staff officers, he left by car for Ismailia. Normally at night the eighty-four-mile trip over a road skirting the desert would have taken less than two hours, but for days low-flying British and French planes had been bombing and strafing the road, so at places it was only barely negotiable. It was 4 A.M. before they reached Ismailia. After a quick inspection of the city he decided to go on to Port Said. Kamal Hussein, whom he had released from his duties as Minister of Education to take charge of the Canal's defenses, argued against it. "The first landings will probably occur at dawn," he said to Nasser. "That's only an hour or two from now. It will take you much longer than that to go the fifty miles to Port Said because of the condition of the road. It would be suicide to try." Finally Nasser was convinced and started back for Cairo. He was still on the way when he heard over the car radio the first Cairo communiqué: "At 7:30 A.M. the enemy dropped paratroopers at Port Said and three other places in the area. The army, police, and populace completely annihilated them." What was the truth? He may have wondered himself as he listened to the propaganda-tinged broadcast. During all of Monday and for the next several days Cairo Radio repeatedly talked about the "annihilation" or "extermination" of all the invaders as fast as they landed from planes and ships. Actually, after it was over and figures could be checked, neutral war correspondents agreed that the total of British-French casualties in the entire invasion was one hundred twenty-five dead and one missing. But all day Monday, as wave after wave of paratroopers floated to earth, Cairo Radio labored to create the myth that "all were exterminated."

As soon as he reached his office he drafted an open appeal to "those who still respect the dignity of man and the supremacy of law in international relations" to come to Egypt's aid with men and arms. The first response was from Moscow. Premier Bulganin sent letters to the Prime Ministers of Britain, France, and Israel announcing that Russia was prepared to use force "to crush the aggressors and restore peace." The notes contained a broad hint that unless Britain and France halted their attack at once, they might touch off the world's first atomic war. Within a few more hours Peiping announced she had nearly three hundred thousand Chinese volunteers ready to fly to Egypt's aid.

From the Canal Zone came reports of hundreds of Egyptian soldiers and civilians killed during the sporadic fighting. Port Said hospital had a thousand casualties. Yet bulletins broadcast from Cyprus told again and again of how much less resistance had been encountered than had been expected. Messages from Ismailia headquarters said many Egyptian volunteers to whom Enfield rifles and light machine guns had been issued had had so little training they were unable to operate these modern weapons. When the waves of invaders hit the canal cities, some of the defenders dropped their guns in panic, discarded their uniforms, and went into hiding in civilian clothes. The worse the news the more Nasser insisted that press and radio feed the Egyptian public stronger and stronger doses of heroic resistance.

One foreign radio report on Monday infuriated him. In Rome, Farouk told a reporter he was ready to return to Egypt to resume the leadership of his country as soon as he was sent for. This was the first time Nasser ever lost his temper about the exiled King.

On Tuesday, at his own order, Cairo Radio throughout the day addressed a message to the people of Port Said: "The enemy who subjugated us for so many years is now in your hands. Kill any number you want. Take revenge, my brothers, for past subjugation. We are now free and we will remain free."

On Wednesday, Anthony Eden, faced with the realization that he had world opinion against him, that his own people were divided, and that he had failed in his scheme to get rid of Nasser, agreed to a withdrawal without conditions. The crisis was over. There would be no need of the Mankabad plan now. Soon he would be able to return home to Manchiet el Bakry and his family.

On Friday, riding in an open car, he went again to Al Azhar. The people in the streets cheered him more hysterically than ever. Once inside the mosque, he walked briskly across the soft red- and blue- and gold-colored rugs covering the immense floor and mounted the narrow, almost perpendicular flight of steps leading to a small platform from which he looked down on the multitude. As he delivered a report of the ten days, he said nothing to dispel any of Cairo Radio's myths. He assured his people that "the whole world is now with us, even free people in Britain herself. Egypt is united, strong, and monolithic, determined and resolved."

He was only partly right. The defeat of Egypt's Sinai army at the hands of the Israelis had been even more humiliating than what had happened in 1948. This time there was no king to blame, no corrupt politicians, no evil dealers in defective weapons. The loss of many millions of dollars' worth of equipment recently received from Eastern Europe was so serious a blow that it must never be admitted in public. The forty-seven sunken ships and the wreckage of two bridges in the Canal might keep the great waterway closed for months, perhaps years. Hundreds of men, women, and children had lost their lives at Port Said. Most of the Air Force planes lay in ruins. The Navy had suffered severe losses. As a result of the rupture of business between Egypt and the West, and the freezing of assets on both sides, the economy of the country would be in a precarious condition for a long time. But the imperialists, as he called them, would have to pay and pay for their folly. Western Europe faced a hard winter. Because oil no longer flowed through the Canal, gasoline was being rationed in some countries; all over Europe prices were skyrocketing. Anticolonial peoples everywhere were now united as never before. Soviet Russia and Communist China had gained the prestige that Britain and France had sacrificed. When the United States sided with the Communists against the invaders, Western unity was gravely damaged. But what was most important, as he saw it, was that sympathy even in some of the Western capitals was on Egypt's side. Battles had been lost, but a war had been won.

His personal situation was a paradox of history. He was a military leader who had come to power by a military revolt. He had repeatedly affirmed his belief in militarism. He had loudly claimed that his army was not the army of Farouk, and his Minister of Defense had boasted that it could never be taken by surprise. It *had* been taken by surprise and put to rout. Yet despite this defeat, he, its leader, was more secure than ever as Egypt's military dictator, and also as a leader of the Arab world.

It was a very self-satisfied Gamal Abdel Nasser who left revolutionary headquarters on Gezira Island and moved back to the mustard-colored house at Manchiet el Bakry.

CHAPTER 21

THE FIRST CIRCLE

Egyptianization was his own idea. Even the word was his. It began one evening late in 1956 with a police raid on the minuscule Jewish colony in Port Said. Nearly every Jewish family there lost someone that night. Twenty-five men, women, and boys were rounded up and led away, without explanation. No one has ever been able to discover what happened to them. They simply vanished. That was the small start. Before he finished he had ordered the mass arrest, internment, or expulsion of a great many of Egypt's fifty thousand Jews.

This was his reaction to the damage the Israeli Army had done in Sinai to his military reputation. For centuries Jews had played a significant part in Egypt's economic and cultural life. Many had their roots deep in the soil. During World War II, when some Egyptians were eager for Hitler's army to win, and again during the war in Palestine, Egypt's Jews suffered little molestation. During the first four post-revolutionary years they had not been singled out for special treatment. But now they were "enemy nationals." They became victims of a wave of hysteria that began at the very top, in the mustard-colored house at Manchiet el Bakry, and extended down to thousands of irresponsible policemen and jailers, who found in Jews a convenient object for the fury they had not been able to unleash against the Israeli, British, and French military forces.

At first, in theory, they took action only against Jews who did not have Egyptian nationality. But day after day early in 1957 new rulings were promulgated, always with Nasser's approval, making more and more Jews liable to arrest and expulsion. Citizenship was automatically taken away from any Jew who had acquired it since 1933. Then from anyone who had ever expressed sympathy for the idea of a Jewish homeland, from any Jew who had acquired citizenship since 1900, from any Jew who had ever been convicted of a crime. Then from those who, though they had acquired citizenship before 1900, had not been in

268

continuous residence since then. Thousands of arrests were made. The knock on the door almost always came at night. Women and children as well as men were taken to camps and prisons. Some of the victims spoke no other language than Arabic, knew no other country than Egypt, but they were about to be expelled anyway. At first deportees were permitted to take the equivalent of twenty dollars in cash and one suitcase of personal belongings. Later the amount of cash was cut and a brown parcel substituted for the suitcase. When the Jewish hospitals at Cairo and Alexandria were sequestered by the government, the patients were turned into the streets and members of the staffs were arrested.

Almost at once the campaign was extended to the British and the French. London filed a protest with the U.N., saying "Thousands of Britons have received orders to leave Egypt within a few days. In many cases they were required to sign declarations in Arabic without ever knowing that the contents confirmed that they were leaving of their free will and renouncing any claim to damages. The indiscriminate character of these expulsion orders is reminiscent of the barbarous methods of mass deportation at short notice which have been practiced in other countries. This operation is being carried out with brutal haste against people who have given service to Egypt and have spent their lives in that country."

As protests mounted, Nasser authorized his Ministry of National Guidance to announce that the Britons and Frenchmen were being "permitted to leave Egypt to save them from the wrath of the Egyptian people." The good will he had won in many parts of the West as a victim of aggression was now being dissipated. He gave no indication that he cared. He read every protest, but instead of ordering some amelioration in the treatment of these people he termed foreigners he accelerated the campaign against them.

One morning a government paper listed nearly five hundred wealthy persons, mostly Jews, whose property had been "placed under government managership," which meant seized. One was Salvatore Circurel, whose department store, Cairo's largest, had been wrecked on Black Saturday, rebuilt, and now was sequestered. The seizures at first were of shops, automobile sales rooms, clubs, private homes, small enterprises, but before long British property worth millions began to be expropriated: banks, insurance firms, a hundred-million-dollar oil company.

One evening during a private discussion of Egyptianization, Nasser said to a friend, "Now we have an excuse to purge the country of all foreign influence, and we'll regret it the rest of our lives if we don't do a thorough job." Very soon he authorized his Minister of Finance to install Egyptians of his own selection as temporary managers of all sequestered firms. Young army officers who knew little about business or finance suddenly found themselves behind huge mahogany desks in banks and insurance companies. He ordered professional associations of lawyers, doctors, engineers, pharmacists, dentists, and architects to drop from their membership rolls all but Egyptians. This meant no foreign professional men would be able to practice in Egypt. British firms had been making a profit of well over a hundred million dollars a year on Egyptian reinsurance. This business must now be transferred to Swiss companies. British and French firms would no longer be permitted to sue in Egyptian courts. Books audited by British and French auditors would not be deemed to have been audited. On his instructions fifty British and French schools were seized, closed, restaffed with Egyptian teachers, and then reopened as all-Egyptian schools. He told his film censors to withdraw from circulation all British and French films, and all Hollywood films made with Jewish talent. He said that the Ministry of Education must break, as quickly as possible, all Egypt's cultural ties with Britain and France, and to remove from the schools all books written by Frenchmen or Englishmen. This would include the works of William Shakespeare, author of his favorite play, and Charles Dickens, whose *A Tale of Two Cities* had had a profound influence on his early thinking. He also ordered all reference to Britain and France deleted from Egyptian textbooks. He told the Ministry, "It is time those receiving their education in this country knew something about Egypt's history."

In the midst of the campaign a complaint came from an unexpected source. Among the diplomatic cables one night was one from the Egyptian Ambassador to Tunisia, who said President Bourguiba had protested against the treatment of Jews in possession of valid Tunisian passports. This irked him. Had Bourguiba forgotten that he, too, was an Arab?

Almost every day the news wires brought dispatches from such Mediterranean ports as Naples telling of the arrival of another shipload of Jewish refugees from Egypt, some of whom always complained that they had been beaten into signing documents that they had left voluntarily, been well treated, had no complaints. One dispatch told of a man who had a million and a half dollars and was permitted to take out only fourteen. These stories apparently did not trouble him, but he was very disturbed one day in January when Ambassador Hare arrived with a complaint from the American State Department about the deportations and a request that he adopt a more modest policy. He considered this outside interference in internal affairs, and said so.

His fight with the West had made him more than ever the darling of the East. The Russian bloc was taking more than half of Egypt's exports. On the anniversary of the Bolshevik Revolution he sent Marshal Voroshilov a cable of "Best wishes for the glory of the peoples of the Soviet Union, with whom our people are bound by the strongest ties of friendship and fraternity." In his public addresses he gave Moscow rather than Washington credit for halting the Anglo-French attack. He allowed the Russians to announce that he would visit their country sometime in 1957. Four Egyptians with strong pro-Soviet feelings now occupied key positions. The Red major, Khaled Mohieddin, had been given three quarters of a million dollars to help him make a success of his new daily newspaper. Ahmed Fouad, who had lent him so many radical books on economics and politics in his Free Officers days, was now director of fourteen companies, including Bank Misr, which controlled most of Egypt's domestic and foreign commerce. Rashed el Barawky, who had translated Marx's *Das Kapital* into Arabic, was director of the Industrial Bank. He appointed Fathy Radwan, who had represented Egypt at the 1951 Communist Peace Congress in Vienna, his Minister of National Guidance. Cairo's bookshops were being flooded with more Arabic and English translations of Russian classics than ever before. A Russian ballet troupe was drawing immense crowds into Cairo's largest theater, and each night between acts a member of the Soviet diplomatic corps made a flattering speech in Arabic to the audience. Moscow sent word that all the exhibits at a recent industrial fair in the Soviet Union would be shipped to Cairo as a gift to "our friends the Egyptians."

When an American reporter asked Nasser just where he stood politically these days, he replied with some pique, "I will not become the stooge or satellite or pawn or hireling of anybody.... Egypt is determined to maintain her independence from all foreign ideologies, such as Marxism, fascism, racism, colonialism, imperialism, and atheism, all of which, incidentally, are of European origin."

One of his minor problems about this time was what to do with Doria Shawfik, the feminist whose magazines he had ordered suppressed. During the past five years many reckless men had risked their lives to plot the overthrow of his regime, but Mrs. Shawfik was the only person in all this time to speak out publicly against him. As a protest against what she called his "dictatorial regime that eventually will lead Egypt to bankruptcy and anarchy," she went on a hunger strike. He told his censors to keep the story out of Cairo papers but to allow it to be cabled abroad. On the sixth day she was taken to a hospital, too weak to talk. On the eleventh she was taken home on a stretcher in the hope her daughters would be able to persuade her to eat. Later, after she was no longer in the public eye, he had her placed under permanent house arrest and denied the right to a passport.

Late in 1956 his Washington Embassy informed him of a White House plan to give economic and military aid to any Middle Eastern country asking for it as a defense against communism: the Eisenhower Doctrine. At first he made no comment, waiting cautiously to see if there was anything worth while in it for him, but he was annoyed by reports that the United States, by use of this device, was trying to fill the "vacuum" caused by the disappearance of Britain and France from the Middle East. The very word vacuum angered him. "This is an insult," he said, "to all Middle Easterners." He celebrated his thirty-ninth birthday in January by receiving a Greek newspaperman and telling him that "while Russia was helping us during the Suez crisis, the United States was freezing fifty million dollars of our assets." Soon, with his permission, the controlled press and radio of Egypt was in full outcry against the Eisenhower Doctrine, terming it "another trick of the evil imperial powers."

In January 1957 coded diplomatic messages from the Egyptian Embassy in Washington informed him that the United States was about to use all the economic weapons at her command to try to accomplish what Britain and France had failed to achieve with their invasion: to isolate him, to prevent him from establishing himself as the strong man of the Middle East, and to bring about his eventual downfall, if possible. His obsession now became an attempt to outwit the State Department. He devoted most of his waking hours to it during 1957, a year that would go down in Middle Eastern history as a time of conniving, intrigue, assassination, plot and counterplot.

He started by gathering together his Arab allies for a show of unity. King Saud arrived in his private plane, equipped with the revolving throne and a built-in juke box. In less than forty-eight hours he would be off to the White House to visit President Eisenhower. It was essential to commit him to neutralism before he left. King Hussein flew in from Amman, resentful that the others had done nothing to implement their offer of financial help for his wobbly kingdom. President Kuwatly flew down from Damascus. This tall, sixty-four-year-old Syrian, who had once tried to commit suicide while a prisoner of the Turks because of their brutality to him, was the one Arab leader he felt he could trust. Their conference was brief but successful, from his own point of view. They signed what he termed "a new solidarity pact." Egypt, Syria, and Saudi Arabia would supply Jordan with arms and money to replace the British subsidy. Although he still became indignant when others tried to impose contractual conditions of any sort on him, he had insisted that in return for this aid Jordan must agree to break all ties with Great Britain and never join the Baghdad Pact. Hussein promised. All four nations rejected the Eisenhower Doctrine and reaffirmed that the Gaza Strip should belong to Egypt. After they had affixed their signatures to the agreement, Saud flew off to Italy to board a ship for New York.

As soon as the tall, partially blind monarch arrived in the United States, it was clear from the dispatches reaching Manchiet el Bakry that he was being accorded the honors usually reserved for the head of a major, friendly nation. To Nasser the purpose was obvious. The United States was going to use Saud to try to extend her own hold on the Middle East. His pride in seeing a fellow Arab treated so well in Washington was overshadowed by his concern about how far Saud might go in looking out merely for his own personal interests. He was also envious. In a newspaper article written by his confidant, Mohamed Heikal, appeared the headline:

EISENHOWER MAY INVITE NASSER TO WASHINGTON

Within a few hours the State Department denied that there was any such intention. This only increased his irritation and intensified his jealousy. Why should the head of a remote country of only six million inhabitants be given such preference over him? But he knew the answer. In addition to their interest in oil the Americans wanted to renew their lease on a vital air base.

One evening Major Gayar brought him a dispatch from Washington that quoted Saud as praising the Eisenhower Doctrine. Less than three weeks had passed since their joint announcement in Cairo rejecting it. Then came news of the Eisenhower-Saud agreement. The King, who already had a personal income of nearly a million dollars a day from oil, was promised fifty million dollars in economic and military aid from the United States Government. All he had to give in return was a lease on the air base for five years and his word that he would try to influence other Arab countries to align themselves with the West. There was no doubt that Egypt and her revolutionary leader were being by-passed, but he felt they were also being intentionally insulted. Vice-President Nixon's tour of Africa was an example. He was going to visit Ethiopia, the Sudan, and Libya, all countries with which Egypt had strained relations, but he would not be coming to Cairo. Worse than that, Washington was helping to make Saud the key figure of the Middle East, and Nasser knew it, so he called a four-power conference at Cairo.

When King Saud arrived he was given a twenty-one-gun salute and an affectionate embrace that disguised his host's real feelings. They were joined at an immense octagonal table in Kubbah Palace by King Hussein and President Kuwatly and their Prime Ministers, and by the military leaders of all four countries. Saud kept his word to Eisenhower. He immediately asked the others to join him in support of the Eisenhower Doctrine and to issue a firm declaration against communism in the Middle East. Turning to Nasser, he asked for a public statement that the Suez Canal would be open to ships of all nationalities. They argued for four days. Often harsh words were spoken. Twice Saud delayed his departure. In the end the conference postponed taking a position on the Eisenhower Doctrine and refused to make any anti-Communist statement, while Nasser declared that the Sinai attack had freed him of any obligation to admit Israeli ships to the Canal. Saud left completely rebuffed.

Nasser had won this round, but he was aware that the fight had only begun. It was going to be a war of nerves. The winner would probably be the man who was most adept at intrigue, and there was no question in his own mind as to who that was. Months before, he had started to put a plan into operation. All his military attachés and most of his Ambassadors to other Middle Eastern countries were young Free Officers. One by one he called them to Manchiet el Bakry for consultations. In no two countries was the problem the same, therefore in no two could they use the same tactics. In some capitals certain key figures had to be removed, preferably by assassination. In others mass rebellion must be sponsored. In this war of subversion great quantities of weapons and munitions might be required. They would have to be smuggled across frontiers and carefully hidden until needed. Meanwhile a hawk eye must be kept for any retaliatory measures against Egypt. He told them that if they were caught it might be impossible to come to their defense. The envoys received their instructions and left. In some ways it was like the old pre-revolutionary days. He shared his secrets with a few men like Amer, but decided not to take the entire Cabinet into his confidence. Yet in an address to his General Staff one night in March he hinted at what was in his mind:

"Those who think unity of the Arabs will come as a result of speeches should open their eyes and look at our Army. But the Army is not the only means. There are special political means. We must work to strengthen opposition groups.... You officers should know that the work of military attachés is very dangerous, but we cannot do without it.... Army officers must be able not only to use guns, but to pursue a war of nerves and to direct commandos."

The first boomerang had been in Beirut. After the mysterious bombing of a number of British and French establishments, a police officer making a routine check of an overloaded automobile belonging to the Egyptian military attaché found it full of explosives, fuses, and detonators. A search was then made of his home, which resembled a well-stocked arsenal.

In Libya the Egyptian military attaché was escorted to the frontier after he had tried to foment mob action.

In Tunisia, President Bourguiba accused Nasser of giving sanctuary to a Tunisian opposition leader charged with plotting the death of Bourguiba.

From far to the south came the next complaint. Haile Selassie said Egypt was trying to create subversion in his Coptic kingdom by stirring up the Moslem minority. Specifically, he demanded the recall of the Egyptian military attaché.

Less than two months after Nasser had kissed King Saud so warmly on both cheeks at Cairo airport, word was flashed to him from the Saudi Arabian capital that mass arrests were being made there, following discovery of a plot to assassinate the King and many members of his family. The Egyptian military attaché was accused of being the instigator.

But the plot that misfired worst was the one in Jordan. A headline in one of the Amman papers called it "A Dangerous Communist-Egyptian Plot to Swallow the Arab World," and published details of how Egypt, Syria, and the Soviet Union planned to get rid of all four Middle Eastern kings and overthrow the Lebanese republic as well. The plotters were working with Palestinian Arabs, who made up two thirds of Jordan's population. Hussein outwitted them by appealing to the loyalty of the Bedouins. One spring day he suddenly placed the Prime Minister under house arrest, surrounded the palace with tanks for his own protection, ordered Syrian troops who had a part in the plot to quit the country, and let it be known that the drift of Jordan into Nasser's orbit had been halted and that all possibility of Jordan's federating with either Syria or Egypt was over. Some of Nasser's friends had to leave Jordan quickly to escape arrest. As Hussein imposed martial law he bluntly accused the Egyptian President of trying to bring about his downfall. He said Nasser had sent a hundred "treacherous criminals" into Jordan from Syria to conduct a wave of assassinations.

In Washington, President Eisenhower issued a statement that the United States regarded the independence and integrity of Jordan "vital to the preservation of world peace." Two days later Gayar rushed into Nasser's office with a bulletin. The American Sixth Fleet had just been ordered to head for the Middle East. Nasser shrugged his shoulders. Gayar, amazed at his chief's reaction, said frantically, "But, Gamal, they say the Sixth Fleet carries atom bombs. What defense do we have against atom bombs?"

Nasser smiled. "The Sixth Fleet and its atom bombs are not within my calculations. If it comes to atomic warfare, I don't think atom bombs will fall on us. They'll be used on larger targets."

The Middle East had become a political whirlpool, with many swirling cross currents. King Saud jumped to the support of Hussein, congratulating him on his bold action and brave talk. Moscow Radio began to attack the young King. Then Saud suddenly flew up to Baghdad and made peace with Iraq's ruler, Faisal, thus patching up a feud that had existed since World War I, when Saud's father seized Mecca in defiance of the Hashemites. The two kings embraced, wept, talked, exchanged gifts, and finally issued a bold rebuke to Nasser: No Arab country should interfere in the affairs of any other Arab country.

As the turmoil spread, Nasser proclaimed a law providing death as the penalty for sabotage, libel, distributing secret leaflets, attempting a *coup d'état,* rumormongering, or even insulting the President of the Egyptian republic. He also seized the Marconi radio, telegraph, and telephone organization and converted it into a government department.

In June, King Saud angered Nasser still further by paying a state visit to King Hussein. Emboldened by this support, the young monarch announced that Egypt's military attaché in Amman had offered a Jordanian soldier "material and moral allurements" if he would arrange a long list of assassinations during the conference of the two kings.

Diplomats began to speculate about whether the thin thread of friendliness between Nasser and Saud could be kept intact much longer. It was still a question which of the two would emerge as the strong man of the Arab world.

Late in the month orders went out from Manchiet el Bakry for an unrestrained press and radio campaign against Jordan. Over the Voice of the Arabs and on the wires of the government-controlled Middle East News Agency, Jordan's Foreign Minister was accused of having committed the unpardonable sin: meeting with Israeli Prime Minister Ben-Gurion to talk peace.

Early in July, Egypt held its first parliamentary election since before the revolution. Anyone who thought he was acceptable enough to win the President's approval as a candidate for one of the three hundred fifty seats to be filled could enter his name, upon payment of a hundred dollars, with the understanding that if he was rejected the money would not be refunded. All those chosen would be candidates of the National Union, the new, unopposed political party, but before their names could go on the ballot their records would be scrutinized by a committee consisting of Nasser, who had appointed himself leader of the party, Amer, Baghdady, and Zakaria Mohieddin. No one even suspected of ever having opposed the regime and no one with any Western connections would be approved. Nasser gave the list of 2469 applicants to his espionage and counterespionage organizations. The names of more than half the candidates were stricken. They not only lost a hundred dollars apiece, but they were given no explanation of why they had failed to pass. There was no recourse. The four-man committee made certain that all members of the Cabinet would be elected to Parliament by disqualifying all rival candidates in their districts. Opposition was also eliminated for thirty-five other close friends of the President, including Sadat, Major Mohieddin, and a Cairene who had just been put in charge of a quarter of a million nationalized trade union members. The election was little more than a popularity contest, with most candidates trying to outdo each other in proving they were more enthusiastic supporters of El Rayis than their rivals. Two women were elected, the first of their sex to hold public office in modern Egypt. Two of Nasser's brothers also gained office.

Several weeks later twenty-one cannon were shot off as he drove to the Parliament building to make what in royalist days had been called "the speech from the throne." But the great gilt chair in which Farouk used to sit had been removed and Nasser's three-hour discourse was announced as "the people's speech." Russian MIGs flew overhead. Diplomats filled the galleries. The address was sprinkled with braggadocio that reached its peak when he said, "Egypt will build the Great Dam herself, without outside economic assistance."

The next day, the country celebrated the fifth anniversary of the revolution with the customary military parade, but this time there was not even a token force from any other Arab country, an indication of how far Egypt's star had fallen. Three days later, on the anniversary of the nationalization of the Suez Canal, he delivered an impassioned speech to a mass of sweltering humanity in Liberation Square, Alexandria. He bitterly accused the United States of trying to destroy Egypt by intrigue. Tahia and the children, listening from the balcony of a nearby building, heard a crowd of a quarter of a million chant his name, interrupt almost every sentence, applaud his shouted grievances.

About this time in a Cairo courtroom thirteen Egyptians, including two former cabinet members, were placed on trial, charged with having been part of an "American imperialist plot" to assassinate Nasser and replace him with Naguib. One witness, when asked how he knew "American imperialism" was involved, replied, "The pistols supplied for the assassination were equipped with silencers and I know that silencers are manufactured only by foreign nations, so I assume the backers of the plot are imperialists." The defendants received long prison terms.

In September, annoyed by what he called Washington's policy of "calculated indifference," he ordered press and radio to intensify their anti-American campaign. At his suggestion the Voice of the Arabs beamed almost daily broadcasts to central Africa about desegregation problems in the United States. In newspaper cartoons Vice-President Nixon was pictured as a villainous munitions salesman, carrying a bomb in one hand and a satchel of assorted weapons in the other as he toured Africa looking for customers. On his order, Cairo's fury was also turned against King Saud, who was accused of having granted an audience to Syrian and Egyptian political refugees while he was at a spa in West Germany.

As Khaled's sixth birthday approached, the boy asked his father this year not to hurry away from the party before the refreshments were served. Nasser promised. "I will tell Major Gayar not to bring me any messages, no matter what happens," he said to Khaled. But he forgot to give Gayar the instructions and after the party was under way the major rushed in just as he had the year before. He held a news bulletin in his hand, and looked almost as excited as he had on October 29, 1956. "What is it this time?" Nasser asked. Gayar handed him the story. Prime Minister Ben-Gurion had been injured, perhaps seriously, by a bomb thrown in the Knesset at Jerusalem by a Jewish fanatic.

Late in the year, after three months of undeclared peace between Cairo and Amman, Nasser gave the order for a renewal of the internecine Arab war with Jordan. Cairo Radio called on both Bedouins and Palestinians to rid themselves of Hussein and his entire family by assassination. The King was accused of having met with Ben-Gurion in a village on the west bank of the Jordan to discuss resettlement of the refugees, in return for a thirty-million-dollar grant. The lie was told, retold, amplified, and embellished so often that many people began to think it must have some foundation. After days of denial Amman Radio began to hit back, referring to Nasser as "a Don Quixote, hopelessly striking with his wooden sword, right and left, but hitting only himself." In Damascus, Palestinian refugees filled the streets, shouting, "Hussein must go! Death to the traitor, Hussein!" while a voice on Cairo Radio kept saying, "His life is in danger. Let him die like the dog, his grandfather."

Kings Saud and Faisal called for an end to this Arab civil war, but Nasser ignored them and ordered the campaign intensified, so Cairo Radio went a step farther and referred to Hussein one night as "that stunted lad, sucking the blood of his people, who calls himself a king." But then the announcers defeated themselves. They told of riots occurring in nonexistent villages, of how a mob had burned down the mansion of the Jordanian Minister of Agriculture, who, as most Jordanians knew, was a Bedouin and lived in a tent, and of another cabinet member crossing into Israel at a time he actually was attending a public function in Amman. When Jordan's papers began to publish the texts of such broadcasts and hold them up to ridicule, Nasser ordered an end to the campaign.

During most of 1957 he had been desperately trying to influence the trend of affairs in the Middle East. He failed in every attempt, most notably in Jordan. In December the young King was more secure on his throne than he had been at the start of the year. Even many who believed that he was too young and too weak to be a ruler felt he had grown in wisdom as a result of the attacks and was more popular with his people than he had ever been.

Gamal Abdel Nasser had one card left. He had been hesitant about playing it because there might be danger for everyone involved. But the situation now demanded drastic action, unless he was willing to turn the leadership of the Arab world over to Saud and to the West. So at five o'clock on the afternoon of February 1, 1958, after weeks of frenetic preparation, he and Syrian President Shukri el Kuwatly stood side by side on the balcony of Abdin Palace in Cairo and waved to a

somewhat bewildered crowd as the Syrian Prime Minister read a proclamation announcing that Syria and Egypt were about to go out of
existence as independent states. In their place would spring up the
United Arab Republic, containing half the population and one fourth
the area of the Arab Middle East. Within a month the people would be
given an opportunity to approve or disapprove in a plebescite, and to
elect a President.

Sound trucks blaring patriotic Syrian and Egyptian songs began to
move slowly through the streets of Cairo. Already city employees were
putting up arches of unity and brotherly love. Pictures of Nasser and
Kuwatly suddenly appeared in shop windows.

The younger man on the balcony, certain he would be the first President of the United Arab Republic because that was the way he was
planning it, embraced the older man, who was sacrificing the independence of his country and his position as head of a state in the interests
of unity. The crowds cheered. The two men had already talked about
the chances of making this into a union of all the Arab states: the first
circle of Nasser's dream in *The Philosophy of the Revolution*. They
agreed there was a possibility, even though the odds might be slim.
They agreed, too, that Syria, with a higher standard of living than
Egypt, a sounder currency, a more stable economy, a better-paid army,
a richer soil, a smaller national debt, might have to make some sacrifices
as a member of the new partnership, but in the arms of Egypt she would
be safe from internal and external subversion, already a threat.

Nasser denied that the U.A.R. was coming into existence as a result
of intrigue on his part. His version was that he agreed to the union only
under pressure. "There were ten political parties in Syria," he said.
"Their leaders came to me saying that everything was in a mess. I met
with all except the Communists. They told me, 'Only you can save us.
Liquidate our parties and join us to Egypt.'"

Geographically their new republic was an unnatural entity, for between the Northern Region and the Southern Region, as Syria and
Egypt were to be called, lay Israel. The only way to go the several
hundred miles from Cairo to Damascus now was by sea or air. But on
this momentous day such obstacles were forgotten. Turning to the
crowd, Nasser shouted to them through a microphone, "Today we look
to the future and feel it will be loaded with power and dignity."

Power for whom?

CHAPTER 22

BELOVED MEN OF BAGHDAD

He knew 1958 was going to be a vital year. The dreams he had revealed in *The Philosophy of the Revolution* seemed to be on the point of bursting into explosive reality. He tried to put his thoughts into words in a speech to the Egyptian Parliament. His voice was low-pitched but vibrant with feeling as he addressed the full benches and crowded galleries. "In the lives of nations," he said, "there are certain generations chosen by destiny to witness decisive turning points in the history of mankind. This generation of Egyptians is one of those ordained by fate to live great moments of transition that are like the pageants of the sunrise. . . . We are witnessing the dawn of our independence, the morning of our freedom, the rebirth of our pride and dignity."

He seemed to confuse the wish with the actuality as he pictured the state he had just helped to create. Instead of a nebulous union facing grave problems of survival, he painted it as a Utopia, born full-blown. "A great state has arisen in this East," he said. "It is neither an intruder nor a usurper. It is without hostility toward anyone. It is a state that protects but does not threaten, strengthens but does not weaken, unites but does not divide . . . a state whose well-being shall have its effect on those around it and on the entire human race."

The hand-picked members of the Egyptian Parliament, spellbound by such oratory, nominated him for the presidency of the U.A.R. and even voted him the right to hand-pick the U.A.R. Parliament.

Early in February Faisal and Hussein, kingly cousins, conferred in the Royal Palace at Amman. After one of their discussions, which lasted the entire night, they sat at a breakfast table and signed a document creating the Arab Federation out of Jordan and Iraq. This was their answer to the United Arab Republic. Each young monarch would retain his own throne, but otherwise the union of the two kingdoms would follow the Egyptian-Syrian pattern.

Nasser received the news soon after finishing his own breakfast that

281

morning. His initial reaction was favorable: barriers were being broken down. This would make it even easier to consolidate the first circle—the Arab world. He dispatched a telegram of congratulations to Faisal, calling the new federation a "blessed step" and expressing the hope that it would bring closer the "days of greater unity." He used flattery on the young King. "There is no doubt that your youth, your faith, and your belief will prove the power that will bring about the dream of all Arabs," he said. Several days later President Kuwatly boldly advanced the opinion that not only Jordan and Iraq but Saudi Arabia, Libya, Tunisia, Algeria, and Yemen would all join the U.A.R. before long. Cairo newspapers said this was not a prediction but "the news of tomorrow."

When days went by with no reply from the telegram to Faisal, Nasser changed his tactics. On his instructions Cairo Radio and Egyptian newspapers began to criticize the Arab Federation. Day by day the attacks grew stronger. Washington had instigated the federation. Israel had approved it. It was a device of foreigners, blessed by the devil.

One day late in February, voters of the two U.A.R. regions were given the opportunity of saying *yes* or *no* to two questions: Do you approve of Egypt and Syria forming the United Arab Republic? Do you approve of Gamal Abdel Nasser as President of the U.A.R.?

The next day, half a million people pushed and jostled their way into Republic Square. When Nasser stepped out onto the balcony and looked down into the sea of upturned, perspiring faces, tears showed in his eyes. The voices of the huge crowd made such a din that few heard the Minister of the Interior announce the results. Seven and a half million ballots had been cast. Only 288 had been against the union; only 451 against Nasser. His percentage of popular support, if the ballot count could be believed, had increased in less than two years from 99.948 to 99.998. When his time to speak came, he talked into the black and silver microphones without referring to his notes. Both his words and his delivery were designed to stir the passions of the throng. The response was loud and wild. He told them one of his first official acts would be to name his dear friend Amer Commander in Chief, with the rank of field marshal.

He made no reference to it in his speech, but he was piqued that day because, although cables granting diplomatic recognition to the U.A.R. were pouring in, and although Marshal Voroshilov had sent a personal letter of congratulation, not a word had come from the United States.

Two days later he made a surprise visit to Damascus to generate enthusiasm for the U.A.R. He had no trouble winning the support of the street in this city that claimed it was the oldest in the world. It took ninety minutes for his automobile to go the first quarter of a mile, the people seemed so determined to see him, to hear his voice, to touch him. At the home of his friend, Shukri el Kuwatly, he made a balcony speech and then started to shake the hands of Syrian notables. This went on all afternoon and long into the night. At the end of each hour he disappeared for a short rest and sometimes a cup of coffee, before resuming the handshaking. The next day, classes were dismissed and schoolchildren paraded in the streets, chanting slogans in praise of Nasser and against imperialism. In the evening he received a report that there had been many automobile accidents caused by zealots pasting such large posters of him on the windshields of their automobiles that they were unable to see the road. On the third day he attacked the Arab Federation, which he had so recently called a "blessed step." Now he said it was doomed to failure and would be "scattered like dry leaves before the wind." Within a few hours Amman Radio replied, quoting Hussein: " 'Lies, intrigue, and conspiracies will only make us more determined to carry home our mission of Arab unity.' " Nasser retorted that the U.A.R. intended to bring together the whole Arab nation, "whether they like it or not." But he hastily added, "because this is the will of the Arab people." The following day, he called the Foreign Ministers of Iraq and Jordan "agents of imperialism whose end is near, my brothers."

Early in March the Crown Prince of Yemen, Said al Islam, arrived in Damascus with his father's authorization to sign a pact of confederation with the U.A.R. Nasser at once ordered a mass meeting to announce the adherence of this minuscule monarchy, the most primitive of all Arabian countries. Facing the crowd, he raised the hand of the dark-skinned man from Yemen and boasted that one more step had now been taken to bring all Arabs together. Yemen could not join a republic, so a new entity was being formed, the United Arab States. He was upset, however, by a report the Crown Prince brought with him. On his way to Damascus he had stopped off to see King Saud, who had flatly declared Saudi Arabia was going to stay out of all federations, unions, and alliances. Nasser reacted at once. He had a bombshell that he had been waiting to set off. Now there was no reason to delay the detonation. He sent for Lieutenant Colonel Abdel Hamid Serraj, the tough young chief of Syria's military intelligence who, like Nasser, was fond of intrigue.

Serraj had played a greater part in preparing the ground for the formation of the U.A.R. than most people knew. Now, on Nasser's orders, he
called a press conference and told a strange story.

One day a man had come to him and identified himself as Assad
Ibrahim, father of one of the wives of King Saud. He said he had been
sent by the King, and produced proof. "Saud is disturbed about the
United Arab Republic," Ibrahim reported. "He calls it Egyptian imperialism. He has sworn by his father's soul that this union shall not
take place, and he puts all his power, moral and financial, at your disposal to prevent it." Serraj was then offered seven million dollars if he
would arrange for the assassination of Nasser, preferably by having his
plane explode en route to Damascus. A first payment of more than five
million dollars was made in the form of three checks drawn on a
Damascus bank. Reporters were given photo copies. Serraj said he had
passed on all the details to Field Marshal Amer, who had told Nasser,
"'The Americans are aware of the plan.'" Serraj quoted Ibrahim as
saying, "'After your coup they will recognize you as the legitimate ruler
of Syria.'" If the plot failed, Serraj was told, the Sixth Fleet would take
the conspirators off to safety somewhere.

The fragile façade of friendship between Nasser and Saud, who had
often embraced each other warmly in front of news cameras, was shattered when Nasser himself took up the attack. In a speech proclaiming
the Constitution of the new republic he said the three checks had been
cashed and the money would be used to help Syria establish heavy
industries. He disregarded the power of Saud's oil wealth and his standing among religious Moslems as keeper of Islam's holy places by linking
him to imperialism and colonialism. He knew he was risking not only
whatever Arab unity existed, but his own future. Perhaps even his own
life. But he decided that this was no time for half measures, and gave
orders for an all-out radio campaign against Saud. Heikal, who had come
to Damascus with him, was ordered to return to Cairo on the first
available plane to spearhead the attack by writing a blistering article
holding the King and his entire family up to ridicule.

In the spring of 1958 the Arab world seemed more bitterly and ir-
revocably fragmented than ever, despite the three amalgamations. State-
controlled radio stations in each of the capitals, and clandestine stations
in hidden places, were spewing hate. Vilification and vituperation were
only thinly disguised as news. Cairo Radio was now using eleven transmitters. Six new ones acquired from Czechoslovakia were about to go
into operation. From dawn until midnight propaganda designed to suit

each situation was beamed in the direction of each Arab country. Hussein, Faisal, Saud, and Chamoun were denounced with equal venom. Most of Cairo's broadcasts urged violent solutions: revolution and assassination. Often a voice beamed at one country would be contradicting a voice speaking at the same moment to another country, but few knew or cared. On all wave lengths Englishmen and Frenchmen were either imperialists, bloodsuckers, or colonialism's stooges, expressions the script writers picked directly out of Nasser's public addresses. Listeners to the Voice of the Arabs were told that Egyptians were being murdered in the United States, and that Dulles was a "power-hungry beast." Nasser's secret Voice of Free Africa referred to Americans in general as "pythons, white dogs, and pigs." Many of the broadcasts gave "news" reports of Arab bombings that had never occurred, Arab riots that had happened only in some writer's imagination, demonstrations in Arab towns that existed on no maps. This was all part of the Nasser technique in winning friends and conquering enemies.

During April he sat back in his office like a military commander, putting pressure on this front, easing it momentarily on another, keeping his enemies on the jump by never letting them know which attack he would press next. In each Arab country he had his army of *agents provocateurs,* his spies, his assassins, ready to take advantage of any schism that might occur. Their instructions were to look for cracks and when they found them to blast them wider.

One morning late in the month he flew off to the Soviet Union, taking with him the fourteen top men in his government. When the party landed at Moscow airport, he was greeted like the leader of a major world power. Premier Khrushchev and most of the other important Soviet political figures were on the field to meet him. Schoolchildren rushed up with armloads of flowers. Troops of the Moscow garrison passed before him in review. Although he was unable to read the newspapers he could see large reproductions of his face on the front pages. The streets were draped with banners welcoming him. He had lunch in the Kremlin, then laid wreaths on the tombs of Lenin and Stalin. He paid a courtesy call on Marshal Voroshilov, Soviet Chief of State, visited an automobile factory, and in the evening was guest of honor at the most elaborate banquet he had ever attended. The food was rich, the courses were many. When the toasts were exchanged, he drank only fruit juice, but that night as he lay in bed in an elaborate apartment in the Kremlin, his head was swimming. He was just forty years old. Six years ago he had been an unknown young army officer. Not even a full colonel. If he had walked down a street in Moscow, no one would have turned a head. Today the Russians treated him like a conquering hero. It was difficult to keep his perspective.

The next day was May Day. In the morning, following close on the heels of Khrushchev, he mounted the reviewing stand atop the Lenin-Stalin mausoleum in the center of Red Square and watched a military display that was even more impressive than he had imagined it would be. The square was loud with the stomp of marching feet and the whine and thunder of military machines. The speech of the day was made by Defense Minister Malinovsky, who, an interpreter explained, was denouncing the United States for failing to follow the Soviet lead in reducing the size of its armed forces. What impressed him most was the nonmilitary parade of hundreds of thousands of Russians representing factories, trade unions, political clubs, and government offices. They scattered the line of march with millions of paper flowers and carried banners calling for peace. It took four hours for them to parade past.

He spent most of his seventeen-day visit touring the Soviet Union by plane, although he conferred often with Khrushchev. Always he tried to maintain a dignified reserve. They talked of disarmament, nuclear weapons, the Middle East situation, the struggle of Africans for freedom, and how to achieve closer military, political, and cultural relations between the U.S.S.R. and the U.A.R. Without much argument he said he would permit the Russians to export to the U.A.R. books, films, information service facilities, professors, scientists, and students in unlimited numbers. But in other fields he drove a hard bargain. He insisted on a large reduction in the prices being charged for arms, a smaller reduction in the price of industrial goods, a unification of credit, and his right to deal with whatever country offered him the best bargains.

May 15 was designated U.A.R.-U.S.S.R. Solidarity Day. Millions of Muscovites took part in feting him. A joint U.S.S.R.-U.A.R. communiqué expressed profound satisfaction at the development of "close and continuously widening relations." After the signing a glittering banquet was held in the Kremlin at which Khrushchev embarrassed him with superlatives, praising his bravery, his understanding, his love of his own people, and his "fearlessness in the face of the colonizers." When his turn to speak came, he pleased his hosts by declaring, "Russia is a peace-loving nation and only imperialistic hostile false propaganda says you are preparing for war." As tokens of their affection for him the Russians gave him an Ilyushin-14 plane for himself, two model earth satellites for his sons, and a cotton research laboratory for Egypt.

He returned to the Middle East to find that his subversion had achieved the most explosive results in Lebanon. At Tripoli a mob sacked and burned a U.S.I.S. library. The Army was called in. Fifteen Lebanese were killed. The rioting spread to Beirut, where another American library was set afire and street fighting broke out. Only the bayonets of soldiers prevented the mob from marching on the American Embassy. Armed bands were crossing into Lebanon from Syria, and Foreign Minister Malik bluntly accused the U.A.R. of instigating the rebellion. Six days after his return Lebanon filed a formal complaint with the U.N. that the U.A.R. was endangering the peace of the Middle East by "a massive, illegal, and unprovoked intervention" in the internal affairs of her neighbor. Each day world tension grew as the Soviet Union openly supported the U.A.R. and the United States began to fly arms to the Beirut government.

One night after he had a long conversation with Heikal, the young editor went back to his newspaper office and wrote an article accusing the United States of offering friendship to the U.A.R. "merely as a tactic in a game aimed at the ultimate destruction of Arab nationalism under Nasser." When Dulles publicly declared the United States would use troops if necessary to help Lebanon preserve her independence, Heikal, after another conference at Manchiet el Bakry, warned Dulles against "the folly of dragging America into a world war."

It was now late in June, and the days were exceedingly hot. Observers from the U.N. arrived in Lebanon to try to assess how much outside intervention there was. Hammarskjold came in the role of trouble-shooter and peacemaker. President Nkrumah of Ghana, who had recently married an Egyptian girl, paid his first state visit to his wife's country. Every day there were more deaths in Tripoli and Beirut. Every day new fears were expressed that some Lebanese city might be the Sarajevo of World War III.

But at three o'clock on the afternoon of June 28, 1958, Nasser waved to a crowd lining the quay at Alexandria and sailed off on the first vacation voyage he and his family had ever taken together. With him were Tahia and their five children; Foreign Minister Fawzi, his wife, and their seventeen-year-old daughter, Hanya; Mohamed Heikal and his young wife, and a shipload of government officials, secretaries, aides, and servants. They sailed on what had been Farouk's favorite yacht, renamed *El Houriah* (*The Freedom*). The King had had it refitted shortly before his abdication at a cost of four million dollars. It was escorted by two Egyptian destroyers, *El Nassr* (*The Victory*) and *El*

Zafar (The Winner). Most of the passengers were in a lighthearted mood, for they had luxurious quarters and were on their way to a strange land, Yugoslavia, to meet a man they knew by reputation, Marshal Tito.

The presidential apartment consisted of bedrooms, a small salon, and a large office paneled in dark wood. While the others roamed the deck or relaxed, Nasser spent nearly all his waking hours at his desk. Occasionally he sent for Fawzi or Heikal. He had ordered the installation of much additional radio equipment, and six extra radio operators had been added to the crew. One radio was always in direct contact with Amer's office in Cairo. Others were tuned in on London, Tel Aviv, Baghdad, Amman, and Beirut. News broadcasts in English, French, and Arabic were monitored. One of his secretaries was on duty in the radio room most of the time, with instructions to bring him without delay any important dispatches.

The first day at sea, a bulletin was received saying: "Ten thousand rebels now control one third of Lebanon. Estimate 1500 dead so far." The second day, a dispatch from Washington said: "If Nasser wins in Lebanon, he may also win before long in Jordan, Iraq, and Saudi Arabia." On the third day, his secretary brought him the message that twelve Jordanian army officers had been arrested for an attempted coup in Amman; that Iraq, in answer to a call of help from Hussein, had agreed to send him five thousand Iraqi troops; that the Lebanese rebel leader had warned he would accept the help of Chinese and Russian volunteers if the West interfered.

It took almost four days to reach Yugoslavia's ancient seaport of Dubrovnik. Marshal Tito stood on the dock waving to them as the pristine white yacht glided into port. He was outfitted completely in white, even to carrying a white fedora. Nasser, in a quiet gray suit, shook hands with him warmly, while Madame Tito embraced Tahia and then took the children in her arms, one by one, paying especial attention to her favorite, six-year-old Abdel-Hamid. Cannons boomed a salute and bands played as the two heads of state drove through Dubrovnik's narrow streets in an open Rolls Royce, followed by their wives in a yellow Cadillac convertible. Nasser allowed Tahia to pose with the Titos for snapshots. This was the first time she had ever been photographed publicly. While the women and children remained in Dubrovnik to shop and sight-see, the men went with Tito into the rugged mountains of South Bosnia to join in a celebration of the climactic battle of World War II between Tito's partisans and the German invaders. It was a long automobile drive over rough roads, but as soon as they reached their destination the sixty-six-year-old marshal insisted on telling his forty-year-old guest the story of Yugoslavia's Valley Forge; how here in 1943 fewer than twenty thousand partisans had been surrounded by one hundred twenty thousand Nazis; how the Yugoslavs buried their field guns to keep them out of enemy hands; how they slaughtered and ate their pack horses; how they lost half their number fighting their way out of encirclement. Nasser listened attentively. That night, the old campaigner and the young conspirator slept in an army hut high above the Sutjeska battlefield. The next day, eighty thousand war veterans and local residents assembled on the field. As the two heads of state walked down the hill from their hut, the valley was suddenly filled with the chant: "Tito—Nasser, Tito—Nasser."

The marshal, who was being denounced almost daily by the Kremlin as an enemy of the Soviet Union, spoke for half an hour. "They attack us from high places," he said, "but we will not be shaken." Nasser, who so recently had been honored in Moscow, made the shortest speech of his career. "The Arab people are fighting for unity," he told the crowd, "and we believe you are with us in that struggle."

When they returned to Dubrovnik they learned that the center of Beirut was under attack by the rebels; that the Lebanese Government claimed three thousand men had infiltrated from the U.A.R.; that Washington was certain Nasser was responsible for the revolt. In reply Cairo Radio shouted: "Let us teach the Americans we do not need their tainted dollars, nor do we require their conditioned aid. No, America! ... We shall fight against you with all our resources, with our hands, our feet, our teeth, but we will not allow you to establish your Zionist-controlled influence over the Middle East."

At Dubrovnik they rejoined their wives and all of them boarded the *Ghaleb* (*Sea Gull*), a Yugoslav naval training vessel that took them to the Island of Brioni, where a villa had been made ready for the Nassers. For days the two heads of state conferred over such matters as positive neutrality and whether Nasser had gone too far in his friendliness toward the Soviet Union. They agreed that it was amusing, and perhaps significant, that not a word about the visit had been printed in any Moscow newspaper.

On the afternoon of July 12 they had all just returned from a swimming party when news was received over the yacht's radio that Hussein had ordered the arrest of sixty army officers, including his aide-de-camp and personal bodyguard. Amman Radio said they were involved in a plot to assassinate the King and seize power, a plot being financed and personally directed by Nasser.

On the morning of July 14 everyone on the island was still asleep when one of the yacht's radio operators received an urgent message from Amer to Nasser. A *coup d'état* had occurred in Iraq. The brigade that occupied Baghdad airport had been led by Nasser's personal and political friend, Abdel Salam Mohamed Aref. Over the radio transmitter in the airport's control tower he had flashed the news of the revolt's success to the control tower at Damascus airport, which in turn had informed Amer. Now Amer was informing his boss, long before the news was generally known anywhere, even in Iraq. The yacht's radio operator had a direct line to Nasser's secretary and passed the message on to him by telephone. He also called Heikal at his hotel. The young editor dressed quickly and hurried to the presidential villa to discuss the development. There the secretary was pacing the floor. "I haven't awakened him yet," he told Heikal. "I'm afraid he'll be annoyed at being disturbed." Heikal was not afraid, so he went to Nasser's bedroom, shook him by the shoulder, and finally aroused him. Because he awakens slowly, it was some time before he understood the import of what had happened. When he did he immediately put in a call for Amer. The rest of the morning he spent in urgent telephone conversations.

The coup had not come as a complete surprise to him. He had been in contact for a considerable time with Brigadier General Abdel Karim Kassem, the leader of the revolt, and knew all about his Free Officers movement. All he did not know was the date.

The yacht's radio picked up Kassem's first broadcast. "By the grace of Allah we have staged a blessed movement and freed Iraq from the party put in power by imperialism for the sake of its personal interest," he said. "The Iraqi Army is part of the people, and you should support it. Go to Al-Rihab Palace and to Nuri's palace and kill them."

Later broadcasts described how the mob had literally carried out the instructions. They had stormed the Royal Palace and brutally killed the twenty-three-year-old King and some members of his family. Nasser was disappointed when he heard that Nuri as-Said, seventeen times Prime Minister, whom he had always considered the arch-villain of imperialism and his own principal enemy in the Arab world, had escaped. Troops had surrounded his house and dynamited it, but the Fox, as the wily old general was called, was not there. A twenty-thousand-dollar reward was offered for him, dead or alive.

After several conversations with Amer, Nasser decided that they should pack up at once and start for home. Marshal Tito advised them against going by sea. He thought they should fly.

"Do you know what nearly happened to our Minister of Defense two years ago?" Nasser asked, and then told him about how Amer's plane had been shot down. "No," he said, "I think I'll risk getting mixed up with the Sixth Fleet rather than getting shot down."

Finally they arrived at a compromise. They would sail on *El Houriah* but Tito would lend them two of his destroyers to assist the Egyptian destroyers in protecting the yacht. They sailed at 4 P.M. that same day, July 14. No one slept much that night. Instead of working in relays the six radio operators stayed at their instruments. Nasser asked them to pay special attention to any reports they could pick up about movements of the Sixth Fleet. News bulletins were pouring into the radio room from all points of the compass. Eisenhower had called for an emergency session of the Security Council. Macmillan had ordered six thousand British troops to prepare for speedy transfer to the Middle East. Iran announced general mobilization. Jordan closed her frontiers. Iraqi troops in Lebanon were instructed to join openly with the rebels. The new Iraqi Minister of Education said, "Iraq will now march with the U.A.R. toward total liberation of the entire Arab motherland." At midnight the convoy left the Adriatic for the open Mediterranean.

The next morning, it was clear to all of them that intervention was inevitable. Ships of the Sixth Fleet were approaching the shores of Lebanon. At 3 P.M. the yacht picked up the news that seven American warships had begun to put thousands of American Marines ashore at Beirut. Nasser conferred quickly with Fawzi about whether they should issue a statement. They decided to radio the Foreign Office to announce: "This is one of the greatest mistakes the United States has made in the Middle East. It is another Suez invasion." At 4 P.M. he sent an urgent radio message to Khrushchev, asking him for his confidential appraisal of the situation. At 7 P.M., while they were all having dinner, one of the Yugoslav destroyers signaled for the entire convoy to stop. Nasser paced the deck nervously, wondering what could have happened. Soon a small boat from the destroyer came alongside. The destroyer's radio operator had received a message for President Nasser. It must be handed to him personally. He ripped open the envelope. It was from Tito and begged him not to proceed any farther but to return at once into the Adriatic and make for the nearest Yugoslav port. There Tito would meet him.

Fawzi said he thought they should take Tito's advice. Just then one of the yacht's radio operators received a reply from Khrushchev. The contents of that message were never divulged, but they made Nasser decide that he had better go to Moscow as quickly as possible and discuss the situation with the Soviet Premier. He sent word to Tito that he was ordering the convoy to head back for the Adriatic port of Pula. As they began the return journey, the commander of the lead Yugoslav destroyer ordered a blackout on all vessels. The Nasser children were excited and curious. The women were nervous. Thus far their husbands had not told them anything about what had happened. Now they were given the news in brief, so they would understand the necessity of going back. They and the children retired early, but the men stayed up the rest of the night listening to news broadcasts and making plans.

During the night, Nasser sent messages to Chou En-lai, Nehru, Nkrumah, and all other members of the Afro-Asian bloc, informing them of his position. He also sent a statement to Cairo for public release, saying any attack on Iraq would be considered an attack on the U.A.R. Then he sent a long radiogram to Amer, informing him of the plan to go to Moscow and telling him that except for Fawzi, Heikal, and his personal staff, no one else knew and no one else was to know, except Tito. Amer was to go to any lengths necessary to keep the public unaware of his actual movements. Perhaps it would be best just to announce that he was en route home by ship. Each day that he was overdue Amer would have to think up some plausible explanation.

As soon as it was light, Nasser, Fawzi, and Heikal, without awakening their families, transferred by small boat to *El Nassr*, which had three times the speed of the yacht. When they reached Pula they were met by Tito and Foreign Minister Popovic. After a dinner conference the Egyptians were driven to the airport. At 3 A.M. they landed in Moscow, where they were met by Deputy Premier Mikoyan and General Serov. To make certain that no one would see them, a heavily curtained limousine was driven out onto the runway and they were taken to a private villa in the suburbs. When Mikoyan left them at 5 A.M. he said Khrushchev would arrive at 10. Heikal decided not to go to bed at all. He was having coffee about 8 A.M. when he remembered he had a friend, Mohamed Kuny, the U.A.R. Ambassador to Moscow, who might be of some help, so he asked the Russians to send a car for Kuny, but not to tell him where he was being taken, or why. An hour later the car returned and a very perplexed man stepped out. When he saw Heikal he gasped, "How did you get here? I thought I was being kidnaped. What's happening?" Just then Fawzi came from the villa. As Kuny slumped into a garden chair in surprise, Fawzi smiled and said, "Why don't you come into the dining room and have breakfast with President Nasser?" Kuny staggered to the door, saw Nasser, put his hand to his head and groaned, "I need an hour of absolute quiet to settle my nerves."

Khrushchev appeared at precisely ten. For two hours he and Nasser discussed whether the Soviet Union intended to confine itself to diplomatic maneuvers and what Nasser should do if American troops entered Iraq and Syria. Khrushchev told him that the Soviet Union would fit its actions to the situation as it developed, but that volunteers would be kept in a state of readiness at Soviet airports and would be dispatched to the U.A.R. whenever he requested them. During a discussion of a possible summit conference Nasser suggested that he should be invited, at least as an observer. Khrushchev nodded. While they were having lunch on a balcony of the villa he offered to supply a plane to take the Egyptians home. He suggested they fly over the Caucasus, Iran, and Iraq, to Damascus, and that they start early the next morning. After lunch he said he would stay "a little while longer," but it was midnight when he finally left.

Each piece of news they received during the day made the situation seem graver. Britain landed two battalions of paratroopers in Jordan at the request of Hussein, and the United States sent two thousand paratroopers to Turkey. Selwyn Lloyd arrived in Washington to confer with Eisenhower. Ben-Gurion gave the British the right to fly military planes over Israel en route to Jordan. But one bulletin brought a smile to Nasser's face. Nuri as-Said, the Fox, had not escaped after all. As he was trying to slip out of Baghdad, disguised as an old woman, he was recognized and killed.

At 4 A.M. Mikoyan arrived at the villa to escort them to the airport. They took off at dawn and landed at Baku in time for breakfast. Hundreds of Russian jet bombers and fighters were in the air. "We're just exercising them because of the emergency," Nasser was told. As they continued their journey, their plane circled low over Baghdad, but they could see no sign of abnormality. They reached Damascus at noon. No advance notice of their arrival had been given, but a communiqué was issued as soon as they left the plane. For ninety-two hours there had been complete silence concerning Nasser's whereabouts. Amer had kept the secret well. One day he had taken the entire Cabinet across the desert to Alexandria to meet El Rayis on his return from Yugoslavia, well knowing the yacht was not going to return that day, or the next, or the next. When he told the Ministers that it had been delayed, some of them angrily accused him of needlessly endangering the life of the Boss. The Ministers returned to Cairo still not knowing the secret.

After approving the communiqué Nasser demanded a quick résumé of what had been happening. He was told that Hussein had issued a statement attacking "certain Arab leaders who have given themselves to the devil" and that Ambassador Hare had delivered to the Foreign Office in Cairo a note from Washington saying that any attack on U.S. forces in the Middle East by any U.A.R. military units would involve grave consequences.

That evening in Damascus, he addressed a hastily assembled crowd and shouted denunciations of the United States and praise of his new Arab allay. "Let us thank Allah," he said, "that our holy march is going from victory to victory." It was an emotional speech, packed with references to God, tyrants, brotherhood, enslavement, the torch of freedom, colonialism's stooges, and holy martyrs. At one point he cried, "We shall not be terrorized by threats of fleets or atom bombs. We are ready for any contingency."

That same evening, he talked with an Iraqi lawyer who had had a leading part in the revolt. The Iraqi gave him a firsthand account of how the mob of civilians and soldiers had set fire to the Royal Palace in Baghdad; young Faisal, his mother, and his uncle, Crown Prince Abdul Illah, fled to the garden with their servants and guards, but they were found and killed. The Crown Prince's body was hung in front of the Ministry of Defense, then taken down and cut into small pieces by the mob.

The next morning, General Aref, now Deputy Prime Minister of Iraq, arrived at the head of a delegation of cabinet members to confer with Nasser. In private they agreed to close military and economic cooperation, but Aref dampened Nasser's hopes that Iraq would immediately join the U.A.R. "Give us a little time," he said. In public, with their arms around each other, they promised the crowd that a new era of Arab co-operation was beginning.

During the day, he received a report that the U.A.R. chargé d'affaires in Amman had gone to the Jordanian Foreign Office for help in obtaining gasoline for his automobile, only to be told that he would have no further use of gasoline, because Jordan had just decided to sever all diplomatic ties with the U.A.R. A few minutes later there was a message saying Lebanon had ordered the U.A.R. Ambassador to leave the country at once.

Two days later, still using the Soviet plane Khrushchev had lent him, he returned to Cairo after an absence of two weeks. The plane then went on to Yugoslavia to bring back the marooned wives and children. The house at Manchiet el Bakry seemed forlorn. This was the first time since his marriage that he had ever been alone in his own home, and it bothered him so much he decided not to sleep there until Tahia and the children returned.

On his first evening in Cairo he spoke to a quarter of a million people jammed together under a great, multicolored Arabesque tent in Republic Square. The July heat was almost unbearable, even for those born to it. There was not the slightest movement of air. Beads of water were rolling down his face and his collar was wilted even before he began to speak. With him on the balcony were six Iraqi officers, four of them members of Kassem's new Cabinet. He addressed them as "you dear and beloved men of Baghdad." To the throng below he said, "My brothers, the guns of imperialism are no longer the strongest guns in the world. . . . Do you remember what Sir Hugh Gaitskell said in Commons to Anthony Eden at the time of the aggression in Egypt? He said, 'If you imagine, Eden, that the world has become a jungle, I would remind you that we are no longer the strongest beasts in the jungle.' " The crowd cheered, clapped, and shouted their approval. When the noise died down, he launched an attack on America for her "armed aggression against Lebanon." He praised Khrushchev and the Russians. He insisted there were no differences between him and the Iraqi leaders. "They said they would sign anything we desired, for our movement is one." He turned his fire on Hussein, condemning him for accepting military aid arriving in planes that had flown over Israel with Ben-Gurion's permission. The people hooted their disapproval of both Hussein and Ben-Gurion.

In the weeks that followed he was certain that he had the Western democracies on the defensive. King Saud, discomfited by the backfire of his assassination plot, delegated management of the country's economy and foreign policy to his brother, Crown Prince Faisal. Nasser considered this a victory. He had been cultivating Faisal for years. During Cairo's propaganda attacks on the royal family he had ordered Faisal spared, for he was certain he could do business with this tough-minded man who had the reputation of being a modernist in his own country. When the Prince finally came to Cairo he was housed in El Tahara guest palace; he conferred with Nasser for hours, day after day. Faisal said he could not go so far as to join Saudi Arabia to the United Arab States, but he did agree to a rapprochement.

The ten Arab countries displayed almost unprecedented unity by obtaining the passage in the U.N. of a joint resolution calling on the Middle Eastern states to abstain from interfering in each other's affairs and requesting the early departure from Jordan and Lebanon of British and American troops. At Nasser's direction Cairo newspapers headlined the story: WE HAVE WON.

In Lebanon a new President was elected and chose as his Prime Minister one of the rebel leaders, Rashid Karami, who earlier had visited Moscow and boldly said he hoped someday to see Lebanon join the U.A.R. The Algerian rebels formed a government in exile and selected Cairo as its headquarters. This gave additional importance to the Egyptian capital as a place for outlawed leaders to stay while plotting revolution and directing battles for independence in their own countries. In Cairo were men from Lahej, Mauretania, Jordan, the French Cameroons, Uganda, Eritrea, the Somalilands, Nigeria, Kenya, and the Sudan—many with a price on their heads.

But as the months passed there were also adverse developments. The worst was the failure of Russia to force the West into a summit conference. This was a personal blow to Nasser because he had been counting on increasing his stature in the eyes of the world by attending such a gathering, even if only as an observer. Then there was the growing independence of Kassem in Iraq. In the beginning the general had been friendly but aloof. Though they had never met, they exchanged personal letters. At first when Kassem was asked why he was not federating with the U.A.R. he replied, "We should not go too fast lest we trip." Later he said, more bluntly, that he did not wish to be the tail to Nasser's kite.

There had been other reverses. Most political experts expected Hussein to fall from his throne the moment British troops left. The troops finally left. Hussein did not fall. Instead he spoke out louder than ever in defiance of Cairo, calling Nasser "international communism's first agent in the Arab world" and declaring that no country in the Middle East was safe from his intrigues. In reply Cairo Radio filled the air waves with vitriol about "this dwarf king, this traitor to the Arabs," but Hussein continued to cling to his throne. In desperation Nasser tried a new tactic. His agents spread a rumor that Hussein was trying to persuade Saud to make peace between himself and Nasser, which gave Nasser the opportunity to say, "I see no need to make a deal with a dead duck." Hussein, to show how secure he felt his regime really was, decided to go to Europe to celebrate his twenty-fourth birthday. While his plane was over Syria it was attacked by two U.A.R. jet fighters. Nasser suggested that Cairo newspapers use the incident to hold the young King up to ridicule, and one paper quoted Hussein as saying to the Queen Mother, "And then, Mom, I jumped from my plane to the enemy plane and I killed the pilot, then I got back into my own plane and came home."

There was also trouble with Nkrumah, who told the first All-African People's Conference, "Do not let us forget that colonialism and imperialism may come to us in a different guise, not necessarily from Europe." And with Bourguiba, who said Nasser was sending army officers into Tunisia to bring about his death and the overthrow of his regime. To this Nasser answered bitterly, "The man is a liar. . . . Assassination is a punishment the people mete out, not the U.A.R." Tunisia shortly broke diplomatic relations with the U.A.R. Then there was a military coup in the Sudan that successfully forestalled a planned pro-U.A.R. coup. There was also trouble in Syria. A large bloc was demanding a looser federation and a return of some of the democratic freedoms. But here the troublemakers were temporarily silenced by the arrest of the hundred top dissenters.

Relations with the United States steadily grew worse. Eisenhower sent Robert Murphy, Deputy Under Secretary of State, to see certain Middle Eastern rulers. On the eve of his arrival in Cairo, Nasser sat up with his aides until almost dawn planning what he was going to say to him, but just before Murphy was to arrive Nasser received a dispatch that the United States was going to insist on a U.N. investigation of Lebanon's charges against the U.A.R. Irked, he snubbed Murphy by canceling the appointment. He finally saw him that evening, and Murphy told him in bold language that the United States would not permit him to subvert the Arab states one by one, and that if Jordan disintegrated Israel would probably seize the west bank of the Jordan River, thus forcing the U.A.R. into a war it obviously did not want. This warning so angered Nasser that he ordered his propaganda machine to begin a new campaign against "American imperialism." Speaking to a convention of co-operative societies, he accused America of intriguing against him all over the Arab world, of inciting Bourguiba, and of trying to drive wedges between Cairo, Beirut, and Khartoum. "It seems to me," he said, "that everything bad that happens in this world must be connected in some way in the eyes of Americans with that devil Nasser." He wound up this three-hour outburst by shouting over the applause of the crowd, "They may not commit murders themselves but they hire assassins. . . . These are the civilized Americans for you!"

In October he sent Amer to Moscow. One evening late in the month he sat in his office and listened to a broadcast describing a reception taking place in the sumptuous St. George's Hall of the Kremlin, attended by the most prominent officials of the Soviet Government and the diplomatic corps. The guest of honor was dark young Field Marshal Amer. To the roomful of expectant men and women Khrushchev defiantly made an announcement: "Because of the friendly relations between our countries, the Soviet Government has agreed to take upon itself the obligation to participate in building the first part of the Aswan Dam, which is so important for the economy of Egypt and the strengthening of her national independence." He then said it was not a simple coincidence that he and Amer found themselves in perfect agreement on all international matters. Amer replied that his people would hear the news "with great joy." In addition to a hundred million dollars in capital, the Soviet Union agreed to supply specialists, technicians, machinery, tools, and materials.

The announcement was received throughout the Arab world with the enthusiasm Nasser had hoped for. He chuckled gleefully as he read in an independent Beirut paper: "Four hundred million Western mistakes are going to build a new pyramid. Thus, and rightfully so, the Soviet Union has taken the place of the West on the banks of the Nile to help Gamal Abdel Nasser at long last to build the pyramid of the twentieth century. If Egypt is said to be the gift of the Nile, the Aswan Dam will be the gift of Moscow, and will be a powerful and probably final dam to Western influence, not only in the Arab world, but in the whole of Asia and Africa."

CHAPTER 23

SPARE PARTS, GAMAL!

There were hardly enough palaces in Cairo to house all the dignitaries who came on visits in January 1959. They kept him busy just shaking hands, presiding at banquets, and performing the role of an agreeable host. Once during the month there were four Prime Ministers either coming or going, all at the same time. Prime Minister Otto Grotewohl of East Germany flew in with an entire planeload of other important East German officials, hopeful of getting official recognition for his country. He was housed in Tiara Palace, but failed in his mission. Prime Minister Rashid Karami flew down from Lebanon to preside over an Arab League economic meeting. He was assigned to the old Farouk guesthouse near the pyramids. Italy's Premier, Amintore Fanfani, dropped in for two days of conferences. He was the President's personal guest at Republican Palace. Prime Minister Kwame Nkrumah arrived from big-game hunting in India with a story of how he had been attacked by a wild elephant and was saved because his host, the Maharajah of Mysore, was such a quick and accurate shot. Spain's Foreign Minister and one of the Iraqi cabinet members came for a financial conference. Eugene Black of the World Bank arrived from New York to discuss Egypt's banking problems. Dag Hammarskjold came on the last leg of a new Middle Eastern tour.

The year started with more tensions and troubles, although he tried to shake them off for an hour or two each afternoon playing tennis. After batting balls around his private court with a professional instructor he plunged more eagerly than ever back into the struggle—the struggle over who was to control the Middle East.

It was now almost seven years since the revolution, yet he had made little progress, even within the first of his three circles. In Iraq, instead of the aged reactionary Nuri as-Said and the youthful Faisal, he now had to contend with a fellow revolutionary. If Kassem had not been so unco-operative they might have come to a working agreement long ago, but he ignored letters Nasser sent to him through diplomatic channels

299

and even turned down a suggestion that they meet on the Iraqi–Syrian frontier for a private talk. The Baghdad newspapers he controlled were now attacking the U.A.R. and its President, calling him an imperialist and accusing him of plotting against revolutionary Iraq "just as he previously plotted against the Iraqi monarchy." Kassem's nephew, Colonel Fadhil Mahwai, a military judge, condemned two former monarchist Prime Ministers to death, but at the same time attacked Nasser's type of Arab nationalism as "reactionary dictatorship." Then Nasser's friend Aref, on whom he had counted to swing Iraq into the U.A.R., was arrested. Aref and Kassem once had slept on the same office floor and called themselves "brothers in revolt," but now the young colonel was accused of trying to assassinate his chief. A military court found him guilty and sentenced him to death. Kassem decided to imprison him instead, but it was a grave blow to those Iraqi rebels who had hung Nasser's pictures in their windows. In Baghdad streets these days Iraqis often fought with axes, guns, and knives because some were pro-Nasser and pro-Aref, while others were loyal to Kassem.

The situation was complicated by the attitude of the Soviets. It was difficult for Nasser to assess Moscow's hidden aim. Why had she sent a two-hundred-man diplomatic mission to Baghdad? Why was she giving Kassem more attention than he was getting? He realized that his attitude toward his own local Communists undoubtedly annoyed Moscow, yet he was convinced that unless he kept them dispersed and disorganized they would constitute a threat to his own tight control. He knew that in Syria they were working actively for union with Iraq, so he instigated raids on clandestine printing shops, shut down three firms publishing propaganda material for the Soviet bloc, jailed hundreds of men suspected of Communist sympathy, and in Damascus ordered a Communist daily newspaper suspended and the door of its shop sealed with red wax. Before long every important Syrian Communist was in jail except Khaled Bakdash, Moscow's principal agent in the Arab world, who had slipped out of the country and was in hiding. That was the situation when, unexpectedly one day late in January, Khrushchev arose before thousands of delegates to the Communist Party Congress in Moscow and sharply attacked the U.A.R. by name, warning her leader that he would err seriously if he continued to harass Communists, "these steadfast supporters of Arab nationalism." The speech infuriated Nasser. He immediately called in Soviet Ambassador Kiselev and told him so. Since Kiselev was going to Moscow the next day, Nasser gave him a letter for Khrushchev demanding that the Soviet Union make known its exact intentions toward the U.A.R. Then he sent for Heikal. The next day, a large red headline appeared on the front page of *Al Ahram:* FRANKLY! Under it was a stinging article reminding Khrushchev of his promise not to meddle in the internal affairs of other countries. Egyptians were friends of the Soviet Union, Heikal wrote, despite and not because of the local Communists.

For more than three weeks Nasser waited for a reply to his letter. It finally came at midnight on February 20, as he sat in his office preparing a speech he was to deliver the next day at a celebration of the first anniversary of the U.A.R. The letter filled ten pages. Khrushchev wanted him to know that he reacted to his good will with equal good will. The fruitful co-operation between them would continue "despite the differences in our political beliefs." The attitude of the U.A.R. toward communism was a matter of internal policy that concerned Nasser and the U.A.R. and no one else.

Seldom if ever had the Kremlin backed down so quickly and completely. It was a letter to make a vain man vainer and a proud man satisfied. He stayed up most of the night revising his speech. By morning he had figured out that the temporary rift between Moscow and Cairo had been the result of "evil agents of imperialism" who had tried to stir trouble between them. At least this is what he told his anniversary audience. Tito, who was in Egypt on another official visit, was on the platform. He and Khrushchev had had no such reconciliation as this, so he made no comment on the rapprochement in his own short speech.

Several weeks later in the Iraqi oilfield city of Mosul, on the banks of the Tigris near the ancient biblical city of Nineveh, an incident occurred that suddenly changed the entire situation. During a demonstration by Kassem's followers a restaurant frequented by Nasser-Aref supporters was burned down. This touched off fighting that turned into a counterrevolution involving several army brigades. By the time it was suppressed, naked mutilated bodies hung from lampposts and the streets of Mosul were littered with burned-out trucks and cars. Kassem charged that Nasser had planned the uprising down to the smallest detail. He declared most members of the U.A.R. diplomatic mission *personae non gratae* and required them to leave Iraq.

Nasser reacted more in pique than anger at first. "If we are hurt, offended, and insulted," he told one public gathering, "we must not be enraged, because that is bound to harm those carrying on our mission."

But in Baghdad there was no restraint. One newspaper used large, boldface type to say: "Abdel Nasser is revealed as the great plotter, enemy, dictator, shedder of blood. Those who proclaim pan-Arabism and raise Abdel Nasser to the rank of prophet have been exposed. Nasser sent arms to Mosul because he wanted to annex Iraq to his kingdom." Another paper called him "a hashish-eater." The next day, Iraqi demonstrators, shouting "Death to Gamal!" burned him in effigy on Baghdad's main thoroughfare. Shops that once had displayed heroic-size portraits of him in their windows now began to sell pictures of donkeys, hyenas, and dancing girls with his grinning face superimposed on them.

To this he finally reacted in kind. From the balcony of the presidential palace in Damascus he made a bitter speech. He said the new Iraqi dictator and "Communist agents of a foreign power" were trying to split the U.A.R. Kassem was reviving the old British idea of a Fertile Crescent: a union of Iraq, Syria, Jordan, and Kuwait. As he concluded his talk, the Syrian crowd began to chant, "Death to the traitor Kassem." Controlled radio stations in the two capitals took up the feud. Baghdad Radio snarled: "The blood of Mosul's free men will haunt you, Gamal." Cairo Radio snapped back: "Iraq is ruled by a Red butcher."

Several days later he heard about Mohamed Said Shihab, an Iraqi officer who had been shot during the fighting at Mosul, fled across the frontier into Syria, and died in a Damascus hospital. Shihab was unknown to the Syrians, but his dead body could be used to advantage, so a state funeral was ordered for him. The next morning, two hundred thousand Syrians either followed the coffin through the streets of Damascus or stood at the curbing, chanting, "There is no other God than Allah. Kassem is against Allah. Down with Kassem." Some of the marchers carried dead dogs and rats labeled "Kassem," hanging from miniature gallows. From the balcony of the presidential palace Nasser delivered his fourth speech in three days. He had made several offers to meet Kassem and all had been rejected, he said. Now reconciliation was impossible. Cairo newspapers took their lead from him and stepped up their campaign of vituperation. Kassem, they said, had gone mad. He was suffering from hysteria and insomnia. Communist doctors gave him morphine injections to enable him to sleep. While he was under the influence of drugs, they obtained his signature on secret documents. At night Communists went to the homes of Nasser supporters and marked the doors with letters. *S* was a signal to armed bands who followed that this house was to be plundered; *Q* meant all inhabitants were to be killed; *SQ* meant loot and kill. Cairo newspapermen competed in the invention of atrocity stories. Even the Middle East News Agency put dispatches on its wires about how Baghdad's streets were littered with dead bodies.

Iraqi newspapers took up the challenge and called Nasser a disciple of Goebbels, Hitler, and Mussolini, the head of Egypt's secret Masonic lodges, a homosexual operating from behind a smoke screen of Islam, just as Hitler had operated behind a smoke screen of Christianity.

Suddenly Nasser's troubles with Moscow began again. As Khrushchev welcomed an Iraqi delegation to the Soviet Union he issued a public rebuke to Nasser for trying to force Iraq into the U.A.R. The Soviet Union, he said, would rush to Iraq's defense whenever she was menaced, because Kassem was a more progressive ruler than Nasser. To demonstrate this faith, Khrushchev signed an agreement giving Iraq one hundred fifty million dollars' worth of economic aid.

That same night, the missing Arab Communist leader, Khaled Bakdash, came out of hiding. Dispatches from Warsaw said he had appeared at a world labor congress as the chief speaker and denounced Nasser as the leader of a corrupt and selfish Egyptian bourgeois movement. Delegates from fifty countries applauded.

As relations with Moscow became increasingly strained, Nasser had his first serious difficulty with Amer. The field marshal kept saying, "Spare parts, Gamal! Please remember we need spare parts." Amer's fear was that a real rupture with the Soviet Union might occur, leaving his army with weapons that could never be repaired. Nasser listened. He respected and trusted Amer more than any other man he knew, but he had to react to Baghdad and Moscow. Reacting was as necessary for him as breathing, and Amer was aware of it. That was why he was concerned about spare parts.

But Amer was not the only one who was worried. One day Nasser found on his desk a subversive pamphlet that accused him of betraying the Arab cause. One of the many questions it asked him was: "How could you forget that Russia sent you millions of dollars' worth of arms that enabled you to resist the Suez attack?" Primarily he was disturbed because no one seemed to know how the pamphlet had reached his desk. It was a chilling reminder of the days when his own Free Officers found ways to get secretly printed leaflets onto the desks of Farouk's officers.

As long as this new crisis continued, he decided he should remain in Damascus. There one day he received reports of an anti-Kassem demonstration in Cairo. All traffic was stopped, most businesses shut down, and offices closed as fifteen thousand organized marchers wound through the capital's streets at funeral pace, carrying banners taunting Kassem. One read: "Death to Kassem, enemy of Allah." Others bore slogans lumping together imperialism, atheism, Zionism, colonialism, communism, and Westernism as enemies of Nasserism, which was called democracy.

A few days later Khrushchev held a press conference in Moscow and branded Nasser "a rather hot-headed young man," adding, "He took upon himself more than his stature permits. This is harmful. He shouldn't do it. He might strain himself."

Nasser's reaction was to mount the presidential balcony in Damascus again and call the Soviet Premier "a meddler."

Khrushchev's latest rebuke stung him more than any other, for he answered it again a few days later by saying, "Except for my hot-headedness our country today would be a Western base for rockets and atom bombs directed at the Soviet Union itself." Then he startled some of his audience by adding, "As for 1956, it was only on November 6, the day the fighting stopped, that the Soviets issued their famous ultimatum to the British and French." Reporters checked with each other to be sure they had heard correctly. The Soviet ultimatum had been issued on November 5, while the fighting did not stop until November 7. For two years Nasser himself had given all credit for ending the attack to the Russians, and almost none to the U.N. or to the United States. Now in his fury he was rewriting his own version of history.

The people of Baghdad celebrated the first day of spring by planting pine trees. It was a traditional ceremony, but this time they chanted as they planted. The words were new: "Today is the day of the tree, and Gamal Nasser is the ground under our shoes." In Arabic *tree* and *shoes* rhyme, and the word they used for ground was not complimentary.

In April, angrier than before over the continually deteriorating situation, he told an Indian editor that the Soviet Union had been one of the Fertile Crescent conspirators; that the real reason the formation of the U.A.R. had been rushed through so quickly—contrary to all his own previous statements—was because Syrian Communists had been getting ready for a coup, and that in the past three weeks he and the U.A.R. had lost all the Soviet good will he had labored so diligently for three years to build up. It was the most outspoken interview he had ever given and disclosed the cynicism he had developed in so short a time. He had extra cause for moroseness: the Arab League, after six days of meetings, failed to pass even a mild resolution supporting him in his fight with Kassem. Iraq, Jordan, Libya, and Tunisia sent no delegates. This was a measure of how far the fragmentation of the Arab world had gone. Only Yemen had been willing to take a pro-Nasser, anti-Kassem stand.

Late in the month he met with Soviet Ambassador Kiselev for the first time in four months. The Ambassador brought a thirty-page letter from Khrushchev and stayed two hours, adding verbal footnotes. Again there was a promise not to interfere in internal Arab affairs, but Nasser did not find it entirely convincing. He waited almost a month before he sent a reply.

Despite all this feuding, ships and planes from Eastern Europe were still arriving at Syrian and Egyptian ports with enormous shipments of war matériel and manufactured goods—often whole factories. In one two-day period the entire equipment for two dozen factories reached Egypt from Russia, and every month or so another submarine would be delivered. Soviet engineers continued to direct preliminary work on the High Dam.

One Sunday in September the Kassem government executed thirteen Iraqi army officers as leaders of the Mosul revolt. Several were men Nasser had known personally. The next day, Cairo newspapers called Kassem "the butcher of humans who sits on top of the dead bodies."

Late in September, Khaled Bakdash caused a new international crisis that occupied Nasser's attention for many days. This time the self-exiled Communist turned up in Peiping at a banquet celebrating the tenth anniversary of the Chinese Communist regime and denounced the U.A.R. and its leader. Nasser was furious that his old friend Chou En-lai, whose autographed photograph occupied a place of honor on the mantelpiece of his salon, was the one who introduced the Syrian renegade at the banquet. Spontaneously he ordered his Foreign Office to file a formal protest, sent the U.A.R. chargé d'affaires in Peiping a cable to come home at once for consultations, and issued detailed instructions to editors and radio executives on how they were to handle the story. The next morning, residents of the U.A.R. were surprised to discover they had a new enemy. All the media of mass communication were stating that Communist China was responsible for increasing international tensions and attempting to subvert the Arab world through local Communist parties. Long articles about Peiping's evil deeds in Tibet, India, and Laos appeared in the morning papers. Edition by edition and day by day the accusations became more virulent. The U.A.R. Embassy in Peiping had been put under a virtual state of siege by the Chinese Government. Visitors to the Embassy were being investigated. U.A.R.

diplomatic cables were delayed. Readers who had grown accustomed in recent months to the idea that Moscow was the real villain now suddenly found their papers telling them that the Soviet Union was genuinely working for world peace, but that Communist China was the enemy of all mankind, especially of the U.A.R. The recriminations went on for several weeks. Then Nasser decided to accept Peiping's "sincere regrets" and the explanation that it was the local Communist party and not the government that had invited Bakdash to speak. Another crisis was over.

On the evening of October 7 Heikal took two American reporters, Wilton Wynn of the Associated Press and Harry Ellis of NBC, to the house at Manchiet el Bakry to interview Nasser. The four men were sitting in the study when their conversation was interrupted by a sharp knock on the door. The aide who entered handed the Boss a small piece of paper. After he read the Arabic words he passed the note on to Heikal, then leaned back in his chair, tilted his head slightly, so that his jaw protruded a little more than usual, and took two long puffs on his cigarette. The first words he spoke were in English: "Radio Baghdad has just announced that Kassem was wounded in an assassination attempt." He and Heikal exchanged significant glances. When he spoke again it was directly to the reporters. "I don't believe in all this terrorism. It only leads to more and more bloodshed," he declared.

After the Americans left, he and Heikal watched additional news bulletins coming in. Shots had been fired at Kassem as he rode in an automobile along Rashaid Street, one of Baghdad's main thoroughfares. The government was imposing a curfew. Late in the evening they heard over the office radio a broadcast by Kassem himself from his hospital room. "We will triumph over the ambitious ones, the traitors, and the criminals," he said.

Late in the year Nasser had a new concern: internal affairs in Syria. Although the old political parties had been formally dissolved, some were still operating underground. There was widespread discontent because union with Egypt had not resulted in improving the living conditions of a majority of the people. The progress of his industrialization and land-reform plans had been slow. Iraq had many partisans among the Syrians. His solution to all these problems was to issue a presidential decree making Amer virtually a *gauleiter* over Syria, responsible only to the President of the U.A.R. Immediately afterward Amer went to Damascus to establish headquarters there.

In November, Nasser decided the time had come to end his feud with the Soviets, so he sent Salah Salem to Moscow in his capacity as editor of *Al Gomhouria.* Salem returned after a week with a notebook full of Khrushchev's reassurances. The Soviet Premier had committed himself on everything from his interest in Palestinian refugees to his willingness to bid for the loan on the second stage of the High Dam. This was quickly followed by a decision of the World Bank to give Nasser more than fifty-six million dollars to deepen the Suez Canal, in spite of his long defiance of the Security Council resolution demanding free passage through the Canal for ships of all nations. He had been barring not only Israeli ships but even ships of other nations carrying Israeli goods. His explanation was that he considered a state of war still existed between Egypt and Israel, although several times during the year he had ignored Prime Minister Ben-Gurion's peace overtures. He had ordered many ships, even though they were not Israeli-owned, to unload their Israeli cargos, which were then confiscated. Once even mail sacks were impounded. He accused Israel of "aggressive intentions" for trying to ship goods through the Canal in foreign bottoms. Because the captain of a ship out of Copenhagen, the *Inge Toft,* refused to unload his cargo of Israeli products, the ship was held immobile for nearly nine months, until the owners finally changed their minds and permitted the cargo to be unloaded and confiscated.

Frequently during 1959 he used Israel as a diversionary target for Arab emotions. Late in the year, when he was embroiled in difficulties with Communist China, the Soviet Union, and some of his Arab neighbors simultaneously, he made several violent attacks on Israel. He said the Jewish state was "a crime established by treachery and imperialism," and threatened her with "extermination." He was especially nettled by Ben-Gurion's public declaration that he considered Kassem a lesser threat to the Middle East than Nasser, and that he would be happy to invite the Iraqi leader to visit Israel.

But there were joys as well as problems. Among the gifts he received were a number of Russian and American movie and still cameras. At first he devoted an hour a day to learning how to operate them. Before long photography became such a hobby with the Nasser family that each member, even the youngest child, had at least one camera of his own. In the spring the San Francisco Ballet came to Cairo for two weeks. Tahia attended the première with several Ministers' wives and enjoyed herself so much that she wanted to go again and she persuaded Nasser to take her, a few nights later. They went incognito, accompanied by Anwar el Sadat and his wife. During the intermission, in the reception room off the royal box, he discussed with the director, the conductor, and the manager of the company how such cultural presentations were financed in the United States.

In June, Tahia's picture appeared in a Cairo newspaper for the first time. She was standing beside him as he greeted Emperor Haile Selassie, but she was not identified in the caption. That same month, he made an effort to persuade Egypt's peasants to discard their galabiyas in favor of a loose-fitting poplin blouse and slacks that he and his Ministers decided were more suitable to twentieth-century life. He was disappointed that the campaign met with little popular enthusiasm. In August he gave his approval to the resumption of cricket matches at the Gezira Sporting Club, once a bastion of British exclusiveness but since 1956 a bastion of bourgeois Egyptian exclusiveness. The rationale was that experts had informed him cricket was not essentially a British game, despite what British dictionaries might say.

Late in the year he began to sprinkle his speeches with the phrase, "a co-operative, socialistic, democratic society," to define his goal for the Arab people. The closest he ever came to explaining the definition was to say he believed "bread for all should be the inevitable prelude to liberty for all." Though all Egyptians and Syrians did not yet have enough bread, he arranged for them to have a small taste of political liberty. Voters of the U.A.R. were allowed to elect forty thousand members of local councils. Anyone who wished to could be a candidate if he was a member in good standing of the National Union, still the only political party permitted. But the act of applying did not assure the person a place on the ballot. Names were carefully screened by government authorities, and all undesirables were eliminated. Each village or voting district had the right to one representative for each five hundred inhabitants. In one town of fifteen thousand a voter had the task of choosing thirty representatives from a list of five hundred candidates. Although there were not nearly that many candidates in Nasser's own district, it took him four minutes to mark his ballot.

In 1959 there was a catastrophe—far removed from politics—that Cairenes would remember for a long time. One hot summer day a two-hundred-ton river steamer, the *Dandara*, licensed to carry sixty passengers, was taking three hundred men, women, and children—government agricultural workers and their families—on an outing up the Nile. Suddenly there was an alarm. The *Dandara* had sprung a leak. In panic the crowd rushed to the side nearest shore and the steamer tipped over. More than half the passengers drowned. The next morning, one of the Cairo papers printed a vivid account of how El Rayis had gone to the scene and taken charge of the search for the bodies. While Nasser was reading the newspapers at breakfast he saw the article. Furious, he left his meal and ordered an aide to get the paper's publisher on the phone. "This is no compliment," he told him. "It looks like a cheap and undignified attempt to gain publicity. Anyone knows that I have men in the government who are capable of occupying themselves with such problems." The journalist responsible for the story was transferred to the Egyptian-Israeli Armistice Commission. "Let Ben-Gurion worry about him," Nasser remarked in suggesting the post.

During 1959 the U.A.R. signed an agreement with the Sudan over the division of the Nile's water, ending a quarrel that had plagued the two countries for thirty years; diplomatic relations were resumed with Jordan, after almost a year of name calling and backbiting without benefit of Ambassadors; and the feud with King Saud was brought to an end when he came to Cairo in August on a four-day visit. In December, Nasser agreed to a resumption of diplomatic relations with Britain, but no sooner had the Union Jack been raised over the British Embassy for the first time in more than three years than an incident occurred that threatened to create a new rupture. One morning Heikal's paper ran an article about the six Egyptian commandos who at Port Said in 1956 kidnaped a young British officer, Lieutenant Anthony Moorhouse, kept him tied up in a tenement for three days, then left him in a steel locker to suffocate to death while British search parties combed the neighborhood looking for him. The six Egyptians had converted the tenement into a museum, where, upon payment of a small fee, visitors could see the locker in which Moorhouse died, his identity card, and even the rope with which he had been bound. Another room contained scurrilous cartoons of Anthony Eden. British newspapers, indignant, called it a deliberate gesture of contempt. In reply Nasser authorized *Al Gomhouria* to ask: "Suppose we make not one but a thousand museums to commemorate the horrible attack on us? What business is that of London?"

Late in 1959 President Eisenhower's choice of countries to visit on his tour of Asia and the Middle East aroused Nasser's ire almost as much as the manner in which Secretary Dulles had withdrawn the offer to finance the Aswan Dam. And for the same reason: he felt he had been intentionally abased in the eyes of the rest of the world. The American President was going to visit such a vest-pocket nation as Greece, yet he planned to bypass Egypt. Worse, the only Arab state he would visit, Tunisia, was ruled by Habib Bourguiba, one of the

U.A.R.'s most persistent critics. Abruptly Nasser called in the American Ambassador. When this brought no satisfaction, he consulted Mohamed Heikal and his other public relations advisers. The next day, a large headline in the *Egyptian Gazette* read: MR. HAGERTY SHOULD BE MORE TACTFUL IN FUTURE. The article below it stated in part: "We are not in any way responsible for the rumor [denied by Press Secretary Hagerty in a published interview] that the U.S. President might visit Cairo, nor have we suggested to him the inclusion of Cairo in the itinerary of his forthcoming journey. As a matter of fact, we are anxious that this visit should not take place, since the prospective visitor is not desirous of coming to this country. . . . We are really at a loss to understand why America should insist upon maintaining her offensive attitude toward us in her newspapers, in her radio broadcasting services, and through repeated declarations made by responsible and semi-responsible sources."

On that note 1959 ended.

Nineteen sixty began with serious military thrusts and reprisals on the Syrian-Israeli frontier. Soldiers of both sides engaged in hit-run battles on land, jet war planes dueled at high altitudes, Arabs and Israelis were killed. Nasser and Ben-Gurion argued in the press over who was to blame, each accusing the other of provocation. Nasser, either misjudging Israel's plans or because of a desire to add to the tension, ordered three Egyptian divisions to take up positions on the Sinai border. Then he went to Syria and stayed there for five weeks. During this time he publicly directed sharp gibes at Great Britain, France, the United States, Dictator Kassem, and King Hussein, but Israel received the brunt of his fury: the threat of military obliteration. He had given U.N. Secretary-General Hammarskjold a tentative promise to grant passage through the Suez Canal, under certain conditions, to non-Israeli cargo ships on their way to and from Israel. Now he publicly vowed that such ships would never go through the Canal again, no matter what action might be taken by any international body. Ralph Bunche of the U.N. came to plead for reconsideration. Then Hammarskjold himself arrived. Persuasion was attempted and inducements were offered, but he shook his head in refusal to all of them. His aides showed him dispatches from Washington speculating that he had deliberately created incidents on the Syrian-Israeli frontier and was being intransigent about Israeli shipping as a diversion from internal troubles in Syria and in the hope of reviving his dwindling prestige as the Arabs' hero against the Jewish state. He read the dispatches and handed them back to his aides for filing, without comment.

When, at the height of the crisis, Prime Minister Ben-Gurion announced that he was going to the United States to accept an honorary college degree, reporters and diplomats agreed the war scare was over, but Nasser, deciding the trip was really an arms-purchasing expedition, shouted to a political meeting at Damascus, "Ben-Gurion is the greatest war criminal of the twentieth century." By the time the Israeli Prime Minister returned to the Middle East the frontier was quiet again, but no ships bound to or from Israel were going through the Canal. This led to the incident of the Egyptian passenger-cargo vessel *Cleopatra*. For several weeks she was held immobile in New York Harbor by the picketing of American dock workers in retaliation for the U.A.R. treatment of Israel-bound ships. Nasser was amused at the State Department's embarrassment but became angry when an amendment was attached to a bill in the U.S. Senate giving the President discretionary authority to withhold aid from nations obstructing free navigation on international waterways. His own unions were ordered to boycott American ships arriving in U.A.R. ports. When, through State Department intervention, the New York picketing came to an end after twenty-four days, he instructed Cairo newspapers to proclaim that Egypt had won a major victory not only over Israel but over the great United States.

During the first half of 1960 he continued to feud with his principal Arab rivals: Kassem of Iraq, Hussein of Jordan, and Bourguiba of Tunisia. The struggle for power was far from settled. Most bothersome to him was Iraqi Dictator Kassem's suggestion that a Palestinian state be re-formed. The United Nations partition plan had provided for the creation of an Arab Palestinian state, but Egypt and Jordan had divided all of Palestine that did not become part of Israel. Now Kassem was proposing that Nasser give up the Gaza Strip and Hussein relinquish the land west of the Jordan River. When the Arab League met in Cairo to discuss the idea of "an immortal Palestine republic," the U.A.R. delegation set out to defeat it. Nasser anticipated an easy victory, for Kassem and Bourguiba had boycotted the gathering and were not represented, and of course Hussein would be on Egypt's side in this controversy. Yet after three weeks of secret meetings the League announced that agreement was impossible, and adjourned. Meanwhile Nasser, in a speech within a short distance of the Iraqi-Syrian frontier, made one of his most unrestrained attacks on the Iraqi Premier. "If Kassem," he said, "is sincere about Palestine, let him send the Iraqi Army to fight with us against Israel on the battle's front line." By midyear four new attempts to overthrow Kassem, some violent, had been made by Nasser's followers in Iraq, perhaps with Nasser's guidance, certainly with his knowledge. None succeeded.

King Hussein of Jordan also still held onto his throne, although he and Nasser continued to exchange epithets and accusations of selfish political motivation.

Early in the year Nasser decided to conduct a battle of written words with Anthony Eden, the man who personified British colonialism for him. Eden's memoirs appeared first in syndicated form in British and American periodicals. In one installment Sir Anthony wrote: "Some say that Nasser is no Hitler or Mussolini. Allowing for a difference in scale, I am not so sure." Nasser's reply was to call in Heikal and start working on his own memoirs of what he called "the 1956 aggression," with a promise to interested book publishers that he would spare no one.

In his relationship with the U.S.A. and the U.S.S.R. he continued his well-tested policy of balance and bargain. The Soviet Union agreed to finance the second stage of the Aswan Dam and signed twenty contracts for the building of new industrial enterprises in the U.A.R. From the United States he obtained another fifty million dollars in economic development loans. Yet frequently in talking to radio audiences or to rally crowds, both at home and abroad, he assailed the West. He told France, Britain, and the United States that their 1950 guarantee of existing Arab-Israeli frontiers against aggression was "dead and buried." To the chagrin of France he opened an office in Cairo for recruiting Arab volunteers to fight against the French in Algeria. He sent Deputy Foreign Minister Zulficar Sabry to Cuba to visit Fidel Castro. To Panama he dispatched a diplomatic delegation much stronger than needed to protect the interests of the few Arab citizens there or to handle the almost nonexistent commercial relationship. Then Panama's Foreign Minister visited Nasser, inspected Egypt's canal, and learned how a small country goes about nationalizing a great international waterway.

By midyear, if Nasser had sat down with a block of paper to make a balance sheet, as he often liked to do, he could have listed on the plus side, from his point of view, that he was still keeping the U.A.R. free of subservience to either the East or the West. That he was still able to collect from either bloc by threatening to ally himself with the other. That he had thus far prevented the creation of a Palestine republic.

On the negative side he would have to list the bitter fact that in eight years he had made little progress in achieving even the first of the three goals he had set for himself in *The Philosophy of the Revolution*. He had managed to bring only Syria into his Arab republic. Kassem was as secure as he had ever been, and Bourguiba and Hussein were perhaps more secure. He had been correct in predicting that Africa would be the scene of "a strange and stirring commotion," but in this second circle neither he nor his country was playing the hero's role he had envisioned for them. And in the third circle the hundreds of millions of Moslems in 1960 were as far from achieving that "unlimited power" as "brethren in Islam" as they had been in 1952, before the revolution.

Much of the support he had won abroad when Egypt was attacked in 1956 he had lost by his subsequent treatment of resident foreigners and his refusal to keep his promise of free passage through the Canal for all ships. Israel still existed and despite the boycott was constantly growing stronger, both industrially and militarily.

Internally the balance sheet would be more encouraging. He was alive after two assassination attempts, the latest a plot, so his secret police said, to poison him. He was still in power despite the variety and the numerical strength of his opponents: Communists, the Moslem Brotherhood, Copts, Jews, the old political parties, the dispossessed landowners, the supporters of Naguib, rival military cliques, and what was left of the foreign colony. Even now Naguib was not a name to be mentioned aloud and he was not permitted visitors. But Nahas, the once powerful pasha, twenty other opposition leaders, and even some of Farouk's relatives and court followers had been given back their civil and political rights. That was the measure of his self-confidence. Most foreigners had been expelled, or encouraged to leave by irresistible economic pressures, or had fled of their own accord, so Egypt was now more Egyptian than she had been in centuries. The successful operation of the Canal since nationalization had done much for Egyptian prestige abroad. Early in the year Nasser himself had set off the charge of dynamite that began work on the great Aswan Dam, and he had opened the country's first hydroelectric station. Hardly a week passed without a ceremony at some new industrial plant, even though separate celebrations of ground-breaking, cornerstone-laying, completion of construction, and shipment of the first products gave the impression that Egypt had many more factories than she actually did have. A start had been made toward reclaiming land from the sea. Egypt now manufactured almost all the cotton products she needed for herself. More and more farmland was being redistributed. Under his guiding hand the old way of life was changing, gradually. Before the end of the year the right of a man to rid himself of a wife merely by saying "I divorce thee!" would be taken away. Henceforth a husband would have to go to court and give good reason: adultery or desertion.

But there was another column on the internal balance sheet. Egypt was still a police state in most respects. All incoming and outgoing mail was opened and censored. Unfavorable comments were eliminated from broadcasts or newspaper dispatches going abroad. Egypt's chief newspapers had been nationalized and placed under management of the single political party, controlled in turn by the government. Now there was nothing even resembling a free press in the Western sense. Telephone lines were tapped. Visitors' rooms were searched. Ambassadors' automobiles were followed. The people dared not discuss, even in whispers, certain subjects, among them the concentration camps hundreds of miles off on the desert where Communists, Moslem Brothers, and other political prisoners were kept, with few guards and no fences because escape meant certain death before water could be reached. Political democracy did not yet exist, despite the frequent promises. No party except the National Union was permitted. Local councils had been elected, but only from candidates who belonged to the single party, and even they had been carefully screened. Poverty was still widespread in Cairo and the villages of Upper Egypt in all its filthy, squalid, diseased, fly-covered, manure-smelling aspects. Clean water had been piped to a few hundred thousand people, but most Egyptians still used the same canals and banks of the Nile for mutually incompatible purposes. The death rate had gone down slightly, but the birth rate was almost as high as ever, with the certainty that by the time the Aswan Dam was completed the land it rescued from the desert would just about feed the increase in the population. During the first three years of the new regime corruption had been eliminated. Now it was common again among the half million civil service workers. Of thirty thousand recently investigated, more than a third were convicted for various offenses.

The newspapers and magazines Nasser read in bed each night continued to refer to him as "the strong man of the Middle East," and during his visit to India in March, Prime Minister Nehru had flattered him in public pronouncements. After his return he had received his first invitation to visit a country in the Western bloc, Greece. Yet New Delhi was not New York and Athens, for all its ancient splendor, was not Washington. He still smarted over the way the West treated him.

Although the campaign he had inaugurated to encourage his people to buy only Egyptian-made products had been partially successful, he himself smoked American cigarettes when he was in the seclusion of his home at Manchiet el Bakry and, like most Egyptians, preferred almost any foreign films to Egyptian ones.

Many of the magazines and newspapers from abroad that Nasser reads speculate about the future. What are his plans? How will he move to achieve his ends? Will he ultimately make peace with Israel? Will the U.A.R. eventually become a friend of the West or join the Communist bloc? He smiles inscrutably when he reads their predictions. Often he says to his aides with a touch of sarcasm, "They seem to know more about it than I do."

INDEX

317

Faluja pocket, 74, 76–78, 81–82
Family names, 8
Fanfani, Premier Amintore, 299
Farida, Queen, 86
Farida School, 22
Farms, size of, 7–9
Farouk, King, 42–45, 69–70, 83–87, 102–
    103, 106, 108, 110–112, 115–116,
    118, 125–127, 134–136, 141, 164, 266
  abdication of, 128–130
  gossip about, 85, 134
  wealth of, 83–87, 134–135
Fatalism, 11
Fath, Mahmud, 176
Fawzi, Mahmoud, 156, 159–160, 196,
    250, 287, 292–293
Fedayeen, 208–209
Federation of Cairo Transport Workers,
    172
Fellahin (peasants), 6–7, 9–11, 38
Feminism, 215
Fertile Crescent, 302, 304
Fertility, Nile and, 6
Fire on the Sacred Land, 60
Flying Palace, plane, 172, 174
Fouad, Ahmed, 50, 94–95, 137, 271
Fouad, King, 85
Fouad II, Prince, 115, 129–130, 135, 159
Fouad University, 102, 135
France, 205, 217, 221, 243, 248, 259, 266–
    267, 272, 312
  (*See also* French, the)
Free Officers, 46–47, 49–50, 52–56, 59–
    61, 66, 87–95, 97, 107–108, 110–113,
    115, 130–135, 138, 149, 153, 155,
    166–167, 182, 274, 290
  credo of, 92
  executive committee of, 91, 95–96, 111–
    112, 133, 135–137
  literature of, 93–95, 98, 109
French, the, 275, 285
  confiscation of property of, 270
  expulsion of, 269
French National Assembly, 250
French planes, 261, 265
French troops, 264

Gaafer, Hussein, 47
Gaitskell, Sir Hugh, 295
Galabiyas, 1, 9, 308
Gamus (*see* Water buffalo)
Gat, 71, 76

Gayar, Major Machmud el, 196, 258,
    261–262, 264–265, 276, 278
Gaza, 62–63, 69–71, 73, 79
Gaza Strip, 189, 204, 208, 263, 311
Germans, 43, 46–48
Germany, 42, 51
  (*See also* East Germany)
Gezira Island, 45, 70, 138, 262
Ghaleb, Yugoslav ship, 289
Ghana, 287
Giro, portrait of Nasser by, 227
Giza, 4, 70
Gleim, Mr., 153
Glubb, Sir John Bagot (Glubb Pasha),
    216–217, 249
  (*See also* Bagot, Sir John)
Goren, Colonel Shlomo, 80
Government (*see* Egyptian Govern-
    ment)
Great Britain, 28, 61, 179, 189, 205, 221,
    244–249, 267, 272, 309
  and Suez Canal, 250–251, 256, 259,
    264
  (*See also* British, the)
Great Pyramid, 4
Greece, 309, 314
Grotewohl, Otto, 299
Guerrillas, 101

Hadi Pasha, Ibrahim Abdel, 89–90, 160–
    161
Hafez, Judge, 129
Hagerty, James, 310
Haifa, 261
Haile Selassie, 213, 275, 308
Hakim, Tewfik, 28, 192
Halim, Prince Abbas, 98
Hammad, Mohamed, 12
Hammarskjold, Dag, 244, 287, 299, 310
Hamza, Mirghani, 180
Hare, Raymond, 259, 271, 294
Hassan, Mohamed, 129
Heikal, Mohamed Hassanein, 60–61, 83,
    112, 122, 125–126, 131, 193–195, 235,
    245, 252, 284, 287, 290, 292, 301,
    306, 310
Helwan, 22
Henderson, Loy, 253
Hilaly, Prime Minister Naguib, 124
Hitler, Adolf, 42, 52, 152–153
Hodeiby, Hassan el, 138, 179, 182–184
Hospitals, Jewish, 269

ABOUT THE AUTHOR

Known throughout the world as a radio commentator and foreign correspondent, Robert St. John is also one of the most important authors writing on international affairs and figures today. *The Boss* is his tenth book, following the success of *Ben-Gurion,* a best-seller in 1959, and translated into many languages. His other well-known books are *From the Land of Silent People, Shalom Means Peace, This Was My World,* and *Foreign Correspondent.* In the past thirty years, he has lived and worked in more than fifty foreign countries, and traveled a million and a half miles. By radio and television he has reported on such diverse subjects as Al Capone and Adolf Hitler, the blitz in London, the Allied landings in France, the liberation of Paris, Franklin D. Roosevelt's death, V-E Day, and the creation of the United Nations in San Francisco. On V-J Day, he established a record, not since equaled, of seventy-two consecutive hours at a microphone.